Workbook to accompany

Personal

Financial

Planning

sixth edition

Lawrence J. Gitman
San Diego State University

Michael D. Joehnk
Arizona State University

Carlene Creviston
Ball State University

THE DRYDEN PRESS
HARCOURT BRACE COLLEGE PUBLISHERS

*Fort Worth Philadelphia San Diego New York Orlando Austin San Antonio
Toronto Montreal London Sydney Tokyo*

Address for Editorial Correspondence
The Dryden Press, 301 Commerce Street, Suite 3700, Fort Worth, TX 76102

Address for Orders
The Dryden Press, 6277 Sea Harbor Drive, Orlando, FL 32887
1-800-782-4479, or 1-800-433-0001 (in Florida)

ISBN: 0-03-076738-5

Printed in the United States of America

3 4 5 6 7 8 9 0 1 2   095   9 8 7 6 5 4 3 2 1

The Dryden Press
Harcourt Brace & Company

Table of Contents

Outlines, Exercises, and Practice Cases

Answers and Solutions

Cases

Outlines, Exercises, and Practice Cases

Chapter 1

Understanding the Financial Planning Process

CHAPTER OUTLINE

I.   The reward of personal financial planning is its impact on your standard of living, consumption patterns, and wealth accumulation.

    A.   Improving your standard of living is a major benefit of personal financial planning.

    B.   Spending your money more wisely is another benefit of financial planning.

        1.   Your current level of consumption is based on the necessities of life and your average propensity to consume.

        2.   A portion of current income should be set aside for deferred (future) consumption.

    C.   Personal financial planning plays a critical role in the accumulation of wealth by directing financial resources to the most productive areas.

II. Personal financial plans are based on your financial goals and cover all the key elements of your financial affairs, from budgeting expenses to retirement and estate planning.

    A.   Financial goals must be defined in the common denominator of money.

        1.   Money is a measure of value used in our economy.

        2.   Money is not only an economic concept. You have a unique personality and emotional makeup that determines the importance of money in your life.

        3.   Types of personal financial goals include: controlling living expenses, increasing total and discretionary income, reducing personal debt, establishing an emergency fund, saving for major assets, and setting up an education fund. Starting a risk management program, establishing a retirement fund, developing savings and investment programs, starting a personal business, and tax and estate planning are other personal financial objectives.

    B.   Financial plans may be categorized as: liability and insurance plans, savings and investment plans, tax plans, retirement and estate plans.

        1.   The typical financial planning life cycle begins with negative income since a child is dependent on its parents. Gradually income increases during the

early and middle years of adulthood. During the retirement years, income usually declines.

2. Liability and insurance planning is a critical aspect of financial planning to protect assets and dependents.

3. The importance of a savings and investment program increases as income increases.

4. Tax planning involves looking at your current and projected earnings and developing strategies that will minimize or defer taxes.

5. Retirement planning must begin long before the actual retirement date.

C. Personal financial planning can be aided considerably by the personal computer.

III. Financial planning must also consider an economic environment impacted by a variety of forces.

A. The key players in the economic environment are government, business, and consumers.
  1. Government provides essential services but also constrains businesses and consumers.
    a. Personal financial decisions should be evaluated on an after-tax basis.
    b. Legal regulations must be taken into consideration when devising a personal financial plan.
  2. Consumers need to understand the role and effects of business on their financial plans since its activities largely affect the cost and availability of goods and services in our economy.
  3. A consumer must learn about and accept the existing financial environment and plan transactions within it.

B. The economy is the result of interaction among government, business, and consumers. A typical economic cycle contains four stages: expansion, recession, depression, and recovery.

C. The economy is based on an exchange system of prices over which the average consumer has no control. A general increase in prices is known as inflation and is a vital aspect of financial planning.

IV. The amount of money you make is determined by your age, your level of education, your career, and geographical location.

A. People with low incomes are generally very young or very old. The period of highest earnings for most people is between the ages of 35 and 55.

B. Heads of households with formal degrees earn higher annual incomes than those with no degrees.

C. The type of job affects earnings potential. The highest earnings tend to occur among professional and managerial workers.

FILL IN THE BLANK

1.   The way you live, the way you spend, and the amount and types of assets you own are all products of the way you manage your ___money___ .

2.   The presence or absence of certain material items, such as a home, cars or jewelry, are commonly associated with your _standard of living_

3.   One trend that has had a profound effect on our standard of living is the _2-income_ family.

4.   Your current level of consumption is based on the _necessities of life_ and your average propensity _to consume_ .

5.   In a carefully drawn financial plan, a portion of current income will be set aside for ___deferred___ or future consumption.

6.   Personal financial planning plays a critical role in the accumulation of ___wealth___ , since it helps direct our financial resources to the most productive areas.

7.   ___real assets___ assets are tangible, physical assets that can be held for either consumption or investment purposes.

8.   ___financial___ assets are intangible, paper assets that are held for the returns they promise.

9.   ___money___ is the common denominator by which all financial transactions are gauged.

10.   The role of money is economic and _emotional_ or _psychological_ .

11.   ___utility___ refers to the amount of satisfaction a person receives from purchasing certain types of goods or services.

12.   A ___liability___ is something we owe and is represented by the amount of debt we have incurred.

13.   ___insurance___ provides a means of protecting our income and our assets.

14.   Financial planning is conducted in an environment in which the ___gov't___ , business, and ___consumers___ are all influential participants and financial decisions are affected by economic conditions and _consumer price behavior_

15. The financial planning environment contains various groups of players: _____gov't_____, _____business_____, and _____consumers_____.

16. The two principal constraints placed upon businesses and consumers by the government from the financial planner's perspective are _____taxes_____ and _____regulation_____.

17. A typical economic cycle contains four stages: _____expansion_____, _____recession_____, _____depression_____, and _____recovery_____.

18. High rates of _____inflation_____ drive up the cost of money.

19. Your income will be affecteed by your _____age_____, your level of _____education_____, and your _____career_____.

20. Typically, people with _____low_____ incomes fall into the very young or very old age groups.

21. The period of highest earnings generally occurs between ages _____35_____ and _____55_____.

CASE PROBLEM

Case 1.1 Jack and Jenny Establish Their Goals

It is January 1993. Jack and Jenny are newlyweds. They feel that it is important to start early to establish and reach their long- and short-term financial goals, which are as follows:

1. To double their combined income in five years.
2. To begin putting money aside for the down payment on a house they hope to buy in five years.
3. To set aside an emergency fund equal to three months of Jack's salary by year end.
4. To buy a second car by year end.
5. To take their first cruise for their third wedding anniversary.
6. To participate in Jenny's employer-sponsored pension fund as much as possible.

With these goals in mind, complete the personal financial goals worksheet that follows. Your main contribution will be to assign priorities to these goals.

PERSONAL FINANCIAL GOALS				
Name(s) _____		Date _____		
Type of Financial Goal	Brief Description	Degree of Priority (High, Medium, or Low)	Target Date	Cost
Increase income				
Gain control over living expenses				
Have more money left over for discretionary/ entertainment purchases				
Set up an education fund for yourself, your spouse, and/or your children				
Establish an emergency fund to meet unexpected expenses				
Implement procedures to keep your tax burden to a minimum				
Put money aside for a home, car, and/or other major expenditures				
Pay off/reduce personal debt; bring monthly debt service requirements down to a more manageable level				
Provide adequate protection against personal risks — life, disability, health, property, and liability insurance				
Start a general savings and investment program to accumulate capital and achieve financial security				
Start your own business				
Set up a retirement fund to supplement social security and employer-sponsored retirement programs				
Maximize the disposition/transfer of estate to heirs				
Other personal financial objectives and goals				

Chapter 2

Measuring Your Financial Standing

CHAPTER OUTLINE

I. Personal financial statements provide a measurement of your current financial standing.

II. The balance sheet or statement of financial position summarizes your financial condition at a certain point. Categories on a balance sheet are assets, liabilities, and net worth.

    A. Assets, the items you own, may be grouped into four broad categories: liquid assets, real property, personal property, and investments. They are recorded at fair market value.

        1. Liquid assets are those financial assets that are held in the form of cash or can be readily converted into cash with little or no loss in value.

        2. Real and personal property are tangible assets that can be lived in, sat on, driven, or worn.

        3. Investments are intangible assets acquired in order to earn a return rather than to provide a service.

    B. Liabilities represent an individual's or family's debts.

    C. Net worth is the amount of actual wealth, or equity, held in owned assets and is determined by subtracting liabilities from assets. If net worth is less than zero, the family is insolvent.

III. An income and expenditures statement provides a summary of income received and money spent over a given period of time, usually one year.

    A. Income shown on the income and expenditures statement includes wages, salaries, bonuses and commissions; earnings on savings and investments (interest and dividends); and the proceeds from the sale of an asset.

    B. Expenditures on the income and expenditure statement represent cash outlays for any purpose.

        1. When income exceeds expenditures, a cash surplus results that should increase net worth.

    2.   When expenditures exceed income, a cash deficit results that decreases net worth.

IV.   Personal finance statements help you to compare past and present financial standing to long-term financial goals.

    A.   Financial statements should be prepared at least once each year, ideally in conjunction with budget preparation.

    B.   After preparation of the financial statements, you should analyze them in order to assess your progress toward your financial goals.

        1.   Focus on the net worth figures on the balance sheet. Two ratios which measure financial stability are the solvency ratio and the liquidity ratio.

        2.   Focus on the bottom line of your income/expense statement. The savings ratio is a measurement of the percentage of your net income you were able to save. The debt service ratio is a measure of your ability to meet your financial obligations.

    C.   Financial statements can be used as forecasting tools to help to assess your progress toward your goals.

FILL IN THE BLANK

1.   Personal _____ are important to the financial planning process, since they provide a system for monitoring your progress toward your goals.

2.   A _____ provides a statement of your financial condition describing the assets you hold, debts you owe, and your net worth at a given point in time.

3.   The _____ provides a measure of financial performance over time; it keeps track of income earned as well as expenditures made over a given period of time.

4.   _____ assets are the cash and near-cash holdings of individuals that are used to meet living expenses, make purchases, and pay bills and loans.

5.   A VCR is an example of _____ property.

6.   A vacation home is an example of _____ property.

7.   _____ are assets that are acquired in order to earn a return rather than provide a service.

8.   A mortgage is an example of a _____.

9. _____ loans include debts, other than mortgages, for which a series of payments are required over a specified period of time and generally finance such purchases as automobiles, appliances, furniture, and boats.

10. _____ is the amount of actual wealth, or equity, held in the owned assets.

11. An income statement prepared on a _____ basis records only the transactions which involve cash receipts or actual cash outlays.

12. _____ consist of the outflow of cash to meet living expenses, purchase assets, pay taxes and reduce debt.

13. When income exceeds expenditures a _____ results; when expenditures exceed income a _____ results.

14. A cash deficit _____ (increases/decreases) net worth.

15. Financial statements should be prepared at least _____ each year, ideally in conjunction with budget preparation.

16. The ratio of total net worth to total assets is the _____ ratio.

17. The liquidity ratio indicates your ability to _____.

18. The ratio of cash surplus to income after taxes is the _____ ratio.

19. The _____ ratio looks at the statement of income and expenditures to see if your debt level is reasonable.

11

EXERCISES

Exercise 2-1

Classify each item as an asset (A) or a liability (L).

a. _____   automobile

b. _____   computer

c. _____   credit card charges

d. _____   installment loan

e. _____   common stock

f. _____   certificate of deposit

g. _____   unpaid tuition

Exercise 2-2

Classify each asset as real property (R), personal property (P), or an investment (I).

a. _____   an ocean front lot

b. _____   a bicycle

c. _____   a certificate of deposit

d. _____   a house

e. _____   cash

Exercise 2-3

Craig is compiling information to prepare his personal balance sheet. Thus far, his total assets amount to $12,000 and his liabilities total $11,500. What is Craig's net worth?

Exercise 2-4

Jennifer has put together the following account balances as a prerequisite to calculating her net worth.

Automobile	$7,500	_____
Outstanding balance on auto loan	5,000	_____
Furniture	3,000	_____
Tuition payment	4,000	_____
Cash savings	3,000	_____
Checking account	500	_____
Personal property (clothes, shoes, etc.)	2,000	_____
Stereo and television	700	_____
Credit card charges	250	_____

a.   Classify each balance as an asset (A) or a liability (L).

b.   Calculate Jennifer's net worth. Assets $_____ minus liabilities

 $_____ equals Jennifer's net worth $_____

c.   Calculate Jennifer's solvency ratio. Total net worth $_____

 divided by total assets $_____ equals solvency ratio _____%

Exercise 2-5

Ron and Jody are compiling information to prepare a year-end income and expenditures statement. They have summarized their income and expenses in the following accounts:

Rent	$ 9,000
Insurance payments	1,500
Car payments	4,000
Food	3,000
Entertainment	1,000
Health care	500
Utilities	2,500
Ron's salary	20,000
Jody's salary	25,000
Credit card payments	1,500
Interest income	300
Clothes, shoes, etc.	2,000
Vacation	1,000
Miscellaneous expenses	700
Taxes	5,000

a.   Prepare Ron and Jody's year-end income statement.
b.   Calculate their savings and debt service ratios on an annual basis.

Exercise 2-6

Ron and Jody have been asked to submit a personal balance sheet as an attachment to a mortgage application for their first home. They have summarized their assets and liabilities as follows:

1984 Subaru		$ 7,000
1985 Chevrolet	6,000	
Furniture		5,000
Certificate of deposit	4,000	
National direct student loan		12,000
Personal property		10,000
Checking account		1,000
Credit card charge balance		200
Loan payable on autos		2,000
Outstanding bills		300
Cash (to be used as a down payment for the house)	10,000	

a. Prepare Ron and Jody's personal balance sheet.
b. Calculate their solvency ratio.

CASE PROBLEMS

Case 2.1 Chris and Judy Prepare Their Financial Statements

Chris and Judy Catania are putting their college degrees to work in a new mail order business that sells sporting equipment to the adventure vacation enthusiast. The first year of business was a success--the business survived without any external financing. However, for the business to reach its potential, Chris and Judy must apply for a small business loan from their local bank. The loan officer has requested that Chris and Judy provide the bank with a personal income and expenditures statement and balance sheet since they will guarantee the loan with their personal assets. Chris and Judy have accumulated the following information about their past year's financial situation. All expenses are stated on an annual basis.

Auto loan payment	$ 3,600
Auto loan balance	7,890
Auto values	15,000
Cash	3,000
Bonds	2,050
Clothing expense	1,500
Dividends	200
Electric expense	1,800
Entertainment expense	1,000
Gasoline and repairs	1,200
Groceries	3,900
Salaries (Chris $15,000; Judy $22,000)	37,000
Healthcare expense	1,000
Household assets	12,400
Insurance expense (auto and homeowners)	1,500
Interest income	300
MasterCard balance	450
Miscellaneous expenses	700
Mortgage balance	65,000
Mortgage payment (including taxes)	10,800
Natural gas	840
Repairs (home)	570
Residence value	80,000
Stocks	5,000
Taxes (income)	5,500
Telephone expense	480
Visa balance	100
Water	240

Questions

1. Prepare an income and expenditures statement for Chris and Judy on the form provided.
2. Prepare a balance sheet for Chris and Judy on the form provided.
3. Calculate their solvency, liquidity, savings, and debt safety ratios.
4. Comment on Chris and Judy's financial performance last year.
5. Forecast their net worth one year from now assuming their income increases 20 percent, the total expenses remain the same and the market value of their assets increase five percent. The auto loan balance and the mortgage loan balance will decrease by the annual total payments, respectively. The credit card balance will remain the same.

INCOME AND EXPENDITURES STATEMENT

Name(s) _____

For the _____ Ending _____

INCOME		
Wages and salaries	Name:	$
	Name:	
	Name:	
Self-employment income		
Bonuses and commissions		
Pensions and annuities		
Investment income	Interest received	
	Dividends received	
	Rents received	
	Sale of securities	
	Other	
Other income		
	(I) Total Income $	

EXPENDITURES		
Housing	Rent/mortgage payment (include insurance and taxes, if applicable)	
	Repairs, maintenance, improvements	
Utilities	Gas, electric, water	
	Phone	
	Cable TV and other	
Food	Groceries	
	Dining out	
Autos	Loan payments	
	License plates, fees, etc.	
	Gas, oil, repairs, tires, maintenance	
Medical	Health, major medical, disability insurance (payroll deductions or not provided by employer)	
	Doctor, dentist, hospital, medicines	
Clothing	Clothes, shoes, and accessories	
Insurance	Homeowner's (if not covered by mortgage payment)	
	Life (not provided by employer)	
	Auto	
Taxes	Income and social security	
	Property (if not included in mortgage)	
Appliances, furniture, and other major purchases	Loan payments	
	Purchases and repairs	
Personal care	Laundry, cosmetics, hair care	
Recreation and entertainment	Vacations	
	Other Recreation and entertainment	
Other items		
	(II) Total Expenditures $	
	CASH SURPLUS (OR DEFICIT) [(I)–(II)] $	

BALANCE SHEET			

Name(s) _____ Dated _____

ASSETS		LIABILITIES AND NET WORTH	
Liquid Assets		**Current Liabilities**	
Cash on hand	$	Utilities	$
In checking		Rent	
Savings accounts		Insurance premiums	
Money market funds and deposits		Taxes	
		Medical/dental bills	
Certificates of deposit (<1 yr. to maturity)		Repair bills	
		Bank credit card balances	
Total Liquid Assets		Dept. store credit card balances	
		Travel and entertainment card balances	
Investments			
Stocks		Gas and other credit card balances	
		Bank line of credit balances	
Bonds			
		Other current liabilities	
Certificates of deposit (>1 yr. to maturity)			
Mutual funds		**Total Current Liabilities**	
Real estate		**Long-Term Liabilities**	
Retirement funds, IRA		Primary residence mortgage	
Other		Second home mortgage	
Total Investments		Real estate investment mortgage	
		Auto loans	
Real Property		Appliance/furniture loans	
Primary residence		Home improvement loans	
Second home		Single-payment loans	
Car(s):		Education loans	
Car(s):		Other long-term loans from parents	
Recreation equipment			
Other		**Total Long-Term Liabilities**	
Total Real Property			
Personal Property			
Furniture and appliances			
Stereos, TVs, etc.			
Clothing		**(II) Total Liabilities**	$
Jewelry			
Other		Net Worth [(I)–(II)]	$
Total Personal Property			
(I) Total Assets		**Total Liabilities and Net Worth**	$

Chapter 3

Planning Your Financial Future

CHAPTER OUTLINE

I.   Budgeting provides direction for future financial activities as well as a method to keep financial transactions on track.

    A.   Financial planning is a process for developing financial goals and related courses of action. A budget is a detailed financial forecast used to monitor and control expenditures and purchases.

    B.   The financial planning process generally involves the following steps:
        1.   Defining financial goals.
        2.   Developing financial plans and strategies to put goals into action.
        3.   Implementing financial plans and strategies.
        4.   Monitoring progress toward specific goals.
        5.   Evaluating results and taking corrective action when necessary.
        6.   Revising and replacing goals as they are achieved or changed.

    C.   Professional financial planners can help in setting up and carrying out fully developed financial plans.
        1.   Financial planners run the gamut from salesmen offering services for a commission to independent, fee-based planners.
        2.   To avoid problems, select a financial planner very carefully.
        3.   Computerized financial plans are also available.

II. The financial planning process begins with the definition of both long-term and short-term financial goals, which in turn provide direction for financial plans and budgets.

    A.   Long-term financial goals should indicate your family's wants and needs for the next 2-5 years on out to the next 30-40 years.
        1.   Financial goals should be initially measured in today's dollar amounts.
        2.   Financial goals should have target dates.

    B.   Short-run financial goals cover a 12-month period.

    C.   Future value calculations help specify long-term goals by estimating the impact of inflation.

III.   Cash budgets are prepared from schedules of estimated income and expenditures for the coming year and provide a system of disciplined spending. The cash budgeting process has three stages: estimating income, estimating expenditures, and finalizing the budget.

    A.   The first step in the cash budget preparation process is to prepare a schedule of estimated income for each month of the coming year.

    B.   The second stage of the cash budgeting process is the preparation of the estimated expenditures. Expenditures should be grouped into categories such as fixed (mortgage or rent payments, other loan payments, insurance, utility bills), flexible (food, medical, gasoline), and periodic (insurance, repairs).

    C.   Finalizing the cash budget requires preparing projected income and expenditures and summarizing the data on a month-to-month and an annual basis.

        1.   If a monthly budget deficit exists, two remedies exist: a) expenditures may be transferred from deficit months to surplus months, and b) income may be transferred from surplus months to deficit months.

        2.   If an annual deficit exists, several solutions may be available: a) liquidate enough savings and investments, or b) borrow the deficit amount; c) cut lower priority expenditure items, or d) increase income.

    D.   A cash budget is valuable only if it is put into use and careful records are kept of actual income and expenditures.

FILL IN THE BLANK

1.   _Financial planning_ is a process by which financial goals and related courses of action are developed.

2.   A _budget_ is a detailed financial forecast that is used to monitor and control expenditures and purchases.

3.   The first step in financial planning is _define fin. goals_.

4.   _Financial planner_ can provide major help in creating your financial plan.

5.   Long-run financial goals should indicate an individual's or family's wants and desires for the next _2-5 to 30 or 40_ years.

6.   Financial goals should be established using today's _dollars_ and _target dates_ should be set.

7.   Short-run financial goals cover a _12 month_ period.

8.   _Cash Budgets_ are prepared from schedules of estimated income and expenditures for the coming year and provide a system of disciplined spending.

9. The cash budget preparation process has three stages: estimating _income_, estimating _expenses_, and _finalizing the budget_

10. A cash budget should be divided into _monthly_ intervals.

11. If a monthly deficit is projected, you could 1) _transfer expenditures_ or 2) _use savings_ to remedy the situation.

12. If an annual deficit is projected, you could: (1) liquidate _savings_, (2) borrow, (3) cut _low priority expenses_, or (4) increase _income_.

13. A _budget control_ schedule provides a summary of how actual income and expenditures compare with the various budget categories and where budget variances exist.

14. A _balanced_ budget is one in which total income for the period equals total expenditures for the period.

CASE PROBLEMS

Case 3.1 Setting Goals

Mick and Megan Harrison are both 27 years old and have been married for three years. They have a two-year-old daughter and another baby is due in five months. Now that their responsibilities are growing and their financial future seems a bit more predictable because of the security of Roy's job, they have decided to begin the personal financial management process by setting long- and short-term goals. These goals include:

1. A $40,000 college fund for each of the children. They will enter college at age 18.
2. A vacation after the baby arrives, which should cost about $1,000.
3. A retirement fund amounting to $250,000 when they retire at age 65.
4. A new house in four years, $150,000 cost ($30,000 down payment needed).
5. A cruise around the world for their twenty-fifth anniversary.
6. A larger apartment in the next few months. Rent will go up $200 to $850 per month.
7. More term life insurance now.
8. A new car in three years.
9. Contribute $100 per month to employer-sponsored retirement fund.
10. Visit friends in Europe in 1995.
11. Net worth in 20 years of $200,000.
12. Net worth in 30 years of $450,000.

It is February 1993. Prepare a statement of personal financial goals which distinguishes between long- and short-term goals. Use the form from text Exhibit 3.4 that follows.

Case 3.2 The Jacksons Prepare a Budget

Lauren and Mark Jackson are a married couple in their late thirties. Lauren is a schoolteacher with an annual take-home pay of $16,500. Mark earns $24,000 after taxes as a bank manager. The Jacksons have three school-age children, Jennifer, Scott, and Margaret. Mark is concerned that they have not been saving enough and has been keeping track of their expenditures to determine where cutbacks can be made. The Jacksons' expenditures for the past year have been summarized below.

Expenditure Category	Amount Spent
Groceries	$ 4,860
Auto expenditures	2,430
Clothing	2,025
Travel	3,215
Dental expenses	1,025
Health care cost (deductible from Mark's employer-provided insurance)	1,000
Mortgage payments	10,125
Property taxes	2,100
Income taxes	4,000
Increase in savings	1,215
Entertainment	1,620
Utilities	1,215
Auto insurance	1,620
Miscellaneous	4,050

In his search for data that will provide a benchmark for comparison, Mark found a study reporting average expenditures for families similar to his. The study follows (on page 26).

PERSONAL FINANCIAL GOALS

Name(s) _____ Date _____

LONG-RUN GOALS

Goal Date	Goal Description

SHORT-RUN GOALS (for the coming year)

Priority	Goal Description	Dollar Outlay
1		
2		
3		
4		
5		
6		
7		
8		
9		
10		

Survey Data	
Expenditure Category	Percent Spent
Housing	30
Food and groceries	15
Transportation	10
Vacation/recreation	5
Health care/insurance	3
Clothing	4
Taxes	15
Savings and investments	6
Other	12
	100%

Questions

1.   Compare the Jacksons' expenditures for the past year with survey data.

Expenditure category	Survey (%)	Jacksons %
Housing		
Food and groceries		
Transportation		
Vacation/recreation		
Health care/insurance		
Clothing		
Taxes		
Savings and investments		
Other		

2.   Which expenditures are above average and below average?

Expenditure category	Above/Below	% Above/Below

3.   Is Mark's concern about saving justified according to comparative data?

Case 3.3 What is Gerald's Monthly Cash Inflow?

Gerald is in the process of putting together his cash budget for next year, 1994. Prepare a statement for him of estimated income from the facts below. Fill out the form that follows, which corresponds to Exhibit 3.5 in the text.

1. Gerald's current take-home pay is $2,100 per month. He expects an eight percent raise in June.
2. His quarterly bonus, paid in January, April, July, and October is usually 20 percent of his monthly take-home pay.
3. He will receive a dividend of $150 in August.
4. His checking account pays monthly interest of approximately $10.

Case 3.4 The Morgenstern's Year Ahead

Jesse and Jennifer Morgenstern's are in the process of preparing their cash budget for 1994. Since their first step is to prepare an annual statement of estimated expenditures, they have assembled the following information.

1. Monthly rent is $850; they expect a four percent increase in September.
2. Gas, electricity, and water are about $150 per month.
3. The telephone bill averages $45 per month.
4. Groceries cost about $300 per month and they spend about $200 per month eating out.
5. They make a $120 auto payment each month.
6. Auto licenses cost $125 each year.
7. Auto maintenance averages $100 per month.
8. All health insurance is provided by Mr. Morgenstern's employer.
9. They spend about $150 per month for clothes.
10. Renters insurance is $220 per year.
11. Auto insurance is $650 annually.
12. Other loan payments are $200 per month.
13. The Morgensterns put $75 per month into their vacation fund.
14. They currently save $100 per month.
15. Charitable contributions are $500 annually.
16. Tuition for an occasional class at the junior college is $100 annually.
17. Subscriptions amount to $250 annually.

Prepare a cash budget statement of annual expenditures using the following worksheet, similar to Exhibit 3.6 in the textbook.

CASH BUDGET: ESTIMATED INCOME

Name(s) _____

For the _____ Ending _____

SOURCES OF INCOME		Jan.	Feb.	Mar.	April.	May	June	July	Aug.	Sep.	Oct.	Nov.	Dec.	Total for the Year
Take-home pay	Name:													
	Name:													
	Name:													
Bonuses and commissions														
Pensions and annuities														
Investment income	Interest													
	Dividends													
	Rents													
	Sale of securities													
	Other													
Other income														
TOTAL INCOME														

CASH BUDGET: ESTIMATED EXPENDITURES

Name(s) _____

For the _____ Ending _____

EXPENDITURE CATEGORIES		Jan.	Feb.	Mar.	Apr.	May	June	July	Aug.	Sep.	Oct.	Nov.	Dec.	Total for the Year
Housing	Rent/mortgage payment (include insurance and taxes, if applicable)													
	Repairs, maint., improvements													
Utilities	Gas, electric, water													
	Phone													
	Cable TV and other													
Food	Groceries													
	Dining out													
Autos	Loan payments													
	License plates, fees, etc.													
	Gas, oil, repairs, tires, maintenance													
Medical	Health, major medical, disability insurance (not provided by employer)													
	Doctor, dentist, hospital, medicines													
Clothing	Clothes, shoes, and accessories													
Insurance	Homeowners (if not covered by mortgage payment)													
	Life (not provided by employer)													
	Auto													
Taxes	Income and social security													
	Property (if not included in mortgage)													
Appliances, furniture, and other	Loan payments													
	Purchases and repairs													
Personal care	Laundry, cosmetics, hair care													
Recreation and entertainment	Vacations													
	Other recreation and entertainment													
Savings and investments	Savings, stocks, bonds, etc.													
Other expenditures	Charitable contributions													
	Gifts													
	Education loan payment													
	Subscriptions, magazines, books													
	Other:													
	Other:													
Fun Money														
TOTAL EXPENDITURES														

Chapter 3 Planning Your Financial Future

Case 3.5 Where Have All the Dollars Gone?

George and Irene Smith have been having some minor financial problems that seem to be related to their expenditures. They feel their spending is out of control. They have decided a cash budget is very important and they especially want a detailed expenditure statement. The following summarizes the expenditures that they anticipate for 1994.

1. The mortgage payment is $789 per month.
2. Repairs and maintenance are about $100 per month.
3. Utilities average $200 per month while the phone costs $75. Cable TV is $26 per month.
4. Groceries are $250 per month and eating out is $350 per month.
5. They have two car loans for a total monthly payment of $750. However, the last payment of $300 on one of the loans is May 1.
6. Auto licenses are $215 annually, paid in July.
7. Auto maintenance and fuel average $125 per month.
8. All health insurance is paid by George's employer. The only significant bill is for the dentist — $80 every January and July.
9. Clothing averages $150 per month.
10. The life insurance premium is due in November and is $600.
11. Auto insurance is due in July and costs $825.
12. Other loan payments are $350 monthly.
13. A vacation in August is expected to cost $1,200 but the cash flow should be about $400 in August and the remainder in September.
14. The Smiths save $80 per month.
15. Charitable contributions are $360 annually and spread out monthly.
16. Subscriptions are $108 per year — $40 in August, $18 in September, $30 in October, and $20 in December.
17. Fun money covers most other incidentals and is $150 per month for each of the two Smiths.

Prepare a statement of monthly cash expenditures using the following worksheet.

Case 3.6 Preparing the Hillman's Cash Budget

Carolyn and Edward Hillman are a married couple in their mid-twenties. Carolyn has just completed her MBA program and has been hired by General Electric as a budget analyst earning $27,000 per year after taxes. Edward is still attending law school and works part-time as a bartender 10 hours per week ($300 per month from September through May). During June, July, and August, Edward is paid $1,440 a month to clerk at a local law firm. Carolyn has decided to set up a monthly cash budget to predict their expenditures and analyze how Edward's law school expenses will be met for the coming academic year. The projected expenditures for the period August, 1993, through August, 1994, are as follows:

CASH BUDGET: ESTIMATED EXPENDITURES		
Name(s)_____		
For the _____ Ending _____		

	EXPENDITURE CATEGORIES	Annual Amounts
Housing (12–30%)	Rent/mortgage payment (include insurance and taxes, if applicable)	$
	Repairs, maint., improvements	
Utilities (4–8%)	Gas, electric, water	
	Phone	
	Cable TV and other	
Food (15–25%)	Groceries	
	Dining out	
Autos (5–18%)	Loan payments	
	License plates, fees, etc.	
	Gas, oil, repairs, tires, maintenance	
Medical (2–10%)	Health, major medical, disability insurance (payroll deductions or not provided by employer)	
	Doctor, dentist, hospital, medicine	
Clothing (3–8%)	Clothes, shoes and accessories	
Insurance (4–8%)	Homeowner's (if not covered by mortgage payment)	
	Life (not provided by employer)	
	Auto	
Taxes (N/A)	Income and social security	
	Property (if not included in mortgage)	
Appliances, furniture and other major purchases (2-8%)	Loan payments	
	Purchases and repairs	
	Other:	
Personal care (1–3%)	Laundry, cosmetics, hair care	
Recreation and entertainment (2–8%)	Vacations	
	Other recreation and entertainment	
Savings and investments (3–10%)	Savings, stocks, bonds, etc.	
Other expenditures (1–10%)	Charitable contributions	
	Gifts	
	Education Loan	
	Subscriptions, magazines, books	
	Other:	
	Other:	
Fun money (1–5%)		
	TOTAL EXPENDITURES	$

Expenditure Category	Monthly Expenditure
Gas and electricity	$ 65
Groceries	100
Telephone	25
Rent	400
Medical	29
Property insurance	20
Auto loan payments	208
Auto insurance	55
Laundry	27
Entertainment and eating out	125
Gas, oil, car repair	40
National Student Direct Loan payments (Carolyn's)	50
Edward's tuition	*
Edward's books	**
Clothing	***
Cable television	22

   * Edward's tuition is $5,500 each term, due in August and January.

  ** Two payments in August and January of $400.

*** Carolyn's professional wardrobe will need to be supplemented in September ($1,200) and in March ($800). Edward's clothing costs amount to $500 and will be spent equally in August, December, March, and June.

Questions

1. Assuming all expenditures except tuition, books, and clothing are budgeted in equal monthly amounts, prepare the Hillman's monthly budget for the period from August 1, 1993 to August 1, 1994. Prepare the monthly cash budget summary that follows.
2. Analyze the budget, and advise the Hillmans on their monthly cash situation.

CASH BUDGET: MONTHLY SUMMARY

Name(s) _____

For the _____ Ending _____

	Jan.	Feb.	Mar.	Apr.	May	June	July	Aug.	Sep.	Oct.	Nov.	Dec.	Total for the Year
INCOME													
Take-home pay													
Bonuses and commissions													
Pensions and annuities													
Investment income													
Other income													
(I) Total Income													
EXPENDITURES													
Housing													
Utilities													
Food													
Autos													
Medical													
Clothing													
Insurance													
Taxes													
Appliances, furniture, and other													
Personal care													
Recreation and entertainment													
Savings and investments													
Other expenditures													
Fun Money													
(II) Total Expenditures													
CASH SURPLUS (OR DEFICIT) [(I) – (II)]													
CUMULATIVE CASH SURPLUS (OR DEFICIT)													

Chapter 3 Planning Your Financial Future

Case 3.7 How Did the Hillmans Do?

The Hillmans of Case 3.6 have been functioning under their budget for several months now and they have actual results for January, February, and March, which are as follows:

Actual Amount

Category	January	February	March
Take-home pay	$2,550	$2,550	$2,550
Housing	400	400	420
Utilities	93	85	80
Food	125	130	110
Autos	196	210	260
Medical	0	45	60
Clothing	0	0	845
Insurance	75	75	75
Tuition	5,500	0	0
Books	390	0	45
Recreation	160	75	30
NSDL	50	50	50
Laundry	30	20	25

1. Complete the Budget Control Schedule that follows. It is from Exhibit 3.9 in the text.
2. Comment on the variants you found.

BUDGET CONTROL SCHEDULE

Name(s) _____

For the _____ Months Ending _____

INCOME	Month: Budgeted Amount (1)	Actual (2)	Monthly Variance (3)	Year-to-Date Variance (4)	Month: Budgeted Amount (5)	Actual (6)	Monthly Variance (7)	Year-to-Date Variance (8)	Month: Budgeted Amount (9)	Actual (10)	Monthly Variance (11)	Year-to-Date Variance (12)
Take-home pay												
Bonuses and commissions												
Pensions and annuities												
Investment income												
Other income												
(I) Total Income												
EXPENDITURES												
Housing												
Utilities												
Food												
Autos												
Medical												
Clothing												
Insurance												
Taxes												
Appliances, furniture, and other												
Personal care												
Recreation and entertainment												
Savings and investments												
Other expenditures												
Fun Money												
(II) Total Expenditures												
CASH SURPLUS (OR DEFICIT) [(I) – (II)]												
CUMULATIVE CASH SURPLUS (OR DEFICIT)												

Key: Col. (3) = Col. (2) – Col. (1); Col. (7) = Col. (6) – Col. (5); Col. (11) = Col. (10) – Col. (9)
Col. (4) = Col. (3); Col. (8) = Col. (4) + Col (7); Col. (12) = Col. (8) + Col. (11)

35

Chapter 4

Managing Your Taxes

CHAPTER OUTLINE

I.   The most recent tax legislation is the <u>Tax Reform Act of 1986,</u> which originally had three purposes: 1) to simplify the tax code for individual taxpayers; 2) to reduce taxpayer abuses by closing many existing loopholes; and 3) to shift a significant amount of the tax burden from individuals to corporations.

   A.   Income taxes provide the major source of revenue for the federal government. Personal incomes are taxed at progressive rates, beginning at 15 percent. The 1986 tax legislation attempted to lessen the impact of inflation on income taxes, often referred to as bracket creep, by making provisions to adjust the income brackets annually to reflect the rate of inflation.

   B.   Income taxes are collected on a pay-as-you-go basis. This is accomplished by requiring your employer to withhold a portion of your income every pay period and to forward it to the IRS.

      1.   The amount of federal withholding taxes deducted from gross earnings each pay period depends on the level of earnings as well as the number of withholding allowances claimed on the W-4 form. Withholding allowances are based on the number of people supported by the taxpayer's income.

      2.   All employed workers (except certain federal employees) have to pay a combined old-age, survivor's, disability, and hospital insurance tax under provisions of the Federal Insurance Contributions Act (FICA). The FICA tax for 1991 is 7.65 percent of the first $53,400 of an employee's income. Your employer is required to match this tax.

      3.   State and local taxes differ from state to state. They may be income taxes, property taxes, sales taxes, estate or inheritance taxes, or licensing fees.

   C.   Taxable income can be found by using the following procedure:

	Gross Income (This includes all income that is subject to Federal taxes.)
Less:	Adjustments from gross income (IRA, alimony paid, etc.)
Equals:	**Adjusted gross income**
Less:	Itemized deductions OR standard deduction
Less:	Personal Exemptions
Equals:	**Taxable income**

1.   The Tax Reform Act of 1986 established three basic types of income: 1) ordinary ("earned") income, 2) investment income, and 3) passive income. Categories 2 and 3 were designed to limit the amount of deductions and write-offs that can be taken. For deduction purposes, investment and passive income cannot be combined with each other or with earned income.

2.   A partial list of adjustments to gross income includes: payments to individual retirement accounts, alimony paid, payments to a self-employed retirement plan, a self-employed health insurance deduction, and penalties for early withdrawal of time deposit savings.

3.   Deducting itemized expenses allows taxpayers to reduce their taxable income. Some common personal expenses that are deductible items are charitable contributions, moving expenses, medical and dental expenses, state and local income and property taxes paid, specified interest expenses, casualty and theft losses, and some employee expenses.

4.   Instead of itemizing personal deductions, a taxpayer can use the standard deduction, a type of blanket deduction.

5.   Deductions based on the number of persons supported by the taxpayer's income are called personal exemptions. A taxpayer can claim an exemption for himself or herself, his or her spouse, and any dependents--which includes children or other relatives that the taxpayer supports who earn less than a stipulated level of income.

6.   A tax credit is a direct reduction of the tax liability. Common tax credits include foreign tax credit, credit for the elderly or permanently disabled, and child and dependent care credit.

D.   Capital gains are taxed at the same rate as any other form of income; preferential treatment is no longer given.

    1.   Homeowners receive special tax treatment in the tax codes. Any taxes on the profits made on the sale of a home may be deferred almost indefinitely as long as another primary residence of equal or greater value is purchased (generally within a 24-month period). People 55 years or older may take a one-time exclusion of $125,000 in capital gains earned from the sale of their principal residences.

E.   Two basic types of returns are the joint return and the individual return.

    1.   A husband and wife may file a joint return if they were married as of the last day of the year. They may also choose to file separate returns.

    2.   A taxpayer may file an individual return as a single person or, if a single person with dependents to support, as head of household.

    3.   Because federal withholding taxes are taken only from income earned on a regular basis, the IRS requires certain people to pay estimated taxes on income earned from other sources.

    4.   The tax year corresponds to the calendar year, January 1 through December 31. Taxpayers should file their returns as soon after the beginning of the year (following the earning year) as possible and must file no later than April 15.

    5.   An automatic four-month extension of time to file, which makes the due date August 15, can be applied for simply by submitting Form 4868. However, taxes must be estimated and a check sent with the extension application. An amended return may also be filed to correct an error in the

original return. An amended return may be filed any time during the three years after the original filing date.

6.   Tax returns may be randomly selected for audit, although the chance is quite slim (1.0 - 1.5% chance).

F.   For information on how to fill out your tax return, a helpful reference source is the IRS Publication 17, <u>Your Federal Income Tax.</u>

1.   The IRS will figure taxes for those taxpayers whose taxable income is less than $50,000 and who do not itemize their deductions.

2.   Many taxpayers use private tax preparation services because they are concerned about accuracy and want to minimize their tax liability as much as possible. They may also believe the complexity of the tax forms makes preparation too difficult or time consuming.

3.   A number of tax software packages are available for PCs that can reduce the hours of figuring all the forms and schedules involved in filing a return. There are basically two software packages: tax planning and tax preparation.

II.   The amount of taxes you pay depends on the rate at which your income is taxed and the amount of taxable income you have.

A.   Tax rates vary not only with the amount of reported taxable income but also according to the filing status used.

1.   For 1991, three marginal tax rates are used: 15%, 28%, and 31%. For a schedule of tax rates, see Exhibit 4.5 in the text. The top tax rate actually represents a surcharge that is levied against taxpayers with high incomes. This surcharge was designed to phase out personal exemptions for wealthy taxpayers.

B.   The IRS requires taxpayers to file their tax returns using specified tax forms.

1.   Form 1040EZ is the simplest, followed by the 1040A, and finally the 1040, the so-called long form, which is also a universal form that can be used by all taxpayers. The 1040 may be accompanied by various forms and schedules to explain items on the tax form.

C.   An illustration of a completed 1040 for Terry and Evelyn Becker is included in the text.

III.   In addition to federal income taxes, individuals pay other types of taxes at the federal, state, and local levels.

A.   Other federal taxes include social security taxes, excise taxes, gift and estate taxes, and other miscellaneous taxes.

1.   The second largest tax for most families is the social security tax or FICA. This tax was 7.65% of gross earnings paid by both the employee and the employer. There is a cap on the amount of FICA tax payable; the maximum taxable income was $53,400 for 1991. Marital status has no effect on the social security tax to be paid.

2.   Taxes levied by the federal government on the purchase of certain luxury items and services are called excise taxes.

3. Gift taxes are levied on a gift (after a stated amount per recipient per year) and are paid by the giver. Estate taxes are levied on the value of an estate left upon the death of its owner.

B. State governments levy taxes to cover their operating expenses; the most important is the sales tax. Other state taxes include income taxes, property taxes, and licensing fees.

C. The majority of local taxes are property taxes, although income taxes, sales taxes and licensing fees may also apply.

IV. Comprehensive tax planning is aimed at reducing taxes and takes both an immediate and long-term perspective; it includes several functions that are closely interrelated with other financial planning activities.

A. Tax planning involves the use of various investment vehicles, retirement programs, and estate distribution procedures that have the effect of reducing, shifting, or deferring taxes.

B. Some popular tax strategies follow:

1. Income shifting is where the taxpayer shifts (through trusts or custodial accounts or outright gifts) a portion of his or her income--and thus taxes-- to relatives in lower tax brackets.

2. Tax shelters are a form of investment that take advantage of tax write-offs allowed in the current tax code.

3. Some investments provide income on which the taxes may be paid at a later date, deferring the tax. The most common example of a tax-deferred investment is an Individual Retirement Account (IRA).

FILL IN THE BLANK

1. The "modern" federal income tax law was outlined in the Internal Revenue Code of _____1939_____.

2. The purpose of the Tax Reform Act of 1986 was 1) to simplify the _____tax code_____ for individuals, 2) to reduce _____taxpayers abuses_____ by closing many of the existing loopholes, and 3) to shift a significant amount of the tax burden from _____individuals_____ to _____corporations_____.

3. The progressive tax structure results in _____lower_____ (higher/lower) average tax rates than stated rates.

4. An important part of the Economic Reform Tax Act of 1981 (ERTA) was its attempt to reduce the impact of inflation on income taxes, referred to as _____bracket creep_____.

5. The IRS expects to collect income taxes on a _____pay as you go_____ basis.

6. The amount of federal withholding taxes deducted from earnings each pay period depends on the level of _____earnings_____ and the number of _____w/holding allowances_____

7. Personal exemptions are based, for the most part, on the _____dependents_____ you support.

8. The Federal Insurance Contributions Act (FICA) levies a tax at a rate of _____7.65%_____ percent against the first $_____53,400.—_____ of the employee's income in 1991.

9. Your gross income, minus adjustments to gross income, minus itemized deductions, and minus _____personal exempt'ns_____ equals taxable income.

10. According to the tax code definition, the three basic types of income are 1) _____actual_____, 2) _____portfolio_____, and 3) _____passive_____.

11. _____active_____ income, the broadest category of income, includes wages, salaries, pension income, and alimony.

12. _____portfolio_____ income is comprised of the earnings generated from various types of investment holdings.

13. _____passive_____ income is a special category of income derived from real estate, limited partnerships, and other forms of tax shelters.

14. The key feature about the categories of income is that they limit the amount of _____deductions_____ and _____write-offs_____ that may be taken.

15. For deduction purposes, the investment and passive income categories _____cannot_____ (can/cannot) be mixed with each other or earned income.

16. You can deduct your contributions to an Individual Retirement Account only if _____not covered under co. retirement plan or annual income < specified amount_____

17. State and local property taxes are an example of personal expenses you might choose to _____itemized_____.

18. Contributions to charitable organizations are allowed to be deducted up to _____ percent of your adjusted gross income.

19. Interest paid on first and second mortgages may be deducted subject to limitations: 1) the mortgages can only be on the _____ and _____ residences, and 2) the amount borrowed can be no more than the _____ price paid for the residence with some adjustments.

20. Job related expenses are deductible only to the extent that they exceed _____ percent of the adjusted gross income.

Chapter 4 Coping With Taxes

21.   Instead of itemizing deductions, a taxpayer can use the
        _____ deduction.

22.   In 1991, each personal exemption claimed is worth $_____.

23.   A _____ is a direct reduction of your tax liability.

24.   There _____ (is/is not) any preferential tax treatment given to
        capital gains.

25.   If a new home is not purchased within 24 months from the date of sale of the old
        home, taxes must be paid on _____ realized from the sale of this
        home and any _____.

26.   A husband and wife may file a _____ tax return if they are married
        as of the last day of the year.

27.   A unmarried taxpayer may file as a _____ or if the taxpayer is a
        single person with dependents, as a _____.

28.   The date by which taxpayers must file their returns is _____.

29.   An automatic _____ month filing extension can be applied for by
        submitting the appropriate form.

30.   Your chances of having your tax return audited are less than _____
        percent.

31.   The three marginal tax rates currently in effect are: _____ percent,
        _____ percent, and _____ percent.

32.   Taxes levied by the federal government on the purchase of certain luxury items and
        services are called _____ taxes.

33.   The largest source of state revenue is the _____ tax.

34.   The primary source of income to cities, counties, school districts and other
        municipalities is the taxation of _____ and _____
        property.

35.   Tax _____ includes illegal activities such as omitting income or
        overstating deductions.

36.   Tax _____ is concerned with reducing taxes in ways that are legal
        and compatible with the intent of Congress.

37.   When a taxpayer shifts a portion of income to family members in lower tax brackets,
        he is attempting to reduce taxes by _____.

38. _____ are certain types of investments that provide write-offs in the form of depreciation, amortization, or depletion.

39. An IRA is an example of a tax_____ investment.

EXERCISES

Exercise 4-1

Mary, Ann, and Susan earn $10,000, $20,000, and $30,000 respectively. Mary's federal income taxes are $667.50, Ann's are $2,167.50, and Susan's amount to $4,200.50. Calculate each woman's average tax rate. How does the average tax rate compare with their individual marginal tax rates?

Exercise 4-2

Tim, Doug, and Brian work for ACSI, Inc. Their salaries are shown below.

a. Calculate the FICA or social security tax each individual must pay per year in 1991.
b. How much FICA tax would the employer pay in each case?

	Annual Salary
Tim	$50,000
Doug	$30,000
Brian	$28,000

Chapter 4 Coping With Taxes

Exercise 4-3

Lee Woods is single and has no dependents. She has listed the financial information below to prepare her 1991 income tax return.

Gross wages	$45,050
Interest paid on mortgage	4,280
Sales taxes paid	1,050
Interest income from savings	6,250
Charitable donation	500
Moving expenses	1,000
IRA contribution	2,000
State income taxes	675
Rental income	24,000
Property taxes	1,500
Expenses incurred on rental property	18,000
Alimony from ex-husband	6,000
Inheritance proceeds from late father	25,000

Given the information above:

a.   Determine in which category each expense or income item belongs: gross income, gross income deduction, itemized deduction, tax exempt, or not allowed.

b.   How much taxable income will Lee have in 1991? Lee is covered by her company's pension plan.

Exercise 4-4

Indicate whether the following types of income are taxable (T) or tax-exempt (E).

a. _____   Profits from tax preparation service run by your spouse.

b. _____   A new car given to you by your parents as a wedding gift.

c. _____   Social security benefits received by a high school student due to her mother's death (her only income).

d. _____   Alimony payments.

e. _____   Grand prize winnings from the state lotto.

f. _____   Insurance proceeds from a life insurance policy covering your father.

g. _____   Christmas bonus from your employer.

h. _____   Gain from sale of rental property.

i. _____   Scholarship based on academic merit used for tuition expenses.

j. _____   A stock dividend received from Beta J, Inc.

Exercise 4-5

For each of the following cases, determine whether the capital gain from the sale of the house may be deferred (D), will be taxed (T), or qualifies for the one-time exclusion (E).

a. _____   Jim and Janet Jones are both in their early thirties. They have just sold their primary residence for $25,000 above the purchase price. The Jones family postpones buying a new home for 36 months.

b. _____   The Pflaums sell their primary residence for $70,000. The original purchase price on this home was $60,000. One month later, they buy a new home for $80,000. (The Pflaums are approaching their late fifties.)

c. _____   The McGills, who are in their mid-forties, sell their primary residence (original purchase price $60,000) for $75,000. One year later, they buy a new home for $60,000.

d. _____   JoAnn and Michael Marks are both 60 years old and have sold their primary residence creating a capital gain of $100,000. They have no plans to purchase another home, but expect to retire to an apartment on the beach.

Exercise 4-6

Calculate the tax liability for each of the following cases according to the tax status and amount of taxable income. (Use Exhibit 4.5 of the text for a schedule.)

Case	Tax Status	Taxable Income	Tax Liability
A	Single	$15,000	_____
B	Joint	$15,000	_____
C	Head of Household	$30,000	_____
D	Joint	$30,000	_____
E	Single	$60,000	_____
F	Married, Filing Separately	$60,000	_____
G	Single	$150,000	_____
H	Joint	$150,000	_____

CASE PROBLEMS

Case 4.1 The Margolis Tax Return (Itemize or Standard Deduction)

Mort and Shirley Margolis are a married couple in their mid-forties living in Chicago. Mort is a trader on the floor of the Chicago Board of Trade and earns $65,000 in commissions. Shirley is a homemaker who owns significant stock in a business left to her and her brother upon the death of her parents. This stock pays dividends of $25,000 per year. The couple have two children who have both graduated from college and are financially independent. For the 1991 tax year, the Margolises have gathered the following financial data for the joint return they will file:

Mortgage interest	$2,500
State income and property taxes	750
Medical and dental expenses	1,000
Mort's business expenses not paid by his employer	345
Donation to the Salvation Army	500

Question

Should the Margolises itemize their deductions or use the standard deduction? Show your calculations to support your decision.

Chapter 5
Managing Your Savings and Other Liquid Assets

CHAPTER OUTLINE

I. Cash management deals with the routine, day-to-day administration of cash and near-cash resources. Liquid financial assets are cash or assets readily convertible into cash with little or no loss in value.

II. Deregulation made it possible for all financial markets and financial institutions to provide a full menu of financial products and services.

    A. Traditional banking institutions--such as banks, savings and loans, mutual savings banks, and credit unions--still hold a large part of the financial market.

        1. Commercial banks are the most common of the traditional financial institutions and offer a full array of services.

        2. Savings and loan associations (S&Ls) channel the savings of individuals into mortgage loans. Most choose not to make consumer loans.

        3. Savings banks are a type of savings institution where the depositors are the actual owners.

        4. A credit union is a special type of mutual association that provides financial services to specific groups of people who share a common bond, such as occupation, religious or fraternal order, or residential area.

    B. A variety of checking and savings accounts are offered by financial institutions.

        1. A demand deposit is an account from which a withdrawal must be permitted whenever demanded by the accountholder. Commonly called checking accounts, most do not earn interest.

        2. A savings account is a type of liquid asset that earns interest. These accounts are frequently called passbook accounts. While financial institutions reserve the right to require a savings accountholder to wait a certain number of days before receiving payment of a withdrawal, most pay withdrawals immediately.

        3. Accounts on which you can write checks and also earn interest may be called NOW accounts, money market deposit accounts (MMDA), or money market mutual funds (MMMF).

            a. Negotiable order of withdrawal (NOW) accounts are interest paying checking accounts. The interest rate is usually related to the balance amount, with higher balances earning somewhat higher interest rates.

    b.   Money market deposit accounts (MMDA), offered by financial institutions, work much like the MMMFs. These accounts, however, are insured by the FDIC.

    c.   A money market mutual fund (MMMF) pools funds from many small investors and purchases short-term marketable securities offered by the U.S. Treasury, major corporations, large commercial banks, and various government organizations. Limited checkwriting privileges are available on MMMFs.

  C.   Deposit insurance protects the funds on deposit (up to a maximum amount) at banks, S&Ls, and credit unions against failure of the financial institution.

III.   Developing sound savings habits is essential to the success of your personal financial planning.

  A.   Some of your financial assets should be liquid to meet your day-to-day needs, and a portion should be set aside for longer-term goals. Most financial planners agree you should keep an amount equal to three to six months take-home pay in a liquid savings reserve.

  B.   Interest can be earned by 1) purchasing investments sold on a discount basis or 2) making investments that pay interest directly. The effective rate of interest can be calculated by using the formula below.

        <u>Amount of interest earned during the year</u>
        Amount of money invested or deposited

    1.   Future Value of a lump sum = Amount deposited x Future Value Factor (see Appendix A). Future Value of a series of deposits = Amount deposited each year x Annuity Factor (see Appendix B).

    2.   Four methods may be used to determine an account balance for interest payment purposes: 1) minimum balance method, 2) the FIFO method, 3) the LIFO method, and 4) the actual balance method.

        a.   Banks using the minimum balance method will pay interest only on the lowest balance in the account during the quarter.

        b.   Financial institutions using FIFO (first-in, first-out) assume withdrawals are charged against the earlier or opening balances of an account.

        c.   When LIFO (last-in, last-out) is used, the bank assumes withdrawals are charged to the most recent deposits or balances.

        d.   The actual balance method is the most accurate and fairest method because it provides full credit for all funds on deposit. It is sometimes called the daily interest method.

  C.   A variety of savings vehicles are available at most financial institutions.

    1.   Money deposited in certificates of deposit (CDs) is expected to remain on deposit for a specified period of time.

    2.   Treasury bills are obligations of the U.S. Treasury issued as part of the funding process of the national debt. They are considered the ultimate

safe investment.

3. Series EE bonds are U. S. Treasury securities that are purchased for half the face value. Interest accrues on the bond while you hold it and is paid only at the time of redemption rather than periodically over the life of the bond. Interest earned on these bonds is exempt from state and local taxes.

4. A central asset account combines banking and investment services like checking and money market accounts, brokerage accounts for executing securities transactions, and bank credit card services.

IV. Maintaining a checking account is a safe and convenient way to pay for goods and services.

A. When you are planning to open a checking account, consider convenience, services provided, and cost.
1. Most checking accounts levy a service charge unless the balance exceeds a specified minimum.
2. Checking accounts may be jointly owned (as may most bank accounts). Joint ownership accounts are usually written with the right of survivorship, specifying that when one of the parties dies, the survivor automatically becomes the sole owner of the account.

B. The checkbook ledger should be carefully maintained.
1. The ledger is a clear record of all transactions in the checking account including checks written, deposits made, service charges, and interest earned.
2. A check written for an amount greater than the current account balance results in an overdraft. Overdraft protection can be arranged with most financial institutions.
3. The most common endorsements are blank, special, restrictive, and conditional.
4. You might issue a stop payment on a check because 1) a check or checkbook has been lost, 2) service or merchandise paid for by check is not satisfactory, or 3) a job for which you paid in advance has not been completed.

C. Monthly statements detailing your checking and deposit transactions will be provided by your financial institution.
1. The reconciliation process is used to correct errors or omissions in recording checks or deposits.
2. The monthly bank statement and/or cancelled checks can be an important tax record.

D. Several types of special checks exist to make your life easier.
1. Cashier's checks can be used by people who do not have checking accounts since the check will be written on the bank's funds. The customer will pay the amount of the check plus a service charge.
2. Traveler's checks provide a safe and convenient form of money for travel. If lost or stolen, traveler's checks can be canceled and new ones issued.
3. A certified check is one that you have written on your own account and

have asked the bank to guarantee that funds are available to cover it.
E.   Other banking services include:
  1.   Safe deposit boxes.
  2.   Automatic teller machines.
  3.   Pre-authorized payments.
  4.   Bank-by-phone accounts.
  5.   Computer-based banking at home.

FILL IN THE BLANK

1.   _____ is an activity that deals with the routine, day-to-day administration of cash and near-cash resources.

2.   _____ assets are cash or other assets that can be readily converted into cash with little or no loss in value.

3.   Financial institutions today usually offer a wide variety of financial products and services available at one location; this is one result of the _____.

4.   A _____ refers to a company that offers extensive financial services.

5.   There are more _____ in the U. S. than any of the other traditional banking institutions.

6.   Most savings and loans are mutual associations where the _____ own the institution.

7.   _____ channel most of their depositors' savings into mortgage loans for home buyers.

8.   _____ banks are found primarily in New England.

9.   A _____ is a special type of mutual association that provides financial services to specific groups of people who share a common bond.

10.   A _____ deposit requires the withdrawal of deposited funds at a financial institution whenever requested by the accountholder.

11.   Financial institutions generally retain the right to require the _____ account holder to wait a specified number of days before receiving a withdrawal.

12.   MMDAs and NOW accounts are examples of _____ accounts.

13.   A money market _____ or a money market _____ combines money from many small investors and purchases marketable securities offered by the U.S. Treasury, major corporations, commercial banks, and various government organizations.

14.   NOW accounts let you earn _____ on a demand deposit.

15.   The _____ protects the funds on deposit (up to a maximum of $100,000) at banks against failure of the institution.

16.   A general consensus among financial planners is that _____ months worth of after-tax income is a sensible target for liquid reserves.

17.   An investment sold for a price lower than its redemption value is sold at a _____ .

18.   The _____ rate of interest is the amount of interest earned during a year divided by the amount of money invested or deposited.

19.   Receiving _____ interest means that you are earning interest on interest that you previously earned.

20.   When you are dealing with the future value of a series of payments you are actually looking at an _____ .

21.   The four ways that a financial institution may determine account balances to earn interest are   1) _____ ,   2) _____ ,   3) _____ , and 4) _____ .

22.   With a _____ , funds are expected to remain on deposit for a specified period of time.

23.   _____ , issued by the U. S. government, are considered the safest security for saving and investment.

24.   _____ bonds are accrued interest securities.

25.   A _____ Account is a comprehensive deposit account that combines checking, investing, and borrowing activities.

26.   If you write a check for more than you have in your account you have created an _____ .

27.   If you endorse a check "for deposit only" you have written a _____ endorsement.

28.   A _____ is an order to your depository institution to refuse payment on an already issued check.

29. The process of balancing your checking account with the bank is also known as
_____.

30. A _____ check is a check drawn on the bank's account.

EXERCISES

Exercise 5-1
Match each type of finanical institution with its characteristic described below.

A. Commercial banks
B. Credit unions
C. Savings banks
D. Savings and loan association

1. _____   The most common type is a mutual association in which depositors actually own the institution.

2. _____   Do not offer regular non-interest bearing checking accounts.

3. _____   A special type of mutual association that provides financial services to specific groups of people who belong to a common occupation, religious or fraternal order, or residential area.

4. _____   The most numerous of the traditional banking institutions.

5. _____   Channels individual's savings into mortgage loans for homes.

6. _____   Offers a full array of financial services, including a variety of savings vehicles, credit cards, several kinds of loans, trust services, and other services.

7. _____   Found primarily in the New England states.

Exercise 5-2

Match each type of account with its characteristic described below.

A. Money market deposit account (MMDA)
B. Negotiable order of withdrawal (NOW)
C. Money market mutual fund (MMMF)

1. _____   A vehicle created by banks to compete with money market mutual funds. Depositors have access through limited checkwriting privileges or automated teller machines.

2. _____   Checking accounts that pay interest.

3. _____   Checking accounts at savings and loans that may also serve as savings vehicles.

4. _____   Pools the funds of many small investors and purchases short-term marketable securities offered by the U.S. Treasury, major corporations, large commercial banks, and various government organizations. Checkwriting privileges are limited to minimum check amounts.

5. _____   Pays the highest rate of any bank account on which checks can be written.

Exercise 5-3

Indicate the amount of deposit insurance coverage allowed by federal guidelines in each of the following cases. Each case represents accounts at a single federally-insured financial institution.

Case	Account Type	Name on Account	Amount on Deposit	Answer
A	Individual MMDA	John Park	$125,000	_____
B	Individual savings	Jane Wiley	85,000	_____
C	Joint savings	Mary & Tom Janks	200,000	_____
D	Individual MMDA	Jason Henry	100,000	_____
	Individual savings	Jason Henry	50,000	
	Individual regular checking	Jason Henry	75,000	_____
E	Joint MMDA	Juan & Maria Joseph	75,000	_____
	Joint savings	Juan & Maria Joseph	50,000	
F	Individual MMDA	Carla Johns	$ 75,000	_____
	Joint savings	Mark & Carla Johns	100,000	
	Individual savings	Mark Johns	85,000	
	Individual IRA	Carla Johns	12,000	

Exercise 5-4

The Foster family has savings that total $75,000. The Fosters have monthly expenses of $2,500. How much should they hold as liquid reserves? How much should they put into savings instruments such as CDs or MMDAs?

Chapter 5 Managing Your Savings and Other Liquid Assets

Exercise 5-5

Calculate the effective rate of interest on each of the following investments.

Investment	Period of Investment	Amount of Interest Earned	Amount Invested
A	6 months	$ 500	$12,000
B	4 months	1,000	30,000
C	1 year	250	5,000
D	2 years	750	4,000
E	9 months	2,000	25,000

Exercise 5-6

Calculate the future value of each deposit described. (Use Appendix A)

Deposit	Amt Deposited	Annual Interest Rate	Length of Deposit
A	$ 1,000	10%	1 year
B	2,000	8	2 years
C	5,000	7	3 years
D	10,000	6	4 years
E	25,000	5	5 years

Exercise 5-7

Calculate the future value of each series of deposits described.
(Use Appendix B)

Deposit	Amount Deposited Per Year	Annual Interest Rate	Number of Deposits
A	$5,000	12%	4
B	2,000	10	10
C	500	7	5

Exercise 5-8

Determine the interest earned for the quarter using the a) minimum balance method, b) FIFO method, c) LIFO method, and d) actual balance method. The interest rate on the account is 8 percent.

Quarterly activity:

Day	Transaction	Account Balance
1	Opening balance	$40,000
30	Withdrawal	5,000
60	Deposit	10,000
90	Ending balance	45,000

Exercise 5-9

Match each type of investment with its characteristic described below.

A. Central asset account
B. Certificate of deposit
C. Series EE savings bonds
D. U.S. Treasury bills

1. _____ Issued as part of its ongoing process of funding the national debt. Sold on a discount basis in minimum denominations of $5,000 to $10,000.

2. _____ Has no specified maturity date.

3. _____ Automatically sweeps excess funds from checking accounts into MMDAs.

4. _____ A savings instrument issued by a financial institution where funds are expected to remain on deposit for a specified period of time.

5. _____ Securities, sold on a discount basis, on which interest accrues prior to redemption. They are exempt from state and local taxes. Issued in denominations of $50 to $10,000.

6. _____ Combines checking account, money market deposit account and brokerage account.

Exercise 5-10

A. Traveler's check
B. Pre-authorized payment
C. Certified check
D. Cashier's check

1. _____ Bank issues a check drawn on itself.

2. _____ Eliminates having to write some checks each month.

3. _____ Most often used by people who do not have checking accounts.

4. _____ Bank guarantees check is good and immediately withdraws amount of check from the account on which it is drawn.

5. _____ May be exchanged for local currencies in most parts of the world.

6. _____ Insured against loss or theft by issuing agency.

Exercise 5-11

Maggie's checkbook register from 7/21 through 8/28 has the following deposits and payments posted.

Check Nbr.	Date	Description of Transaction	Pmt/ Debit	Dep/ Credit	Balance
		Balance Forward			$1,500.00
501	7/21	Garfield's Department Store	$ 50.00		1,450.00
502	7/25	Consolidated Edison	125.14		1,324.86
503	7/25	Piggly Wiggly Markets	68.96		1,255.90
504	7/26	VISA	305.17		950.73
505	8/01	Pee Wee Day Care	60.00		890.73
506	8/05	1st National Bank	551.42		339.31
507	8/05	3rd National Bank	152.00		187.31
508	8/13	Cable Vision, Inc.	25.50		161.81
509	8/14	General Telephone	31.29		130.52
510	8/15	Saks Fifth Avenue	57.91		72.61
511	8/20	Community Clean	20.00		52.61
512	8/21	Roscoes Restaurant	29.35		23.26
513	8/28	GAI, Inc.	14.00		9.26
	8/28	Salary Deposit		2,050.00	2,059.26

The transactions summary statement for the month follows. Reconcile Maggie's checking account using the blank worksheet which follows. It is the same as Exhibit 5.9 in the text.

Transactions Summary Statement

Checking Account Activity

Previous Balance	$1,500.00	Beginning date	7/20/92
Deposits/Credits	6.50	Ending date	8/30/92
Checks/Debits	1,367.39		
New Balance	139.11		

Deposits/Credits

Date	Description	Amount
8/25	Interest earned	$ 6.50

Checks/Debits

Date	Check No.	Amount	Date	Check No.	Amount
7/24	501	50.00	8/05	507	152.00
7/29	502	125.14	8/20	508	25.50
7/30	503	68.96	8/21	509	31.29
8/01	504	305.17	8/22	510	57.91
8/06	506	551.42			

57

CHECKING ACCOUNT RECONCILIATION

For the Month of _____ , 19_____

Accountholder Name(s) _____

Type of Account _____

1. Ending balance shown on bank statement _____ $_____

Add up checks and withdrawals still outstanding:

Check Number or Date	Amount	Check Number or Date	Amount
	$		$
	TOTAL	$	

2. Deduct total checks/withdrawals still outstanding from bank balance _____ − $_____

Add up desposits still outstanding:

Date	Amount	Date	Amount
	TOTAL	$	

3. *Add* total deposits still outstanding to bank balance _____ + $_____

A **Adjusted Bank Balance** (1 - 2 + 3) _____ $_____

4. Ending balance shown in checkbook _____ $_____

5. *Deduct* any bank service charges for the period _____ − $_____

6. *Add* interest earned for the period _____ + $_____

B **New Checkbook Balance** (4 - 5 + 6) _____ $_____

Note: Your account is reconciled when line A equals line B.

Chapter 6

Making Housing and Other Major Acquisitions

CHAPTER OUTLINE

I.   A family's housing needs depend on age, income level, and number of children. Housing needs can be met in a variety of ways--from single family homes to condos and apartments.

   A.   The average American home is 1,500 square feet, costs close to $100,000, and has three bedrooms and two baths.
      1.   Most families prefer a single family home that stands alone on its own lot.
      2.   A manufactured home is a factory-produced living unit that can be transported to a desired location, connected to facilities, and used as a residence.
      3.   A condominium owner receives title to an individual unit and shares joint ownership of common areas and facilities. Owners are assessed a monthly fee for maintaining the common areas.
      4.   Apartment buildings in which the tenant owns a share of the corporation that owns the building are cooperative apartments. Residents lease their unit from the corporation and are assessed monthly in proportion to their ownership shares, which are based on the amount of space they occupy.

II.   To decide how much housing you can afford, you will need to consider the down payment, closing costs, the monthly mortgage payment, property taxes, and homeowner's insurance.

   A.   People buy homes for many reasons, including pride of ownership, a feeling of permanence, a sense of stability, and a financial payoff.
      1.   Home ownership provides a tax shelter since the homeowner can deduct property taxes and the interest paid on the mortgage when itemizing on his federal (and some state) taxes.
      2.   Home ownership also provides an inflation hedge during most economic cycles.
   B.   There are several items to consider when evaluating the cost of home ownership and determining how much you can afford: 1) the down payment, 2) points and closing costs, 3) mortgage payments, 4) insurance and property taxes, and 5) home maintenance and operating expenses.
      1.   To determine the amount of down payment required, lenders use the loan-to-value ratio that specifies the maximum amount of money the lender will

loan relative to the total value of the property. Most lenders prefer an 80 percent to 85 percent loan-to-value ratio.

2. Mortgage points are fees charged by lenders at the time they grant the mortgage loan. Each mortgage point equals one percent of the amount borrowed.

3. Closing costs are the other expenses that borrowers ordinarily pay at the time the loan is closed and title of the property is conveyed. Closing costs may include such items as: 1) loan application fees, 2) loan origination fees, 3) points, 4) title search and insurance, 5) attorney's fees, 6) appraisal fees, and 7) other miscellaneous fees.

4. Monthly mortgage payments are made up of principal and interest charges. Part of each payment pays the lender for the use of his money that month, and part is applied to reducing the loan balance.

    a. Affordability ratios are often used to determine if a loan applicant qualifies for a loan. The ratio compares the applicant's monthly income to the mortgage payment. A commonly used criteria is that the monthly mortgage payment should not exceed 25 percent to 30 percent of the monthly gross income. If the applicant has several other installment loan obligations, the ratio may be adjusted downward.

5. The monthly mortgage payment often includes property tax payments and homeowners insurance payments (PITI).

6. Homeowners also incur maintenance and operating expenses.

C. People may choose, or be forced, to rent because they do not have enough funds for a down payment. They may anticipate having to make a move in their jobs or have a family situation that is unsettled. Some people just do not want the responsibilities associated with home ownership.

1. Renting requires signing a rental contract or lease agreement. (Although oral leases are enforceable, you should insist upon a written lease.) The rental contract will likely include the amount of the monthly payment, the payment date, penalties for late payment, the length of the lease agreement, deposit requirements, a statement about who pays for utilities and repairs, renewal options, and any restrictions.

2. There are many factors to consider when deciding whether buying or renting fits your particular situation. See Exhibit 6.6 in the text for a method of analysis.

III. After you have found the right house at the right price, you have to make a financing decision.

A. Most home buyers rely on a real estate agent to locate a home with the desired characteristics. The real estate agent's primary responsibility is to the seller, who pays the commission.

B. Real estate buy-sell agreements must be in writing and conform to certain requirements. These include names of buyers and sellers, a description of the property, specific price and terms, and (usually) the signatures of the buyer and seller. This agreement will be accompanied by some earnest money which can be kept by the seller if the buyer backs out of the agreement for any reason not mentioned as a contingency (being unable to secure a loan is a common contingency).

C. The prospective home buyer should familiarize him or herself with the various lenders who grant mortgage loans and the types of mortgage contracts available in the community.

1. Sources of mortgage money are savings and loan associations, commercial banks, mutual savings banks, mortgage banking companies, and credit unions.

D. Sellers may also finance the mortgage. Seller financing can be a contract with balloon payments or a buy-down agreement.

1. A balloon payment note involves a single, very large principal payment due at some specified future date.

2. A buy-down is generally an arrangement with a builder to buy a home with prearranged financing at special low interest rates. The buyer, however, will pay for the reduced interest in the form of a higher home purchase price.

E. There are several types of mortgages available in most localities.

1. The fixed rate mortgage is characterized by a fixed interest rate and a level monthly mortgage payment over the term of the loan.

2. The adjustable rate mortgage (ARM) has its interest rate linked to a specific interest index and is adjusted at specific intervals. There will be caps on the periodic adjustments, and there will be a cap on the maximum interest rate for the loan.

3. A conventional mortgage is one offered by a lender who assumes all the risk of loss.

4. A mortgage may be insured by the Federal Housing Administration or a private insurer or guaranteed by the Veterans Administration. In case the buyer defaults, the lender will be protected.

F. The closing process involves three important parts: 1) the RESPA statement, 2) the title check, and 3) the closing statement.

1. The Real Estate Settlement Procedures Act (RESPA) requires advance disclosure of all closing costs to buyers.

2. To make sure the title is free from all encumbrances and that owners who are conveying title have the legal interest which they claim, a title search is made.

3. The closing statement provides the buyer and seller with a summary of the monies which change hands during the closing procedures.

G. When interest rates drop, it may become beneficial to refinance an existing mortgage.

IV. Other big-ticket assets such as automobiles, furniture, appliances, and recreational equipment are expensive and require careful consideration and deliberation before purchasing or leasing.

FILL IN THE BLANK

1. Buildings in which each tenant owns shares of the corporation that owns the building are known as _____ apartments.

2. Buyers of _____ receive title to an individual housing unit and share joint ownership of any common areas and facilities.

3. For many homeowners, the biggest financial payoff from owning a home is the _____ shelter it can provide.

4. _____ taxes and _____ paid on a mortgage are tax deductible housing costs.

5. There are five items which should be considered when determining home affordability: 1) the down payment, 2) _____, 3) _____, 4) insurance and property taxes, and 5) home maintenance and operating expenses.

6. The _____ ratio specifies the percent of the total value of the property the lender is willing to loan.

7. _____ are charged by lenders at the time they grant the mortgage loan. In effect, they increase the cost of borrowing money.

8. Closing costs are expenses levied by lenders on _____, which ordinarily must be paid at the time the loan is closed and title to the property is conveyed.

9. _____ include loan application fees, loan origination fees, points, title search and insurance, attorney's fees, and appraisal fees.

10. The ratio of the borrower's total monthly installment loan payments to his gross monthly income is a _____ ratio.

11. The monthly mortgage payment may contain these components 1) _____ 2) _____, 3) _____, and 4) _____.

12. The portion of the mortgage that goes for taxes and insurance is paid into an _____ account.

13. Homeowner's insurance protects the replacement value of the house and its contents but not the _____.

14. A real estate contract must be in writing and conform to certain requirements to be legally enforceable. It should contain 1) names of buyers and sellers, 2) _____, 3) _____, and 4) signatures of buyers and sellers.

15. _____ is the money the prospective buyer of a home is asked to pledge at the time the offer to purchase is made.

16. You would be most likely to get a home mortgage at a _____.

17. Two forms of seller financing are _____ and _____.

18. A builder-developer has arranged with a financial institution for mortgage financing at interest rates that are below the market rates. The builder-developer will sell this home at a premium price but with a lower interest rate. He has engaged in a _____.

19. When both the interest rate and the monthly mortgage payment remain the same over the life of the loan, you have a _____ mortgage.

20. A 15-year mortgage will have a _____ (lower/higher) monthly payment than a 30-year mortgage.

21. The rate of interest on an _____ mortgage is linked to a specific interest rate index and will be adjusted at specific intervals.

22. A _____ mortgage is one offered by a lender who assumes all the risk of loss.

23. If your monthly mortgage payment is not large enough to cover the interest cost, this is known as _____ amortization.

24. The _____ provides lenders mortgage insurance on high loan-to-value ratio loans.

25. The three key components necessary in closing a real estate transaction are 1) the RESPA statement, 2) _____, and 3) _____.

26. Federal legislation, known as the _____, requires lenders to provide the borrower information about the settlement costs of the real estate transaction.

27. A _____ is done to ensure that the property is free of all liens and encumbrances.

28. When mortgage interest rates have declined significantly, it may be advisable to _____ your current mortgage.

29. _____ is a loss in value of an automobile as the vehicle is driven.

30. The biggest fixed cost associated with owning and operating most automobiles is the
     _____ .

31. Automobile operating costs can be characterized as _____ or
     _____ .

32. The written agreement to purchase an automobile is called a _____ .

33. Besides ownership, the most popular form of automobile financing is the
     _____ .

34. When purchasing furniture or major appliances it is often very helpful to consult
     some consumer _____ .

EXERCISES

Exercise 6-1

First National Bank requires that mortgage loan applicants make a down payment so the loan-to-value ratio is no higher than 75 percent. The Helmsleys have applied for a mortgage loan with First National Bank for a property which will cost $250,000.

a.   The Helmsleys will need to make a down payment of at least $_____

b   The maximum amount the bank will loan on this property is $_____

Exercise 6-2

Don and Amy are borrowing $100,000 for their home. If the lender requires that 2 points be paid, how much will Don and Amy owe in mortgage points?

Exercise 6-3

1.   Use the Table of Monthly Mortgage Payments in Exhibit 6.5 of the text to calculate the monthly mortgage payments for each of the following mortgages.

Case	Rate of Interest(%)	Loan Maturity (Years)	Mortgage Amount
A	8	15	$100,000
B	12	10	50,000
C	9.5	30	75,000
D	14	20	30,000
E	10	25	65,000

2.   For each mortgage calculate the total amount of interest that would be paid over the life of the loan.

Chapter 6 Making Housing and Other Major Acquisitions

Exercise 6-4

Affordability guidelines stipulate:

* monthly mortgage payments should not exceed 25 to 30 percent of the borrower's monthly gross income.

* total monthly installment obligations should not exceed 33 to 38 percent of the borrower's gross income.

Calculate the maximum mortgage advisable in each of the following cases.

Case	Gross Income	Other Installment Loan Obligations
A	$4,000	$ 500
B	1,200	100
C	3,000	250
D	5,000	1,000

Exercise 6-5

The West family is comparing the costs of renting versus buying a home. Jean West has compiled all of the relevant costs of each option. Using the form provided compare the costs of each option and recommend whether the West family should rent or buy their home.

Costs of Renting

Monthly payment	$ 1,000
Renter's insurance	750

Costs of Buying

Purchase price of home	$100,000
Mortgage payments	1,290
Homeowner's insurance	625
Property taxes	3,750
Maintenance	2,500
Principal reduction in loan balance	1,730
Annual interest (year 1)	13,750
Marginal tax rate	28.0%
Expected appreciation in the value of the home	2.5%
Down payment and closing costs	20,000
After-tax rate of return	5.0%

RENT-OR-BUY ANALYSIS			
A. COST OF RENTING			
1. Annual rental costs (12 x monthly rental rate of $ _____)			
2. Renter's insurance			
Total cost of renting			
B. COST OF BUYING			
1. Annual mortgage payments (Terms: $ _____ , _____ months, ___ %) (12 x monthly mortgage payment of $ _____)			
2. Property taxes (___% of price of home)			
3. Homeowner's insurance (___% of price of home)			
4. Maintenance (___% of price of home)			
5. After-tax cost of interest lost on down payment and closing costs ($ _____ x ___% after-tax rate of return)			
6. Total costs			
Less:			
7. Principal reduction in loan balance (see note below)			
8. Tax savings due to interest deductions* (Interest portion of mortgage payments $_____ x tax rate of ___%)			
9. Tax savings due to property tax deductions* (line B.2 x tax rate of ___%)			
10. Total deductions			
11. Annual after-tax cost of home ownership (line B.6 – line B.10.)			
12. Less: Estimated annual appreciation in value of home (___% of price of home)			
Total cost of buying (line B.11 – line B.12.)			

Exercise 6-6

Karen purchased a new car on January 1 this year for $12,000 and plans to keep it three years. At the end of three years, the car is estimated to be worth 35 percent of its original value.

a.   What will be the value of the car in three years?

b.   Determine the depreciation cost per year and per month.

Exercise 6-7

Brian, age 22, is shopping for a new car. He is looking at the costs of the two cars shown below and must decide if he can afford the luxury sedan which is his preference or if he must be satisfied with the economy model. He has budgeted $700 per month for an auto. Brian drives approximately 20,000 miles per year.

Automobile Operating Costs

	Luxury Sedan	Economy Model
Purchase price	$15,000	$8,000
Monthly loan payment	380	203
License plates/yr.	30	30
Emissions test/yr.	15	15
Personal property tax/yr.	500	250
Auto insurance/yr.	1,000	700
Repairs/5,000 miles	75	50
Maintenance/5,000 miles	50	35
Fuel cost per mile	4.0 cents	2.5 cents
Depreciation in 1st year	20.0%	25.0%

a.   Using the following blank page, calculate the total operating cost of each car on an annual basis and a cost per mile basis.

b.   What is your recommendation to Brian? Can he afford the sedan?

CASE PROBLEMS

Case 6.1 Fixed-rate versus Adjustable-rate Mortgages

Michael and Megan Wright are negotiating the purchase of their second home. Their first home has already been sold, leaving them with $57,000 in cash. The home they have chosen to buy has a purchase price of $183,000 which would be financed with one of the following types of mortgages.

<u>1st National Bank</u>
  Fixed-rate mortgage

15 year, $126,000 principal amount, 8 1/2% rate, $1,241 payment per month.
*Lenders points: 2 points with 30% down
                       3 points with 20% down
*Other closing costs: 4% of the purchase price of the home

<u>Merchant's Bank</u>
  Adjustable rate mortgage

30 year, $126,000 principal amount, 7 3/4% rate adjustable annually based on U.S. Treasury securities. The periodic cap is 2% and the overall cap is 5%. $903 payment per month initially.
*Lenders points: 1.75 points with 30% down
                       2.50 points with 20% down
*Other closing costs: 4.5% of the purchase price of the home

The insurance costs are expected to be $1,350 per year, taxes are expected to be $2,430 per year, and annual utility bills are estimated at $2,100.

First National Bank will allow mortgage payments to equal 25 percent of the Wright's monthly gross income. Merchant's Bank requires that mortgage payments not exceed 29 percent of their monthly gross income.

Michael and Megan have a combined gross income of $54,000 per year.

Questions

1. If Michael and Megan use the $57,000 in cash for their down payment, how much will lenders points and other closing points amount to for both mortgages?
2. Do the Wrights qualify for the 25 percent and 29 percent affordability ratios?
3. Compare the fixed-rate mortgage with the adjustable-rate mortgage described. What are the advantages and disadvantages of each? Which would you recommend in this instance?

Case 6.2 What Can The Kominskis Afford?

John and Marylou Kominski have been saving for their own house for six years. They have accumulated $29,500 to be used as a down payment and to cover closing costs. Their combined annual income is $65,000. They expect that homeowners insurance and taxes will be about $300 monthly.   The lender uses a 30 percent affordability ratio and the interest rate is currently 10 percent on a 30 year loan with a minimum 15 percent down payment.

Use the above information and the following worksheet from Exhibit 6.6 in the text to determine the maximum purchase price the Kominskis could pay for a home.

	HOME AFFORDABILITY ANALYSIS*	
Name _____ Date _____		

Item	Description	Amount
1	Amount of annual income	$ _____
2	Monthly income (Item 1 ÷ 12)	$ _____
3	Lender's affordabiilty ratio (in decimal form)	_____
4	Maximum monthly mortgage payment (PITI) (Item 2 x Item 3)	$ _____
5	Estimated monthly tax and homeowner's insurance payment	$ _____
6	Maximum monthly loan payment	$ _____
7	Approximate average interest rate on loan	_____
8	Planned loan maturity (years)	_____
9	Mortgage payment per $10,000 (using Item 7 and Item 8 and Monthly Mortgage Payment Table in Exhibit 6.5)	$ _____
10	Maximum loan based on monthly income ($10,000 x Item 6 ÷ Item 9)	$ _____
11	Funds available for making a down payment and paying closing costs	$ _____
12	Funds available for making a down payment (Item 11 x .67)	$ _____
13	Maximum purchase price based on available monthly income (Item 10 + Item 12)	$ _____
14	Minimum acceptable down payment (in decimal form)	_____
15	Maximum purchase price based on down payment (Item 12 ÷ Item 14)	$ _____
16	Maximum home purchase price (lower of Item 13 and Item 15)	$ _____

Case 6.3 Should the Limb's Refinance Their Mortgage

Chan and Karen Limb have lived in their current home for three years. They bought it when interest rates were pretty high. Rates are considerably lower today, and since they plan to stay in their house for at least another five years, they want to consider refinancing their current mortgage.

Here are the facts about their current mortgage and the best new loan they have found:

```
Current monthly payment excluding
     taxes and insurance .......... $ 674
There is no prepayment schedule
New loan payment would be ........ 582
Closing costs on the new loan
     would be  ................. 1,250
```

Using the following analysis form which is like Exhibit 6.9 in the text, analyze the Limb's situation. Should they refinance their old loan?

Case 6.4 Should Henry Lease or Buy a Car?

Henry Eaton needs a new car. He has selected the make and model and now must consider the financing alternatives. The price of the car is $16,700. Under the closed-end lease, Henry would make a $500 security deposit and monthly payments of $375 for four years. If Henry purchases the car, he will have to put $2,500 down, pay a 7 percent sales tax on the purchase price, and make monthly payments of $375. The current interest rate on Henry's savings is 5.5 percent. The car would have a resale value of about $5,000 in four years.

Use the worksheet from Exhibit 6.11 that follows to determine whether Henry should buy the car or lease it.

MORTGAGE REFINANCING ANALYSIS

Name _____ Date _____

Item	Description	Amount
1	Current monthly payment (Terms: _____)	$_____
2	New monthly payment (Terms: _____)	_____
3	Monthly savings, pretax (Item 1 – Item 2)	$_____
4	Monthly savings times your tax rate (____%)	_____
5	Monthly savings, after-tax (Item 3 – Item 4)	$_____
6	Costs to refinance:	
	a. Prepayment penalty $_____	
	b. Total closing costs (after-tax) _____	
	c. Total refinancing costs (Item 6a + Item 6b)	$_____
7	Months to break even (Item 6c + Item 5)	_____

AUTOMOBILE LEASE VERSUS PURCHASE ANALYSIS

Name _____ Date _____

LEASE

Item	Description	Amount
1	Security deposit required	$ _____
2	Term of lease and loan (years)*	_____
3	Term of lease and loan (months) (Item 2 × 12)	_____
4	Monthly lease payment	$ _____
5	Total payments over term of lease (Item 3 × Item 4)	$ _____
6	Interest rate earned on savings (in decimal form)	_____
7	Opportunity cost of security deposit (Item 1 × Item 2 × Item 6)	$ _____
8	Payment/refund for market value adjustment at end of lease ($0 for closed-end leases) and/or estimated end-of-term charges	$ _____
9	Total cost of leasing (Item 5 + Item 7 + Item 8)	$ _____

PURCHASE

Item	Description	Amount
10	Purchase price	$ _____
11	Down payment	$ _____
12	Sales tax rate (in decimal form)	_____
13	Sales tax (Item 10 × Item 12)	$ _____
14	Monthly loan payment (Terms: $ _____ , _____ months, ___ %)	$ _____
15	Total payments over term of loan (Item 3 × Item 14)	$ _____
16	Opportunity cost of down payment (Item 2 × Item 6 × Item 11)	$ _____
17	Estimated value of car at end of loan	$ _____
18	Total cost of purchasing (Item 11 + Item 13 + Item 15 + Item 16 – Item 17)	$ _____

DECISION

If the value of Item 9 is less than the value of Item 18, leasing is preferred; otherwise the purchase alternative is preferred.

Chapter 7
Borrowing on Open Account

CHAPTER OUTLINE

I.   Consumers, businesses, and governments rely heavily on the use of credit to make transactions.

    A.   Credit is a means of purchasing goods and services when the total outlay is too large to be paid out of current resources.
        1. People borrow for 1) large outlays, 2) financial emergencies, 3) convenience, and 4) investment purposes.
        2. The benefits of borrowing are the ability to pay for expensive goods or services in a series of installments and to have an itemized record of the transaction.
        3. Avoid using credit for 1) routine basic living expenses, 2) impulse purchases, and 3) non-durable short-lived goods and services.
    B.   Lenders will look at many factors when assessing a borrower's creditworthiness such as present earnings, net worth and credit history.
        1. Your credit history tells whether you are a dependable, reliable, and responsible borrower.
        2. Things to do when establishing credit: 1) open checking and savings accounts, 2) open and use charge accounts periodically, and 3) obtain a small loan.
        3. Married women must take special care to establish credit histories in their own legal names.
    C.   A good credit guideline is not to allow the monthly debt repayment to exceed 20 percent of your monthly take-home pay. (The debt safety ratio.)

II. An open credit account is a form of credit extended to the consumer in advance of any transactions.

    A.   A credit statement summarizing the credit transactions will be prepared monthly. This statement will provide a summary of transactions, the new balance, and the minimum payment.
    B.   Open credit accounts are available from 1) financial institutions and 2) retail stores/merchants.
        1. Retail charge cards are issued by retail merchants and allow customers to use credit when purchasing goods and services. The accounts are subject to a credit limit and periodic repayment of the debt.

77

2.   Bank credit cards are issued by commercial banks and other financial institutions and allow their holders to charge purchases at a variety of establishments.

3.   The 30-day, or regular charge account, requires the customer to pay the full amount 10 to 20 days after the billing date. These accounts do not involve a charge card.

4.   Travel and entertainment cards enable the holder to charge purchases at entertainment-related establishments.

5.   Prestige cards offer more advantages and features than other credit cards. They usually have higher annual fees.

6.   Affinity cards are standard bank credit cards issued in conjunction with some charitable, political, or other sponsoring group.

7.   A revolving line of credit does not involve the use of credit cards but is accessed by writing checks on a common demand deposit account or a specially designated credit line account. There are three basic accounts: 1) overdraft protection, 2) an unsecured personal line of credit, and 3) a home equity line of credit.

C.   Obtaining an open line of credit requires making a formal application.

1.   A credit application may ask for personal/family information, housing, employment and income, assets and liabilities, existing charge accounts, and credit references.

2.   A credit investigation with the local credit bureau will usually be conducted as a result of a credit application.

3.   A credit bureau gathers and sells information about the credit history of individual borrowers.

4.   Some creditors make the credit decision by using a credit scoring system.

D.   Consumer credit legislation protects in several ways.

1.   The Equal Credit Opportunity Act makes it illegal for creditors to discriminate on the basis of sex, marital status, race, national origin, religion, age, or the receipt of public assistance when considering a credit application.

2.   The Fair Credit Reporting Act protects your rights in the collecting and disclosure of credit information.

3.   The Fair Credit Billing Act addresses issues in mailing bills, error complaints, and discounts for cash purchases.

4.   The Truth in Lending Act requires lenders to make full disclosure of finance charges and annual percentage rates (APR).

5.   One section of the Consumer Protection Act limits the liability of the cardholder if a credit card is lost or stolen.

6.   The Fair Credit Billing Act allows the cardholder recourse on unsatisfactory purchases.

7.   The Fair Debt Collection Practices Act extended protection against unreasonable collection practices.

E.   Credit card insurance protects the cardholder if the card is lost or stolen. Passage of the Consumer Protection Act has made this protection unnecessary.

F.   The biggest danger of consumer credit is the propensity to overspend, which may lead to insolvency and eventual bankruptcy.

1.   People who cannot resolve insolvency on their own may petition the bankruptcy court for 1) a wage earner plan or 2) straight bankruptcy.

        a.   A wage earner plan is an extended debt repayment schedule.

        b.   Straight personal bankruptcy is a legal procedure that discharges most debts. However, there are some debts and some assets that remain.

        c.   Professional legal advice is recommended if you are considering personal bankruptcy.

III.   Several methods of computing finance charges may be used with retail charge cards.

    A.   There are four basic techniques for computing finance charges.
        1.   The previous balance method is the most expensive for the consumer since interest is charged on the outstanding balance at the beginning of the billing period.
        2.   The average daily balance method computes the interest based on the average amount owed each day over the billing period.
        3.   The adjusted balance method applies interest charges to the balance remaining at the end of the billing period.
        4.   The past due balance method does not charge any interest for customers who pay their account in full before a specified period of time; otherwise the finance charge is imposed under one of the three preceding methods.

IV.   There are several advantages and disadvantages in using retail charge cards.

    A.   The most significant advantage of charge cards is that customers can delay payment until the end of the billing period. Other advantages include:
        1.   Interest free loans for the credit period.
        2.   Recordkeeping, recourse in unsatisfactory purchases, and credit for returns.
        3.   A preferred customer status.
        4.   The convenience of writing a single check for payment.
        5.   Use in emergencies.

    B.   The use of credit cards has two major disadvantages.
        1.   The tendency to overspend.
        2.   High interest costs on unpaid balances.

V.   Banks and other financial institutions offer credit cards, and several other types of open account credit, including overdraft protection, unsecured personal lines, and home-equity credit lines.

    A.   The basic features of bank credit cards include:
        1.   The line of credit limits the credit card holder to a maximum amount that can be owed at any point.
        2.   Purchases may be made from a variety of merchants who honor a particular bank card.
        3.   Cash advances are available and reduce the credit limit accordingly.
        4.   Interest rates on bank credit cards are among the highest in consumer credit.

5. Other fees such as an annual fee and transaction charges on cash advances may also be a cost of using bank credit cards.
6. A monthly statement is provided showing all transactions, payments, account balances, finance charges, available credit and the minimum payment.
7. Interest may be avoided by making a payment of the full balance at the end of every month. By paying only the minimum payment due, an interest charge will be made on the remaining balance.
8. The return of merchandise to the merchant will result in a credit on the statement.
B. Bank credit cards have advantages and disadvantages.
1. Interest free loans and consolidated statement of expenses are advantages.
2. The tendency to overspend is the major disadvantage.
C. A debit card provides direct access to your checking account and works just like writing a check. It is not credit.
D. The three major forms of an open credit line are overdraft protection lines, unsecured personal lines of credit, and home equity credit lines.
1. An overdraft protection line is a line of credit linked to a checking account that enables a depositor to overdraw his or her checking account up to a predetermined limit.
2. An unsecured personal line of credit is a method of borrowing money from the bank without going through lengthy application procedures each time a loan is needed.
3. A home equity line of credit is a secured second mortgage on a home.

FILL IN THE BLANK

1. _____ is a means of purchasing goods and services in which the total outlay is too large to be paid out of current resources.

2. The major reasons for personal borrowing are 1) large outlays, 2) _____, 3) _____, and 4) _____.

3. To avoid the misuse of credit avoid using credit for 1) _____, 2) _____, and 3) _____.

4. Lenders will consider these factors when assessing a borrower's creditworthiness: 1) _____ earnings, 2) net _____, and 3) credit _____.

5. A good credit guideline is not to allow the monthly debt repayment to exceed _____percent of the monthly take-home pay.

6. An _____ account is a form of credit extended to the consumer in advance of any transactions.

7.   The _____ charge account does not involve a charge card.

8.   _____ charge cards are issued by merchants.

9.   _____ charge cards are issued by financial institutions.

10. _____ charge cards offer more advantages and features than other credit cards.

11. The American Express card is an example of a _____ card.

12. _____ charge cards are issued in conjunction with some charitable, political, or other sponsoring organization.

13. The three types of revolving credit lines are _____, _____, and _____.

14. _____ gathers and sells credit histories of individual borrowers to lenders.

15. _____ is a method used to make the credit decision by assigning points to various characteristics of creditors.

16. The _____ _____ _____ Act makes it illegal for the creditor to discriminate on the basis of sex, marital status, race, national origin, religion, age or receipt of public assistance.

17. The _____ _____ _____ Act includes numerous provisions protecting the consumers' rights in the disclosure of credit information.

18. The Truth in Lending Act requires lenders to make full disclosure of _____.

19. The Consumer Protection Act limits the liability of the cardholder in the event _____.

20. The Fair Credit Billing Act gives the cardholder recourse on _____ goods and services charged to their account.

21. Personal insolvency has two legal remedies through the bankruptcy court. They are 1) _____ and 2) _____.

22. In a personal insolvency, Chapter 13, also known as _____, involves a debt repayment schedule.

23. In a personal bankruptcy, _____ and _____ are examples of liabilities that are not forgiven while _____ and _____ are some assets that may be kept.

Chapter 7 Borrowing on Open Account

24. The _____ method of computing finance charges is the most expensive for the consumer since interest is charged on the outstanding balance at the beginning of the billing period.

25. The _____ method of computing finance charges applies interest charges to the balance remaining at the end of the billing period.

26. The _____ method of computing finance charges usually ignores purchases and returns made during the billing period.

27. The _____ method of computing finance charges does not charge any interest for customers who pay their account in full before a specified period of time.

28. Cash advances are available on _____ credit cards.

29. Interest rates on bank credit cards are among the _____ (lowest/highest) in consumer credit.

30. The most common fees charged on bank credit cards in addition to interest charges are _____ and _____ .

31. A _____ card provides direct access to a checking account and works like writing a check.

32. The three major forms of an open credit line are 1) _____ , 2) _____ , and 3) _____ .

33. A _____ is a secured second mortgage on a home.

34. An _____ is a line of credit linked to a checking account that enables a depositor to overdraw his or her checking account up to a predetermined limit.

35. An _____ is a method of borrowing money from the bank without going through lengthy application procedures each time a loan is made.

EXERCISES

Exercise 7-1

Match each type of open credit account with its characteristic described below.

A. 30-day charge account
B. Retail charge account
C. Bank credit charge card
D. Travel and entertainment charge account
E. Prestige charge accounts
F. Revolving lines of credit

1. _____ This does not involve a credit card and is accessed by writing checks on common demand deposit accounts.

2. _____ The customer is required to pay the full amount billed within 10 to 20 days after billing date and generally does not involve a credit card.

3. _____ The customer may buy goods and services offered by the issuing firm up to a predetermined credit limit.

4. _____ Issued by financial institutions, these allow the holder to charge purchases at a variety of stores.

5. _____ Typically offered by gas and electric companies.

6. _____ Similar to bank credit cards, these allow holders to charge purchases at hotels, motels, restaurants, and airlines.

7. _____ More advantages and features are offered, along with a higher credit limit than most.

8. _____ May be added to a regular checking or NOW account as overdraft protection.

9. _____ The major source of open account credit.

Chapter 7 Borrowing on Open Account

Exercise 7-2

Match the following consumer credit legislation with the consumer rights that are protected.

A. Equal Credit Opportunity Act
B. Fair Credit Reporting Act
C. Fair Credit Billing Act
D. Consumer Credit Protection Act
E. Fair Debt Collection Practices Act

1. _____ Credit reports must contain accurate, relevant, and recent financial information about credit applicants.

2. _____ Bills must be mailed at least 14 days prior to the payment due date.

3. _____ Recourse is made available on unsatisfactory purchases.

4. _____ Gives the customer the right to be informed in writing of 1) how much money is owed, 2) to whom, and 3) steps that can be taken if the debt is disputed.

5. _____ A creditor may not discriminate on the basis of sex, marital status or religion.

6. _____ If a husband and wife open a joint credit account, the creditor must report the information to the credit bureau in the names of both parties.

7. _____ Allows merchants to give cash discounts to customers who pay cash.

8. _____ Lenders must disclose both the dollar amount of the finance charges and the annual percentage rate charged.

9. _____ A credit card must contain a form of user identification.

10. _____ Limits the liability of the cardholder to $50 in the event the card is lost or stolen.

Exercise 7-3

Bill has monthly take-home pay of $2,500 and on average total monthly consumer credit payments of $625. Calculate Bill's debt safety ratio. Can Bill increase his monthly credit expenditures? Should he reduce his monthly credit expenditures?

Exercise 7-4

Jenna's bank credit card statement is shown for the month of August. Compute the monthly finance charge for her statement using the 1) previous balance method, 2) average daily balance method, and 3) adjusted balance method.

Billing Date: August 31   Interest Rate 1.5% per month or 18% APR
Previous balance (July 31): $315.25

Transactions	Charges	Amount
8/02	Schnuck's Grocery	$ 75.89
8/05	Rite Aid Pharmacy	29.40
8/10	Charlie's Restaurant	25.10
8/12	The Sharper Image	152.00
8/14	Joe's Hair	45.00
8/20	B. Dalton Bookstores	19.50
8/25	May Co. Department Stores	195.27
8/25	Trans World Airlines	654.00
8/30	**Payment**	$500.00
	New Balance	$696.16

Chapter 8

Using Consumer Loans

CHAPTER OUTLINE

I. Consumer loans can be made as single-payment installment loans but are more likely to have monthly installment payments. They are widely used to finance the purchase of expensive assets such as cars.

A. Long-term liabilities are commonly used to finance durable goods that are too expensive to purchase out of current funds. Consumer loans differ from open account credit in the formality of the lending arrangement.
   1. Consumer loans help finance autos, furniture, appliances, education, and personal items, or are used to consolidate several debts.
   2. Consumer loans can be broken into categories based on the type of repayment arrangement--single-payment or installation loan. A single-payment loan is made for a specified period of time, at the end of which payment in full is due. An installment loan is repaid in a series of fixed, scheduled payments (usually monthly) rather than a lump sum.
   3. Consumer loans may be made at a fixed or variable interest rate.
   4. Interest costs rise and fall due to market conditions. The tax subsidy on interest expense has been eliminated. As costs change, the question of whether or not to borrow at this time becomes relevant.

B. Consumer loans can be obtained from a number of sources, including commercial banks, consumer finance companies, credit unions, savings and loan associations, sales finance companies, life insurance companies, and friends and relatives.
   1. Commercial banks generally charge lower rates than most other lenders because they take only the best credit risks and are able to obtain relatively inexpensive funds from their depositors.
   2. Consumer finance companies make secured and unsecured loans at high rates to predominantly high risk borrowers.
   3. Credit unions offer consumer loans only to their members. It is often the least expensive borrowing.
   4. Businesses that sell expensive items often provide installment financing to purchasers of their products. These installment contracts are then sold to sales finance companies.

        5.   Life insurance policyholders can obtain loans against the cash value of their life insurance policies. This type of loan has no stated maturity date.

    C.   Borrowing to make major acquisitions must be managed carefully.

        1.   When shopping for credit:

            a.   The size and number of payments should fit comfortably in your spending and savings plans.

            b.   Both the purchase price of the item and the cost of the credit must be known.

            c.   Know what collateral is to be pledged on the loan.

            d.   Understand the payment date, time period of the credit obligation, penalties for late payment, and prepayment penalties.

        2.   Always be aware of the amount of consumer debt that has been accumulated. The debt safety ratio is a quick way to assess your debt position.

 II.   Single-payment loans are usually secured with collateral and generally carry a term to maturity of one year or less. Their cost depends on the stated rate of interest and the type of interest used.

    A.   Important loan features include the loan application, loan collateral, loan maturity, and loan repayment.

        1.   Loan collateral is the asset used to secure the loan. In default this asset can be sold to repay the loan.

        2.   Loan maturity is the time period over which the loan is granted, at the end of which the loan must be repaid.

        3.   Loan repayment is the date on which the loan is expected to be repaid. Early payment may involve a prepayment penalty or reduced finance charges depending on the lender's policy.

    B.   The two basic methods of computing finance charges on a single-payment note are the simple interest method and the discount method.

        1.   In the simple interest method, interest is charged only on the actual loan balance outstanding. The mathematical expression for computing simple interest is:

F_s = principal amount of loan x stated annual rate of interest x term of loan stated in years

The Annual Percentage Rate (APR) is calculated with the equation:

$$\text{APR} = \frac{\text{average annual finance charge}}{\text{average loan balance outstanding}}$$

        2.   In the discount method, the finance charges are calculated, then subtracted from the amount of the loan. The APR on a discounted loan will be higher than on a simple interest loan and is calculated in a similar way.

III. Installment loans are paid off with a series of payments over time, can either be secured or unsecured, and have maturities from 6 months to 10 years.

A. The installment purchase contract specifies the obligations of both the borrower and the lender. It will contain four basic components: a sales contract, a security agreement, a note, and an insurance agreement.
1. The security agreement indicates whether or not the lender has control over the item being purchased.
2. The note is the formal promise on the part of the borrower to repay the lender as specified in the sales contract.
3. Credit life insurance is sometimes a condition of receiving an installment loan. Credit life insurance provides insurance to pay off the obligation if the borrower dies. Disability insurance will pay if the borrower becomes disabled.
4. Special features in the installment loan agreement include additional collateral, default, repossession, and balloon payments.
a. An add-on clause enables the lender to add certain assets to the loan's collateral that are acquired after the contract has been signed. (This clause will not be enforced by the courts.)
b. The acceleration clause allows the lender to demand immediate repayment of the entire amount of the unpaid debt if the borrower misses a payment.
c. A recourse clause specifies the type of action the lender can take in the event the borrower defaults. This includes garnishment or repossession.
B. Finance charges, monthly payments, and APRs for installment loans vary.
1. When simple interest is used on an installment loan, interest is charged only on the outstanding balance of the loan.
2. When the add-on method of charging interest is used on an installment loan, the finance charges are calculated using the original balance of the loan and then added to it. This type of loan is one of the most costly forms of consumer credit.
3. The Rule of 78 may be used to determine the monthly interest charges on add-on installment loans.
C. Assuming that you have sufficient liquid reserves, if it costs more to borrow the money to buy something than you can earn in interest on your cash savings, then do not finance the purchase. Use your savings instead.

FILL IN THE BLANK

1. The two major types of consumer loans are _____ and _____.

2. Consumer loans differ from open account credit in the formality of the _____.

3. _____ loans account for nearly half of all consumer loans.

4. _____ for a loan can be repossessed by the lender in the event the buyer fails to make the payments.

5. If you have overextended your credit, a _____ loan can help to straighten out the situation.

6. A _____ loan is made for a specified period of time, at the end of which payment in full is due.

7. A _____ loan generally has a maturity of no longer than one year.

8. An _____ loan is repaid in a series of fixed, scheduled payments rather than a lump sum.

9. _____ interest is no longer tax deductible.

10. _____ typically have lower rates than other lenders of consumer credit.

11. _____ generally make secured or unsecured small loans to high risk borrowers.

12. Only members can obtain installment and single-payment loans from _____.

13. _____ specialize in mortgage lending, but they also make consumer loans.

14. _____ buy installment contracts from businesses which sell more expensive items and provide installment financing to purchasers of their products.

15. GMAC and GECC are examples of _____.

16. Life insurance policyholders may take a loan against the _____ of their life insurance policies.

17. Life insurance loans do not have a stated _____.

18. _____ is the asset that secures a loan.

19. A quick way to assess a personal debt position is to compute the _____ ratio.

20. A financial guideline on the level of consumer credit recommends that the debt safety ratio should not exceed _____ percent.

21.   The three most important features of debt are _____,
      _____, and _____.

22.   Lenders do not take physical possession of collateral; instead they file a
      _____.

23.   When borrowers maintain possession or title to movable property designated as
      collateral, the instrument that gives lenders title to the property in the event of
      default is called a _____.

24.   If lenders hold title to the collateral, the agreement giving them the right to sell
      these items in case of default is a _____.

25.   A _____ is a set percentage of the interest that would have been
      paid over the remaining life of the loan and charges when early repayment is made.

26.   If you are unable to meet the payment date on a single-payment loan, you may be
      able to arrange a loan _____.

27.   The two basic methods used to calculate the finance charges on a single-payment
      loan are _____ and _____.

28.   Interest is charged only on the _____ in the simple interest method.

29.   With the _____ method, the finance charges are calculated and then
      subtracted from the amount of the loan.

30.   The discount method yields a _____ (lower/higher) APR than
      the simple interest method.

31.   The _____ specifies the obligations of both the borrower and the
      lender and has four basic components: a sales contract, a security agreement, a note,
      and an insurance agreement.

32.   The formal promise on the part of the borrower to repay the lender as specified in
      the sales contract is outlined in the _____.

33.   _____ insures the lender against the death of the borrower.

34.   An _____ clause enables the lender to add certain assets to the
      loan's collateral that are acquired after the contract has been signed.

35.   An _____ clause allows the lender to demand immediate payment of
      the entire amount of the unpaid debt if the purchaser misses a payment.

36.   A _____ is an attempt on the part of the lender to collect part of
      the borrower's salary without a court order.

37. _____ is the legal procedure that will require an employer to pay a portion of the borrower's wages to the lender.

38. The act of seizing collateral when the borrower defaults on an installment loan is _____.

39. _____ loans are one of the most costly forms of consumer credit.

40. The _____ is used to determine monthly charges on add-on installment loans.

41. If your after-tax earnings on your savings is greater than the cost of borrowing, you should _____.

EXERCISES

Exercise 8-1

Calculate the monthly installment loan payment for the following simple interest loans. Use Exhibit 8.8 of the text for monthly payment factors.

a. 12 months, 10%, $25,000.
b. 24 months, 15%, $10,000.
c. 48 months, 8%, $ 5,000.

Exercise 8-2

Calculate the payment necessary at the maturity date of the following single payment notes using the simple interest method.

	Principal	Interest Rate	Term of Loan
a.	$1,000	5%	3 years
b.	5,000	7%	5 years
c.	7,000	10%	10 years

Exercise 8-3

Calculate the finance charge and the annual percentage rate on the following single payment loans using the discount method.

	Principal	Interest Rate	Term of Loan
a.	$7,500	8%	2 years
b.	5,000	9%	1 year
c.	12,000	10%	3 years

Exercise 8-4

Calculate the finance charge and the monthly payment on a $15,500 add-on installment loan with an interest rate of 7.5 percent and a term of two years.

Chapter 8 Using Consumer Loans

Exercise 8-5

Compare the total finance charges of the two loans described below. (Use Exhibit 8.8 of the text for the monthly payment factors for the simple interest loan.)

Loan 1:   A simple interest installment loan to be repaid in monthly payments at a 9 percent stated interest rate, $10,000 principal value, and a one year maturity term.

Loan 2:   An add-on installment loan to be repaid in monthly payments at a 9 percent stated interest rate, $10,000 principal value, and a one year maturity term.

Exercise 8-6

Calculate the APR for the following add-on loans with monthly installments.

	Principal	Interest Rate	Term of Loan
a.	$20,000	10%	2 years
b.	15,000	9%	3 years
c.	3,500	6%	5 years

Exercise 8-7

Laura borrowed $7,500 to be repaid in 48 monthly installments; the loan was made at an add-on interest rate of 6 percent. If Laura repays the loan after 12 months, how much will the lender receive as the loan "payoff"?

CASE PROBLEMS

Case 8.1 Integrative-Evaluation of Consumer Loans

Keron is considering purchasing a new Honda motor scooter to commute to work. The scooter will cost $3,450 including all taxes and supplemental equipment (helmet and storage bins). Keron cannot pay cash and must finance the purchase. He has surveyed the local financial institutions about the available consumer loans and summarized his findings below. Evaluate each loan and recommend to Keron which loan to take.

Honda Dealer's Loan Association
Installment loan, 12 percent simple interest, 3 years.

Society Bank
Installment loan, 10 percent add-on interest, 3 years.

General Finance Company
Single payment loan, 15 percent simple interest, 18 months.

Case 8.2 Keeping Track of the Smith's Consumer Debt

Gene and Joan Smith are worried about their level of consumer debt. They need to buy a second car and they do not know if they could qualify for another loan based on what they already owe. Their combined take-home pay is $3,800 per month. They borrowed $2,000 on a personal installment loan. The monthly payment is $75 and they still owe $1,400. They bought a car about two years ago. Their monthly payment is $311 and they still owe $6,000. They use credit cards extensively and make only the required minimum payments. Here is what they owe on various cards.

Visa	$35 per month	$1,500 due
MasterCard	$45 per month	$1,250 due
Shell Oil	$25 per month	$ 400 due
Macy's	$75 per month	$1,700 due
Discover	$55 per month	$2,000 due

They have also done some remodelling in their house using a home equity credit line. The monthly payment is $265 and the remaining balance is $9,800. Finally, Joan is attending night school for her masters degree. She has a student loan of $2,500 and payments of $100 monthly. Using the following worksheet which is from Exhibit 8.3 in the text, make an inventory of the Smith's debts and calculate their debt safety ratio.

Case 8.3 Which Way to Go: Cash or a Loan?

Louann needs new furniture. She has the money in her savings account, but she would rather take out a loan if it would be to her advantage. The loan is for two years at 12 percent interest. The principal is $2,500 and it would be a simple interest installment loan. (Use Exhibit 8.8 to find the monthly payment.) Her savings are in a special credit union account that pays 6.5 percent interest. She is in the 28 percent tax bracket.

Use the following worksheet from Exhibit 8.12 in the text to help Louann with her decision.

AN INVENTORY OF CONSUMER DEBT

Name _____ Date _____

Type of Consumer Debt		Current Monthly Payment[a]	Latest Balance Due
Auto loans	1.	$	$
	2.		
	3.		
Education loans	1.		
	2.		
Personal installment loans	1.		
	2.		
Home improvement loan			
Other installment loans	1.		
	2.		
Single-payment loans	1.		
	2.		
Credit cards (retail charge cards, bank cards, T&E cards, etc.)	1.		
	2.		
	3.		
	4.		
	5.		
	6.		
	7.		
Overdraft protection line			
Personal line of credit			
Home equity credit line			
Loan on life insurance			
Margin loan from broker			
Other loans	1.		
	2.		
	3.		
Totals		$	$

$$\text{Debt safety ratio} = \frac{\text{Total monthly payments}}{\text{Monthly take-home pay}} \times 100 = \frac{\$}{\$} \times 100 = \underline{\quad\quad} \%$$

[a] Leave the space blank if there is *no* monthly payment required on a loan (e.g., as with a single-payment or education loan).

BUY ON TIME OR PAY CASH			

Name _____   Date _____

■	**Cost of Borrowing**		

1.	Terms of the loan
	  a. Amount of the loan
	  b. Length of loan (in years)
	  c. Monthly payment
		$ _____
		
		$ _____	

2.	Total loan payments made (monthly loan payment x length of loan in months) _____ per month x _____ months		$ _____
3.	Less: Principal amount of the loan		$ _____
4.	Total interest paid over life of loan (line 2 – line 3)		$ _____

5.	Tax considerations:
	• Is this a home-equity loan (where interest expenses
	  can be deducted from taxes) ....yes ☐ no ☐
	• Do you itemize deductions on your federal tax returns................................yes ☐ no ☐
	• If you answered yes to BOTH questions, then proceed to *line 6;*
	  if you answered no to *either one or both* of the questions, then
	  proceed to *line 8* and use *line 4* as the after-tax interest cost of the loan.		

6.	What Federal Tax Bracket are you in? (use either 15, 28, or 31%)	____ %	
7.	Taxes saved due to interest deductions (line 4 x tax rate, from line 6: **$** _____ x ___%)		$ _____
8.	Total after-tax interest cost on the loan (line 4 – line 7)		$ _____
■	**Cost of Paying Cash**		
9.	Annual interest *earned* on savings (Annual rate of interest earned on savings x amount of loan: ____% x _____)		$ _____
10.	Annual after-tax interest earnings (line 9 x [1 – tax rate] — e.g., 1 – 28% = 72%: $ _____ x ___%)		$ _____
11.	Total after-tax interest earnings over life of loan (line 10 x line 1-b: $ _____ x _____ years)		$ _____
■	**Net Cost of Borrowing**		
12.	Difference in cost of borrowing vs. cost of paying cash (line 8 minus line 11)		$ _____
BASIC DECISION RULE: *Pay cash* if line 12 is positive; *borrow the money* if line 12 is negative.			
Note: For simplicity, compounding is ignored in calculating *both* the cost of interest and interest earnings.			

Chapter 9
Insuring Your Life

CHAPTER OUTLINE

I. The purpose of life insurance is to protect your family from financial loss in the event of your untimely death. Sound insurance planning requires a basic understanding of your exposure to risk and how insurance can provide protection against it.

  A. Insurance planning involves thinking about the losses to which your assets and income are exposed and how you can provide protection against such losses by weaving insurance into your financial plan.

  B. Most employees rely on the benefits supplied by their employers to provide many insurance needs, especially health insurance.
    1. Many employees provide variable benefits in a cafeteria-style plan which allows employees to select the benefits needed.

  C. Insurance companies must earn sufficient money from premiums and investment income to pay claims expenses and still earn a profit.

  D. An insurance policy is a contract between you and an insurance company under which the insurance company promises to pay for your losses according to specified terms. You pay premiums in return for this promise.

  E. Risk is the uncertainty with respect to economic loss.
    1. Risk avoidance is the act of avoiding any opportunity of loss by not participating in an activity. Some risks cannot be avoided.
    2. Loss prevention is any activity that reduces the probability that a loss will occur or lessens the severity of the loss should it occur.
    3. Risk assumption is the choice of accepting and bearing the risk of loss.
    4. Insurance permits society to reduce individual financial risks and share losses.

  F. Insurance is an ideal method of handling risk if the following criteria are met:
    1. There must be a large number of similar exposures to loss.
    2. The potential loss must be fortuitous.
    3. The cost of insurance must be relatively low.
    4. Losses must be non-catastrophic.

  G. Underwriting involves a decision regarding whom the company can insure and the determination of applicable rates.

Chapter 9 Insuring Your Life

II. There are three approaches widely used to help you calculate how much life insurance is right for you: 1) the human life value approach, 2) the multiple earnings approach, and 3) the needs approach.

    A. The human life approach attempts to convert your future earnings into a present value. This approach does not consider either your financial obligations or the external resources available to your family.

    B. The multiple earnings approach is a simple technique which bases life insurance needs on an arbitrary multiple of gross annual earnings. This method also fails to consider financial obligations and external resources.

    C. The needs approach does consider the financial obligations and financial resources available to the insured person and his or her family. The three steps to this method are 1) estimating total economic resources needed, 2) determining all financial resources that would be available, and 3) subtracting the amount of resources from the amount needed in order to determine the amount of additional life insurance required to provide for the insured's family.

        1. Life insurance covers some of the financial loss resulting from death. Money is available for:

            a. family income (care of children, college funds).

            b. additional expenses (medical bills, funeral expenses).

            c. debt liquidation (mortgage, car loans).

            d. augmenting the surviving spouse's income.

            e. special requirements (training a spouse to enter the labor force).

            f. liquidity (for estate taxes).

        2. After estimating the financial needs that a family must meet upon the death of a family member, a list of all available resources for meeting those needs must be prepared. These include social security benefits, other insurance, pension funds, and income produced by other family members.

        3. The final step in determining the amount of life insurance required is to subtract the amount of available resources from the total needed to satisfy all of the family's financial objectives.

    D. A detailed illustration of the needs approach appears in the text.
       This approach is believed by most financial planners to be the best.

III. The three basic types of life insurance are term, whole life, and universal life.

    A. Term insurance, the purest form of life insurance, provides a stipulated amount of life insurance (death benefits). Since there are no investment features associated with term insurance, there is no cash value.

        1. The most common types of term insurance are straight term, renewable term, convertible term, and decreasing term.

            a. Straight term policies are written for a given number of years.

            b. A renewable term policy may be renewed at its expiration for another term of equal length without taking another medical examination. The premium will increase to reflect your increase in age.

            c. Convertible term insurance allows the insured to convert coverage into a whole life or endowment life insurance policy.

     d.   Decreasing term maintains a level premium while the amount of protection decreases each year.

    2.   The primary strength of term insurance is that it can offer an economical way to purchase a large amount of protection against financial loss resulting from death. The primary weakness of term insurance is that rates increase as the insured ages.

B.   Whole life insurance is designed to offer financial protection for the whole life of the individual. Whole life insurance has a savings feature called cash value.

    1.   The major types of whole life policies are continuous premium, limited payment, and single premium.

         a.   Under a continuous premium whole life policy, individuals pay a level premium amount each year until they die or exercise a forfeiture right. Continuous premium whole life offers the greatest death protection and the least savings per dollar of premium paid for lifetime protection.

         b.   A limited payment whole life policy offers coverage for the entire life of the insured but schedules payments to end after a limited period.

         c.   A single premium whole life policy is purchased on a cash basis. One premium payment at the inception of the contract buys life insurance coverage for the rest of the insured's life.

    2.   The premium payments for whole life insurance contribute toward building an estate. The most frequently cited disadvantages of whole life insurance are that more death protection can be purchased with term insurance, and higher yields can be obtained from other investment vehicles.

C.   Universal life insurance combines term insurance with a tax-deferred savings/investment account that pays interest at competitive market rates.

    1.   Universal life insurance is a type of whole life insurance. The special aspect of a universal life policy is that the cost of protection (the pure insurance portion) and the savings element portion are identified separately in its premium. These policies enjoy favorable tax treatment, with the interest credited to the policy generally accumulating tax free.

    2.   The basic structure of a universal whole life policy is as follows: the premium paid for the policy, the annual contribution or annual outlay, is deposited into a fund known as an accumulation account; the insurer credits the interest to the account at a current rate and deducts from it the cost of the death benefits and other expenses. Universal life policies may either provide a level death benefit or provide a stated amount of insurance plus the accumulated cash value.

    3.   A primary advantage of the universal life policy is the flexibility it provides.

    4.   Before buying universal life, understand what interest rate is being used in the salesman's presentation. Your actual accumulation account balance will depend on interest rates as they really are (not as projected). Try to evaluate the expense charges or fees that are levied by the insurance company.

D. Variable life insurance, credit life insurance, mortgage life insurance, industrial life insurance, special purpose policies, group life insurance, and other types of insurance are also available.

   1. In variable life insurance policies, the benefits payable to the beneficiary are related to the value of the insurance company's assets that support the policy's obligations. The unique feature of this policy is that the consumer may select and periodically change the type of investments to be used with his or her savings/investment plan. Accordingly, the amount of profits or losses associated with the investment opportunity may vary.

   2. Credit life insurance is sold in conjunction with installment loans. It is an expensive way to buy life insurance and usually should be avoided.

   3. Mortgage life insurance is a form of credit life insurance designed to pay the mortgage balance upon the death of the borrower.

   4. Industrial life insurance or home service life is a whole life or endowment life insurance that is issued in policies with small face amounts. The cost per dollar of protection is very high.

   5. Deferred premium life insurance is generally marketed to college students. Students borrow the first (sometimes the first and second) year's premium and sign a promissory note to repay sometime in the future. Since most college students don't need life insurance, and they certainly don't need an additional debt, deferred premium life insurance is not recommended.

   6. Group life insurance is nearly always term insurance with the premium based on the characteristics of the group as a whole rather than related to any specific individual.

IV. All life insurance contracts have various provisions that establish the rights and obligations of the policyholder and the insurance company.

A. The key features found in most life insurance contracts are the beneficiary clause, settlement options, policy loans, payment of premiums, nonforfeiture options, policy reinstatement, and change of policy.

   1. The beneficiary clause details who should receive the death benefit.

   2. The settlement options stipulate how the funds will be distributed to the beneficiary. Options include interest only, payments for a stated period, payments of a stated amount, and life income.

   3. Policyholders may borrow from the cash value of their life insurance policies. This loan becomes a lien against the face and will be deducted from the face value if it has not been repaid before death.

   4. The frequency of paying the policy premiums is stipulated in the contract. Paying annually will be the least expensive method.

   5. A nonforfeiture option provides the policyholder with some benefits when a policy is terminated prior to its maturity.

      a. Under a reduced amount option, the policyholder receives a paid-up policy with a lower face value.

      b. The extended term option provides that upon the relinquishment of the policy, the company issues a term life insurance policy for the same face value that will remain in effect for a specified time.

6. Policy reinstatement may be made by paying all of the back premiums plus interest at a stated rate and providing evidence that the insured can pass a physical exam and meet other insurability requirements.
7. Many life insurance policies contain a provision that permits the insured to switch from one type of policy to another.

B. Other key contractual features may include a grace period, multiple indemnity clause, disability clause, insurability options, suicide clause, incontestability clause, misstatement of age or sex clause, exclusions of types of losses covered, and participation in policy dividends.

C. Competitive features of life insurance policies include 1) protection from creditors, 2) medium for savings, and 3) tax benefits.
   1. Insurance proceeds paid to a named beneficiary will not become part of the estate of the decedent and cannot be attached by his creditors.
   2. Life insurance can be used for savings. The principal is safe, competitive interest rates are usually paid, the cash value is readily available, and it creates some forced savings for those with little will power.
   3. Life insurance proceeds are not subject to state or federal income taxes; however, interest earned on the proceeds will be taxable.

D. Before buying life insurance, you should estimate the amount of life insurance necessary to meet your and your family's financial requirements, consider the types of policies available, and familiarize yourself with the various provisions that life insurance contracts typically include.
   1. Investigate the insurance company offering the policy. Best's Insurance Reports can give you an idea of the company's financial condition.
   2. Look for an agent with a Chartered Life Underwriter designation and seek recommendations from other professionals who deal with agents.

FILL IN THE BLANK

---

1. The purpose of _____ is to protect your family from financial loss in the event of your untimely death.

2. Many workers receive most of their insurance through _____.

3. Flexible benefits are usually available through _____.

4. _____ is any activity that reduces the probability that a loss will occur or lessens the severity of the loss should it occur.

5. _____ is the choice of accepting and bearing the risk of loss.

6. _____ is an ideal method of handling risk if the following criteria are met: 1) there are a _____ number of similar exposures to loss, 2) the potential loss must be _____, 3) the cost of _____ must be relatively low, and 4) losses must be _____.

7. _____ determine whom companies will insure and at what rates.

8. The three approaches in determining how much insurance is necessary for an individual or a family are 1) the _____ approach, 2) the _____ approach, and 3) the _____ approach.

9. The _____ approach is a simple technique that bases life insurance needs on an arbitrary multiple of gross annual earnings.

10. The _____ approach attempts to convert your future earnings into a present value.

11. The _____ approach considers the financial obligations and financial resources available to the insured's family.

12. The three basic types of life insurance are 1) _____, 2) _____, and 3) _____.

13. The primary strength of _____ insurance is that it offers an economical way to purchase a large amount of protection against the financial loss resulting from death.

14. A term insurance policy that allows the insured to change coverage into a whole life or endowment life insurance policy is _____ term.

15. _____ term requires a level premium over the term of coverage, but the amount of protection decreases.

16. _____ insurance is designed to offer financial protection for your entire life.

17. _____ and _____ insurance have a savings and investment feature.

18. _____ insurance combines term insurance with a tax-deferred savings/investment account that pays interest at competitive rates.

19. A _____ whole life policy is one that offers coverage for the entire life of the insured but schedules payments to end after a limited period.

20. Under a _____ premium whole life policy, individuals pay a level premium amount each year until they die or exercise a forfeiture right.

21. In _____ insurance, the premiums contribute toward building an estate.

22. A primary advantage of the _____ policy is the flexibility it provides.

23. _____ life insurance is sold in conjunction with installment loans.

24.   In _____ life insurance policies, the benefits payable are related to the value of the investment portfolio that supports the policy obligations.

25.   The _____ in a life insurance contract stipulate how the funds should be distributed to a beneficiary.

26.   The _____ clause in a life insurance contract details who should receive the death benefit.

27.   The _____ feature in a life insurance contract provides the policyholder with some benefits when a policy is terminated prior to its maturity.

28.   Life insurance may be an attractive medium for savings when you consider_____, _____, _____, and _____ .

29.   Life insurance proceeds are generally not subject to _____ .

30.   _____ insurance is best if you have absolutely no risk tolerance or self-discipline when it comes to saving and investing.

31.   _____ insurance is best if you simply want inexpensive, but solid life protection.

32.   _____ insurance is best if you need a tax shelter and are an experienced, risk-tolerant investor.

33.   _____ insurance is best if you would like a combination insurance/savings plan and you are somewhat flexible and self-directed when it comes to money matters.

EXERCISES

Exercise 9-1

Match each type of life insurance policy with the appropriate characteristic.

A. Term
B. Whole life
C. Universal life
D. Straight term
E. Renewable term
F. Convertible term
G. Decreasing term
H. Continuous premium whole life

I. Limited payment whole life
J. Single premium whole life
K. Endowment life
L. Variable life
M. Credit life
N. Mortgage life
O. Group life
P. Deferred premium life

Chapter 9 Insuring Your Life

1. _____   The benefits payable are related to the value of the insurance company's assets, which support the policy's obligations.

2. _____   Contains no investment features.

3. _____   Allows the insured to convert term coverage into a whole life or endowment life insurance policy.

4. _____   The pure insurance portion and the savings portion are identified separately in its premium.

5. _____   Generally sold in conjunction with installment loans.

6. _____   Frequently marketed to college students who have little current cash.

7. _____   Cost is based on the characteristics of a group rather than those of an individual.

8. _____   Maintains a level premium but the amount of protection decreases over time.

9. _____   A whole life policy for which insureds pay a level premium amount each year until they die or exercise forfeiture.

10. _____   A whole life policy that requires payments for a limited length of time but provides death protection to insureds for their entire lives.

Exercise 9-2

Match each key feature of the life insurance contract with its description.

A. Beneficiary clause
B. Settlement option
C. Policy loan
D. Payment of premiums
E. Nonforfeiture options
F. Policy reinstatement
G. Change of policy

1. _____   A cash advance against the cash value of the policy.

2. _____   Details who should receive the death benefit.

3. _____   The policyholder receives a paid-up policy with a lower face value than the terminated policy.

4. _____   The policyholder must pay all back premiums plus interest and meet other insurability requirements in order to exercise this option.

5. _____ Stipulates how the funds will be distributed to the beneficiary.

CASE PROBLEMS

Case 9.1 What Type of Life Insurance is Right for Jennifer?

Jennifer is a divorced mother of two young children, Rebecca, 5, and Micah, 8. She works full time as a physical therapist at the local hospital earning $28,000 per year. She does receive child support from her ex-husband but still must live on a limited budget. She has recently been considering the purchase of a life insurance policy to provide for the children's care in the event of her death prior to the children reaching majority.

Questions

1. Which type of life insurance--term, whole life, universal life--best fits Jennifer's financial situation and goals?
2. If you were a life insurance agent, what additional information would you want about Jennifer and her family in order to assess her life insurance needs more thoroughly?

Case 9.2 A Life Insurance Choice for the Ketterings

Paul and Vivian Kettering are a wealthy couple in their forties who have just sold a large manufacturing company that they founded 20 years ago. They need to invest the funds from the sale of their business. They both are sophisticated financial planners who self-direct most of their vast portfolio of investments. A life insurance policy making their three children equal beneficiaries is under consideration.

Questions

1. What investment considerations other than life insurance should the Ketterings make?
2. What type of policy would you recommend to the Ketterings? Why?

Chapter 9 Insuring Your Life

Case 9.3 How Much Life Insurance Is Right for This Family?

Family Profile

Husband - John Talbot, professional musician, 40, salary $45,000
Wife   - Shirley Talbot, university professor, 40, salary $39,000

Children: Megan, 12
          Jonathon, 9

Annual combined income	$79,000
Equity in primary residence	50,000
Total installment loans	12,000
Mortgage balance on primary residence	70,000
Cash and investments	63,000
Anticipated final burial expenses	7,000
Survivors benefits of social security for children	1,200/mo.

Should either John or Shirley die, they feel that living expenses until Jonathon turns 18 would be $4,500 per month. However, as noted below, the Talbots want to replace all lost income during this time, not just cover expenses. Once the children are in college, monthly living expenses should drop to $3,900. At retirement, age 65, they should decline further to $3,300. The retirement Social Security payment should be about $800 per month for either John or Shirley. Other retirement income is estimated at $1,200 per month. For ease of calculation and because John and Shirley are the same age, it is estimated that either, as the surviving spouse, would live to age 85. In their income calculations, they are assuming that Shirley is the survivor.

John and Shirley Talbot are reviewing their insurance needs. Their life insurance goals are:

- to provide their children until they become 18 with an income equal to their current income.
- to provide a means to pay off the liabilities should either spouse die.
- to provide a college education fund that would provide $15,000 per child for four years.

Currently John has a term life policy with a death benefit of $50,000. Shirley is covered under a group policy which provides a $30,000 death or disability benefit.

Questions

1. Use the multiple earnings approach (factors appear in Exhibit 9.1 of the text) to find the amount of life insurance if they want to replace 65 percent of their lost earnings.
2. Use the needs approach to determine the amount of life insurance that meets the Talbots goals. Are the Talbots adequately insured? (Use the following worksheet from Exhibit 9.3.)
3. What type of life insurance and what amounts of insurance would you recommend for the Talbots?

Insured's
Name _____ Date _____

				Totals
A. **Family Income Needs**				
1. Debt Liquidation:				
a. House mortgage	$			
b. Other loans	$			
c. Total debt (a+b)				$
2. Final expenses				$
3. Annual income needs:	Period 1	Period 2	Period 3	
a. Monthly living expenses	$	$	$	
b. Less: Social security survivor's benefits				
c. Less: Surviving spouse's income				
d. Less: Other pension benefits and income				
e. Net monthly income needed (a – b – c –d)				
f. Net yearly income needed (12 x e)				
g. Number of years in period				
h. Funding needed each period (f x g)				
i. Total living needs (add line h for each period)				$
4. Spouse reeducation fund				$
5. Children's opportunity fund				$
6. Other needs				$
7. TOTAL INCOME NEEDS (add right column)				$
B. **Financial Resources Available**				
1. Savings and investments	$			
2. Group life insurance	$			
3. Other life insurance	$			
4. Other resources	$			
TOTAL RESOURCES AVAILABLE (1 + 2 + 3 + 4)				$
C. **Additional Life Insurance Needed (A – B)** (Note: no additional insurance is needed if number is negative.)				$

Chapter 10

Insuring Your Health

CHAPTER OUTLINE

I. Health care coverage is an essential element of your personal financial planning process because of the protection it provides for your financial plans.

    A. In the 1930s, the modern concept of broadly-based health care insurance was born. Since then, many plans have been developed by private insurers, physicians' groups, and the federal and various state governments.

    B. Many people may be covered by multiple health care plans: employer-sponsored group plans, social security, workers' compensation, automobile-related medical payments, veteran's benefits, and individually-purchased coverage.

    C. The choices of where to go for health care include health maintenance organizations, neighborhood emergency centers, individual practice associations, and preferred provider organizations as well as the traditional personal physician and community hospital.

    D. Health insurance is quite complex, and designing the best way to meet your health care needs requires a systematic approach.

II. Several types of health care coverages are available. They fall into the major categories of 1) hospital, 2) surgical expense, 3) physicians expense, 4) major medical, 5) comprehensive major medical, 6) dental, 7) long-term care, 8) other special coverages, and 9) disability income.

    A. Hospital insurance policies offer reimbursement plans covering the costs of hospital room and board and other expenses incidental to hospitalization.

    B. Surgical expense insurance provides coverage for the cost of surgery (Second opinions may be required for elective surgical procedures to reduce the number of unnecessary surgeries).

    C. Physicians expense insurance can cover the cost of such services as physician fees for nonsurgical care in a hospital, at home, in a clinic, or in the doctor's office. Routine office calls are not covered.

    D. Major medical insurance provide benefits for nearly all types of medical expenses resulting from accidents or illnesses. To give insureds an incentive to avoid unnecessary medical costs, major medical plans typically contain provisions for deductibles, participation or coinsurance, and internal limits.

113

      1.   Because major medical plans are designed to supplement the basic hospital, surgical, and physicians expense policies, they frequently have relatively large deductibles.

      2.   A participation or coinsurance clause stipulates that the company will pay some portion of the amount of the covered loss in excess of the deductible rather than the entire amount. The most common share for the insurance company is 80 percent.

      3.   Internal limits place constraints on the amounts that will be paid for certain specified expenses, such as a maximum dollar amount per day for room and board, even if the overall policy limits are not exceeded by the claim.

  E.   A comprehensive major medical insurance plan combines the basic hospital, surgical, and physicians expense coverages with major medical protection in a single policy.

  F.   Dental insurance covers necessary dental health care as well as dental injuries sustained through accidents.

  G.   Long-term care insurance is becoming more of an issue due to our aging population. Long-term care can be financially-devastating for the patient and/or the family.

  H.   Other special types of coverage include travel, "dread disease," and hospital income policies.

  I.   Disability income insurance is designed to provide families with weekly or monthly payments to replace income when an insured person is unable to work as a result of a covered illness, injury, or disease.

      1.   Disability insurance should enable you to maintain a standard of living at or near your present level.

      2.   During most of your working years, there is a greater probability that you will be disabled than you will die.

III.   To compare the health insurance coverages offered by different insurers, you need to evaluate whether they contain liberal or restrictive provisions. Generally, these provisions can be divided into two categories: terms of payment and terms of coverage.

  A.   How much your health care insurance will pay is determined by 1) deductibles, coinsurance, and waiting periods, 2) duration of benefits, 3) policy limitations, 4) coordination of benefits, and 5) method of payment.

      1.   In order to reduce administrative costs of frequent and/or small claims, nearly all types of health insurance policies include deductible, coinsurance, or waiting period clauses.

      2.   How long benefits will be paid is a major concern. There may be limits per incident or per year.

      3.   Policy limits place a cap on the amount the insurer will pay.

      4.   A coordination of benefits clause prevents the insured from collecting multiple payments for the same accident or illness under different policies.

      5.   The financing method used to pay your covered medical expenses will be specified as 1) the indemnity approach, 2) the valued approach, or 3) the service approach.

B. The major terms of a health insurance policy will show 1) persons and places covered, 2) definition of accident, 3) change of occupation, 4) definition of disability, 5) house confinement, 6) cancellation, 7) renewal, 8) continuation of group coverage, 9) rehabilitation, 10) pre-existing conditions, 11) pregnancy and abortions, and 12) mental illness.

IV. There are five traditional sources of financial aid available for losses arising from accidents or illness: 1) social security, 2) workers' compensation, 3) group health insurance, 4) Blue Cross/Blue Shield, and 5) individual health insurance coverage.

    A. Social security can provide disability income from two separate programs 1) Medicare and 2) disability income.
        1. Medicare, which covers Americans when they reach the age of 65 (a few other groups are also covered) is a health plan with two primary components: (1) basic hospital insurance, and (2) supplementary medical insurance.
            a. Under the basic hospital insurance coverage of Medicare (Part A), inpatient hospital services are paid. Deductibles and co-payments are part of the program.
            b. The supplementary medical insurance program under Medicare (Part B) provides payment for a variety of medical expenses. Those wanting Part B must pay monthly premiums.
        2. Disability income from the social security system may be available to those who have contributed to the system for 20 quarters of the 40 quarters immediately preceding the date of disability. The disability must have lasted for at least 5 months and be expected to prevent employment for at least 12 months. The Social Security Administration will decide if you meet its disability definition.
    B. Workers' compensation provides compensation to workers for job-related injuries or illness. The premium is paid by the employer.
    C. Group health insurance contracts are written between a group and an insuring organization. Premiums are usually paid totally or partially by the employer. In a few cases, the employee pays the entire premium.
    D. Blue Cross/Blue Shield contracts are nonprofit prepaid hospital expense plans.
    E. Individual health insurance provides protection directly to policyholders and their families. These policies are more expensive than group policies.
    F. Subscribers/users may contract with and make monthly payments to an organization that provides health care to the subscriber and his family as needed.
        1. The traditional Health Maintenance Organization (HMO) provides comprehensive health care services by a group of doctors who are employed by the organization.
        2. The Individual Practice Association is similar to an HMO except that the services are not offered only in one central location.
        3. A Preferred Provider Organization offers comprehensive services to its subscribers within a network of physicians and hospitals.

VI.   The best way to buy health insurance is to match your insurance needs with the various types of coverage available.

    A.   Most people need protection against two types of losses that can result from accident or injury: 1) loss of income, and 2) additional expenses for medical bills and rehabilitation.

    B.   In preparing a health care plan, there are four methods of dealing with risk: 1) risk avoidance, 2) loss prevention and control, 3) risk assumption, and 4) insurance.

        1.   Risk avoidance means avoiding the exposure that creates potential for loss--not always possible.

        2.   Loss prevention and control can reduce many health problems.

            a.   Prevention of illness would increase if a wellness orientation were adopted by society.

            b.   Abiding by the speed limit and wearing a safety belt are two ways of reducing injuries or avoiding automobile accidents.

    C.   Match your present resources with your present needs. This required evaluating and updating plans as resources and needs change.

    D.   Shopping for coverage means looking for a quality agent and company.

FILL IN THE BLANK

1.   In the _____, the modern concept of broadly-based health care insurance was begun.

2.   Most hospital-related health care expenses are paid by _____ insurance.

3.   Second surgical opinions are usually paid by _____insurance.

4.   _____ insurance provides benefits for nearly all types of medical expenses resulting from either accident or illness.

5.   Because major medical plans are designed to supplement the basic hospital, surgical, and physicians expense policies, they frequently have a large _____.

6.   Another name for coinsurance is _____.

7.   A _____ insurance plan combines the basic hospital, surgical, and physicians expense coverages with major medical protection to form a single policy.

8.   As the population ages, there will be a greater need for _____ insurance protection.

9. _____ insurance is designed to provide families with payments to replace income when the insured person is unable to work as a result of a covered illness or accident.

10. In order to reduce administrative costs of small claims, nearly all types of health insurance policies have _____, _____, and/or _____ clauses.

11. A coordination of benefits prohibits the insured from collection for health care costs _____.

12. One purpose of a deductible is to reduce the chance the insured will _____ illness and incur unnecessary health care costs.

13. Insurance companies can pay for covered medical expenses using 1) the _____ approach, 2) the _____ approach, or 3) the _____ approach.

14. If you lose your job and your group insurance benefits, federal legislation, known as _____, will allow you temporary continued coverage.

15. Government-administered sources of financial aid available for losses arising from accidents or illness are _____ and _____.

16. Social security might provide disability income from two separate programs: _____ and _____.

17. Medicare is a health plan with two primary components: 1) Part A, _____ insurance and 2) Part B, _____ insurance.

18. Medicare provides health care payment for persons _____ of age. The insured must _____ for Part B of this insurance.

19. Disability income from social security may be available if the disabled who person meets these qualifications: _____ and _____.

20. _____ is a government-administered disability program for which the employer pays the premiums.

21. Blue Cross/Blue Shield can be viewed as _____ hospital expense plans.

22. A _____ provides comprehensive health care services by a group of doctors at a central location for a prepaid monthly charge.

23. A _____ offers comprehensive services to its subscribers within a network of physicians and hospitals.

24. Health insurance generally must cover two basic types of losses

1) _____, including rehabilitation, and 2) _____.

25.   In order to determine your health insurance purchase plans you must match your _____ with your _____.

CASE PROBLEMS

Case 10.1 Roger's Health Insurance Coverage

Roger Strader and his brother manage a small tree trimming business. Both receive an annual salary of $20,000. The Straders purchased health insurance for each employee, a major medical policy with a $500 deductible, an 80 percent coinsurance clause, internal limits of $190 per day on hospital room and board, and overall limit protection of $100,000.

On October 1, Roger was trimming an elm tree. As he prepared to cut a limb, he slipped and the chain saw deeply lacerated his arm. Roger was rushed to the local Urgi-Care Center and was immediately transferred to a local hospital where he underwent surgery. Roger then spent 30 days in the hospital. The expenses from the Urgi-Care Center and the ambulance totalled $250. Surgery and anesthesia cost $1,000; hospital room and board cost $230 per day. Drugs and rehabilitative care totalled $850.

Questions

1.   How much of Roger's medical bills will be paid under his insurance policy? How much must he pay personally?
2.   What expenses may be questioned by Roger's insurance company?
3.   Comment on Roger's health insurance coverage.

Case 10.2 Disability Insurance for a Young and Growing Family

Stacey and Mike have four sons under the age of six. Stacey is an aspiring actress and has also worked for national advertisers. She tours with a national acting troupe six months per year. Her salary from the acting company is $5,000 per month after taxes (for six months) and her income from TV commercials is $500 per month after taxes (for 12 months). She is covered by the acting troupe's group insurance. The policy provides disability coverage of

60 percent of the employee's monthly take-home pay. (Since Stacey works only six months per year, the disability benefit is based on earning $2,500 per month). In case of complete disability, Stacey would also be eligible for $500 per month from social security.

Stacey's husband, Mike, who is self-employed, earns $3,000 per month after taxes. Mike has purchased a comprehensive health care/disability policy that would provide disability income of 70 percent of his monthly take-home pay. Mike would be eligible for social security disability benefits of $800 per month if he qualified.

Stacey and Mike currently spend 75 percent of their combined take-home pay to meet their living expenses. Another 5 percent is spent on entertainment and travel. The remaining 20 percent is put into savings and investments.

Questions

1. How much disability insurance do Stacey and Mike, individually, need to insure adequate protection if they became disabled? (Use the worksheets provided.)
2. Are Stacey and Mike currently adequately covered?
3. What recommendations would you make to Stacey and Mike regarding their disability coverage?

DISABILITY BENEFIT NEEDS		
Name(s) _____	**Date** _____	

1.	Estimate current monthly *take-home* pay		$ _____
2.	Estimate existing benefits:	$ _____	
	a. Social security benefits	_____	
	b. Other government benefits	_____	
	c. Company programs	_____	
	d. Group disability policy benefits	_____	
3.	Total existing disability benefits (2a + 2b + 2c + 2d)		$ _____
4.	Estimated monthly disability benefits needed ([1] − [3])		$ _____

Chapter 11

Protecting Your Property

CHAPTER OUTLINE

I. The basic principles of property and liability insurance pertain to types of exposure, criteria for an insurable exposure, the principle of indemnity, and coinsurance.

   A. Most individuals face two basic types of exposure: physical loss of property and loss through liability.
      1. Most property insurance contracts define the property covered in the policy and name the perils for which the insurance proceeds will be available. The insured should develop a complete property inventory and identify the perils against which protection is desired.
         a. A property inventory should be prepared to aid in the selection of coverage and to help settle a claim if a loss occurs.
         b. The insured should determine the perils against which he wishes the insured property to be protected.
      2. Liability insurance is available to protect you from financial losses resulting from negligently causing property damage or bodily injury to someone else.
         a. You are said to have performed a negligent action when your behavior has been inconsistent with the reasonable person doctrine.
         b. The two most common defenses to a charge of negligence are assumption of risk and contributory negligence.
   B. Criteria for an insurable exposure for property and liability losses are the same as for other types of insurance. The following conditions must be met: 1) a large number of similar exposure units, 2) the loss covered is fortuitous, 3) the cost is relatively low, and 4) losses are non-catastrophic.
   C. The principle of indemnity states that the insured may not be compensated by the insurance company for an amount exceeding the actual economic loss.
      1. The principle of indemnity limits the amount the insured may collect to the actual cash value, which is defined as the replacement cost less depreciation. Replacement cost coverage is available in some policies.
      2. Insurable interest means that people who insure property must stand to lose financially if the property is damaged or destroyed. They cannot receive more in payment than their financial interest in the property.
      3. After an insurance company pays the claim, its right of subrogation allows it to demand reimbursement from the person who caused the loss (or from his or her insurance company).

4. The "other insurance" clause prohibits insured persons from insuring property with two or more insurance companies and then collecting for a loss in full from each company.
D. Coinsurance is a provision commonly found in property insurance contracts requiring policyholders to buy a minimum amount of insurance equal to a specified percentage of the value of their property.

II. Your home should be insured properly since it is likely to be your single-most expensive asset. Homeowner's policies are classified as HO-1, HO-2, HO-3, HO-4, HO-6, and HO-8.

A. A named perils policy lists the perils covered in the policy.
1. Section I provides coverage for the home and its contents.
2. Section II provides coverage in case of negligence on the part of the insured.
B. The homeowner's policy offers property protection under Section I for the dwelling unit, other unattached structures, and the personal property of homeowners and their families.
C. Renters insurance is needed to protect a tenant's personal property.
D. You can suffer three different types of property-related loss when misfortune occurs: 1) the direct loss of property, 2) an indirect loss through the loss of the use of damaged property, and 3) extra expenses resulting from direct and indirect losses.
1. The homeowner's policy covers the persons named in the policy and the members of their families who are residents of the household.
2. The homeowner's policy offers coverage worldwide and does not have territorial exclusions.
E. In addition to the principle of indemnity, replacement cost, policy limits, and deductibles can influence the amount an insurance company would pay for a loss.
1. The amount necessary to repair, rebuild, or replace an asset at today's prices is its replacement cost.
2. In Section I of the homeowner's policy, the amount of coverage on the dwelling unit establishes the amounts applicable to the accompanying structures, the unscheduled personal property, and temporary living expenses. In Section II, the standard liability limit and the medical payments limit are established.
a. Deductibles place limits on what a company must pay for small losses and therefore reduce the premium charged.

III. Your automobile involves great exposure to loss and should be adequately covered. The greatest exposure to loss can come from liability claims against you as a result of an accident in which you are at fault.

A. The first four parts of the personal auto policy (PAP) are: 1) liability coverage, 2) medical payments coverage, 3) uninsured motorists coverage, and 4) coverage for damage to your auto.
1. Liability coverage provides coverage for bodily injury and property damage for which you become legally obligated to pay due to an

automobile accident. It will also help settle or defend any claim or suit asking for damages.

    a.   Although insurance provides both bodily injury and property damage liability insurance, there will be a dollar limit up to which it will pay for damages for any one accident.

  2. Medical payments coverage provides for payment to a covered person of an amount no greater than the policy limits for all reasonable and necessary medical expenses incurred within three years after an automobile accident.

  3. Uninsured motorists coverage is available to meet the needs of innocent accident victims negligently injured by uninsured, underinsured, or hit-and-run motorists.

  4. Coverage for physical damage to an auto includes collision and comprehensive coverage.

    a.   Collision insurance is a first-party property damage coverage that pays for collision damage to an insured automobile regardless of fault.

    b.   Comprehensive automobile insurance protects against loss to an insured automobile caused by any peril other than collision.

B.   No-fault automobile insurance was introduced because of a need for more medical coverage for victims of serious accidents.

  1. No-fault automobile insurance is based on the belief that the liability system should be replaced by a system that reimburses without regard to negligence.

C.   The automobile insurance premium is based on a combination of many factors: 1) geographic territory, 2) amount of use the automobile receives, 3) personal characteristics of the driver, 4) type of automobile, 5) driving record of the insured, and 6) applicable discounts.

D.   Financial responsibility laws require motorists to buy liability insurance.

E.   A clause in your car financing contract will require you to buy physical damage insurance on the car you are buying.

IV.   A variety of other insurance policies are available. They include 1) personal property floaters, 2) umbrella personal liability, 3) mobile home insurance, 4) boat insurance, 5) recreational vehicle insurance, 6) automobile repair insurance, 7) earthquake insurance, 8) flood insurance, and 9) professional liability insurance.

V.   When buying property and liability insurance, first develop an inventory of exposures to loss and arrange them from highest to lowest priority.

A.   Most property insurance agents are classified as captive (those who represent only one insurance company) and independent (those who represent several companies). Look for a Certified Property Casualty Underwriter (CPCU) designation for an agent with above-average knowledge and experience.

B.   A few notes on settling claims follow.

  1. After an accident, record the names and addresses of all witnesses, drivers, occupants, and injured parties, along with the license numbers of the automobiles involved. Notify the police and your insurance company. Do not admit any liability. Cooperate with your insurance company.

123

2. The typical insurance claim involves four steps: 1) giving timely notice to the insurance company a loss has occurred, 2) having the claim investigated, 3) proving your loss, and 4) having the company decide on the validity of the claim.
    a. If the loss is complex, a claims adjustor will be assigned to the case.
        i. The claims adjustor will work either for the insurance company or as an independent adjustor and will primarily look out for the interests of the company.
        ii. A public adjustor or attorney may be necessary to negotiate a claim.

FILL IN THE BLANK

1. The effective use of property and liability insurance rests on the understanding of the _____ and _____ .

2. Before you buy property loss insurance contracts, you should develop an _____ and identify _____ .

3. A _____ is a cause of loss.

4. Examples of perils which are excluded from the usual HO policy are _____ , _____ , _____ , _____ , and _____ . _____ and _____ could not be insured by making additions to your policy.

5. Protection against negligent acts is _____ insurance.

6. You are said to have been _____ when your behavior has been inconsistent with the reasonable person doctrine.

7. The two most common defenses to a charge of negligence are _____ and _____ .

8. Under the _____ defense, the allegation is that some action of the plaintiff relieved the defendant of his or her duty to protect the plaintiff.

9. Under the _____ defense, the defendant maintains that the plaintiff contributed to his or her own loss by his or her actions.

10. The principle of _____ states that the insured may not be compensated by the insurance company in an amount exceeding his economic loss.

11. The concept of _____ means that the individuals who insure property must stand to lose something if that property is subject to loss.

12. _____ is the replacement cost minus depreciation.

13. After an insurance company pays a claim, its right of _____ allows it to request reimbursement from the person who caused the loss or from his or her insurance company.

14. The _____ clause prohibits insured persons from insuring their property with and collecting on two or more insurance policies.

15. _____ is a provision commonly found in property insurance requiring insureds to carry an amount of insurance equal to a specified percentage of the value of their property.

16. All homeowner's forms are divided into two sections. Section I applies to _____ and Section II applies to _____.

17. HO-1 is known as the _____ form, HO-2 is the _____ form, and HO-3 is the _____ form.

18. _____ insurance covers only personal belongings and furnishings because the insured has no insurable interest in the structure.

19. A person can suffer three different types of property-related loss when misfortune occurs: 1) _____ of property, 2) _____ through the loss of use of damaged property, and 3) _____.

20. A _____ policy provides comprehensive coverage on a blanket basis for virtually all of the insured's personal property.

21. The amount necessary to repair, rebuild, or replace an asset at today's prices is the _____ cost.

22. _____ limit what the insurance company must pay on small losses and reduce insurance premiums.

23. Probably no asset involves more exposure to loss than your _____.

24. The _____ is a comprehensive automobile policy designed to be easily understood by the "typical" insurance purchaser.

25. When a motorist who is involved in an automobile accident is covered under two or more liability insurance contracts, the coverage on the _____ is primary.

26. _____ insurance is available to meet the needs of "innocent" accident victims negligently injured by uninsured, underinsured, or hit-and-run motorists.

27.   Three points must be proven in order to receive payment through uninsured motorists insurance: 1) _____ was at fault, 2) this motorist has no _____, and 3) _____ were incurred.

28.   _____ insurance is a first-party property damage coverage that pays for collision damage to an insured automobile regardless of fault.

29.   _____ insurance protects against loss to an insured automobile caused by any peril other than collision.

30.   _____, _____, and _____ are the key personal characteristics which affect the premium charged for automobile insurance.

31.   In some states, automobile owners are required to show evidence that they have liability insurance prior to receiving registration for their motor vehicles. In other states, motorists must prove they have liability insurance after they have been involved in an accident. These are examples of _____ laws.

32.   A _____ insurance agent is one who represents only one insurance company.

EXERCISES

Exercise 11-1

Identify the appropriate concept involved in the principle of indemnity in each of the following statements.

A. Insurable interest
B. Actual cash value
C. Subrogation
D. Other insurance

1. _____   A fire destroys a small office with business equipment that originally cost $20,000. The replacement cost is $22,000 and the average age of the equipment was 3 years old. The equipment had a useful life of 10 years.

2. _____   Martha is injured in an auto accident and is reimbursed by her insurance company for her medical expenses and the repairs to her car. The insurance company then sues the insurance company of the party at fault.

3. _____   John insures his apartment building for property loss. He subsequently goes bankrupt and defaults on the mortgage to the apartment building.

The bank that issued the mortgage seized the collateral (the apartment building). When the apartment building is later damaged by vandals, John places a claim with the insurance company since his policy had not been cancelled. The insurance company denies payment.

4. _____ A fire destroys a building valued at $150,000. The building is insured by two insurance companies for $150,000 each. Each insurance company pays $75,000 on the fire claim.

Exercise 11-2

Murray and Jeanette Wilson own a small corner grocery that is insured by a fire policy containing a 75 percent coinsurance clause. When the building is destroyed by fire, the value of the building and its contents is estimated at $400,000. The Wilson's policy provides coverage of $250,000.

    a. How much will the insurance company pay?

    b. If the Wilsons had carried sufficient insurance to meet the 75 percent coinsurance clause, could they have received $400,000?

Exercise 11-3

Max and Maxine Otterman have an HO2 policy that offers protection against a variety of perils. For each situation described, mark a (C) if the loss is covered or an (N) if the loss is not covered by this policy.

1. _____ Their garage is struck by lightning and burns to the ground.

2. _____ Max leaves gardening implements on the sidewalk to his home and a guest falls and breaks a leg.

3. _____ Maxine is sued for slandering a guest at a cocktail party in her home.

4. _____ At a graduation party at their house, their teenage son picked a fight with a classmate. The classmate sustained minor injuries requiring medical attention.

5. _____ A large oak tree in the front yard was damaged by a storm.

6. _____ The Otterman's quarter horse is killed when the barn on their property collapses.

7. _____ Their youngest son's scooter, which is parked in the driveway, is damaged by a falling tree limb.

8. _____ A stamp collection packed away in their basement is damaged by rising water during a rainy spring.

9. _____ The Otterman house has burned to the ground. While their new home is being built, they live at the local Holiday Inn.

10. _____ The Otterman housekeeper claims to have sustained a back injury while working in their home. She sues for damages, and they run up a substantial amount of legal expenses defending this case.

11. _____ Maxine has her diamond ring stolen while on vacation in Caracas, Venezuela.

12. _____ The live-in nanny trips over the youngest son's roller skates and sustains a broken ankle.

13. _____ The Otterman daughter, a college student, is home for the summer and trips over a rug in the dining room and sprains her wrist.

Exercise 11-4

A home located in the Five Oakes Historical District is a grand architectural structure with 5,000 square feet of living space including a sun porch, a solarium, a mahogany-panelled study, and various other turn-of-the-century amenities. Even though the replacement value of this home is $350,000, the market value is only $100,000 due to its location. If the house is insured with an HO-8 policy, what is the maximum amount of insurance the owners of this house can carry?

Exercise 11-5

Your automobile is insured with a standard Personal Auto Policy (PAP) with these coverages: liability, medical payments, uninsured motorists, collision and comprehensive. For each situation described, mark a (C) if the loss is covered or an (N) if the loss is not covered by a standard PAP.

1. _____ Due to an automobile accident, you are sued by a business property owner for lost business for the partial destruction of her building. You incur significant legal fees in defending your case, which is eventually adjudged in your favor.

2. _____ Your PAP has bodily injury liability loss limits of $25,000/$50,000. In an accident, you injure three pedestrians. The medical costs for these people are $20,000, $15,000, and $17,000.

3. _____ You are driving up a one-way street (the right direction) and are hit by a motorist driving the wrong way. She is cited by the traffic patrol who also finds out she has no insurance.

4. _____ Your son who lives in your household damages a covered auto while pulling into the garage.

5. _____ Your son's girlfriend, without permission, takes your covered auto and backs it into a parked car, damaging both cars.

Exercise 11-6

For each of the following situations, determine who will most likely pay the higher premium based on the factors described.

	Use of Automobile	Personal Characteristics of Drivers	Type of Automobile	Driving Record
Person A	Pleasure	Unmarried, 26 year old woman	Aries station wagon	Clean
Person B	Business	Unmarried, 21 year old man	Datsun 280ZX	2 traffic violations

Answer: _____

	Use of Automobile	Personal Characteristics of Drivers	Type of Automobile	Driving Record
Person A	Business	Unmarried, 25 year old woman	Audi 5000	Clean
Person B	Business	Married, 25 year old woman	Audi 5000	Clean

Answer: _____

	Use of Automobile	Personal Characteristics of Drivers	Type of Automobile	Driving Record
Person A	Pleasure	Unmarried, 25 year old woman	Toyota Camry	2 traffic violations
Person B	Pleasure	Unmarried, 28 year old man	Cadillac Seville	1 traffic violation

Answer: _____

Chapter 12

Investing in Stocks and Bonds

CHAPTER OUTLINE

I. A clear understanding of your investment objectives and alternatives is essential to developing a successful investment program. Investment is differentiated from speculation by its long-term perspective and stability.

    A.   Several prerequisites are essential to successful investment: 1) ample insurance and liquidity, 2) some money, 3) knowledge and know-how, and 4) a broker and some vehicle in which to invest.

    B.   You can reach your financial goals through investing by defining specific objectives, working out a savings plan to come up with the investment capital, and developing an investment plan.

        1.   Estimate a reasonable rate of return to be earned on the investment and determine how much capital is needed to reach your target. You could invest a lump sum or make systematic deposits to a savings plan.

        2.   Next, set up a written investment plan which specifies how the accumulated capital will be invested.

    C.   Your investment objectives will determine the specific kinds of investment you make.

        1.   Investments may be made to enhance current income, to save for a major expenditure, to accumulate funds for retirement, and to shelter income from taxes.

        2.   Some types of investments are either not taxed at all or taxed at low effective rates.

    D.   Various corporate investments can be used to satisfy various investment objectives.

        1.   Common stock is an equity investment that represents an ownership interest in a corporation.

        2.   Bonds represent liabilities to the issuer. The bondholder loans money to the issuing corporation.

        3.   Preferreds and convertibles are forms of hybrid securities. Preferred stocks have a stated dividend rate, payment of which is given preference over dividends to holders of common stock. A convertible security is a special type of fixed income obligation (preferred stock or bonds) with a conversion feature permitting the investor to convert it into a specified number of shares of common stock.

        4.   A mutual fund is a company that invests in a diversified portfolio of securities.

5. Investments in real estate range from raw land speculation to limited partnership shares in commercial property.
6. Commodities and financial futures are contracts to buy commodities or financial instruments at a given price by some future date. Options give the holder the right to buy or sell common stocks at a set price over a specified period of time.
7. Precious metals and collectibles are specialized investments sometimes associated with hobbies. Liquidity and price are uncertain.

E. When selecting investments, the possible risks or uncertainties associated with them must be considered.
1. If you invest in a business firm by purchasing its stocks or bonds, you face the possibility that the issuing firm will fail. This is business risk.
2. Financial risk, also associated with stock or bond investments, is related to the amount of debt financing used by the firm.
3. Market risk results from the behavior of investors in the securities market.
4. Purchasing power risk refers to changes in price levels within the economy. A high rate of inflation decreases the purchasing power of fixed value securities.
5. Fixed income securities, which include preferred stocks and bonds, offer owners a fixed periodic return and are most affected by interest rate risk.
6. Liquidity risk is the risk of not being able to liquidate an investment conveniently and at a reasonable price.
7. Event risk refers to unexpected situations that significantly and immediately affect the underlying value of the investment.

F. All investment vehicles have just two basic sources of return: current income and/or capital gain. Together, these make up the total return from an investment.
1. Income is a cash flow from dividends on stock, interest from bonds, or rent from real estate.
2. Capital appreciation (or growth) is reflected in an increase in the market value of investments.

G. The ability to earn interest-on-interest will affect future returns.

H. The amount of risk associated with a given investment vehicle is directly related to its expected return; i.e., the higher the expected return, the more risk the investor faces.

I. The value of an investment depends on the amount of return it is expected to provide the investor relative to the amount of perceived risk involved.
1. The only return that matters is the expected future return since past returns are no guarantee as to future performance.
2. You can obtain a close estimation of return by computing the investment's approximate yield.

Approximate yield = $[CI + (FP - CP) / N)] / [(CP + FP) / 2]$ where

      CI = average annual current income
      FP = expected future price of investment
      CP = current price of investment
      N = investment period

An investment is acceptable if it generates a rate of return that meets or exceeds your desired rate of return.

II. Common stocks are popular because of the attractive returns they offer investors in the form of price appreciation or payment of dividends (or both).

A. Shares of common stock are issued by corporations in any line of business.
1. Publicly-traded issues are shares that are readily available to the general public and that are bought and sold in the open market. Rights offerings are used when a firm with a new issue of common stock must, under state law, allow the current stockholders to purchase new shares in proportion to their existing share ownership; this is known as a preemptive right. A warrant gives an investor the right to purchase shares of stock at a certain price over some specified period of time.
2. Par value is the stated (face) value on a stock certificate. Since it is virtually meaningless, most new issues have no par value.
3. Income received in the form of dividends is taxed as ordinary income. Income earned as the result of selling a security for more than its original purchase price is a capital gain. For most taxpayers, capital gains will be taxed at their ordinary income rate.
B. The holders of common stock normally receive voting rights. Usually stockholders may cast one vote for each share they own.
C. Corporations pay dividends, usually on a quarterly basis, to their common stockholders in the form of cash and/or additional stock. Cash dividends are the most common and are determined by the firm's directors. A dividend yield is a measure of common stock dividends stated as a percent. It is computed as follows:

$$\text{Dividend yield} = \frac{\text{Annual dividends received per share}}{\text{Market price per share of stock}}$$

Stock dividends represent new shares of stock issued to existing stockholders. Stock dividends have no immediate value, since they represent the receipt of something already owned by the stockholder.
They do not represent taxable income.

D. Common stock performance can be described in a number of ways.
1. Book value is an accounting measure determined by subtracting the firm's liabilities and preferred stocks from the value of its assets.
2. Profit margin is the ratio of the firm's net profits to its sales.
3. Return on equity reflects the profitability of the firm. It is net profit relative to stockholder's equity.
4. The firm's annual earnings are usually measured and reported in terms of earnings per share (EPS). EPS translates total corporate profits into profits on a per share basis and provides a convenient measure of the amount of earnings available to stockholders.

$$\text{EPS} = \frac{\text{Net profit after taxes - Preferred dividends paid}}{\text{Number of shares of common stock outstanding}}$$

5. When the prevailing market price per share is divided by the annual earnings per share, the result is the price/earnings ratio. The PE ratio is an indication of investor confidence and expectations.

6. Beta is an index of the inescapable market risk in a share of common stock. It indicates how responsive the stock is to the stock market. The beta for a given stock is determined by applying various statistical techniques that relate the stock's historical returns to the market (market beta is 1.0). The higher a stock's beta, the more risky it is considered to be.

E. The above measurements of value are a part of fundamental analysis and are used to determine the underlying value of stock. The notion of fundamental analysis is that the value of a stock is determined by its expected stream of future earnings.

F. Common stocks are often classified on the basis of their quality, level and stability of dividends, or rate of growth in earnings.
1. Blue chip stocks are those stocks known to provide a stable and safe return.
2. Growth stocks are stocks that have experienced, and are expected to continue experiencing, consistently high rates of growth in operations and earnings.
3. Stocks whose appeal is based primarily on the dividends they pay are known as income stocks.
4. Speculative stocks are purchased in the hope that their prices will increase in a short time.
5. Stocks whose price movements tend to follow the business cycle are called cyclical stocks. Conversely, defensive stocks are expected to remain stable during periods of contraction in business activity.

G. Common stock investing involves selecting a desired rate of return, finding companies that promise that return, and timing the investment decision.
1. You might invest in stock to accumulate and increase capital, and/or to receive a cash flow.
2. The advantages of stock investment include both the potential returns as well as the long-term capital gains. Risk, the problem of timing purchases and sales, and the uncertainty of dividends are all disadvantages of common stock ownership.
3. Unless you need to live off the income, the basic investment objective for any security is to earn an attractive, fully compounded rate of return. Reinvestment is the key.

III. Bonds are fixed-income securities issued by corporations and various government levels or agencies that provide investors with a secure and regular source of current income. Bonds represent a form of debt capital, meaning that funds raised through their sale are borrowed funds.

A. Bonds provide investors with both current income through interest payments and limited capital gains that may be realized if market interest rates fall.

B. A bond is a negotiable (except for government savings bonds), long-term debt that carries certain obligations on the part of the issuer. The amount of interest due is stated as a percentage (coupon). Interest will be paid in two semi-annual installments until maturity or call. The principal amount of a bond, also known as its par value, specifies the amount of capital that must be paid at maturity. Whenever an issue's coupon differs from the prevailing market rate of interest, debt securities will trade at market prices that differ from their principal (or par) values.

1. Bonds can be differentiated by the type of collateral required. Senior bonds are secured obligations, since they are backed by collateral. Junior bonds (debentures) are backed only with a promise by the issuer to pay interest and principal on a timely basis.

2. The sinking fund specifies the annual repayment schedule that will be used to pay off the issue and indicates how much principal will be retired each year.

3. A call feature stipulates the conditions under which the bond can be retired prior to its maturity date. Call features are used most often to replace an issue with one that carries a lower interest rate.

4. Regardless of the type of collateral or kind of issue, any bonds issued today will be registered. Bearer bonds may no longer be issued, although a few have not yet matured and may be available on the bond market.

C. Today's bond market offers issues to meet just about any type of investment objective and to suit virtually any investor.

1. Treasury bonds issued by the U.S. Treasury are of the highest quality, a feature that along with their liquidity, makes them extremely popular with individuals and institutions.

2. Agency bonds are issued by political subdivisions of the U.S. government, but their securities are not direct obligations of the Treasury.

3. Municipal bonds are tax-free issues of states, counties, cities, and other political subdivisions, such as school districts and water and sewer districts. To determine what return a fully taxable bond would have to provide in order to match the after-tax return on a lower-yielding tax-free issue, compute the municipal's fully taxable equivalent yield:

$$\text{Fully taxable equivalent yield} = \frac{\text{Yield of municipal bond}}{(1 - \text{Tax rate})}$$

4. The major nongovernmental issuers of bonds are corporations, including industrials, public utilities, rail and transportation bonds, and financial issues.

5. Zero coupon bonds pay no annual interest. Instead, they are sold at a deep discount from their par values and then increase in value over time at a compound rate of return that makes them worth, at maturity, much more than their initial investment. Junk bonds are high-yield bonds that are considered very speculative and receive low quality ratings.

D. Bond ratings are like a letter grade assigned to a bond issue designating its investment quality. A bond rating is assigned at the time of issue that indicates the ability of the issuing organization to service its debt in a timely fashion.

E. The market price of a bond is determined by its coupon, maturity, and movement of market interest rates. The extent to which bond prices move in a given direction depends on the magnitude of interest rate movements, as well as the bond's coupon and maturity.

1.   The yield on a bond is the rate of return that would be earned if the bond were held for a stated period of time. Current yield reflects the amount of annual interest income the bond provides relative to its current market price:

Current yield = Annual interest income/Market price of bond

The annual rate of return that a bondholder would receive if he or she held the issue to its maturity is calculated in the bond's yield to maturity:

$$\text{Approximate yield to maturity} = \frac{CI + [(\$1000 - CP)/N]}{[(CP + \$1000)/2]}$$

where,
   CI = annual current income,
   CP = current price, and
   N = the investment period.

IV.   Preferred stocks and convertible securities are corporate issues that combine the features of both equity and debt securities.

   A.   Preferred stocks carry a fixed dividend that is paid quarterly and stated either in dollar terms or as a percentage of their par or stated value.
      1.   They are considered hybrid securities because they possess features of both common stocks and corporate bonds.
         a.   Most preferred stock is cumulative--any dividends passed by the directors in previous periods must be paid prior to distributing dividends to common stockholders.
         b.   As a rule, preferred stocks are nonparticipating--the preferred stockholders receive only the stated amount of dividends and do not receive higher payments as corporate profits increase.
      2.   Dividend yield, found by dividing annual dividend income by the market price of the stock, is used to compare preferred stock with other investment opportunities.
   B.   Although convertible issues possess the features and performance characteristics of both a fixed income security and equity, they should be viewed as equity. Both bonds and preferred stock can be convertible.
      1.   A convertible bond is issued as a debenture, with the provision that, within a stipulated time period, it may be converted into a certain number of shares of the issuing company's common stock. The conversion ratio specifies the number of shares of common stock into which the bond can be converted.
      2.   Conversion value is an indication of what a convertible issue would trade for if it were priced to sell on the basis of its stock value. Conversion values are found by multiplying the conversion ratio of the issue by the current market price of the underlying common stock.

3. Convertible securities appeal to investors who want the price potential of a common stock along with the stability and reduced risk of a corporate bond.

FILL IN THE BLANK

1. The four most frequently cited investment objectives are 1) to enhance _____; 2) to save for _____; 3) to accumulate funds for _____; and 4) to _____.

2. _____ is a form of equity investment that represents an ownership interest in a corporation.

3. _____ represent liabilities to the issuer. The holder actually loans money to the issuer.

4. _____ stocks have a stated dividend rate, payment of which is given preference over dividends to holders of common stock.

5. A _____ security is a special type of fixed income obligation that carries a conversion feature permitting the investor to exchange it for a specified number of shares of common stock.

6. A _____ is a company that invests in a diversified portfolio of securities.

7. The possibility that a firm will fail due to economic or industry factors or mismanagement is called _____ risk.

8. _____ risk relates to the amount of debt used to finance the firm.

9. Changes in security prices due to changes in political, economic or social conditions, and/or in investor tastes and preferences is usually called _____ risk.

10. Changes in price levels within the economy result in _____.

11. Interest rate risk means that when interest rates rise the prices of securities will _____.

12. Liquidity risk refers to the inability to sell securities _____ and at a reasonable _____.

13. _____ risk occurs when something happens to a company which has a sudden and significant impact on its financial condition.

14.   Any investment vehicle has two basic sources of return: _____ and _____ .

15.   The key element of return for the investor is the reinvestment of income or _____ interest.

16.   The amount of _____ associated with a given investment is directly related to its expected return.

17.   The only return that matters when investing is the _____ .

18.   After the initial sale of common stock when a corporation is formed, subsequent sales of additional shares may be made in a _____ offering.

19.   _____ offerings are used when a firm with a new issue of common stock must, under state laws, let the current stockholders purchase new shares in proportion to their existing shares. This is known as a _____ right.

20.   A _____ gives an investor the right to purchase shares of stock at a certain price over some specified period of time.

21.   It _____ (is/is not) desirable to exercise warrants immediately after they are issued.

22.   Corporations have annual _____ at which new directors are elected and special issues are voted on. Since most small stockholders are unable to attend, they may assign their votes by _____ .

23.   _____ value is a stated value placed on some stock certificates which is not intended to represent the value of the stock.

24.   Corporations pay _____ to their common stockholders in the form of cash and/or additional stock.

25.   _____ is an accounting measure that is determined by subtracting the firm's liabilities and preferred stocks from the value of its assets.

26.   The ratio of a firm's net profits to its sales is called the _____ .

27.   The profitability of the firm to its shareholders is reflected in the _____ .

28.   When the difference between the net profit after taxes and the preferred dividends paid is divided by the number of shares of stock outstanding, the result is _____ .

29.   The _____ is viewed as an indication of investor confidence and expectations.

30. _____ is an index of the inescapable market risk in a share of common stock.

31. _____ stocks are known to provide a stable and safe return.

32. _____ stocks have experienced, and are expected to continue experiencing, consistently high rates of increase in operations and earnings.

33. Stocks whose primary appeal is the dividends they pay are _____ stocks.

34. _____ stocks are purchased in the hope that their prices will increase in a short period of time.

35. Stocks whose price movements tend to follow the business cycle are called _____ stocks while _____ stocks are expected to remain stable during periods of contraction in business activity.

36. To facilitate the marketing of bonds, issues are broken down into standard principal amounts known as _____.

37. _____ bonds sell below their par value while _____ bonds sell above it.

38. _____ bonds are secured debt obligations, backed by collateral. _____ bonds are backed only by the promise of the issuer.

39. A _____ is an unsecured bond.

40. An annual principal repayment schedule on a bond to aid in retiring the issue is called a _____.

41. In an attempt to compensate investors who have their bonds called, a _____ is added to the par value of the bond and paid to the investor.

42. _____ bonds are issued to specific owners and the names of the bondholders are registered with the issuer. However, any holder of a _____ bond is considered to be the owner, since the issuing organizations keep no record of ownership.

43. _____ bonds are the highest quality type of bonds, because of their backing by the U.S. government.

44. _____ bonds are issued by some political subdivisions of the U.S. government but are not the direct obligation of the U.S. Treasury.

45. Interest earned on _____ bonds will be tax-frees at the federal (and some states) level.

46. _____ bonds are highly speculative, low quality, and pay a high yield.

47. A bond's investment quality is usually designated by its S&P or Moody's _____.

48. The price of a bond is determined by its _____, _____, and _____.

49. _____ stocks and _____ bonds are hybrid securities because they possess features of both common stocks and corporate bonds.

50. The current income from interest payments on the convertible bonds normally _____ (does/does not) exceed the income from dividends that would be received from the comparable investment in the underlying common stock.

51. The conversion value of a convertible equals its _____ times the - _____ of the common stocks.

EXERCISES

Exercise 12-1

Match each descriptive statement with the appropriate investment vehicle.

A. Common stock
B. Bonds
C. Preferred stock
D. Convertible bond
E. Mutual fund
F. Real estate
G. Commodities, financial futures and stock options

1. _____ Liabilities issued by governments and corporations which pay a stated rate of interest.

2. _____ An equity interest in a corporation which has a stated dividend rate.

3. _____ Contracts to buy staple goods or financial instruments at a given price by some future date.

4. _____ A company that invests in a diversified portfolio of securities.

5. _____ Includes investment in raw land, limited partnership shares and commercial property.

6. _____ Return depends solely on the change in price of the underlying asset.

7. _____ A form of equity that represents an ownership interest in a corporation and does not have a stated dividend rate.

8. _____ An investment vehicle that can be transformed from a creditor relationship to an equity relationship.

Exercise 12-2

Match each descriptive statement with the appropriate types of investment risk.

A. Business risk
B. Financial risk
C. Market risk
D. Purchasing power risk
E. Interest rate risk
F. Liquidity risk
G. Event risk

1. _____ Relates to the mix of debt and equity financing.

2. _____ Caused by changes in price levels within the economy.

3. _____ The possibility of not being able to liquidate an investment conveniently and at a reasonable price.

4. _____ Affects company value unexpectedly, significantly and immediately.

5. _____ Affects preferred stock and bonds by causing the prices of these securities to fluctuate as interest rates change in the market place.

6. _____ Results from behavior of the investors in the securities markets.

7. _____ The possibility that the firm issuing the security will fail.

Chapter 12 Investing in Stocks and Bonds

Exercise 12-3

Calculate the approximate yield of the following investments.

Investment Type	Price	Purchase Price	Sale Cash Flows	Investment Period
a. Common stock	$ 90	$100	$5 dividends/year	5 years
b. Preferred stock	$ 75	$60	$2.50 dividends/yr	2 years
c. Bond	$1,000	$950	$70 interest/year	6 months
d. Note	$ 400	$550	$0 interest/year	3 years

Exercise 12-4

Calculate the dividend yield for each of the stocks listed.

a. Common stock with a current market price of $100, paying quarterly dividends of $1.50.

b. Common stock currently selling at $50 per share with a 10 percent stock dividend.

c. Preferred stock (par value $75) with a current market price of $125, paying annual $15 cash dividends.

Exercise 12-5

Hasset Video Systems, Inc. has the following financial characteristics.

Net sales	$60,000,000
Total assets	$36,000,000
Total liabilities	$14,400,000
Total preferred stock	$ 5,400,000
Total annual preferred stock dividends	$ 432,000
Net profits after taxes	$ 4,500,000
Number of shares of common stock outstanding	750,000
Current market price of common stock	$75.00/share
Annual common stock dividends	$ 3.75/share

Using the financial information provided, calculate the:

a.   stock's dividend yield
b.   book value per share
c.   earnings per share
d.   P/E ratio
e.   net profit margin

Chapter 12 Investing in Stocks and Bonds

Exercise 12-6

For the common stock described below, predict how the return on the stock will be affected based on the market movement in each situation.

a.   Stock A has a beta of .75, the market rate of return increases by 12 percent.
b.   Stock B has a beta of 1.00, the market rate of return decreases by 15 percent.
c.   Stock C has a beta of 1.2, the market rate of return increases by 5 percent.

Exercise 12-7

Match each descriptive statement with the appropriate type of stock.

A. Income stock
B. Speculative stock
C. Cyclical stock
D. Defensive stock

1. _____   Characterized by fast growing firms with fluctuating P/E ratios.

2. _____   When the economy is in recovery, the price of the stock goes up; when the economy declines, the price of the stock declines.

3. _____   Stocks that have low betas.

4. _____   Stock that almost always has a positive beta.

5. _____   A stock whose appeal is based primarily on the dividends paid.

6. _____   Stock that may have a negative beta.

Exercise 12-8

Janice has $25,000 to invest. She can buy a corporate bond with a yield of 8 percent or a municipal bond with a yield of 6 percent. Janice is in the 28 percent tax bracket. Based on yield, which bond is most attractive?

Exercise 12-9

Calculate the current yield and the approximate yield on the $1,000 par value bonds described below.

Bond	Coupon Rate	Maturity in	Market Value of the Bond
A	10%	10 years	$1,000
B	8%	5 years	950
C	12%	15 years	1,200
D	5%	20 years	1,050

Exercise 12-10

William owns 100 shares of Berry Co. preferred stock that is cumulative and pays a stated dividend of $5 per year. Berry Co. has passed the preferred dividend for the past two years. Before any dividends may be paid to the common shareholders, how much will William receive in dividends?

Exercise 12-11

Marcus is considering buying a $1,000 convertible bond of the Parapline Co. which may be converted into common stock at $50 per share. Currently, the Parapline Co. common stock is selling for $42 per share. Marcus expects within one year the stock price will rise to $55 per share due to rumors of a merger.

a.   Calculate the conversion ratio of the bond.
b.   If Marcus were to convert the bond today, how much would he realize?
c.   If the stock price increases to $55 per share, how much profit will Marcus realize?

CASE PROBLEMS

Case 12.1 The Armanis Wonder, What Does Retirement Cost Today?

Kevin and Joyce Armani, who are self-employed, are planning to retire in 20 years. They have not been very systematic about their retirement savings so they don't want to waste any more time. They estimate that they will need $250,000 cash at retirement in addition to their other assets and that they can earn 10 percent on their investments. They could make a lump sum investment because of some excess cash from their business or, they could save systematically each year and put the extra cash into the business. Using the following worksheet from Exhibit 12.1 in the text, estimate what lump sum payment the Armanis could make and the annual payments that are an alternative.

DETERMINING AMOUNT OF INVESTMENT CAPITAL

Financial goal: _____

_____

_____

1. Targeted Financial Goal (see Note 1)	$
2. Projected Average Return on Investments	
A. Finding a Lump Sum Investment:	

3. Future Value Factor, from Appendix A
  ■ based on _____ years to target date and a projected average
   return on investment of _____	

4. Required Lump Sum Investment ■ line 1 ÷ line 3	$
B. Making a Series of Investments Over Time:	
5. Amount of Initial Investment, if any (see Note 2)	$

6. Future Value Factor, from Appendix A
  ■ based on _____ years to target date and a projected
   average return on investment of _____	

7. Terminal Value of Initial Investment ■ line 5 × line 6	$
8. Balance to Come From Savings Plan ■ line 1 − line 7	$

9. Future Value Annuity Factor, from Appendix B
  ■ based on _____ years to target date and a projected
   average return on investment of _____	

10. Series of Annual Investments Required Over Time ■ line 8 ÷ line 9	$

Note 1: The "targeted financial goal" is the amount of money you want to accumulate by some target date in the future.

Note 2: If you're starting from scratch—i.e., there is no initial investment—enter a zero in line 5, skip lines 6 and 7, and then use the total targeted financial goal (from line 1) as the amount to be funded from a savings plan; now proceed with the rest of the worksheet.

Chapter 13

Making Securities Investments

CHAPTER OUTLINE

I. Stocks, bonds, and other securities are traded in a highly efficient market network that includes both organized exchanges and over-the-counter markets. The securities markets include the capital markets for long-term securities and the money markets for short-term securities.

   A. The primary market where new securities are sold to the public and the secondary market where old securities are traded comprise the securities market.
   1. Investment banking firms specialize in underwriting new security issues and may either sell them themselves or arrange for a selling group to do so. On very large issues, underwriting syndicates may be formed to spread the risks. Individuals rarely buy securities in this market.
   2. The secondary market includes various securities exchanges, which handle transactions of larger, better known companies, and the over-the-counter market, which handles those of small, less known firms.

   B. Listed securities are traded on organized exchanges in various cities. These exchanges operate under strict sets of rules devised by the exchanges and the federal government.
   1. Known as the "big board," the New York Stock Exchange is the largest and most prestigious organized securities exchange in the world. Membership is limited and listing requirements are stringent.
   2. The American Stock Exchange is the second largest organized stock exchange in terms of companies listed with membership costs and listing requirements less stringent than the NYSE.
   3. Several regional exchanges deal primarily in securities with local and regional appeal.

   C. Unlisted securities are traded in the over-the-counter (OTC) market, This is not a specific institution but rather a telecommunications network of direct transactions between investors and security dealers. The OTC market is linked through the National Association of Securities Dealers Automated Quotation System (NASDAQ), which provides up-to-date bid and ask prices on several thousand securities.

   D. The Securities and Exchange Commission was established to enforce the Securities Exchange Acts of 1933 and 1934. Most states, as well as the exchanges themselves, have laws regulating the sale of securities.

E. Prices go up in bull markets, which are associated with investor optimism, economic recovery, and governmental stimulus. Prices go down in bear markets, which are associated with investor pessimism and economic slowdowns.

II. Investors use brokers to buy and sell securities.

A. Stockbrokers, or account executives, buy and sell stocks, bonds, convertibles, mutual funds, options, and other types of securities for their customers. The largest brokerage firm is Merrill Lynch, Pierce, Fenner and Smith, Inc.
1. It is important to select a broker who understands your investment objectives and can effectively assist you in pursuing them.
2. Brokerage houses offer many services, including free information, research staffs, monthly statements, up-to-the-minute stock price quotations, and world news.
3. An odd lot transaction consists of fewer than 100 shares of a security, while a round lot is 100 shares or a multiple thereof.
4. Even though brokerage fees are said to be negotiated, for small transactions most firms have established fee schedules. Brokerage fees differ for different kinds of securities.
B. Discount brokers have low overhead operations and offer little or no customer services. They can save investors 30 to 80 percent of full-service brokers' commissions.
C. Investors can use several kinds of orders when making transactions depending on their goals and expectations with respect to the given transaction.
1. A market order is an order to buy or sell a security at the best price available at the time the order is placed.
2. An order to buy at a specified price (or lower) or to sell at a specified price (or higher) is known as a limit order.
3. An order to sell a stock when the market price reaches or drops below a specified level is a stop-loss order.
D. Buying on margin allows investors to use borrowed money to make security transactions, thereby magnifying both returns and losses. Federal Reserve Board margin requirements specify the amount of equity necessary, the percentage of the money the investor must provide. Money is usually borrowed directly from the brokerage firm.
E. A short sale occurs when a broker borrows a security and then sells it on the investor's behalf. The investor anticipates that the value of the stock will drop. If it does, he can buy the stock and replace it at a lower price, thereby making a profit.

III. Basing investment decisions on sound information is the heart of most successful investment programs.

A. Every publicly-traded corporation is required to provide its stockholders and other interested parties with annual reports containing information such as balance sheets, income statements, and summarized statements for prior years.

B. Financial information is available in local newspapers, national newspapers, and magazine publications.
   1. Economic data include news items about government actions, political and international events, and statistics related to price levels, interest rates, the federal budget, and taxes.
   2. Market data describe the general behavior of the securities markets, usually in the form of averages or indexes.
      a. The Dow Jones Industrial Average is made up of four parts: 1) an industrial average based on 30 stocks, 2) a transportation average based on 20 stocks, 3) a utility average based on 15 stocks, and 4) a composite average based on all 65 industrial, transportation, and utility stocks.
      b. The Standard & Poor's indexes include: 1) an industrial index based on 400 stocks, 2) a transportation index of 20 stocks, 3) a public utility index of 40 stocks, 4) a financial index of 40 stocks, 5) a composite index for all 500 stocks used to determine the first four indexes, and 6) the MidCap Index made up of 400 medium sized companies.
      c. The three most widely followed exchange-based indexes are those of the New York Stock Exchange, the American Stock Exchange, and the National Association of Securities Dealers Automated Quotation for the OTC market.
   3. Industry data and information about specific companies can be obtained from local newspapers, financial publications and industry trade associations.
   4. Stock price quotations consist of the highest and lowest prices over the past 52 weeks, the cash dividend expected to be paid on each share during the year, the dividend yield (%), the P/E ratio (current market price divided by earnings per share for the most recent 12-month period), the daily volume (in round lots), the high, low and close prices for the day, and the net change in closing price from the day before. Prices are given in dollars and eighths of dollars (as 44 1/8 = $44.125).
   5. Bond quotations include the coupon (interest rate), the year the bond matures, the current yield, the number of bonds traded, the closing price for the day, and the net change in closing price from the day before. All bonds are quoted as a percent of par; a quote of 89 translates into .89 x $1,000 = $890.
C. Another source of information is the reports that major brokerage firms write for their customers and the investing public, which include economic and market analyses, industry and company reports, and lists of securities classified as either "buy" or "sell."
D. There are a number of subscription advisory services that provide information and recommendations on various industries and specific securities.
E. Professional investment advisors attempt to develop investment plans consistent with the financial objectives of their clients.
F. Personal computers provide assistance in the security selection process by computerizing huge data bases of investment information.

IV. Your portfolio of investment holdings must be diversified by putting your funds into a variety of securities. The portfolio should reflect your personal characteristics and investment objectives.

A. Diversification is desirable because it leads to improved return and/or reduced risk.
1. The following personal characteristics of the investor are vital: level and stability of income, family factors, net worth, experience and age, and disposition toward risk.
2. You must establish your objectives: high current income, significant capital appreciation, liquidity, safety, etc.
3. Once goals are established, diversification is achieved through the process of asset allocation. The goal is to reduce the effects of negative market changes and to conserve capital. Once the general contents of the portfolio are determined, security selection begins.
B. It is important to monitor investment holdings by knowing how they have performed over time and whether or not they have lived up to your expectations.

FILL IN THE BLANK

1. The securities markets consist of the _____ markets for long-term securities, and the _____ markets for short-term securities.

2. New securities are offered for the first time in the _____ market; old securities are bought and sold in the _____ market.

3. Investment banking firms specialize in _____ new security issues.

4. Potential investors must be provided with a _____, a document describing the firm and the issue.

5. Within the secondary market, _____ handle transactions of larger, better known companies, while the _____ market tends to handle transactions of small, lesser known firms.

6. Membership on an organized exchange is called a _____.

7. Companies traded on organized exchanges are said to be _____.

8. Known as the "big board," the _____ is the largest and most prestigious organized securities exchange in the world.

9. The _____ is the second largest (in terms of companies listed) organized stock exchange in the U.S.

10. The Midwest Stock Exchange is an example of a _____ stock exchange.

11. The over-the-counter market is linked through the _____.

12. The _____ price represents the highest price offered to purchase a given security. The _____ price is the lowest price at which the security is offered for sale.

13. Buyers and sellers of less active OTC securities, which are not a part of the NASDAQ system, must find each other through _____, who specialize in making markets in certain securities.

14. The _____ was established to enforce the Securities Exchange Acts of 1933 and 1934.

15. _____ laws are state laws designed to protect investors by preventing firms from attempting fraudulent sales.

16. Prices go up in _____ markets and down in _____ markets.

17. _____, or account executives, buy and sell securities for their customers.

18. Securities held for a client by a brokerage firm are said to be held in _____ name.

19. If your broker goes bankrupt, you are protected against the loss of securities held by this broker by the _____, an agency of the federal government that insures each customer's account against financial failure of the brokerage firm.

20. An _____ lot transaction consists of fewer than 100 shares of a security, while a _____ lot represents a 100-share multiple.

21. _____ have lower overhead costs and offer little or no customer services. They may be able to save investors 30 to 80 percent of full-service brokers' commissions.

22. A _____ order is an order to buy or sell a security at the best price available at the time it is placed.

23. An order with a specified price is a _____ order.

24. An order to sell a stock when the market price reaches or drops below a specified level is a _____ order.

25. Buying on _____ allows investors to use some borrowed money to make security transactions.

26. The _____ sets margin requirements that specify the amount of equity necessary.

27. A _____ has occured when a broker borrows a security and then sells it on the investor's behalf.

28. Every publicly traded corporation is required to provide its stockholders and other interested parties with annual _____.

29. Two of the most widely followed market indexes are the _____ and the _____.

30. By investing in a variety of securities, you will achieve _____ in your portfolio which should improve return and/or reduce risk.

31. The general make-up of the portfolio is determined by _____.

EXERCISES

Exercise 13-1

Thomas bought 25 shares of IBM common stock at $138 per share and 10 K Mart bonds for $1,310 per bond. Using Exhibit 13.5 and the information in the text, calculate the brokerage commission Thomas will pay on the common stock. Calculate the brokerage commission on the bonds if the broker charges 1 percent on the par value of the bonds on bond transactions.

Exercise 13-2

Jordan purchased 200 shares of American Express at 40 1/4 per share on margin one year ago. The margin requirement on the stock is 60 percent and the interest rate on borrowed funds is 9 percent. Jordan sold the stock today for 50 1/2 per share.

a. What is Jordan's total dollar investment considering she bought the stock on margin?
b. What is Jordan's net profit after the sale of the stock?
c. What is the return on investment on the transaction?
d. What would the return on investment have been if Jordan had not purchased the stock on margin?

Exercise 13-3

Four months ago, Kay sold two stocks short: 100 shares of Dana Corporation at 34 7/8 and 150 shares of Chris Craft at 50 1/4. Currently, Dana Corporation is selling at 28 and Chris Craft at 73 5/8. If Kay decides to cover her short sales, what profit or loss will she realize on each transaction? (Ignore any commissions.)

Exercise 13-4

High	Low	Stock	Div.	%	PE	Vol	High	Low	Close	Chg
25 1/4	14 7/8	Bally Mfg	.24	1.1	20	1113	22 1/4	21 3/4	22 1/4	+5/8

Answer these questions for Bally Mfg. stock:
1. What was the closing price per share on this day?
2. How many shares were traded this day?
3. What would you expect your quarterly dividends per share to be?
4. Compute the EPS for Bally.

Bond Quote:

		Cur Yld	Vol	Close	Net Chng
OcciP	10 1/2 03	9.0	15	116 5/8	+1/8

For Occidental Petroleum bonds answer the following questions:
1. What is the coupon rate on the bond?
2. How much interest in dollars will be received per year by the holder of one bond?
3. When does the bond mature?
4. How many Occidental Petroleum bonds were sold on this day?
5. How much did one Occidental bond sell for at the close of this day?
6. How much would the owner of this bond receive at maturity?

Exercise 13-5

Imagine you have just received $100,000 and plan to invest all of it. Use the model portfolio described in Exhibit 13.11 of the text that best describes your current situation: newlywed couple, two-income couple, divorced mother or older couple. If you are single, use the newlywed couple model since it allows for the most risk. With the guidelines in the exhibit and a current financial publication, create your portfolio on the form provided. Plan to keep track of the investment's performance. Pick a date three to six months from now to end the exercise. You may also sell an investment before the period ends. Analyze your performance. Are you glad it was only on paper or do you wish you really had invested some hard cash? The Inventory of Investment Holdings worksheet provided on the following page is from Exhibit 13.12.

AN INVENTORY OF INVESTMENT HOLDINGS

Name(s): _____   Date: _____

Type of Investment	Description of Investment Vehicle	Date Purchased	Amount of Investment (Quote—$ Amount)	Amount of Annual Income from Dividends, Interest, Etc.	Latest Market Value (Quote—$ Amount)	Comments/ Planned Actions
TOTALS						

Instructions: List number of shares of *common and preferred stock* purchased as part of the description of securities held; then put the price paid *per share* under the "Quote" column and total amount invested (number of shares x price per share) under the "$ Amount" column. Enter the principal (par) value of all *bonds* held in place of number of shares; "$ Amount" column for bonds = principal value of bonds purchased x quote (for example, $5,000 x .755 = $3,775). List *mutual funds* as you did for stock. For *real estate*, enter total market value of property under "Quote" column and amount actually invested (down payment and closing costs) under "$ Amount." Ignore the "Quote" column for *savings* vehicles. For "Amount of Income" column, list *total* amount received from dividends, interest, and so on (for example, dividends per share x number of shares held). Under "Latest Market Value," enter market price as of the date of this report (for instance, in December 1988, Emory Air Freight was trading at 4¹/₂). The latest market value for *real estate* is entered as an *estimate* of what the property would likely sell for (under "Quote") and the *estimated* amount of equity the investor has in the property (under "$ Amount").

CASE PROBLEMS

Case 13.1 Gregory Invests His Court Award

Gregory has just received a $250,000 judgment as a result of a legal claim he made against a negligent driver. In a automobile accident, Gregory sustained significant injuries, which will limit his physical activities for the remainder of his life. He is currently a 28-year-old credit manager of a small lumber distributor where he earns $30,000 per year and has monthly expenditures of $1,500.

Some of Gregory's friends are forming a partnership to buy turn-of-the-century homes in an up-and-coming section of town and renovate them for resale. Each partner must contribute $100,000 toward buying a section of homes and paying for the labor and materials used in renovation. Gregory has been invited to participate in this investment. His friends are certain the $100,000 investment will double after the sale of the homes.

Gregory figures he will join the partnership and invest the rest of his cash in blue-chip common stock ($75,000), Aaa-rated bonds ($50,000) and money market instruments ($25,000).

Questions

1. What should Gregory's investment objectives be?
2. Comment on Gregory's projected investment plan.
3. What investment strategy would you recommend to Gregory?

Chapter 14

Investing in Mutual Funds, Real Estate, and Derivative Securities

CHAPTER OUTLINE

I. With a mutual fund, an investor buys an ownership position in a professionally managed, widely diversified portfolio of securities and participates in all the dividends and capital gains of the portfolio in proportion to the number of shares owned in the fund.

   A. Mutual funds have grown tremendously in the past quarter century and are a powerful force in the securities markets and a major financial institution in our economy.
   B. A mutual fund is an investment company that is in the business of investing and managing other people's money. The two basic types of investment companies are open-end and closed-end companies.
      1. Open-end mutual funds (which sell an unlimited number of ownership shares) are the dominant type of investment company. Since investors actually buy their shares from and sell them back to the mutual fund itself, there is never any trading among individuals. The fund's net asset value represents the value of a share in a particular mutual fund.
      2. Closed-end investment companies operate with a fixed number of shares outstanding and do not regularly issue new ones. These shares are traded in the secondary stock market.
   C. The cost of investing in an open-end mutual fund depends on whether the fund is a load or no-load fund.
      1. Load funds charge a commission when the shares are purchased.
      2. A no-load fund has no commission when shares are purchased.
      3. Either of these may charge a redemption or back load when shares are sold.
      4. Some funds charge a separate, annual marketing fee called a 12(b)-1 fee. All funds charge an annual management fee regardless of how well or how poorly the fund does. These fees will be deducted before any money is distributed to owners.
      5. Fees can be very complex and all mutual funds must fully disclose all fees on a fee table as part of the prospectus.
   D. For closed-end investment companies, the buying and selling of funds is no different from buying and selling common stock on a listed exchange.
   E. Purchasing shares from an open-end fund is quite different. In a load fund, investors buy the stocks from a broker or through salespeople employed by the fund. In a no-load fund, the investor deals directly with the management company.

F. Mutual funds may specialize in certain types of investments or may have specific investment objectives: growth, income, tax-exempt income, preservation of investment capital, or some combination thereof.
1. The objective of a growth fund is capital appreciation and is recommended for an aggressive investor who wants to build capital and has little interest in current income.
2. Maximum capital gains funds are highly speculative funds that seek large profits from capital gains.
3. Equity-income funds invest in high-yielding common stocks for income and capital preservation.
4. Balanced funds are designed to earn both capital gains and current income.
5. Growth-and-income funds emphasize capital growth over income as they invest mainly in equities.
6. Bond funds invest exclusively in various kinds and grades of bonds with income being the primary objective.
7. Money market mutual funds can be classified as general purpose money funds, tax-exempt money funds, and government securities funds.
8. Sector funds are mutual funds that restrict their investments to a particular sector of the market (pharmaceuticals, for example).

G. Investors choose mutual funds for several reasons: 1) to achieve diversification, 2) to obtain services of professional money managers, 3) to generate an attractive rate of return on their investment capital, and 4) for the convenience they offer.

H. Mutual funds may offer services such as: 1) automatic reinvestment plans, 2) regular income, 3) conversion or exchange privileges, and 4) retirement plans.

I. Fund performance is measured by its return during the year.
1. Mutual funds have three potential sources of return:
1) dividend income, 2) capital gains distribution, and 3) change in the fund's NAV (from increased market values of the fund's securities). The return on a mutual fund may be measured by calculating an approximate yield. (The formula was introduced in Chapter 12.)

$$\text{Approx. yield} = \frac{[\text{Dividends + capital gains distribution + (ending price - beginning price)}]/1 \text{ yr time period}}{[(\text{ending price/beginning price})/2]}$$

2. Future performance is the key to a successful mutual fund. Mutual fund investors must consider the future direction of the market as well as the past performance of the mutual fund.

J. Information on the objectives, characteristics, management, and past performance of a mutual fund can be obtained from the fund's prospectus or financial publications like the <u>Wall Street Journal.</u>

II. Individuals seeking attractive profit opportunities may choose real estate investments, which can take such forms as speculating in raw land, buying income-producing properties, investing in limited partnerships, and purchasing REITs.

A. Some of the basic factors to be considered in a real estate investment are cash
flow, taxes, appreciation in value, risk versus return, and the use of leverage.
 1. The investor's cash flow, or annual cash earnings, depends not only on the
project involved but also on depreciation and taxes.
 2. A total assessment of a proposed real estate investment should include
estimates of expected changes in value as well as cash flow projections.
 3. The anticipated level of return on the investment as well as the stability of
those periodic returns (the risk) is another important consideration in
evaluating a proposed real estate investment.
 4. Leverage is the use of borrowed money to magnify returns. If the total
return on the investment is greater than the cost of borrowing (the net
profit on a leveraged investment is greater than the cost of borrowing), the
net profit on a leveraged investment will be proportionately greater than
on an investment that does not use leverage. The risk of default that comes
with leverage must be considered along with the potential benefits.
B. The key to speculating in raw land is to purchase property in the areas of
potential population growth or real estate demand.
C. Income property is a relatively common type of real estate investment that can
provide both attractive returns and a tax shelter for investors. The real estate
purchased is leased to tenants to generate income in the form of rent receipts.
The real estate may also increase in value over time.
 1. Apartments, duplexes, and rental houses are all examples of residential
property that provides income.
 2. Office buildings, stores, strip shopping centers, and mobile home parks are
examples of commercial property. Commercial property is considerably
more risky than residential property for the novice investor.
D. Limited partnerships are professionally managed real estate syndicates that
invest in various types of real estate. Managers assume the role of general
partner, which means that their liability is unlimited, while the other investors
are limited partners, meaning they are legally liable for only the amount of
their original investment.
 1. The two types of real estate limited partnerships are single property and
blind pool syndicates. The single property syndicate is established to raise
money to purchase a specific piece of property. The blind pool syndicate is
formed in order to raise a given amount of money to be invested at the
discretion of the general partner.
 2. The primary returns from real estate limited partnerships lie in the gains
that occur from appreciation in property values. The goals of the
syndicate, the expected return, and the perceived risks should all be
carefully evaluated before purchasing units in a real estate syndicate.
Recent tax law changes have removed many of the tax-based reasons for
investing in these partnerships.
E. Real Estate Investment Trusts (REIT) are closed-end investment companies that
invest in mortgages and various types of real estate investments. The three
basic types of REITs are: those that invest in properties (property or equity
REIT); mortgage REITs; and hybrid REITs, which invest in both properties and
mortgages.

III.   Derivative securities are so called because they derive their value from the price behavior of some real or financial asset. They include commodities, financial futures, and options.

A.   Commodities markets provide a mechanism through which producers of certain commodities can protect themselves against future price declines on their products. Commodities are sold by contract at a predetermined price prior to the time they become available. This method protects the seller and the buyer of the commodity against price fluctuation. Individuals who are neither producers or users of commodities can trade commodities (futures contracts) on organized exchanges. Futures trading is accompanied by an enormous amount of risk.
   1.   A futures contract is a commitment to deliver a certain amount of a particular item at some specified future date.
   2.   Futures contracts can be bought and sold through local brokerage offices. Most futures contracts are sold on very low margins of 5 percent to 10 percent.
B.   Financial futures contracts cover many financial items--from foreign currencies to corporate and treasury bonds to the stock market. Financial futures are designed and traded in a similar fashion as commodities except the dollar size of the contracts is much larger. The stock index futures are an example of a financial futures.
C.   An option is a type of contract that gives an individual the right to buy or sell a specific security or some other financial instrument. The stock option is the most popular.
   1.   A stock option is a negotiable instrument that gives the holder the right to buy or sell 100 shares of common stock in a given company at a specified price (the striking price) for a designated period of time. Options are traded on organized exchanges.
   2.   An option to sell something is called a put and an option to buy is a call. Put and call options are created by investors rather than the company which has issued the stock and are traded on the organized exchanges.
   3.   While there are several ways of investing in options, buying puts and calls for speculation is the simplest technique and is the most popular with individual investors. Puts and calls can give you a large return from your investment dollar since they offer a leverage effect. The level of risk is relatively high.
   4.   To make an options transaction, contact a securities broker who can execute the trade through the CBOE, AMEX, or other options exchanges.

FILL IN THE BLANK

1.   With a _____, an investor buys an ownership position in a professionally managed, diversified portfolio of securities.

2. The two basic types of investment companies are _____ end, which sell an unlimited number of ownership shares, and _____ end, which issue only a limited number.

3. The dominant type of investment companies are_____ mutual funds in which investors actually buy their shares from and sell them back to the mutual fund itself.

4. The shares of a _____ mutual fund are traded in the secondary stock market while the shares of a _____ mutual fund are never traded among individuals.

5. A mutual fund that does not charge an acqution commission is called a _____ fund.

6. _____ funds are highly speculative mutual funds that seek large profits from capital gains.

7. _____ funds are mutual funds that restrict their investments to a particular industry in the market.

8. A _____ fund is best suited for an aggressive investor who wants to build capital and has little interest in current income.

9. _____ funds provide cash flow on a regular basis mainly from common stocks.

10. _____ funds invest primarily in short-term money market investments like government securities, commercial paper, and certificates of deposit.

11. The primary objective of a bond fund is _____.

12. _____ funds emphasize capital appreciation and income rather than capital preservation.

13. _____ funds are designed to earn both capital gains and current income from stocks and bonds.

14. The basic reasons for investing in mutual funds are 1) to achieve _____, 2) to obtain the services of professional _____, 3) to generate an attractive _____ on invested capital, and 4) for the _____ they offer.

15. Mutual funds have three potential sources of return: 1) _____ income, 2) _____ distribution, and 3) change in the _____.

Chapter 14 Investing in Mutual Funds, Real Estate, and Derivative Securities

16. Phone switching refers to the use of _____ by phone among mutual fund families.

17. _____ plans assure that income earned on a mutual fund can be compounded.

18. Mutual fund future performance is influenced by _____ and _____.

19. Some basic factors to be considered in a real estate investment are: 1) _____ flow and taxes, 2) appreciation in _____, 3) risk versus _____, and 4) the use of _____.

20. _____ is the use of borrowed money to magnify returns.

21. The key to speculating in raw land is to purchase property in areas of _____.

22. _____ are professionally managed real estate syndicates that invest in various types of real estate. All investors except the manager are liable only for their original investment.

23. A _____ syndicate is a limited partnership established to raise money for a specific piece of property.

24. A _____ syndicate is a limited partnership established to raise money to be invested at the general partner's discretion.

25. A _____ is a closed-end investment company that may invest in mortgages or other types of real estate investments.

26. _____ futures markets provide a mechanism through which producers of staples such as coffee, sugar, and soybeans can protect themselves against a future price decline on their products.

27. _____ futures are contracts on such items as foreign currencies and corporate and treasury bonds.

28. An _____ is a negotiable instrument giving the holder the right to buy or sell 100 shares of common stock in a given company at a specified price for a designated period of time.

29. An option to sell something is called a _____ and an option to buy something is called a _____.

30. If you believe the price of a stock is going to fall, you would buy a _____ option. If you believe the price of a stock is going to rise, you would buy a _____ option.

EXERCISES

Exercise 14-1

Indicate whether the statement describes an open-end (O) or a closed-end (C) mutual fund.

1. _____ Can sell an unlimited number of ownership shares.

2. _____ Operates with a fixed number of shares outstanding and does not regularly issue new ones.

3. _____ The minority of mutual funds are of this type.

4. _____ Shares are directly purchased from and sold to the fund itself.

5. _____ There is no trading of shares among individuals.

6. _____ Allows phone switching.

Exercise 14-2

Indicate whether the statement describes a no-load (N), load (L), low-load (LL), or back-end load (B) fund.

1. _____ A commission is charged when the shares are sold.

2. _____ There is no commission on purchases or sales.

3. _____ A purchase commission of up to 8 1/2 percent of the purchase price is charged.

4. _____ Discounts are offered to investors who buy in large blocks.

Chapter 14 Investing in Mutual Funds, Real Estate, and Derivative Securities

Exercise 14-3

On September 12, the market value of all securities held by the SSS Mutual Fund was $10,500,000. SSS had $2,000,000 in liabilities with 1,500,000 shares. On that day, the Wall Street Journal reported an offer price of $4.92.

a. Calculate the NAV for SSS Mutual Fund.
b. Calculate the load charge per share for the fund.

Exercise 14-4

Identify the type of mutual fund described in each statement.

A. Growth fund
B. Maximum capital gain fund
C. Equity-income fund
D. Balanced fund
E. Growth-and-income fund
F. Bond fund
G. Money market mutual fund
H. Sector fund

1. _____ A mutual fund that restricts its investments to a particular industry.

2. _____ A mutual fund which invests exclusively in various kinds and grades of liability instruments.

3. _____ The primary investment objective is current cash flow and preservation of capital.

4. _____ High performance funds which seek large profits from capital gains through speculation.

5. _____ The primary investment objective is to earn both capital gains and current income.

6. _____ The primary investment objective is capital appreciation with income from common stocks.

7. _____ The primary investment objective is capital appreciation.

8. _____ Invest in a variety of money market investment instruments.

Exercise 14-5

Compare the three no-load mutual funds by calculating the approximate yield of each for the year.

No-load Fund	Dividends	Capital Gains Distributions	Beginning Fund Price Per Share	Ending Fund Price Per Share
1	$1.25	.75	$13.25	$14.50
2	.50	.10	4.00	5.00
3	2.00	.05	12.00	13.50

Exercise 14-6

In March, Marshall purchased a 25,000 pound copper contract in the commodities market for delivery in June at a price of 62.75 cents per pound. At the time of delivery, the price of copper had gone up to 64 cents per pound. The margin on the transaction was 20 percent.

a. How much did Marshall have to put up to purchase the futures contract?
b. How much did Marshall profit on the transaction?
c. What was Marshall's return on invested capital?

Exercise 14-7

Compute the profit (if any) and rate of return on each put or call based on the data below.

	Stock Option	Option Price	Common Stock Striking Price	Current Market Price	Number of Shares
(1)	Call	$ 200	$45	$55	100
(2)	Put	900	55	35	200
(3)	Call	1,200	65	75	300
(4)	Call	1,250	75	65	400
(5)	Put	400	85	95	500

Chapter 14 Investing in Mutual Funds, Real Estate,
    and Derivative Securities

Exercise 14-8

Tammy Tucker is evaluating the purchase of a residential duplex for $175,000. Tammy can pay cash for the property or put up $105,000 and borrow the remaining $70,000 at 12 percent interest. The expected annual cash flow from the property is $20,000 after all expenses except interest and income taxes. Tammy is in the 28 percent tax bracket.

a.   Calculate her return on investment assuming she pays cash.
b.   Calculate her return on investment assuming she borrows $70,000.
c.   Which method of financing should Tammy choose to buy the duplex?

CASE PROBLEMS

Case 14.1 Phil Wabar's Investment Options

Phil Wabar is a chemical engineer at a large construction company which specializes in building chemical processing plants. Phil earns $42,000 per year and has saved $51,000 over the past five years. Up until this point, he has invested his funds in certificates of deposit at his local bank. Phil wants to save approximately $100,000 so that he can finance the development of an invention that he has been working on for some time. Even though he saves a large portion of his salary, he feels at his current savings rate, someone else will bring a similar invention to market before he has a chance. His friends have advised him that he should invest in real estate or options in order to earn more than a modest return on his funds. They have made two specific recommendations:

1.   A limited partnership in a shopping mall in a developing metropolitan area. Minimum investment is $50,000.
--OR--
2.   A commodities future contract in cotton. Minimum investment is 50,000 pounds at 65¢ per pound.

Questions

1.   Outline the pros and cons of the limited partnership.
2.   Outline the pros and cons of the commodities contract.
3.   What advice would you give Phil about investing his savings?

Chapter 15

Meeting Retirement Goals

CHAPTER OUTLINE

I. Retirement planning is a key element of financial planning which, to be most effective, should begin relatively early and involve a strategy of systematically accumulating retirement funds.

    A.   Retirement planning includes 1) setting retirement goals--your desired standard of living, your desired income level, and other special retirement goals, and 2) formulating an investment program.

    B.   Two basic factors should be considered when setting retirement goals: 1) age at retirement, and 2) financial position and goals.

    C.   Because the economy changes, the plan you make today may need revision within three to five years. The strategy, therefore, is to plan retirement in a series of short-runs. Stating your retirement income needs is frequently based on a percentage of your present earnings. Using a worksheet can make it easier to determine future retirement needs.

    D.   Many financial planning software packages designed for home computers contain retirement planning programs.

    E.   The three principal sources of income for retired people are social security, income-producing assets, and employer pension plans.

II. Although social security is an important source of income for retired people, it should not be the only source.

    A.   The basic elements of social security are:

        1.   Financing. The cash benefits under social security come from the payroll taxes (FICA) paid by covered employees and their employers. The system no longer operates entirely on a current funding basis but is now more like a pension fund.

        2.   Solvency. Since revenues to pay benefits are now creating a surplus, funds should be available to pay benefits for the next 40 to 50 years.

        3.   Investment. Social security should not be viewed as an investment but rather as a social insurance system which insures workers and their families against poverty resulting from retirement, early death, or disability.

    B.   Social security covers most gainfully employed workers except two major classes of employees: 1) federal civilian employees hired before 1984 who are covered under the Civil Service Retirement System, and 2) employees of state and local governments who have chosen not to be covered.

    1.   In order to qualify for social security benefits nearly all workers must be employed in a job covered by social security for at least 40 quarters. A spouse and/or dependent children of a deceased worker will be eligible for monthly benefits if the worker was fully insured at the time of death.

  C.   Old-age and survivor's benefits are important to retired people and their dependents.

    1.   Workers who are fully insured may receive old-age benefits for life once they reach the age of 65 or receive reduced benefits at age 62. The minimum age goes up starting in the year 2000.

    2.   If a covered worker dies, the spouse can receive survivor's benefits from social security if (s)he has dependent children under 16 or is at least 60 him or herself.

  D.   The amount of social security benefits to which an eligible person is entitled is set by law and defined according to a complex formula.

    1.   Up to half your social security benefits may be taxable in some circumstances.

  E.   A rule of thumb to plan for social security benefits is that the average married retired wage earner will receive about 40 to 60 percent of his or her pre-retirement wages.

    1.   The Social Security Administration will provide a Personal Earnings and Benefit Estimate Statement upon request.

III.   The two basic types of pension programs are employer-sponsored and self-directed.

  A.   More than 50 percent of all wage and salaried workers in the U.S. are covered by employer-sponsored pension plans. Employers sponsor benefit plans to: 1) attract and retain quality employees, 2) meet the demands of collective bargaining, and 3) provide benefits to owners and key managers of the firms.

    1.   Employer-sponsored retirement plans are important in two ways. First, payments under these plans represent a needed source of income to retired workers and their dependents. Second, assets in these retirement funds have a tremendous impact on the U.S. security markets.

  B.   Employers can sponsor two types of retirement programs: 1) basic plans, in which all employees automatically participate after a certain period of employment and 2) supplemental plans, which are voluntary.

    1.   There may be participation requirements based on years of service, minimum age, level of earnings, and employee classification.

    2.   In a noncontributory pension plan, the employer pays the total cost of the benefits. In a contributory plan, the employee shares in the contribution. Pension plans impose criteria that must be met before the employee can obtain a nonforfeitable right to a pension (vested rights). ERISA established maximum periods in which the employee could be vested.

3. Retirement plans specify at what age an eligible employee is entitled to benefits.

4. The two most common methods of computing benefits are defined contribution and defined benefit plans. A defined contribution plan is one that specifies the amount of contribution that employee and employer must make. At retirement, the worker is awarded whatever level of monthly benefits those contributions will purchase. In a defined benefit plan, employees will receive specified payments regardless of the performance of the retirement fund. Any investment short falls must be made up by employers.

5. Pension plans are funded in two ways: 1) an unfunded plan allows the employer to make payments to retirees from current income, while 2) a funded plan formally establishes charges against income to allow for the pension liabilities as they accrue.

6. The IRS permits a corporate employer making contributions to a qualified pension plan to deduct its contribution to the plan from taxable income. Employees, on whose behalf the contributions are made, do not include these benefits as taxable income until they are actually received.

C. Supplemental employer-sponsored plans are usually voluntary and enable employees to increase the amount of funds being held for retirement. The three basic types of supplemental plans are profit-sharing, thrift and savings, and salary reduction plans.

   1. Profit-sharing plans permit employees to participate in the earnings of their employer.

   2. Thrift and savings plans require employers to contribute to savings plans by a partial matching of employee contributions.

   3. A salary reduction plan gives employees the option to divert a portion of their salaries to a company-sponsored tax-sheltered savings account. The most popular kind of plan is the 401(K).

D. Self-directed retirement programs include Keogh plans for self-employed individuals and individual retirement accounts (IRAs), for all gainfully employed people. Whether or not the IRA contribution is tax deductible is determined by income level and participation in an employer-provided pension plan.

   1. Keogh plans allow self-employed individuals to establish tax-deferred retirement plans for themselves and their employees.

   2. An IRA can be invested in many types of investments.

   3. The IRS imposes penalties for withdrawing funds from Keoghs and IRAs prior to age 59 1/2.

E. Two major areas of government influence on pension plans are the Internal Revenue Code requirements for plan qualifications and the rules and regulations established by the Employee Retirement Income Security Act (ERISA) of 1974.

IV. An annuity is a type of tax-sheltered investment that systematically pays out benefits, usually over an extended period of time.

A. Annuities are the opposite of life insurance. They provide for the systematic liquidation of an estate to protect against the economic difficulties that could result from outliving personal financial resources.

B. Annuities can be classified according to several key characteristics, including method of paying premiums, disposition of proceeds, beginning date of benefits, and method of calculating benefits.

   1. The two methods used to purchase an annuity are the single premium and installment contributions.

   2. The four most widely used options in the distribution of annuity proceeds are the life annuity with no refund, the guaranteed minimum annuity, the annuity certain, and the temporary life annuity.

      a. The life annuity with no refund provides the annuitant with a specified amount of income for life. Upon death of the annuitant, the income ceases and no refund is made.

      b. The guaranteed minimum annuity may be a life annuity, period certain where the annuitant is guaranteed a stated amount of monthly income for life for a minimum number of years.

      c. Another form of guaranteed minimum annuity is the refund annuity which provides that upon death of the annuitant, monthly payments will be made to the designated beneficiary until the purchase price of the annuity has been refunded.

      d. The annuity certain pays a specified amount of monthly income for a specified number of years. If the annuitant dies, payments are made to a designated person until the specified period has passed.

      e. The temporary life annuity continues benefits for a specified period only if the annuitant survives.

   3. An annuitant usually has the choice of receiving monthly benefits immediately upon buying an annuity or of deferring benefits for a number of years.

   4. Annuity contracts are written as fixed-dollar or variable. A fixed-dollar annuity provides a fixed monthly payment amount. A variable annuity has an adjustable annuity payment depending on the actual investment experience of the insurer.

C. Life insurance companies are the leading source of annuities.

D. The timing and the type of annuity purchases should coincide with the needs of the individual and his or her family.

E. Surrender of an annuity is subject to IRS penalties and seller-imposed surrender fees.

FILL IN THE BLANK

1. The best time to start thinking about retirement is _____.

2.   The two major steps in retirement planning are 1) _____ and 2) _____.

3.   The three principal sources of retirement income for most people are 1) _____, 2) _____, and 3) _____.

4.   The _____ Act established a number of social programs, including the widely-known Old Age, Survivor's, Disability, and Health Insurance programs.

5.   The cash benefits under the social security program are derived from _____ paid by covered employees and their employers.

6.   Social security has moved from a total _____ basis more to a _____ basis.

7.   By 2027 a person will have to be _____ years old before receiving full social security retirement benefits.

8.   Social security should not be thought of as an _____ but a social insurance system.

9.   In order to qualify for social security retirement benefits, a worker must be employed by a job covered by social security benefits for at least _____ quarters.

10.   Qualified persons may receive reduced social security retirement benefits at age _____.

11.   If a covered worker dies, the spouse may receive _____ from social security.

12.   It is now possible to learn what your social security benefits are by requesting a _____.

13.   Sixty-five year-old retired social security recipients will have their benefits reduced if they have an earned income in excess of $_____. The general rule is that for each $2 earned in excess of this amount, the beneficiary loses $_____ in benefits.

14.   Social security benefits are _____ (never/sometimes) taxable.

15.   Pension plans have been developed by employers for these reasons: 1) _____, 2) _____, and 3) _____.

16.   In a _____ pension plan, the employer pays the total cost of the benefits.

17.   When a nonforfeitable right to pension benefits is secured by an employee, the employee is _____.

18. One of the principal purposes of the Pension Reform Act of 1974 was to require covered employers to grant employees _____ rights according to certain standards.

19. In _____ vesting, the employee is fully vested in five years with no partial vesting before that time, while in _____ vesting, partial vesting accrues each year with full vesting in seven years.

20. A defined _____ plan is one that specifies the amount of pension benefit contribution that the employer and employee must make.

21. A defined _____ plan permits the employee to know before retirement how much their monthly retirement income will be.

22. In an _____ pension plan, the employer makes payments to retirees from current income.

23. In a _____ pension plan, charges are made against current income to allow for pension liabilities as they accrue.

24. A _____ pension plan is voluntary and enables employees to increase the amount of funds being held for retirement.

25. A 401(K) plan is a salary _____ plan.

26. A _____ plan allows self-employed individuals to establish tax-deferred retirement plans for themselves and their employees.

27. Keogh plans and IRAs are _____ investment plans.

28. An _____ is a type of investment vehicle that systematically pays out benefits, usually over an extended period of time.

29. The period in which premiums are paid into an annuity is called the _____ period.

30. A _____ annuity contract is one that is bought with a lump sum payment.

31. Under the life annuity, _____, the annuitant is guaranteed a stated amount of monthly income for life and is guaranteed payment for a minimum number of years regardless of whether the annuitant lives or dies.

32. The _____ provides that upon the death of the annuitant, monthly payments will be made to the designated beneficiary until the total purchase price of the annuity has been paid back.

33. Under the life annuity, with _____, the annuitant receives a specified amount of income for life regardless of whether the period over which income is distributed turns out to be 1 or 50 years.

34. A specified amount of monthly income for a specified number of years without consideration of any life contingency is provided by the _____.

35. The _____ provides benefits for a specified period of time only if the annuitant survives.

36. Most annuities are written as _____ annuities.

37. A _____ adjusts the monthly income provided according to the actual investment experience of the insurer.

38. _____ companies are the leading source of annuities.

EXERCISES

Exercise 15-1

In each of the following descriptions of a personal situation, determine whether the person would or would not be covered under the Old Age Survivors Benefits of the Social Security Administration. (Covered = C, Not Covered = N)

1. _____   A worker who was employed in a job covered by social security from June 1965, to May 1969, and has reached age 65.

2. _____   A worker who was employed in a job covered by social security from April 1970 to June 1973 and then from December 1975 to August 1980 and has reached age 65.

3. _____   A 65-year-old fully insured worker in the year 2027 wishing to receive full retirement benefits.

4. _____   A 17-year-old high school student who is the child of a deceased father who was fully insured.

5. _____   A 55-year-old widow of a fully insured worker whose youngest child is 21 years old.

6. _____   A 15-year-old dependent of a fully insured disabled worker.

Chapter 15 Meeting Retirement Goals

Exercise 15-2

C. D. Heath has the opportunity to contribute 15 percent of his pay to a 401(k) plan administered by his employer. C. D. is currently in the 28 percent tax bracket and earns $40,000 per year.

a. What tax savings will result from contributing the maximum amount to the 401(K)?
b. As a result of the tax savings, C. D.'s out-of-pocket contribution to the 401(K) will be
    $_____.

Exercise 15.3

Paul is 30 years old and self-employed. He is starting a Keogh plan for himself this year. His business has been so successful that he is confident he can put $30,000 into the plan each year until age 60 when he will retire. He should earn 10 percent on this contribution. How much money will he have accumulated when he retires?

CASE PROBLEMS

Case 15.1 Retirement Income and Investment Needs

Robert and Debbie Mescon are both 30 years old and have two children entering middle school. Now that they are in a financially sound position with respect to their family goals, they have begun to think about retirement planning. The Mescons have reviewed their current household expenditures of $62,000 and estimate that their retirement household expenses could be maintained at 75 percent of the current amount.

Both Robert and Debbie have high career earnings and upon retirement would qualify for the maximum benefit from Social Security. Other sources of income will come from their respective companies' pension plans which they estimate will total $20,000 annually. They currently have a portfolio of investments with a value of $40,000. Inflation is expected to average 5 percent over the next 35 years and the expected rate of return on any assets held before and after retirement is 8 percent.

Questions

1.   Using the worksheet provided, project the Mescon's retirement income and investment needs. (The Mescons plan to retire in 35 years. Use 1991 social security benefits Exhibit 15.6.)

2.   Does this analysis allow for any special goals the Mescons may set like travel or a vacation home? What special provisions should be made for these types of goals?

3.   Are there any factors about the Mescon financial situation this analysis does not take into account?

PROJECTING RETIREMENT INCOME AND INVESTMENT NEEDS

Name(s) _____ Date _____

I. **Estimated Household Expenditures in Retirement:**

    A. Approximate number of years to retirement .... _____

    B. *Current* level of annual household
       expenditures, excluding savings .... $ _____

    C. Estimated household expenses in retirement *as a*
       percent of current expenses .... _____

    D. Estimated annual household expenditures
       in retirement (B x C) .... $ _____

II. **Estimated Income in Retirement:**

    E. Social security, annual income .... $ _____

    F. Company/employer pension plans,
       annual amounts .... $ _____

    G. Other sources, annual amounts .... $ _____

    H. Total annual income (E + F + G) .... $ _____

    I. Additional required income, or *annual* shortfall (D – H) .... $ _____

III. **Inflation Factor:**

    J. Expected average annual rate of inflation
       over the period to retirement .... _____

    K. Inflation factor (in Appendix A):
       Based on _____ years to retirement (A) and an expected
       average annual rate of inflation (J) of _____ .... _____

    L. Size of inflation-adjusted
       annual shortfall (I x K) .... $ _____

IV. **Funding the Shortfall:**

    M. Anticipated return on assets held
       after retirement .... _____

    N. Amount of retirement funds required—size of nest egg (L + M)............................. $ _____

    O. Expected rate of return on
       investments *prior* to retirement .... _____

    P. Compound interest factor (in Appendix B):
       Based on _____ years to retirement (A) and an expected
       rate of return on investments of _____ (O) .... _____

    Q. Annual savings required to fund
       retirement nest egg (N + P)... $ _____

Note: Parts I and II are prepared in terms of current (today's) dollars.

Case 15.2 Pension Plan Considerations

Laura is a professional marketing manager of a major corporation. After her four children began high school, she enrolled in the local university where she earned her MBA. Beginning her career at age 50 has not left her much time to explore the various employers in her chosen field before retirement. After five years with her current employer, she is considering a job move to another company offering her a higher level position. Her current employer offers a pension plan in which vesting of benefits becomes complete for eligible employees after seven years. What financial considerations should Laura make before finalizing her career decision?

Chapter 16

Preserving Your Estate

CHAPTER OUTLINE

I.   The overriding objective of estate planning is to insure the orderly transfer of as much of your estate as possible to heirs and/or designated beneficiaries. Uncontrolled planning occurs when the estate owner fails to arrange for the disposition of assets and the minimization of tax and other estate settlement costs. Various state and federal laws will determine how the estate will be dispersed and taxed when there is no will and/or no estate planning.

   A.   Some form of estate planning is necessary for almost all adults.
      1.   People planning means anticipating the psychological and financial needs of those people and organizations you care about--not only providing security but assuring your beneficiaries that they have enough income or capital or both to insure a continuation of their way of life.
      2.   From the standpoint of wealth alone, estate planning is essential for anyone with an estate exceeding $600,000.
   B.   Quite often, when people die, their estates die with them--not because they have done anything wrong but because they have not done anything.
      1.   Last illness and funeral expenses are examples of first-level death-related costs.
      2.   Second-level death-related expenses consist of the attorneys', appraisers', and accountants' fees; probate expenses; administrative costs; federal estate taxes; and state death taxes.
      3.   Failure to moniter an estate plan can impair the ability of both fundamental and investment assets to provide steady and adequate levels of financial security. The ravages of inflation cannot be ignored.
      4.   Improper management of the decedent's business or other assets included within the estate can result in a rapid decline of their value.
      5.   Lack of liquidity (insufficient cash to cover death costs and other estate obligations) can force sacrifice sales of assets.
      6.   Incorrect use of vehicles of transfer can cause estate impairment.
      7.   A prolonged and expensive disability of a family wage earner is often called a living death and can quickly diminish the value of the estate.
   C.   Your estate consists of whatever property you own. Your probate estate consists of the real and personal property that you own in your own name that can be transferred according to the terms of a will at death. Your gross estate includes all property subject to federal estate tax at death, both probate and nonprobate.
   D.   The estate planning process consists of four important steps: 1) gathering comprehensive and accurate data on all aspects of the family, 2) categorizing

the data into problem areas and estimating estate transfer costs, 3) formulating the estate plan and preparing for its implementation, and 4) finally, testing and implementing the proposed plan.

II.   A will is a written legal expression of your wishes as to the disposition of your property to take effect upon your death.

A.   Intestacy exists when a person dies without a valid will. State statutes delineate certain preferred classes of survivors to receive your estate. If there are no survivors at all (including very distant cousins), the state normally takes all the property.

B.   A will allows the maker of the will (the testator) to determine the disposition of property at his or her death. It may be changed any time prior to the testator's death.

1.   A properly prepared will should 1) provide a plan for distributing the testator's assets in accordance with his or her wishes, the beneficiaries' needs, and federal and state dispositive and tax laws, 2) consider the changes in family circumstances that might occur after execution, and 3) be unambiguous and complete.

2.   Will drafting, regardless of the size of the estate, should be done by an attorney.

C.   Although there is no absolute format, most wills contain eight distinct parts.

1.   The introductory clause includes the testator's name, a declaration of residence and a revocation of prior wills and codicils.

2.   The direction of payments directs the estate to pay certain expenses, such as debts and funeral costs.

3.   The dispositive provisions include the distribution of personal effects, money and residual assets. A pecuniary legacy is a clause that passes money to a specified party.

4.   The appointment clause is used to appoint executors, alternates and guardians.

5.   A tax clause specifies that the appropriate taxes be taken from the estate. Without this provision, the apportionment statutes of the testator's state may allocate the burden of taxes among the beneficiaries.

6.   The common disaster clause makes provision for the marital deduction to be taken in case of a common disaster or simultaneous death.

7.   The execution and attestation clause is a precaution against fraud.

8.   State laws require that a will be signed by a specific number of witnesses, usually two or three. All witnesses must sign the will in the presence of one another.

D.   There are three requirements for a valid will.

1.   The maker must be mentally competent. The testator must have 1) a full and intelligent knowledge of the act in which he is involved, 2) an understanding of the property he possesses,
3) a knowledge of the dispositions he wants to make of it.

2.   The testator must have freedom of choice at the time the will is made and executed. Coercion or duress will invalidate a will.

      3.   Most state have statutes specifying who may make a will, the form and execution a will must have, and requirements for witnesses.

   E.   Wills can be revised at any time and any number of times prior to the testator's death. Revisions should be made in the event of changes in health or financial circumstances, family structure, or tax laws.

      1.   If only a minor modification is necessary, a codicil can be drawn up.

      2.   A testator can revoke a will by: 1) making a later will that expressly revokes prior wills, 2) writing a codicil that expressly revokes any wills, 3) making a later will that is inconsistent with a former will, 4) physically destroying the will with the intention of revoking it. State law may revoke a will in cases of divorce, marriage, birth or adoption, or murder.

      3.   The "right of election" allows a survivor to take a specified portion of the probate estate regardless of what the will provides.

   F.   The original will should be kept in a safe deposit box together with deeds, contracts, and other valuable papers.

   G.   The letter of last instructions contains thoughts and instructions that people want conveyed that cannot properly be included in their wills. This is not a legally binding document.

   H.   The executor of an estate will guide the will through the probate process. Money owed is collected, creditors are satisfied, and the remaining estate is distributed appropriately by the executor.

   I.   Joint ownership, which may be joint tenancy (any two or more people) or tenants by the entirety (husband and wife only), permits the interest of a decedent to pass directly to the surviving joint tenant. In joint tenancy, each joint tenant can unilaterally sever the tenancy, but a tenancy by the entirety can be severed only by mutual agreement, divorce, or conveyance by both spouses to a third party.

III.   A trust is a relationship created when the grantor, also called the settler or creator, transfers property to a second party, the trustee, for the benefit of the third parties, the beneficiaries, who may or may not include the grantor.

   A.   Trusts may be created for a number of reasons.

      1.   The burden of paying taxes on the income produced by securities, real estate, and other investments can be shifted from a high-bracket taxpayer to a trust itself or to its beneficiary, both of whom may be subject to lower income tax rates than the grantor.

      2.   Management and conservation of trust property is provided for minors, spendthrifts, incompetents, and others who cannot or do not want to take the time to learn to handle large sums of money and other property. The Tax Reform Act of 1986 introduced some limits to this transfer.

   B.   A competent trustee will 1) possess sound business knowledge and judgment, 2) have intimate knowledge of the beneficiary's needs and financial situation, 3) be skilled in investment and trust management, 4) be available to beneficiaries, and 5) be able to make decisions impartially.

   C.   There are several types of trusts:

      1.   A living or inter vivos trust is created during the grantor's lifetime.

        a.   The grantor reserves the right to revoke the trust and regain the trust property in a revocable living trust.

        b.   Grantors who establish irrevocable living trusts relinquish title to the property held in the trust as well as the right to revoke or terminate the trust.

2.   A trust created by a deceased's will is called a testamentary trust.

3.   A will can be written so that it "pours over" certain assets into a previously established trust.

IV.   Federal tax law provides for a gift tax on certain gifts made during your lifetime. The donor is primarily liable for the tax.

    A.   Almost all property can be the subject of a transfer on which the gift tax must be paid. Exceptions to this include services that one person performs for another and rent-free use of property.

    B.   Usually, a gift is considered to be made when the donor relinquishes dominion and control over the property or property interest is transferred.

    C.   All that is transferred by an individual is not necessarily subject to a gift tax.

        1.   An annual exclusion is available for gift transfers by a donor of amounts up to $10,000 to each of any number of donees.

        2.   Gift splitting is permitted in order to equate the tax treatment of married taxpayers domiciled in common law states with the tax treatment of taxpayers domiciled in community property states.

        3.   Federal law permits an unlimited deduction for gift tax purposes for property given by one spouse to another.

    D.   There are several tax-oriented reasons that estate planners recommend gift giving.

        1.   A single individual can give any number of donees up to $10,000 each year entirely tax free. If the donor is married and the donor's spouse consents, this amount can be raised to $20,000.

        2.   Regardless of the size of a gift--and even if it is made less than three years before the donor's death--it typically will not be treated as part of the donor's gross estate.

        3.   One of the most important reasons for making a lifetime gift is that the appreciation on the gift from the time it is made will not be included in the donor's estate.

        4.   Because of the credit that can be used to offset otherwise taxable gifts, gift taxes currently do not have to be paid on gifts totaling $600,000 or less.

        5.   The gift tax marital deduction allows spouses to give an unlimited amount of money or other property entirely gift tax free to each other.

V.   The federal estate tax is levied on the value of the property that the deceased transfers or is deemed to transfer to others. One of the goals of estate planning is to minimize the amount of estate taxes paid.

A. The computation of federal estate tax involves determining the gross estate, the adjusted gross estate, the taxable estate, the estate tax payable before credits, and the net federal estate tax payable.

B. More individuals are subject to state death taxes (estate and/or inheritance) than are liable for federal estate taxes.
1. An inheritance tax is a tax on the right to receive a decedent's property.
2. A state estate tax is imposed on the deceased's right to transfer property and is measured by the value of the property transferred.
3. The credit or gap estate tax is designed to bridge the gap between the state's inheritance and estate taxes and the maximum state death tax credit allowed against the federal estate tax.
4. Other factors can affect the amount of state death tax due.
    a. Certain exemptions for property transferred to the United States, the state, and charitable organizations and deductions for funeral and administrative costs are allowed.
    b. While real estate and tangible personal property can be taxed in only one state, intangible personal property may be taxed in multiple states.
    c. The rates at which transfers or receipts of property are taxed vary widely from state to state.

C. Estate shrinkage can be minimized and financial security maximized by judicious use of tax-oriented arrangements and maneuvers.
1. Each time a new tax-paying entity can be created, income taxes will be saved and estate accumulation stimulated.
2. Any dollar that is deductible from taxable income is more useful to the taxpayer than a nondeductible dollar.
3. Tax burden can be minimized by spreading income over more than one tax year or deferring the tax to a later period so that the taxpayer can invest the tax money for a longer period of time.
4. Estate taxes may be paid by buying flower bonds or special types of life insurance policies.

FILL IN THE BLANK

1. When the estate owner fails to arrange for the disposition of her assets by writing a will, the _____ will make the determination for her.

2. _____ means anticipating both psychological and financial needs of those people and organizations you care about.

3. From the standpoint of wealth alone, estate planning is essential for anyone with an estate exceeding $_____.

4. Last illness and funeral expenses are examples of _____ death related costs.

5. _____ death related expenses are various professional fees, probate expenses, administrative cost, federal estate taxes, and state death taxes.

6. Lack of _____ can result in insufficient cash to cover death costs and other obligations.

7. A prolonged and expensive disability of a family wage earner is often called a _____.

8. Your _____ consists of all your property.

9. Your _____ estate consists of the real and personal property that you own in your own name that can be transferred according to the terms of a will at death.

10. Your _____ estate includes all the property subject to federal estate tax at death, both probate and nonprobate.

11. Properly arranged _____ is not included as a part of your estate, though the benefits go to your family.

12. _____ payments to a surviving spouse or minor children generally are neither probate assets nor subject to any estate taxes.

13. A _____ is a written legal expression of a person's wishes concerning the disposition of his or her property at death.

14. _____ is the situation that exists when a person dies without a valid will.

15. The writer of a will is called the _____.

16. Will drafting, regardless of the size of the estate, should be done with the help of an _____.

17. The _____ clause includes the testator's name, a declaration of residence and a revocation of prior wills and codicils.

18. The _____ directs the estate with respect to certain payments of expenses, such as debts and funeral expenses.

19. The _____ provisions include the distribution of personal effects, money and residual assets.

20. A _____ is a clause that passes money to a specified party.

21. The _____ clause is used to appoint executors, alternates and guardians.

22. A _____ clause specifies that the appropriate taxes be taken from the estate.

23. In case both spouses died in an automobile accident, a _____ clause would allow the marital deduction to be taken.

24. The _____ and _____ clauses are a precaution against fraud.

25. The witness clause should contain the signatures of _____ or _____witnesses (depending on state law), all signing in the presence of one another.

26. The three requirements for a valid will are _____, _____, and _____.

27. Threats, misrepresentations, inordinate flattery, or mental or physical coercion employed to destroy the testator's freedom of choice are all types of _____.

28. If only a minor modification to a will is necessary, a _____ is usually drawn up rather than rewriting the entire will.

29. The _____ allows a survivor to take a specified portion of the probate estate regardless of what the will provides.

30. Some states provide for _____ of the will, a mechanism for filing and safekeeping it in the office of the probate court.

31. The _____ contains thoughts and instructions that people want conveyed that should not be included in their wills.

32. In a process of liquidation called a _____, money owed is collected, creditors are satisfied, and what remains is distributed to heirs by the executor.

33. Two forms of joint ownership are _____ and _____.

34. A _____ is a relationship created when one party, the _____, also called the settler or creator, transfers property to a second party, _____, for the benefit of the third parties, the _____.

35. The property placed in a trust is called _____ or _____.

36. A _____, such as a trust company or bank that has been authorized to perform trust duties, should have investment experience and be impartial.

37. A trust created by a deceased's will is called a _____ trust.

38. For federal income tax purposes, the _____ of a revocable living trust is treated as the owner of the property in the trust.

39. A _____ trust is one in which the grantor controls investment decisions and management policy until he or she is unable or unwilling to do so, at which time the trustee assumes that role.

40. A _____ trust contains income-producing assets.

41. Federal tax law provides for a _____ tax on certain gifts made during your lifetime. Death-time gifts may trigger the _____ tax.

42. An annual exclusion is allowed for gift transfers of amounts up to $_____ to each of any number of donees.

43. The _____ is the amount you may bequeath tax free.

44. An _____ tax is a tax on the right to receive a decedent's property, while an _____ tax is imposed on the deceased's right to transfer property.

45. The _____ or _____ estate tax is designed to bridge the gap between the state's inheritance and estate taxes and the maximum state death tax credit allowed against the federal estate tax.

46. Techniques of estate planning can be summarized by the four D's: _____, _____, _____, and _____.

CASE PROBLEMS

Case 16.1 Jonathan Marcum's Video Will

Jonathan Marcum is a well paid executive in a film production company. While he has accumulated a variety of valuable assets, until now he has given little thought to the disposition of the assets in the event of his death. Jonathan is married and has three school-age children. His assets are listed below.

Primary residence	$ 675,000
Ski chalet in Jackson Hole, Wy	245,000
Common stock in film production company	8,125,000
Corporate bonds	4,500,000
Personal collection of antiques	314,000
Cash and marketable securities	135,000
Real estate limited partnership shares	575,000
Other assets	259,000
TOTAL ASSETS	$14,828,000

Jonathan would like to leave his entire estate to his wife, Meredith. Jonathan plans to videotape his will after it has been drafted with the aid of his attorney. Jonathan intends to name his business partner, Sid Goldberg, the executor of the will.

Questions

1. Answer this question based on the information in the chapter in Exhibit 16.3. If Jonathan fails to create a will before his death, what would happen to his estate?
2. Outline the key components which should be included in Jonathan's will.
3. What options are available to Jonathan should he change his mind about his beneficiary?
4. Is Jonathan's video will valid?
5. What role will Sid Goldberg play as executor? What are his duties? Is Sid a good choice as executor?

Case 16.2 Computing Estate Taxes on the Reisman Estate

Daniel Reisman of Fort Lauderdale, Florida, died in 1975, leaving his entire estate to his wife of 40 years, Corinne. Last month when Corinne died, the remaining estate had an asset value of $3,575,657 with debts of $215,000. Corinne's funeral costs amounted to $7,900. The cost of administering the estate was $13,510. These items were the only applicable deductions from the gross estate. Corinne named her son, Patrick, and daughter, Ellen, equal heirs to receive the balance of the estate after all debts and taxes were paid and a contribution of $25,000 was made to the American Cancer Society. In the past five years, Corinne has been gifting her assets to her children and has paid the tax on these transfers totaling $49,200. Using the following worksheet as a guide to calculations, answer the following questions:

Questions

1. Compute the value of Corinne's adjusted gross estate at the time of her death using the following worksheet from Exhibit 16.6.
2. Determine the taxable estate.
3. Determine the net federal estate tax payable.
4. Comment on the shrinkage of the estate. How could the estate have been preserved?

COMPUTING NET FEDERAL ESTATE TAXES PAYABLE

Name _____ **Date** _____

Line	Computation	Item	Amount	Total Amount
1		*Gross estate*		$ _____
	Subtract sum of:	(a) Funeral expenses	$ _____	
		(b) Administrative expenses	_____	
		(c) Debts	_____	
		(d) Taxes	_____	
		(e) Losses	_____	
2	Result:	*Adjusted gross estate*		$ _____
	Subtract sum of:	(a) Marital deduction	_____	
		(b) Charitable deduction	_____	
3	Result:	*Taxable estate*		$ _____
4	Add:	*Adjusted taxable gifts*		$ _____
5	Result:	*Tentative tax base*		$ _____
6	Compute:	*Tentative estate tax*	$ _____	
7	Subtract:	Gift taxes payable on post-1976 gifts	_____	
8	Result:	*Estate tax payable before credits*		$ _____
9	Subtract sum of:	(a) Unified tax credit	$ _____	
		(b) State death tax credit	_____	
		(c) Credit for tax on prior transfers	_____	
		(d) Credit for foreign death taxes	_____	$ _____
10	Result:	*Net federal estate tax payable*		$ _____

Answers and Solutions

CHAPTER 1

FILL IN THE BLANK ANSWERS

1. money
2. quality of life (standard of living)
3. two-income
4. necessities of life, to consume
5. deferred
6. wealth
7. Real
8. Financial
9. Money
10. emotional or psychological
11. Utility
12. liability
13. Insurance
14. government, consumers, consumer price behavior
15. government, business, consumers
16. taxes, government regulation
17. expansion, recession, depression, recovery
18. inflation
19. age, education, career
20. low
21. 35, 55

SOLUTIONS TO CASE PROBLEMS

Case 1.1

See worksheet that follows.

PERSONAL FINANCIAL GOALS

Name(s) __Jack & Jenny__   Date __January 1993__

Type of Financial Goal	Brief Description	Degree of Priority (High, Medium, or Low)	Target Date	Cost
Increase income	To double it	High	Long range	1998
Gain control over living expenses				
Have more money left over for discretionary/ entertainment purchases	1st Cruise	Low	Long range	Winter 1995
Set up an education fund for yourself, your spouse, and/or your children				
Establish an emergency fund to meet unexpected expenses	Set up for 3 month's salary	High	Short range	1994
Implement procedures to keep your tax burden to a minimum				
Put money aside for a home, car, and/or other major expenditures	House — downpayment Car — downpayment	Medium High	Long Short	1998 1994
Pay off/reduce personal debt; bring monthly debt service requirements down to a more manageable level				
Provide adequate protection against personal risks — life, disability, health, property, and liability insurance				
Start a general savings and investment program to accumulate capital and achieve financial security				
Start your own business				
Set up a retirement fund to supplement social security and employer-sponsored retirement programs	Jenny's employer's plan	Medium	Short & long range	Start now to retirement
Maximize the disposition/transfer of estate to heirs				
Other personal financial objectives and goals				

CHAPTER 2

FILL IN THE BLANK ANSWERS

1. financial statements
2. balance sheet
3. income and expenditures statement
4. Liquid
5. personal
6. real
7. Investments
8. liability
9. Consumer installment
10. Net worth
11. cash
12. Expenditures
13. cash surplus, cash deficit
14. decreases
15. once
16. solvency
17. pay current debts
18. savings
19. debt safety

SOLUTIONS TO EXERCISES

Exercise 2-1

a.	automobile	A
b.	computer	A
c.	credit card charges	L
d.	installment loan	L
e.	common stock	A
f.	certificate of deposit	A
g.	unpaid tuition	L

Exercise 2-2

a.	an ocean front lot	R
b.	a bicycle	P
c.	a certificate of deposit	I
d.	a house	R
e.	cash	P

Exercise 2-3

Total assets - total liabilities = net worth
 $12,000   - $11,500   = $500

Exercise 2-4

a.

Automobile	$7,500	A
Outstanding balance on auto loan	5,000	L
Furniture	3,000	A
Tuition payment	4,000	L
Cash savings	3,000	A
Checking account	500	A
Personal property (clothes, shoes, etc.)	2,000	A
Stereo and television	700	A
Credit card charges	250	L

b.   Total assets - total liabilities = net worth
 $16,700   - $9,250   = $7,450

c.   Solvency ratio = Total net worth/total assets
= $7,450/$16,700
= .45 or 45%

This tells us Jennifer could withstand a 45 percent decline in the market value of her assets before she would be insolvent.

Exercise 2-5

Income

Ron's salary	$20,000
Jody's salary	25,000
Interest income	300
Total income	$45,300

Less: Expenditures

Rent	$ 9,000
Car payments	4,000
Food	3,000
Utilities	2,500
Clothes, shoes, etc.	2,000
Credit card payments	1,500
Insurance payments	1,500
Entertainment	1,000
Vacation	1,000
Health care	500
Miscellaneous expenses	700
Taxes	5,000
Total expenditures	$31,700

Contribution to
savings or investment $13,600

Savings ratio = $13,600/$45,300 - $5,000 = .337 or 33.7%

Debt Service ratio = $4,000/$45,300 = .088 or 8.8%

Exercise 2-6

BALANCE SHEET FOR RON AND JODY

Assets		Liabilities and Net Worth	
Cash	$10,000	NDS loan	$12,000
Checking account	1,000	Auto loan	2,000
Certificate of deposit	4,000	Outstanding bills	300
Automobiles	13,000	Credit card charges	200
Furniture	5,000	**Total liabilities**	$14,500
Personal property	10,000	Net worth	$28,500
Total assets	$43,000	**Total liabilities**	
		and Net worth	$43,000

Solvency ratio = $28,500/$43,000 = .663 or 66.3%

SOLUTIONS TO CASE PROBLEMS

Case 2.1

1. See worksheet on following page.

2. See worksheet on following page.

3. Solvency ratio $\quad$ = Total net worth/Total assets
    $$= \$44,010/\$117,450$$
    $$= 37.4\%$$

    Liquidity ratio $\quad$ = Liquid assets/Total current debts
    $$= \$3,000/(\$550 + \$3,600 + \$10,800)$$
    $$= \$3,000/\$14,950$$
    $$= 20.1\%$$

    Savings ratio $\quad$ = Cash surplus/Income after taxes
    $$= \$2,870/(\$37,500 - \$5,500)$$
    $$= \$2,870/\$32,000$$
    $$= 9.0\%$$

    Debt safety ratio = Total monthly loan payments/Monthly gross income
    $$= (\$3,600 + \$10,800)/\$37,000$$
    $$= \$14,400/\$37,000$$
    $$= 38.9\%$$

4. Solvency ratio: Chris and Judy could withstand about a 37 percent decline in the market value of their assets before they would be insolvent.

    Liquidity ratio: Chris and Judy can cover only about 20 percent of their existing one-year debt obligations with their current assets or about 2 1/2 months of coverage. If an emergency took place that curtailed their income, their liquid reserves would be exhausted very quickly. They should strengthen their liquidity position by additional savings or the transfer of some fixed assets to hard assets.

    Savings ratio: Chris and Judy have a relatively high savings ratio. (The American average is from 4 to 6 percent.)

    Debt safety ratio: This ratio is also relatively high. It is generally advisable to keep this ratio below 35 percent.

INCOME AND EXPENDITURES STATEMENT

Name(s) *Chris & Judy Catania*

For the **Year**   Ending **January 1993**

INCOME

Wages and salaries	Name: **Chris**	$ 15,000
	Name: **Judy**	22,000
	Name:	
Self-employment income		
Bonuses and commissions		
Pensions and annuities		
Investment income	Interest received	300
	Dividends received	200
	Rents received	
	Sale of securities	
	Other	
Other income		
	(I) Total Income	$ 37,500

EXPENDITURES

Housing	Rent/mortgage payment (include insurance and taxes, if applicable)	10,800
	Repairs, maintenance, improvements	570
Utilities	Gas, electric, water	2,880
	Phone	480
	Cable TV and other	
Food	Groceries	3,900
	Dining out	3,600
Autos	Loan payments	
	License plates, fees, etc.	1,200
	Gas, oil, repairs, tires, maintenance	
Medical	Health, major medical, disability insurance (payroll deductions or not provided by employer)	
	Doctor, dentist, hospital, medicines	1,000
Clothing	Clothes, shoes, and accessories	1,500
Insurance	Homeowner's (if not covered by mortgage payment)	
	Life (not provided by employer)	
	Auto	1,500
Taxes	Income and social security	5,500
	Property (if not included in mortgage)	
Appliances, furniture, and other major purchases	Loan payments	
	Purchases and repairs	
Personal care	Laundry, cosmetics, hair care	
Recreation and entertainment	Vacations	1,000
	Other Recreation and entertainment	700
Other items		
	(II) Total Expenditures	$ 34,630
	CASH SURPLUS (OR DEFICIT) [(I)–(II)]	$ 2,870

BALANCE SHEET		

Name(s) **Chris & Judy Catania**   Dated **January 1993**

ASSETS			LIABILITIES AND NET WORTH		
Liquid Assets			**Current Liabilities**		
Cash on hand	$ 3,000		Utilities	$	
In checking			Rent		
Savings accounts			Insurance premiums		
Money market funds and deposits			Taxes		
Certificates of deposit (<1 yr. to maturity)			Medical/dental bills		
			Repair bills		
			Bank credit card balances	550	
Total Liquid Assets		3,000	Dept. store credit card balances		
			Travel and entertainment card balances		
Investments					
Stocks	5,000		Gas and other credit card balances		
Bonds	2,050		Bank line of credit balances		
Certificates of deposit (>1 yr. to maturity)			Other current liabilities		
Mutual funds			**Total Current Liabilities**		550
Real estate			**Long-Term Liabilities**		
Retirement funds, IRA			Primary residence mortgage	65,000	
Other			Second home mortgage		
Total Investments		7,050	Real estate investment mortgage		
Real Property			Auto loans	7,890	
Primary residence	80,000		Appliance/furniture loans		
Second home			Home improvement loans		
Car(s):	15,000		Single-payment loans		
Car(s):			Education loans		
Recreation equipment			Other long-term loans from parents		
Other					
Total Real Property		95,000	**Total Long-Term Liabilities**		72,890
Personal Property					
Furniture and appliances	12,400				
Stereos, TVs, etc.					
Clothing			(II) Total Liabilities		$73,440
Jewelry					
Other			Net Worth [(I)–(II)]		$44,010
Total Personal Property		12,400			
	(I) Total Assets	$117,450	**Total Liabilities and Net Worth**		$117,450

5.

	Current Year	Forecasted Year
Wages and salaries	$ 37,000	$ 44,400
Other income	500	500
Expenditures	34,630	34,630
Cash surplus	$ 2,870	$ 10,270
Assets	$117,450	$123,323
Liabilities *	73,440	59,040
Net worth	$ 44,010	$ 74,553 **

* Auto Loan	7,890	4,290 (7,890 - 3,600)
	65,000	54,200 (65,000 - 10,800)

** Assets + Cash Surplus - Liabilities = Forecasted Net worth

CHAPTER 3

FILL IN THE BLANK ANSWERS

1. Financial planning
2. budget
3. to define your financial goals
4. Professional financial planners
5. 2 to 5 years on out to the next 30 to 40
6. dollars, target dates
7. 12-month
8. Cash budgets
9. income, expenditures, finalizing the budget
10. monthly
11. transfer expenditures from deficit months to surplus months, transfer income from surplus months to deficit months
12. savings or investments, borrow, low priority expenditures, income
13. budget control schedule
14. balanced

SOLUTIONS TO CASE PROBLEMS

Case 3.1

Solution on worksheet follows this page.

PERSONAL FINANCIAL GOALS

Name(s) __Mick & Megan__   Date __February 1993__

LONG-RUN GOALS

Goal Date	Goal Description
1995	European Trip
1996	New car
1997	New house — $150,000 value
2009	College fund, first child — $40,000
2011	College fund, second child
2013	Net worth of $200,000
2015	Around the World cruise
2023	Net worth of $450,000
2031	Retirement fund $250,000

SHORT-RUN GOALS (for the coming year)

Priority	Goal Description	Dollar Outlay
1	Term life insurance	unknown
2	Larger apartment $+200/mo.	$850/mo.
3	Retirement contribution	$100/mo.
4	Fall vacation	$1,000
5		
6		
7		
8		
9		
10		

Case 3.2

1.

	Survey Data (%)	Jackson Family (%)
Housing	30	28
Food and groceries	15	12
Transportation	10	10
Vacation/recreation	5	11.9
Health care/insurance	3	5
Clothing	4	5
Taxes	15	15.1
Savings and investments	6	3
Other	12	10

2.

	Comparison to Average	Deviation (%)
Housing	Below	-2
Food and groceries	Below	-3
Transportation	Equal	0
Vacation/recreation	Above	+6.9
Health care/insurance	Above	+2
Clothing	Above	+1
Taxes	Above	+0.1
Savings and investments	Below	-3
Other	Below	-2

3.   Yes. The Jacksons seem to be using surplus cash for vacation and recreation.

Case 3.3

See following worksheet.

Case 3.4

See following worksheet.

Case 3.5

See following worksheet.

Case 3.6

1.   See following worksheet.

2.   The Hillmans have a monthly deficit for 8 of 12 months but end the academic year in July with a net surplus of $5,728. Unless they have resources saved before August, they will need to borrow to cover their needs through April.

CASH BUDGET: ESTIMATED INCOME

Name(s): _Gerald_

For the _Year_ Ending _December 31, 1994_

SOURCES OF INCOME		Jan.	Feb.	Mar.	April.	May	June	July	Aug.	Sep.	Oct.	Nov.	Dec.	Total for the Year
Take-home pay	Name: Gerald	$2,100	$2,100	$2,100	$2,100	$2,100	$2,310	$2,310	$2,310	$2,310	$2,310	$2,310	$2,310	$26,670
	Name:													
	Name:													
Bonuses and commissions		420			420			462			462			1,764
Pensions and annuities														
Investment income	Interest	10	10	10	10	10	10	10	10	10	10	10	10	120
	Dividends								150					150
	Rents													
	Sale of securities													
	Other													
Other income														
TOTAL INCOME		$2,530	$2,110	$2,110	$2,530	$2,110	$2,320	$2,782	$2,470	$2,320	$2,782	$2,320	$2,320	$28,704

205

CASH BUDGET: ESTIMATED EXPENDITURES

Name(s) *Jesse & Jennifer Morgenstern*

For the _____ *Year* _____ Ending *December 31, 1994*

EXPENDITURE CATEGORIES		Annual Amounts
Housing (12–30%)	Rent/mortgage payment (include insurance and taxes, if applicable)	$ 10,336
	Repairs, maint., improvements	
Utilities (4–8%)	Gas, electric, water	1,800
	Phone	540
	Cable TV and other	
Food (15–25%)	Groceries	3,600
	Dining out	2,400
Autos (5–18%)	Loan payments	1,440
	License plates, fees, etc.	125
	Gas, oil, repairs, tires, maintenance	1,200
Medical (2–10%)	Health, major medical, disability insurance (payroll deductions or not provided by employer)	
	Doctor, dentist, hospital, medicine	
Clothing (3–8%)	Clothes, shoes and accessories	1,800
Insurance (4–8%)	Homeowner's (if not covered by mortgage payment)	220
	Life (not provided by employer)	
	Auto	650
Taxes (N/A)	Income and social security	
	Property (if not included in mortgage)	
Appliances, furniture and other major purchases (2-8%)	Loan payments	2,400
	Purchases and repairs	
	Other:	
Personal care (1–3%)	Laundry, cosmetics, hair care	
Recreation and entertainment (2–8%)	Vacations	900
	Other recreation and entertainment	
Savings and investments (3–10%)	Savings, stocks, bonds, etc.	1,200
Other expenditures (1–10%)	Charitable contributions	500
	Gifts	
	Education Loan	100
	Subscriptions, magazines, books	250
	Other:	
	Other:	
Fun money (1–5%)		
	TOTAL EXPENDITURES	$ 29,461

CASH BUDGET: ESTIMATED EXPENDITURES

Name(s) George & Irene Smith

For the Year   Ending December 31, 1994

EXPENDITURE CATEGORIES		Jan.	Feb.	Mar.	Apr.	May	June	July	Aug.	Sep.	Oct.	Nov.	Dec.	Total for the Year
Housing	Rent/mortgage payment (include insurance and taxes, if applicable)	$789	$789	$789	$789	$789	$789	$789	$789	$789	$789	$789	$789	$9,468
	Repairs, maint, improvements	100	100	100	100	100	100	100	100	100	100	100	100	1,200
Utilities	Gas, electric, water	200	200	200	200	200	200	200	200	200	200	200	200	2,400
	Phone	75	75	75	75	75	75	75	75	75	75	75	75	900
	Cable TV and other	26	26	26	26	26	26	26	26	26	26	26	26	312
Food	Groceries	250	250	250	250	250	250	250	250	250	250	250	250	3,000
	Dining out	350	350	350	350	350	350	350	350	350	350	350	350	4,200
Autos	Loan payments	750	750	750	750	750	450	450	450	450	450	450	450	6,900
	License plates, fees, etc.							215						215
	Gas, oil, repairs, tires, maintenance	125	125	125	125	125	125	125	125	125	125	125	125	1,500
Medical	Health, major medical, disability insurance (not provided by employer)													
	Doctor, dentist, hospital, medicines	80						80						160
Clothing	Clothes, shoes, and accessories	150	150	150	150	150	150	150	150	150	150	150	150	1,800
Insurance	Homeowners (if not covered by mortgage payment)													
	Life (not provided by employer)											600		600
	Auto							825						825
Taxes	Income and social security													
	Property (if not included in mortgage)													
Appliances, furniture, and other	Loan payments	350	350	350	350	350	350	350	350	350	350	350	350	4,200
	Purchases and repairs													
Personal care	Laundry, cosmetics, hair care													
Recreation and entertainment	Vacations								400	800				1,200
	Other recreation and entertainment													
Savings and investments	Savings, stocks, bonds, etc.	80	80	80	80	80	80	80	80	80	80	80	80	960
Other expenditures	Charitable contributions	30	30	30	30	30	30	30	30	30	30	30	30	360
	Gifts													
	Education loan payment													
	Subscriptions, magazines, books								40	18	30		20	108
	Other:													
	Other:													
Fun Money		300	300	300	300	300	300	300	300	300	300	300	300	3,600
TOTAL EXPENDITURES		$3,655	$3,515	$3,515	$3,515	$3,515	$3,215	$4,395	$3,715	$4,093	$3,305	$3,875	$3,295	$43,908

CASH BUDGET: MONTHLY SUMMARY

Name(s) Carolyn & Edward Hillman

For the ___Period___ Ending ___August 31, 1994___

INCOME	Jan.	Feb.	Mar.	Apr.	May	June	July	Aug.	Sep.	Oct.	Nov.	Dec.	Total for the Year
Take-home pay	$2,550	$2,550	$2,550	$2,550	$2,550	$3,690	$3,690	$3,690	$2,550	$2,550	$2,550	$2,550	$34,020
Bonuses and commissions													
Pensions and annuities													
Investment income													
Other income													
(I) Total Income	$2,550	$2,550	$2,550	$2,550	$2,550	$3,690	$3,690	$3,690	$2,550	$2,550	$2,550	$2,550	$34,020
EXPENDITURES													
Housing	$400	$400	$400	$400	$400	$400	$400	$400	$400	$400	$400	$400	$4,800
Utilities	90	90	90	90	90	90	90	90	90	90	90	90	1,080
Food	100	100	100	100	100	100	100	100	100	100	100	100	1,200
Autos	248	248	248	248	248	248	248	248	248	248	248	248	2,976
Medical	29	29	29	29	29	29	29	29	29	29	29	29	348
Clothing	0	0	925	0	0	125	0	125	1,200	0	0	125	2,500
Insurance	75	75	75	75	75	75	75	75	75	75	75	75	900
~~Taxes~~ Tuition	5,500							5,500					11,000
Appliances, furniture, and other													
~~Personal care~~ Books	400							400					800
Recreation and entertainment	147	147	147	147	147	147	147	147	147	147	147	147	1,764
Savings and investments													
~~Other expenditures~~ NDSL	50	50	50	50	50	50	50	50	50	50	50	50	600
~~Fun Money~~ Laundry	27	27	27	27	27	27	27	27	27	27	27	27	324
(II) Total Expenditures	$7,066	$1,166	$7,091	$1,166	$1,166	$1,291	$1,166	$7,191	$2,366	$1,166	$1,166	$1,291	$28,292
CASH SURPLUS (OR DEFICIT) [(I) − (II)]	$(4,516)	$1,384	$(4,541)	$1,384	$1,384	$2,399	$2,524	$(3,501)	184	$1,384	$1,384	$1,259	$5,728
CUMULATIVE CASH SURPLUS (OR DEFICIT)	$(4,516)	$(3,132)	$(2,673)	$(1,289)	95	$2,494	$5,018	$1,517	$1,701	$3,085	$4,469	$5,728	$5,728

Case 3.7

1. See following worksheet.

2. The Hillmans have done very well. That they are living within their budget is
    indicated by the positive cumulative cash surplus for the three months of $214.
    Looking at individual categories over the last three months, the Hillmans have been
    careful about their use of utilities. Although auto expense is below expectation, this
    may just be seasonal. If not, it is important to do proper maintenance on any vehicles.
    Apparently Carolyn was able to get the office clothing she needed at good prices.
    They have also reduced their recreation spending. Being a student and new employee
    can be very stressful and it is hoped that the drastic reduction in this category is not
    eroding their ability to relax. The laundry savings is marginal.

    There are very few overspent categories. Food was higher than expected, which may
    mirror the decline in recreation spending. Medical expenses were down, but this is
    usually not a very controllable item as long as preventive care is not being neglected.
    Books were higher than anticipated. Sometimes this expense is also not easy to
    control.

    All in all, the Hillmans did a fine job and seem to have their expenses well under
    control.

BUDGET CONTROL SCHEDULE

Name(s): _____

For the _____ Months Ending _____

	Month:				Month:				Month:			
	Budgeted Amount (1)	Actual (2)	Monthly Variance (3)	Year-to-Date Variance (4)	Budgeted Amount (5)	Actual (6)	Monthly Variance (7)	Year-to-Date Variance (8)	Budgeted Amount (9)	Actual (10)	Monthly Variance (11)	Year-to-Date Variance (12)
INCOME												
Take-home pay	$2,550	$2,550	-0-	-0-	2,550	$2,550	-0-	-0-	$2,550	$2,550	-0-	-0-
Bonuses and commissions												
Pensions and annuities												
Investment income												
Other income												
(I) Total Income	2,550	2,550	-0-	-0-	2,550	2,550	-0-	-0-	2,550	2,550	-0-	-0-
EXPENDITURES												
Housing	$ 400	$ 400	-0-	-0-	$ 400	$ 400	-0-	-0-	$ 400	$ 420	$ 20	20
Utilities	90	93	3	3	90	85	(5)	(2)	90	80	(10)	(12)
Food	100	115	25	25	100	130	30	55	100	110	10	65
Autos	248	196	(52)	(52)	248	210	(38)	(90)	248	260	12	(78)
Medical	29	-0-	(29)	(29)	29	45	16	(13)	29	60	31	18
Clothing	-0-	-0-	-0-	-0-	-0-	-0-	-0-	-0-	925	845	(80)	(80)
Insurance	75	75	-0-	-0-	75	75	-0-	-0-	75	75	-0-	-0-
~~Taxes~~ Tuition	5,500	5,500	-0-	-0-			-0-	-0-			-0-	-0-
Appliances, furniture, and other												
~~Personal care~~ Books	400	390	(10)	(10)	-0-	-0-	-0-	(10)	-0-	45	45	35
Recreation and entertainment	147	160	13	13	147	75	(72)	(59)	147	30	(117)	(176)
Savings and investments												
~~Other expenditures~~ NDSL	50	50	-0-	-0-	50	50	-0-	-0-	50	50	-0-	-0-
~~Fun Money~~ Laundry	27	30	3	3	27	20	(7)	(4)	27	25	(2)	(6)
(III) Total Expenditures	$7,066	$7,019	(47)	(47)	$1,166	$1,090	(76)	(123)	$2,091	$2,000	(91)	(214)
CASH SURPLUS (OR DEFICIT) [(I) – (III)]	$(4,516)	$(4,469)	47	47	$1,384	$1,460	76	123	$459	$550	91	214
CUMULATIVE CASH SURPLUS (OR DEFICIT)												

Key: Col. (3) = Col. (2) – Col. (1); Col. (7) = Col. (6) – Col. (5); Col. (11) = Col. (10) – Col. (9)
Col. (4) = Col. (3); Col. (8) = Col. (7) + Col. (4); Col. (12) = Col. (8) + Col. (11)

CHAPTER 4

FILL IN THE BLANK ANSWERS

1. 1939
2. tax code, taxpayer abuses, individuals, corporations
3. lower
4. bracket creep
5. pay-as-you-go
6. gross earnings, withholding allowances
7. number of people
8. 7.65%, $53,400
9. personal exemptions
10. active income, portfolio income, passive income
11. Active
12. Portfolio
13. Passive
14. deductions and write-offs
15. cannot
16. you are not covered by a qualified company-sponsored retirement program or your annual income is below a specified minimum
17. itemize
18. 50 percent
19. primary, secondary, original
20. 2 percent
21. standard
22. $2,150
23. tax credit
24. is not
25. all capital gains, any previous homes
26. joint
27. single person, head of household
28. April 15
29. four
30. 1.5 percent
31. 15, 28, 31
32. excise
33. sales
34. real estate, personal
35. evasion
36. avoidance
37. income shifting
38. Tax shelters
39. deferred

SOLUTIONS TO EXERCISES

Exercise 4-1

Mary's average tax rate = $ 667.50/$10,000 = 6.7% vs. 15%
Ann's average tax rate   = $2,167.50/$20,000 = 15.0% vs. 15%
Susan's average tax rate = $4,200.50/$30,000 = 14.0% vs. 28%

All of the average tax rates are below the marginal tax rate. (The marginal tax rate is the highest rate at which part of the total taxable income is taxed.) Under the progressive tax structure, personal income tax rates are scaled at increasing rates. As income increases, the average tax rate will approach the marginal tax rate. Note Ann and Susan's marginal rates: Susan earns $10,000 more than Ann and her average tax rate is correspondingly higher.

Exercise 4-2

		Tim	Doug	Brian
a.	FICA paid by the employee	$3,825.00	$2,295	$2,142
b.	FICA paid by the employer	same	same	same

Social security withholding rate for this year is 7.65 percent; same rate paid by employer.

Exercise 4-3

Taxable income can be derived by the following procedure:

	Gross income
Less:	Adjustments to gross income
Equals:	Adjusted gross income
Less:	Itemized deductions
Less:	Exemptions
Equals:	Taxable income

From the information gathered, first determine in which categories each expense or income item belongs, if any.

		Category
Gross wages	$45,050	Gross income
Interest paid on mortgage	4,280	Itemized deduction
Sales taxes paid deduction	1,050	Not an allowed
Interest income from savings	6,250	Gross income
Charitable donation	500	Itemized deduction
Moving expenses	1,000	Itemized deduction
IRA contribution deduction	2,000	Not an allowed
State income taxes	675	Itemized deduction
Rental income	24,000	Gross income
Property taxes	1,500	Itemized deduction
Expenses incurred on rental property	18,000	Deduction from rental income
Alimony from ex-husband	6,000	Gross income
Inheritance proceeds from late father	25,000	Tax exempt

Calculation of Lee Wood's Taxable Income

	Gross income	$63,300
Less:	Adjustments to gross income	0
Equals:	Adjusted gross income	$63,300
Less:	Itemized deductions	7,955
Less:	Personal Exemptions	2,150
Equals:	Taxable income	$53,195

Exercise 4-4

a. T
b. E
c. E
d. T
e. T
f. E
g. T
h. T
i. E
j. T

Exercise 4-5

A. T
b. D or E
c. D
d. E

Exercise 4-6
(See Exhibit 4.5 - Tax Rate Schedules)

Case
A	$2,250
B	$2,250
C	$4,851
D	$4,500
E	$14,475.50
F	$15,157.75
G	$42,375.50
H	$39,615.50

SOLUTIONS TO CASE PROBLEMS

Case 4.1

Itemized deductions are:
Medical and dental	$ 0 (under limit)
Mortgage interest	2,500
State taxes	750
Contributions	500
Business expense	0 (under limit)
Total	$ 3,750

The standard deduction is $5,700. Mort and Shirley should use the standard deduction.

CHAPTER 5

FILL IN THE BLANK ANSWERS

1. Cash management
2. Liquid
3. deregulation (Depository Institutions Deregulation and Monetary Control Act of 1980)
4. financial supermarket
5. commercial banks
6. depositors
7. Savings and loans
8. Savings
9. credit union
10. demand
11. savings
12. interest-bearing checking
13. mutual fund, deposit account
14. interest
15. FDIC
16. three to six
17. discount
18. effective
19. Compound
20. annuity
21. minimum balance method, FIFO method, LIFO method, actual balance
22. certificate of deposit
23. Treasury bills
24. Series EE
25. Central Asset Account
26. overdraft
27. restrictive
28. stop payment
29. reconciliation
30. cashier's

SOLUTIONS TO EXERCISES

Exercise 5-1

1. D, C, B
2. D, C, B
3. B
4. A
5. D
6. A, B, D
7. C

Exercise 5-2

1. A
2. B
3. B
4. C
5. A

Exercise 5-3

Case	Deposit Insurance Coverage
A	$100,000
B	85,000
C	100,000
D	100,000
E	100,000
F	272,000 *

*   Note: all of the accounts are titled differently. Although Carla has two accounts in her name, one is an IRA which qualifies on its own for $100,000 of insurance.

Exercise 5-4

Liquid reserves:
$ 2,500 x 3 months = $ 7,500 minimum
$ 2,500 x 6 months = $15,000 maximum

Savings-type instruments:
$75,000 x 10% = $ 7,500 minimum
$75,000 x 25% = $18,750 maximum

Exercise 5-5

$$\text{Effective rate of interest} = \frac{\text{Amount of interest earned over the course of 1 year}}{\text{Amount of money invested or deposited}}$$

Investment
A	($500 x 2)/$12,000 = 8.3%
B	($1,000 x 3)/$30,000 = 10%
C	$250/$5,000 = 5%
D	($750/2)/$4,000 = 9.4%
E	($2,000 x 1.33)/$25,000 = 10.6%

Exercise 5-6

Future value = Amount deposited x Future value factor (Appendix A)

Deposit	Amount Deposited		Future Value Factor		Future Value
A	$ 1,000	x	1.100	=	$ 1,100
B	2,000	x	1.166	=	2,332
C	5,000	x	1.225	=	6,125
D	10,000	x	1.262	=	12,620
E	25,000	x	1.276	=	31,900

Exercise 5-7

Future value = Amount deposited each year x Annuity factor (Appendix B)

Deposit	Amount Deposited per year		Future Value Annuity Factor		Future Value
A	$5,000	x	4.779	=	$23,895
B	2,000	x	15.937	=	31,874
C	500	x	5.751	=	2,876

Exercise 5-8

a. Minimum balance method:
$35,000 x .08 x (90/360) = $700

b. FIFO method:
$35,000 x .08 x (90/360) = $700
$10,000 x .08 x (30/360) = _67_
$767

c. LIFO method:
$35,000 x .08 x (90/360) = $700
$10,000 x .08 x (30/360) = _67_
$767

d. Actual balance method:
$40,000 x .08 x (30/360) = $266.67
35,000 x .08 x (30/360) = 233.33
45,000 x .08 x (30/360) = _300.00_
$800.00

Exercise 5-9

1. D
2. C, A
3. A
4. B
5. C
6. A

Exercise 5-10

1. D
2. B
3. D
4. C
5. A
6. A

Exercise 5-11

See following worksheet.

218

CHECKING ACCOUNT RECONCILIATION

For the Month of __July__ , 19__93__

Accountholder Name(s) __Maggie__

Type of Account __Checking__

1. Ending balance shown on bank statement _____ | $ 139.11 |

Add up checks and withdrawals still outstanding:

Check Number or Date	Amount	Check Number or Date	Amount
505	$ 60.00		$
511	20.00		
512	29.35		
513	14.00		
	TOTAL $ 123.35		

2. Deduct total checks/withdrawals still outstanding from bank balance _____ − $ 123.35

Add up desposits still outstanding:

Date	Amount	Date	Amount
8/28	2,050		
	TOTAL $ 2,050		

3. *Add* total deposits still outstanding to bank balance _____ + $ 2,050

[A] **Adjusted Bank Balance** (1 - 2 + 3) _____ $2,065.76

4. Ending balance shown in checkbook _____ $2,059.26

5. *Deduct* any bank service charges for the period _____ − $

6. *Add* interest earned for the period _____ + $ 6.50

[B] **New Checkbook Balance** (4 - 5 + 6) _____ $2,065.76

Note: Your account is reconciled when line A equals line B.

219

CHAPTER 6

FILL IN THE BLANK ANSWERS

1. cooperative
2. condominiums
3. tax
4. Property, interest
5. points and closing costs, mortgage payments
6. loan-to-value
7. Mortgage points
8. borrowers
9. Closing costs
10. affordability
11. principal, interest, property taxes, homeowner's insurance
12. escrow
13. land
14. a description of the property sufficient to provide positive identification, specific price and other terms
15. Earnest money
16. savings and loan association
17. balloon payments, buy-downs
18. buy-down
19. fixed-rate
20. higher
21. adjustable rate
22. conventional
23. negative
24. Federal Housing Administration or Private Mortgage Insurance
25. title check, closing statement
26. Real Estate Settlement Procedures Act
27. title check
28. refinance
29. Depreciation
30. installment loan payment
31. fixed, variable
32. sales contract
33. closed-end lease
34. buying guide

SOLUTIONS TO EXERCISES

Exercise 6-1

a. (.25)($250,000) = $62,500   b.   (.75)($250,000) = $187,500

Exercise 6-2

$(.02)(\$100,000) = \$2,000$

Exercise 6-3

	(1)	(2)	(3)
1.	Amount	Loan	
	of loan/	Payment	(1) x (2)
Case	10,000	Factor*	Monthly Payment
A	10	95.57	$955.70
B	5	143.48	717.40
C	7.5	84.09	630.68
D	3	124.36	373.08
E	6.5	90.88	590.72

* From Exhibit 6.5

2. Formula is monthly payment times number of payments minus
    loan principal equals interest paid.

A	$955.70 x 180 months = $172,026 - $100,000 =	$72,026.00
B	$717.40 x 120 months = $86,064 - $50,000 =	$36,064.00
C	$630.68 x 360 months = $227,044.80 - $75,000 =	$152,044.80
D	$373.08 x 240 months = $89,539.20 x $30,000 =	$59,539.20
E	$590.72 x 300 months = $177,216 - $65,000 =	$112,116.00

Exercise 6-4

			Maximum total monthly installment loan payments		Other installment loan payments	Maximum monthly mortgage payment
A	(.38)($4,000)	=	1,520	-	$ 500	= $1,020
B	(.38)($1,200)	=	456	-	100	= 356
C	(.38)($3,000)	=	1,140	-	250	= 890
D	(.38)($5,000)	=	1,900	-	1,000	= 900

Exercise 6-5

See following worksheet.

The West family should rent a home since the annual costs are less expensive. However, this looks only at current costs. Rents may increase and property values and principal reduction could swing the analysis toward purchase quickly.

RENT-OR-BUY ANALYSIS

A. COST OF RENTING			
1. Annual rental costs			
(12 x monthly rental rate of $ **1,000**)		$12,000	
2. Renter's insurance		750	
Total cost of renting			$12,750
B. COST OF BUYING			
1. Annual mortgage payments (Terms: $ _____ , _____ months, ___ %)			
(12 x monthly mortgage payment of $ **1,290**)	$15,480		
2. Property taxes			
(___% of price of home)	3,750		
3. Homeowner's insurance			
(___% of price of home)	625		
4. Maintenance			
(___% of price of home)	2,500		
5. After-tax cost of interest lost on down payment and closing costs			
($ **20,000** x **5** % after-tax rate of return)	1,000		
6. Total costs		23,355	
Less:			
7. Principal reduction in loan balance (see note below)	1,730		
8. Tax savings due to interest deductions*			
(Interest portion of mortgage payments $ **13,750** x tax rate of **28** %)	3,850		
9. Tax savings due to property tax deductions*			
(line B.2 x tax rate of **28** %)	1,050		
10. Total deductions		6,630	
11. Annual after-tax cost of home ownership			
(line B.6 – line B.10.)		16,725	
12. Less: Estimated annual appreciation			
in value of home (**2.5** % of price of home)		2,500	
Total cost of buying (line B.11 – line B.12.)			$14,225

Exercise 6-6

a. $12,000 x .35 = $4,200
b. $7,800/3 years = $2,600 depreciation per year
     $7,800/36 months = $216.67 depreciation per month

Exercise 6-7

AUTOMOBILE OPERATING COSTS

| | Annual Costs | | Monthly Costs | | Costs per mile (20,000 miles) | |
	Sedan	Economy Model	Sedan	Economy Model	Sedan	Economy Model
(1) Fixed Costs						
Installment loan payment	$4,560	$2,436	$380.00	$203.00	$.228	$.122
Auto insurance	1,000	700	83.33	58.33	.050	.035
License plates	30	30	2.50	2.50	.002	.002
Personal property taxes	500	250	41.67	20.83	025	.013
Emissions test	15	15	1.25	1.25	.001	.001
Total fixed costs	$6,105	$3,431	$508.75	$285.91	$.306	$.173
(2) Variable Costs						
Repairs	$ 300	$ 200	$ 25.00	$ 16.67	$.015	$.010
Maintenance	200	140	16.67	11.67	.010	.007
Fuel	800	500	66.67	41.67	.040	.025
Total var. costs	$1,300	$ 840	$108.34	$ 70.01	$.065	$.042
(3) Depreciation	$3,000	$2,000	$250.00	$166.67	$.150	$.100
Total Operating Costs [(1) + (2) + (3)]	$10,405	$6,271	$867.09	$522.59	$.521	$.315

The luxury sedan costs $867.09 per month and the economy model costs $522.59 per month to operate. Since Brian has $700 per month for auto expenses, the economy model better fits his limited budget. However, when actual cash outlays are considered, the luxury sedan costs $617.12 per month, which Brian could afford with $700 each month.

SOLUTIONS TO CASE PROBLEMS

Case 6.1

1. <u>1st National Bank</u>
    $57,000/$183,000 = 31.2% down payment

    .02 x $126,000 = $2,520 lenders points
    .04 x $126,000 = <u>$5,040</u> closing costs
    $7,560

    <u>Merchant's Bank</u>
    .0175 x $126,000 = $2,205 lenders points
    .045 x $126,000 = <u>$5,670</u> closing costs
    $7,875

2. <u>1st National Bank</u>--affordability ratio = 25%
    $1,241/$4,500 = 27%

    <u>Merchant's Bank</u>--affordability ratio = 29%
    $903/$4,500 = 20%

    Michael and Susan meet both affordability ratios.

3.

Regular Payment	Total Interest Paid over Life of Loan	
$1,241	$ 97,380 *	1st National Bank
903	$199,080 **	Merchant's Bank

    * $1,241 x 15 years x 12 months/year = $223,380 total paid
    $223,380 - $126,000 = $97,380

    ** $903 x 30 years x 12 months/year = $325,080 total paid
    $325,080 - $126,000 = $199,080

    The advantages of the fixed-rate mortgage are 1) the total interest paid over the life of the loan is less than half of the alternative mortgage; 2) the payment is fixed and won't increase; and 3) the total closing costs are lower.

    The disadvantages of the fixed-rate mortgage are 1) the monthly payment is higher; and 2) the interest rate is fixed (should interest rates decline significantly, no change will be made in the monthly payment).

    The advantages of the adjustable-rate mortgage are 1) the monthly payment is lower; and 2) the interest rate is adjustable in the event of a decline in mortgage rates.

The disadvantages of the adjustable-rate mortgage are 1) the amount of interest paid over the life of the loan is higher since it has a 30-year term; 2) the closing costs are higher; and 3) the payment is uncertain since the rate may change.

The 15-year fixed rate mortgage is recommended since it has lower closing costs and less interest paid over the life of the loan.

Case 6.2

The worksheet solution follows.

Based on the analysis, the Kominskis can afford a home valued at $131,113.

Case 6.3

See following worksheet.

Chan and Karen should refinance their old mortgage because they will break-even on expenses in 13 months and they plan to stay in the house for 60 months.

Case 6.4

See following worksheet.

Based on the analysis, Henry would be better off in the long-run if he chose to purchase the car because the cost of leasing is $18,110 while the cost of buying is only $17,219.

HOME AFFORDABILITY ANALYSIS*

Name _John & Marylou Kominski_   Date _January 1993_

Item	Description	Amount
1	Amount of annual income	$ 65,000
2	Monthly income (Item 1 ÷ 12)	$ 5,417
3	Lender's affordabiilty ratio (in decimal form)	.30
4	Maximum monthly mortgage payment (PITI) (Item 2 x Item 3)	$ 1,625
5	Estimated monthly tax and homeowner's insurance payment	$ 300
6	Maximum monthly loan payment	$ 1,340
7	Approximate average interest rate on loan	.10
8	Planned loan maturity (years)	30
9	Mortgage payment per $10,000 (using Item 7 and Item 8 and Monthly Mortgage Payment Table in Exhibit 6.5)	$ 87.76
10	Maximum loan based on monthly income ($10,000 x Item 6 ÷ Item 9)	$ 152,689
11	Funds available for making a down payment and paying closing costs	$ 29,500
12	Funds available for making a down payment (Item 11 x .67)	$ 19,765
13	Maximum purchase price based on available monthly income (Item 10 + Item 12)	$ 172,454
14	Minimum acceptable down payment (in decimal form)	.15
15	Maximum purchase price based on down payment (Item 12 ÷ Item 14)	$ 131,767
16	Maximum home purchase price (lower of Item 13 and Item 15)	$ 131,767

226

MORTGAGE REFINANCING ANALYSIS

Name **Chan & Karen Limb**   Date **January 1993**

Item	Description		Amount
1	Current monthly payment (Terms: _n/a_)		$ **674**
2	New monthly payment (Terms: _n/a_)		**582**
3	Monthly savings, pretax (Item 1 – Item 2)		$ **92**
4	Monthly savings times your tax rate (_n/a_%)		**n/a**
5	Monthly savings, after-tax (Item 3 – Item 4)		$ **n/a**
6	Costs to refinance:		
	a. Prepayment penalty	$ **0**	
	b. Total closing costs (after-tax)	**$1,250**	
	c. Total refinancing costs (Item 6a + Item 6b)		$ **1,250**
7	Months to break even (Item 6c ÷ Item 5) **(Item 6c ÷ Item 3)**		**14 months**

AUTOMOBILE LEASE VERSUS PURCHASE ANALYSIS

Name **Henry Eaton**   Date **January 1993**

LEASE

Item	Description	Amount
1	Security deposit required	$ 500
2	Term of lease and loan (years)*	4 years
3	Term of lease and loan (months) (Item 2 x 12)	48 months
4	Monthly lease payment	$ 375
5	Total payments over term of lease (Item 3 x Item 4)	$ 18,000
6	Interest rate earned on savings (in decimal form)	.055
7	Opportunity cost of security deposit (Item 1 x Item 2 x Item 6)	$ 110
8	Payment/refund for market value adjustment at end of lease ($0 for closed-end leases) and/or estimated end-of-term charges	$ -0-
9	Total cost of leasing (Item 5 + Item 7 + Item 8)	$ 18,110

PURCHASE

Item	Description	Amount
10	Purchase price	$ 16,700
11	Down payment	$ 2,500
12	Sales tax rate (in decimal form)	.07
13	Sales tax (Item 10 x Item 12)	$ 1,169
14	Monthly loan payment (Terms: $ _____ , _____ months, ___ %)	$ 375
15	Total payments over term of loan (Item 3 x Item 14)	$ 18,000
16	Opportunity cost of down payment (Item 2 x Item 6 x Item 11)	$ 550
17	Estimated value of car at end of loan	$ 5,000
18	Total cost of purchasing (Item 11 + Item 13 + Item 15 + Item 16 – Item 17)	$ 17,219

DECISION

If the value of Item 9 is less than the value of Item 18, leasing is preferred; otherwise the purchase alternative is preferred.

228

CHAPTER 7

FILL IN THE BLANK ANSWERS

1. Credit
2. financial emergency, convenience, investment purposes
3. routine basic living expenses, impulse purchases, non-durable short-lived goods and services
4. present, worth, history
5. 20 percent
6. open credit
7. 30-day or regular charge account
8. Retail
9. Bank
10. Prestige
11. travel and entertainment
12. Affinity
13. overdraft protection, unsecured personal credit line, home equity credit line
14. A credit bureau
15. Credit scoring
16. Equal Credit Opportunity Act
17. Fair Credit Reporting Act
18. finance charges (APR, # payments, monthly payment, etc.)
19. the card is lost or stolen
20. unsatisfactory
21. a wage earner plan, straight bankruptcy
22. wage earner plan
23. child support and alimony payments and certain government payment benefits, home equity up to $7,500, a car up to $1,200 and other personal items
24. previous balance
25. adjusted balance
26. average daily balance
27. past due balance
28. bank
29. highest
30. annual fees, transaction fees on cash advances
31. debit
32. overdraft protection lines, unsecured personal lines of credit, home equity credit lines
33. home equity line of credit
34. overdraft protection line
35. unsecured line of credit

SOLUTIONS TO EXERCISES

Exercise 7-1

1. F
2. A

3. B
4. C
5. A
6. D
7. E
8. F
9. C

Exercise 7-2

1. B
2. C
3. B
4. E
5. A
6. A
7. C
8. D
9. D
10. D

Exercise 7-3

Debt safety ratio = $\dfrac{\text{Total monthly consumer credit payments}}{\text{Monthly take-home pay}}$

= \$625/\$2,500

= .25 or 25%

The guideline for consumer credit levels recommends that the maximum debt safety ratio should not exceed 20 percent. Since Bill's exceeds 20 percent, he should probably reduce his expenditures.

Exercise 7-4

1) Previous balance method:
$315.25 x .015 = $4.73

2) Average daily balance method:

	Number of Days	Balance	Weighted Balance
	30	$315.25	$9,457.50
	1	- 184.75*	-184.75
Total	31		$9,272.75

$$\text{Average daily balance} = \frac{\$9,272.75}{31 \text{ days}} = \$299.12$$

Interest expense = $299.12 x .015 = $4.49

3) Adjusted balance method:
$315.25 - 500 = -$184.75. Therefore, no interest is due.

CHAPTER 8

FILL IN THE BLANK ANSWERS

1. single-payment, installment loan
2. lending arrangements
3. Auto
4. Collateral
5. consolidation
6. single-payment
7. single-payment
8. installment
9. interest
10. Commercial banks
11. Consumer finance companies
12. credit unions
13. Savings and loan associations
14. Sale finance companies
15. captive finance companies
16. cash value
17. maturity date
18. Collateral
19. debt safety
20. 20
21. loan collateral, loan maturity, loan repayment
22. lien
23. chattel mortgage
24. collateral note
25. prepayment penalty
26. rollover
27. simple interest method, discount method
28. actual loan balance outstanding
29. discount
30. higher
31. installment purchase contract
32. note
33. Credit life insurance
34. add-on clause
35. acceleration
36. wage assignment
37. Garnishment
38. repossession
39. Add-on
40. Rule of 78
41. borrow

SOLUTIONS TO EXERCISES

Exercise 8-1

Using Exhibit 8.8, the monthly payments are:

a. ($25,000/$1,000) x 87.92 = $2,198.00
b. ($10,000/$1,000) x 48.49 = $484.90
c. ($5,000/$1,000) x 24.42 = $122.10

Exercise 8-2

$$Fs = P \times r \times t$$

where

F_s = finance charge, simple interest method
P = principal amount of loan
r = stated annual rate of interest
t = term of loan stated in years

a. F_s = $1,000 x .05 x 3 = $150

Principal amount + finance charge = total payment due at the maturity date
$1,000 + $150 = $1,150

b. F_s = $5,000 x .07 x 5 = $1,750

$5,000 + $1,750 = $6,750

c. F_s = $7,000 x .10 x 10 = $7,000

$7,000 + $7,000 = $14,000

Exercise 8-3

a. F_d = P x r x t = $7,500 x .08 x 2 = $1,200

$$APR = \frac{\text{average annual finance charges}}{\text{average loan balance outstanding}}$$

Average annual finance charges = $1,200/2 = $600

Average loan balance outstanding = $7,500 - $1,200 = $6,300

APR = $600/$6,300 = 9.5%

b. $F_d = \$5,000 \times .09 \times 1 = \$450$

$$APR \frac{\$450}{(\$5,000 - \$450)}$$

$$= \$450/\$4,550 = 9.9\%$$

c. $F_d = \$12,000 \times .10 \times 3 = \$3,600$

$$APR = \frac{(\$3,600/3)}{(\$12,000 - \$3,600)}$$

$$= \$1,200/\$8,400 = 14.3\%$$

Exercise 8-4

$F = P \times r \times t$
 $= \$15,500 \times .075 \times 2$
 $= \$2,325$

Monthly payments $= \dfrac{\$15,500 + \$2,325}{24} = \$742.71$

Exercise 8-5

Loan 1: Using Exhibit 8.8, the monthly payment is $874.60.

   ($10,000/$1,000) x 87.46 = $874.60
   12 payments x $874.60 = $10,495.20
   $10,495.20 - $10,000 = $495.20 interest

Loan 2: $F = P \times r \times t$
        $= \$10,000 \times .09 \times 1$
        $= \$900$ interest

The add-on method results in nearly double the interest paid over the term of the loan.

Exercise 8-6

Approximate APR $= \dfrac{M(95N + 9)F}{12N(N+1)(4P+F)}$

   where
      M = number of payments in a year
      N = number of loan payments scheduled over life of a loan
      F = total finance charges
      P = principal portion of loan

a.

$$\text{APR} = \frac{12[95(24) + 9]\$4,000}{12(24)(24 + 1)[(4 \times \$20,000) + \$4,000]}$$

$$= \frac{109,872,000}{604,800,000} = 18.2\%$$

b.

$$\text{APR} = \frac{12[95(36) + 9]\$4,050}{12(36)(36 + 1)[(4 \times \$15,000) + \$4,050]}$$

$$= \frac{166,649,400}{1,023,775,200} = 16.3\%$$

c.

$$\text{APR} = \frac{12[(95)(60 + 9]\$1,050}{12(60)(60 + 1)[(4 \times \$3,500) + \$1,050]}$$

$$= \frac{71,933,400}{660,996,000} = 10.9\%$$

Exercise 8-7

Sum of the digits = (Number of payments/2) x (Number of payments + 1)
$$= (48/2) \times (48 + 1)$$
$$= 24 \times 49$$
$$= 1,176$$

The lender is entitled to (48 + 47 + 46 + 45 + 44 + 43 + 42 + 41 + 40 + 39 + 38 + 37)/1,176
$$= .4337 \times \text{total finance charges}$$
$$= (.4337 \times \$1,800[1]) = \$780.66$$
($1,800 - 780.66 = $1,019.34 interest due borrower)

Amount of loan including add-on finance charges	$9,300.00
Less: Interest refunded to borrower	1,019.34
Less: Payments to date (12 x $193.75[2])	2,325.00
Loan Payoff	$5,955.66

[1]Total finance charges: $\quad F = P \times r \times t$
$$= \$7,500 \times .06 \times 4$$
$$= \$1,800$$

[2]Payment: ($7,500 + $1,800)/48 = $193.75

SOLUTIONS TO CASE PROBLEMS

Case 8.1

To evaluate these loans, calculate the monthly payment (when applicable), the total finance charge, and the total interest and principal paid over the period.

	Total Monthly payment	Total interest finance charges	plus principal over period
Honda Dealer's Loan Assoc.	$114.61*	$ 675.96**	$4,125.96
Society Bank	124.58	1,034.88	4,484.88
General Finance Company	N/A	776.25***	4,226.25

  * See Exhibit 8.8 for factors.
 ** ($114.61 x 36) - $3,450 = $675.96
*** ($3,450 x .15 x 1.5) - $776.25

The Honda Dealer's Loan Assoc. results in the least amount of interest paid over the term. Note that the stated interest rate on the Society Bank appears lowest but because it is an add-on loan the APR is much higher. Keron should take the HDLA installment loan.

Case 8.2

The worksheet solution follows.

Based on the analysis the Smiths would have difficulty qualifying for more consumer debt because their debt safety ratio is 25.9 percent versus an acceptable maximum of 20 percent.

Case 8.3

The worksheet solution follows.

The loan payment is ($2,500/$1,000) x $47.05 = $117.63

According to the analysis, it is more costly for Louann to borrow the money rather than pay cash so she should not make the loan. She should reduce her savings and pay cash.

AN INVENTORY OF CONSUMER DEBT

Name _Gene & Joan Smith_   Date _____

Type of Consumer Debt		Current Monthly Payment[a]	Latest Balance Due
Auto loans	1. 2 year old car	$ 311	$ 6,000
	2.		
	3.		
Education loans	1. night school	100	2,500
	2.		
Personal installment loans	1.		
	2.		
Home improvement loan			
Other installment loans	1.		
	2.		
Single-payment loans	1.		
	2.		
Credit cards (retail charge cards, bank cards, T&E cards, etc.)	1. Visa	35	1,500
	2. Master Card	45	1,250
	3. Shell Oil	25	400
	4. Macy's	75	1,700
	5. Discover	55	2,000
	6.		
	7.		
Overdraft protection line			
Personal line of credit			
Home equity credit line	remodeling	265	9,800
Loan on life insurance			
Margin loan from broker			
Other loans	1.		
	2.		
	3.		
Totals		$ 911	$ 25,150

Debt safety ratio = $\dfrac{\text{Total monthly payments}}{\text{Monthly take-home pay}} \times 100 = \dfrac{\$\ 986}{\$3800} \times 100 = \underline{25.9}\%$

[a] Leave the space blank if there is *no* monthly payment required on a loan (e.g., as with a single-payment or education loan).

237

BUY ON TIME OR PAY CASH

Name **_Louann_**   Date **_June 1, 1993_**

■   **Cost of Borrowing**

1.	Terms of the loan
	  a. Amount of the loan
	  b. Length of loan (in years)
	  c. Monthly payment
		$ 2,500
		2
		$ 117.63	

2.	Total loan payments made (monthly loan payment x length of loan in months) 117.63 per month x **24** months		$ 2,823.12
3.	Less: Principal amount of the loan		$ 2,500.00
4.	Total interest paid over life of loan (line 2 – line 3)		$ 323.12

5.	Tax considerations:
	• Is this a home-equity loan (where interest expenses
	  can be deducted from taxes) ....yes ☐ no ☒
	• Do you itemize deductions on your federal tax returns ....yes ☒ no ☐
	• If you answered yes to BOTH questions, then proceed to *line 6;*
	  if you answered no to *either one or both* of the questions, then
	  proceed to *line 8* and use *line 4* as the after-tax interest cost of the loan.		

6.	What Federal Tax Bracket are you in? (use either 15, 28, or 31%)	%	
7.	Taxes saved due to interest deductions (line 4 x tax rate, from line 6: $_____ x ___%)		$
8.	Total after-tax interest cost on the loan (line 4 – line 7)		$ 323.12

■   **Cost of Paying Cash**

9.	Annual interest *earned* on savings (Annual rate of interest earned on savings x amount of loan: **6.5** % x **2,500**)		$ 162.50
10.	Annual after-tax interest earnings (line 9 x [1 – tax rate] — e.g., 1 – 28% = 72%: $ 162.50 x **72** %)		$ 117.00
11.	Total after-tax interest earnings over life of loan (line 10 x line 1-b: $ **117** x **2** years)		$ 234.00

■   **Net Cost of Borrowing**

12.	Difference in cost of borrowing vs. cost of paying cash (line 8 minus line 11)		$ 89.12

BASIC DECISION RULE: *Pay cash* if line 12 is positive; *borrow the money* if line 12 is negative.

Note: For simplicity, compounding is ignored in calculating *both* the cost of interest and interest earnings.

CHAPTER 9

FILL IN THE BLANK ANSWERS

1. life insurance
2. employee benefit plans
3. cafeteria-style plans
4. Loss prevention
5. Risk assumption
6. Insurance, large, fortuitous, insurance, non-catastrophic
7. Underwriters
8. human life, multiple earnings, needs
9. multiple earnings
10. human life
11. needs
12. term, whole life, universal life
13. term
14. convertible
15. Decreasing
16. Whole life
17. Whole life, universal life
18. Universal life insurance
19. limited payment
20. continuous
21. whole life
22. universal life
23. Credit
24. variable life insurance
25. settlement options
26. beneficiary
27. nonforfeiture
28. safety of principal, competitive return, liquidity, forced savings
29. state or federal income taxes
30. Whole life
31. Term
32. Variable life
33. Universal life

SOLUTIONS TO EXERCISES

Exercise 9-1

1.	L	7.	O
2.	A	8.	G
3.	F	9.	H
4.	C	10.	IG
5.	M		
6.	P		

Exercise 9-2

1. C
2. A
3. E
4. F
5. B

SOLUTIONS TO CASE PROBLEMS

Case 9.1

1. Jennifer is on a limited budget so she should be shopping for the life insurance that provides the most coverage per insurance dollar premium spent. Term insurance is the least inexpensive type of policy and will provide solid life protection.

2. Other information necessary to more accurately assess Jennifer's life insurance needs may include:
    Jennifer's financial obligations and financial resources.
    Jennifer's savings and investing goals.
    Other sources of money available to her children if she should die (social security, father taking custody of the children, etc.).

Case 9.2

1. Since the Ketterings have a large portfolio of investments, their primary objective is most likely not death protection for their children. They are probably considering the investment and tax benefits of purchasing life insurance. An attractive feature of life insurance for those planning the passing of a large estate is that insurance policy proceeds can pass to named beneficiaries free of any estate taxes. Of course, some restrictions apply. To qualify for the estate tax exemption, insureds must relinquish various "incidents of ownership," including the right to change the beneficiary, to take the policy's cash surrender value, and to choose a settlement option. These last items were not covered in the text, but may be interesting for discussion.

2. To fit the Ketterings' goals and situation, either a universal life or variable life policy is recommended for their investment features. The choice between the

240

universal and variable life policies would depend on the Ketterings' risk tolerance. The universal life policy is somewhat more flexible and well-suited for those who are self-directed in money matters. If the Ketterings are more risk tolerant and well versed in equity investments, the variable life policy may be more appropriate.

Case 9-3

1. Multiple earnings approach

John	(8.6)($40,000) =	$344,000	
Shirley	(8.6)($39,000) =	335,400	
		$679,400	

2. See following worksheet.
   The Talbots are grossly underinsured to meet their current goals.

3. The two basic goals of providing a steady income stream until 18 years of age for the children and setting up an education fund can be met in a variety of ways. A term life insurance policy can provide the death protection and the cash for the education fund (only in the event of a death). Or a whole life or universal life policy can provide the death protection and also, through its savings feature, provide the education fund (not contingent upon death).

Since the Talbots have a large insurance need, it is most economical to purchase a term insurance policy. To provide for the education fund, they have two choices: 1) buy a whole life or universal life policy for the savings/investment feature, or 2) buy term insurance with a large enough death benefit to cover all needs in the event of a death while establishing an independent savings plan. The term policy could be decreasing term which sets a level premium but a decreasing death benefit. This would coincide with the independent savings plan which would have an increasing balance simultaneously.

Insured's Name	John & Shirley Talbot	Date	January 1993

					Totals
A.	**Family Income Needs**				
	1. Debt Liquidation:				
	a. House mortgage	$ 70,000			
	b. Other loans	$ 12,000			
	c. Total debt (a+b)				$ 82,000
	2. Final expenses				$ 7,000

		Period 1	Period 2	Period 3	
	3. Annual income needs:				
	a. Monthly living expenses	$6,583	$3,900	$3,300	
	b. Less: Social security survivor's benefits	1,200	0	800	
	c. Less: Surviving spouse's income	3,250	3,250	0	
	d. Less: Other pension benefits and income	0	0	1,200	
	e. Net monthly income needed (a – b – c –d)	2,133	650	1,300	
	f. Net yearly income needed (12 x e)	25,596	7,800	15,600	
	g. Number of years in period	9	16	20	
	h. Funding needed each period (f x g)	230,364	124,800	312,000	
	i. Total living needs (add line h for each period)				$ 667,164
	4. Spouse reeducation fund				$ –0–
	5. Children's opportunity fund				$ 120,000
	6. Other needs				$ –0–
	7. TOTAL INCOME NEEDS (add right column)				$ 876,164
B.	**Financial Resources Available**				
	1. Savings and investments	$ 63,000			
	2. Group life insurance	$ 30,000			
	3. Other life insurance	$ 50,000			
	4. Other resources	$ 50,000			
	TOTAL RESOURCES AVAILABLE (1 + 2 + 3 + 4)				$ 193,000
C.	**Additional Life Insurance Needed (A – B)** (Note: no additional insurance is needed if number is negative.)				$ 683,164

CHAPTER 10

FILL IN THE BLANK ANSWERS

1. 1930s
2. hospital
3. surgical expense
4. Major medical
5. deductible
6. participation
7. comprehensive major medical
8. long-term care
9. Disability income
10. deductible, coinsurance, waiting period clause
11. from two or more policies
12. fake
13. indemnity, valued, service
14. Consolidated Omnibus Budget Reconciliation Act or COBRA
15. social security, workers' compensation
16. disability income, medicare
17. basic hospital, supplementary medical
18. 65 years, pay a premium
19. have had the disability at least five months and is expected to last at least twelve months
20. Workers' compensation
21. nonprofit
22. Health Maintenance Organization
23. Preferred Provider Organization
24. medical expenses, lost income
25. resources, needs

SOLUTIONS TO CASES

Case 10.1

1.   Roger's Total Health Care Expenses

Urgi-Care and ambulance	$ 250
Surgery and anesthesia	1,000
Hospital room and board ($250/day)	7,500
Drugs and rehabilitative care	850
Total	$9,600

<u>Roger's Expenses Covered by Insurance</u>

Urgi-care and ambulance	$ 250(.80)	$ 200
Surgery and anesthesia	1,000(.80)	800
Hospital room and board		
30 days x 230/day x (.80)*		5,520
Drugs and rehabilitative care	850(.80)	680
Total		$7,200
Less: $500 Deductible		500
		$6,700

Total expenses - Insurance benefits = Expenses paid by Roger
$9,600 - $6,700 = $2,900
     *$230/day x .80 = $184 (does not exceed internal limits)

2.   The drugs and rehabilitative expenses may be questionable. The rehabilitative expenses coverage is not a standard feature of every policy.

3.   Roger has incurred most of the expenses which he must pay himself for three reasons: the $500 deductible, the 80 percent coinsurance, and the daily room rate at the more costly hospital. Roger had to pay More than 30 percent of the total costs personally. This is a significant debt considering Roger's salary of $20,000 per year.

Case 10.2

1.   See following worksheets.

2.   Stacey is inadequately covered by $1,000 per month. Mike is only $100 short of recovering his monthly take-home pay (disability insurance plus social security) should he become disabled.

3.   Stacey should seek additional disability coverage since Mike's salary could not maintain their present disability needs. Stacey and Mike would face an annual deficit and not be able to meet their savings and investment goals or be able to enjoy entertainment or travel.

Present Annual Expenditures		Annual Expenditures (Stacey is disabled)	
Income	$72,000	Income	$60,000*
Less: Living Expenses (.75)	54,000	Living Expenses	54,000
Entertainment and Travel (.05)	3,600	Entertainment and Travel	3,600
Savings and Investment (.20)	14,400	Savings and Investment	14,400
	$ -0-		- $12,200

Mike could adequately compensate the shortfall of his disability with a slight increase in savings.

*Includes Stacey's disability income.

DISABILITY BENEFIT NEEDS

Name(s) _Stacey_   Date _January 1993_

1.	Estimate current monthly *take-home* pay		$ 3,000
2.	Estimate existing benefits:	$ 500	
	a. Social security benefits	0	
	b. Other government benefits	0	
	c. Company programs		
	d. Group disability policy benefits	1,500	
3.	Total existing disability benefits (2a + 2b + 2c + 2d)		$ 2,000
4.	Estimated monthly disability benefits needed ([1] − [3])		$ 1,000

DISABILITY BENEFIT NEEDS

Name(s) _Mike_   Date _January 1993_

1.	Estimate current monthly *take-home* pay		$ 3,000
2.	Estimate existing benefits:	$ 800	
	a. Social security benefits	0	
	b. Other government benefits	0	
	c. Company programs	2,100	
	d. Group disability policy benefits		
3.	Total existing disability benefits (2a + 2b + 2c + 2d)		$ 2,900
4.	Estimated monthly disability benefits needed ([1] − [3])		$ 100

CHAPTER 11

FILL IN THE BLANK ANSWERS

1. types of losses to which you are exposed, how best to cover them
2. complete inventory of property in need of insurance coverage, the perils against which protection is desired
3. peril
4. flood, earthquake, mud slides, nuclear radiation, wear and tear; nuclear radiation, wear and tear
5. liability
6. negligent
7. assumption of risk, contributory negligence
8. assumption of risk
9. contributory negligence
10. indemnity
11. insurable interest
12. Actual cash value
13. subrogation
14. other-insurance
15. Coinsurance
16. structure and contents, personal liability
17. basic, broad, special
18. Renter's insurance
19. the direct loss, an indirect loss, extra expenses resulting from these losses
20. personal property floater policy
21. replacement
22. Deductibles
23. automobile
24. personal auto policy (PAP)
25. automobile
26. Uninsured motorists
27. another motorist, insurance, damages
28. Collision
29. Comprehensive automobile
30. Age, sex, marital status, driving record
31. financial responsibility
32. captive

SOLUTIONS TO EXERCISES

Exercise 11-1

1. B
2. C
3. A
4. D

Exercise 11-2

The 75 percent coinsurance clause requires that the policy limits must equal or exceed 75 percent of the building (.75 x $400,000 = $300,000). Since the building is not insured adequately according to the coinsurance clause, the insurance company would be obligated to pay only $250,000/$300,000 of the claim up to the policy limit.

($250,000/$300,000) x $250,000 = $208,333

b.   No.   They would have received the $300,000 policy limits.

Exercise 11-3

1.	C	8.	C
2.	C	9.	C
3.	N	10.	C
4.	N	11.	C
5.	C	12.	C
6.	N	13.	N
7.	N		

Exercise 11-4

The HO-8 policy allows the homeowners to get their property repaired up to the full amount of their loss or up to its market value, whichever is less. If the house is totally destroyed, the homeowners will recover $100,000.

Exercise 11-5

1.   C
2.   C--but not fully covered since the policy limit for all injured parties is $50,000.
3.   C
4.   C
5.   N

Exercise 11-6
1.   Person B
2.   Person A
3.   Person B

CHAPTER 12

FILL IN THE BLANK ANSWERS

1. current income, major expenditures, retirement, shelter income from taxes
2. Common stock
3. Bonds
4. Preferred
5. convertible
6. mutual fund
7. business
8. Financial
9. market
10. purchasing power
11. fall
12. quickly, price
13. Event
14. current income, capital gain
15. compound
16. risk
17. expected rate of return
18. public
19. Right, preemptive
20. warrant
21. is not
22. stockholders meetings, proxy
23. Par
24. dividends
25. Book value
26. profit margin
27. return on equity
28. earnings per share
29. price/earnings ratio
30. Beta
31. Blue chip
32. Growth
33. income
34. Speculative
35. cyclical, defensive
36. denominations
37. Discount, premium
38. Senior, Junior
39. debenture
40. sinking fund
41. call premium
42. Registered, bearer
43. Treasury
44. Agency
45. Municipal

46. Junk
47. rating
48. coupon, maturity, market interest rates
49. Preferred, convertible
50. does
51. conversion ratio, market price

SOLUTIONS TO EXERCISES

Exercise 12-1

1.	B	5.	F
2.	C	6.	G
3.	G	7.	A
4.	E	8.	D

Exercise 12-2

1. B
2. D
3. F
4. G
5. E
6. C
7. A

Exercise 12-3

$$\text{Approximate yield} = \frac{CI + [(FP - CP)/N]}{(CP + FP)/2}$$

where

CI = average annual current income
FP = expected future price of investment
CP = current price of investment
N = investment period

a.

$$\text{Common stock approximate yield} = \frac{\$5 + [(\$100 - \$90)/5]}{(\$100 + \$90)/2}$$

$$= \quad \$7/\$95 = 7.4\%$$

b.

$$\text{Preferred stock approximate yield} = \frac{\$2.50 + [\$75 - \$60)/2]}{(\$75 + \$60)/2}$$

$$= \quad \$10/\$67.50 = 14.8\%$$

c.   Bond approximate yield $= \dfrac{\$35 + [(\$950 - \$1,000)/0.5]}{(\$950 + \$1,000)/2}$

$= -\$65/\$975 = -6.7\%$

d.   Note approximate yield $= \dfrac{\$0 + [(\$550 - \$400)/3]}{(\$550 + \$400)/2}$

$= \$50/\$475 = 10.5\%$

Exercise 12-4

Dividend yield = Annual dividend received per share/market price per share

a. Dividend yield = $1.50/$100 = 1.5 percent per quarter or 6 percent per year
b. Dividend yield is not relevant; a stock dividend is not cash
c. Dividend yield = $15/$125 = 12 percent

Exercise 12-5

a.   Dividend yield = Annual dividend received/market price per share
$= \$3.75/\$75.00 = 5\%$

b.   Book value per share $= \dfrac{\text{Assets - (liabilities + preferred stock)}}{\text{Number of shares outstanding}}$

$= \dfrac{\$36,000,000 - (\$14,400,000 + \$5,400,000)}{750,000}$

$= \dfrac{\$16,200,000}{750,000} = \$21.60$ book value per share

c.   Earnings per share $= \dfrac{\text{(Net profits after taxes - preferred dividends paid)}}{\text{Number of shares of common stock outstanding}}$

$= \dfrac{\$4,500,000 - \$432,000}{750,000} = \$5.42$

d.   P/E ratio = Price per share/EPS = $75.00/$5.42 = $13.84

e.   Net profit margin = net profit after tax/net sales
$= \$4,500,000/\$60,000,000$
$= .075$ or 7.5%

Exercise 12-6

a. $(12\%)(.75) = 9\%$ Stock A is predicted to <u>increase</u> 9%.
b. $(15\%)(1) = 15\%$ Stock B is predicted to <u>decrease</u> by 15%.
c. $(5\%)(1.2) = 6\%$ Stock C is predicted to <u>increase</u> by 6%.

Exercise 12-7

1. B
2. C
3. D
4. C
5. A
6. D

Exercise 12-8

$$\text{Fully taxable equivalent yield} = \frac{\text{Yield of municipal bond}}{(1 - \text{tax rate})}$$

$$= 6 \text{ percent}/(1 - .28)$$
$$= 8.3 \text{ percent; choose the municipal bond}$$

Exercise 12-9

Current yield = Annual interest yield/Market price of bond

$$\text{Approximate yield to maturity} = \frac{CI + [(\$1,000 - CP)/N]}{(CP + \$1,000)/2}$$

	Current Yield	Approximate Yield to Maturity
Bond A:	$[(.10)(\$1,000)]/\$1,000 = 10\%$	$\dfrac{(\$100)+[(\$1,000 - \$1,000)/10]}{(\$1,000 + \$1,000)/2}$ $= 10\%$
Bond B:	$[(.08)(\$1,000)]/\$950 = 8.4\%$	$\dfrac{(\$80) + [(\$1,000 - \$950)/5]}{(\$950 + \$1,000)/2}$ $= \$90/\$975 = 9.2\%$
Bond C:	$[(.12)(\$1,000)]/\$1,200 = 10\%$	$\dfrac{(\$120)+[(\$1,000 - \$1,200)/15]}{(\$1,200 + \$1,000)/2}$ $= \$106.67/\$1,100 = 9.7\%$
Bond D:	$[(.05)(\$1,000)]/\$1,050 = 4.8\%$	$\dfrac{(\$50) + [(\$1,000 - \$1,050)/20]}{(\$1,050 + \$1,000)/2}$ $= \$47.50/\$1,025 = 4.6\%$

Exercise 12-10

2 years in arrears x $5/share = $10/share
    Current year x $5/share = <u>$ 5/share</u>
                                 $15/share

100 shares x $15 = $1,500 total dividends

If the stock had been noncumulative, William would have received only the current year dividend of $5 per share.

Exercise 12-11

a. $1,000/$50 per share = 20 shares
b. $42 x 20 shares = $840; of course, Marcus would not exercise his conversion since it would result in a loss.
c. $55 x 20 shares = $1,100
       $1,100 - $1,000 = $100 profit

SOLUTIONS TO CASE PROBLEMS

Case 12.1

See worksheet following this page.

DETERMINING AMOUNT OF INVESTMENT CAPITAL

Financial goal: *To accumulate $250,000 cash for their retirement in 20 years.*

1. Targeted Financial Goal (see Note 1)	$ **250,000**
2. Projected Average Return on Investments	**10%**
A. Finding a Lump Sum Investment:	
3. Future Value Factor, from Appendix A ■ based on **20** years to target date and a projected average return on investment of **10%**	**6.72**
4. Required Lump Sum Investment ■ line 1 ÷ line 3	$ **37,202**
B. Making a Series of Investments Over Time:	
5. Amount of Initial Investment, if any (see Note 2)	$ **-0-**
6. Future Value Factor, from Appendix A ■ based on **20** years to target date and a projected average return on investment of **10%**	**6.72**
7. Terminal Value of Initial Investment ■ line 5 × line 6	$ **-0-**
8. Balance to Come From Savings Plan ■ line 1 − line 7	$ **250,000**
9. Future Value Annuity Factor, from Appendix B ■ based on **20** years to target date and a projected average return on investment of **10%**	**57.2**
10. Series of Annual Investments Required Over Time ■ line 8 ÷ line 9	$ **4,371**

Note 1: The "targeted financial goal" is the amount of money you want to accumulate by some target date in the future.

Note 2: If you're starting from scratch—i.e., there is no initial investment—enter a zero in line 5, skip lines 6 and 7, and then use the total targeted financial goal (from line 1) as the amount to be funded from a savings plan; now proceed with the rest of the worksheet.

CHAPTER 13

FILL IN THE BLANK ANSWERS

1. capital, money
2. primary, secondary
3. underwriting
4. prospectus
5. securities exchanges, over-the-counter market
6. seat
7. listed
8. New York Stock Exchange
9. American Stock Exchange
10. regional
11. National Association of Securities Dealers Automated Quotation System (NASDAQ)
12. bid, ask
13. market makers
14. Securities and Exchange Commission
15. Blue sky
16. bull, bear
17. Stockbrokers
18. street
19. Securities Investor Protection Corporation (SIPC)
20. odd, round
21. Discount brokers
22. market
23. limit
24. stop-loss
25. margin
26. Federal Reserve Board
27. short sale
28. stockholders reports
29. Dow Jones Industrial Average, Standard & Poor's Index
30. diversification
31. asset allocation

SOLUTIONS TO EXERCISES

Exercise 13-1

Stock: 25 shares at $138 per share = $3,450
Bonds: 10 bonds at $1,310 per bond = $13,100

Brokerage commission on stock:	$29.50 + (.013)($3,450)	
	$29.50 + $44.85 =	$ 74.35
Brokerage commission on bonds:	$10 per bond x 10 bonds =	$100.00
Total commissions		$174.35

Exercise 13-2

Transaction		Without Margin	With Margin
	Dollars invested:		
a.	Jordan's investment	$ 8,050	$ 4,830
	Borrowing	0	3,220
	Total purchase	$ 8,050	$ 8,050
	Sale of stock gross proceeds	11,700	11,700
	Less: Interest at 9 percent borrowing	0	290
	Net proceeds	$11,700	$11,410
	Less: Total investment	8,050	8,050
b.	Net profit/loss	$ 3,650	$ 3,360

$$\text{Return on investment} \qquad d. \quad \frac{\$3,650}{\$8,050} = 45\% \quad c. \quad \frac{\$3,360}{\$4,830} = 70\%$$

Exercise 13-3

Dana Corporation: $34.88 - $28.00 = $6.88/share gain
$ 6.88 x 100 shares = $688.00 gain

ChrisCraft: $50.25 - $73.63 = $23.38 loss
$23.38 x 150 shares = $3,507 loss

This large loss on ChrisCraft proves Kay should pay more attention to her portfolio or place a stop loss order on the short sale.

Exercise 13-4

52 Weeks						Vol				Net
High	Low	Stock	Div	%	P-E	100s	High	Low	Close	Chg.
25 1/4	14 7/8	Bally Mfg	.24	1.1	20	1113	22 1/4	21 3/4	22 1/4	+5/8

a. (1) $22.25 per share
 (2) 111,300
 (3) $.24/4 = $.06
 (4) P-E ratio = 20
   P/E = 22.25/20 = 20
   PE is a multiple of EPS; therefore $22.25/20 = $1.1125

Bonds		Curr Yld	Vol	Close	Net Chg.
Occi	10-1/2 03	9.0	15	116 5/8	+1/8

b. (1) 10.5 percent coupon rate
 (2) $1,000 x .105 = $105.00 interest per year
 (3) 2003
 (4) 15

(5) $1,166.25. Bond prices are quoted as a percentage of the bond's face ($1,000).
116.625% x $1,000 = $1,166.25

(6) $1,000. Corporations are obligated to pay face value.

Exercise 13-5

There is no solution available since the data is subjective.

SOLUTIONS TO CASE PROBLEMS

Case 13.1

1. Gregory has received a legal judgment based on his physical disability. Should he in the future not be able to work at all, he will need this cash to live on. Gregory's investment objectives should be to preserve his principal by being a conservative investor. Since he is currently employed and makes enough money to cover his expenses, he does not need current income from his investments.

2. Gregory is planning to invest 40 percent of his cash in speculative real estate. Even though his friends feel assured their investment will be successful, it is too great a sum for Gregory to gamble. Of the remainder of his portfolio, 30 percent is in blue-chip common stocks, 20 percent is in Aaa-rated bonds, and 10 percent in money market instruments. This mix is satisfactory based on Gregory's investment goals since they are relatively safe and do provide current income in the event Gregory needs additional cash.

3. Gregory should not commit $100,000 to a speculative real estate investment. If he could invest a smaller amount, say $20,000, the risk of losing the cash would not be devastating. The rest of the portfolio could remain in the investment choices he has made with the addition possibly of a small percentage of growth stocks or a growth mutual fund.

CHAPTER 14

FILL IN THE BLANK ANSWERS

1. mutual fund
2. open, closed
3. Open-end
4. closed-end, open end
5. no load
6. Maximum capital gains
7. Sector funds
8. growth fund
9. Equity-income
10. Money market mutual
11. income
12. Growth-and-income
13. Balanced funds
14. diversification, money managers, return, convenience
15. dividend, capital gains, NAV
16. conversion privileges
17. Automatic reinvestment
18. the future course of the market, past performance of the fund itself
19. cash, value, return, leverage
20. Leverage
21. potential population growth or real estate demand
22. Limited partnerships
23. single property syndicate
24. blind pool syndicate
25. Real Estate Investment Trust
26. Commodities
27. Financial
28. stock option
29. put, call
30. put
31. call

SOLUTIONS TO EXERCISES

Exercise 14-1

1. O
2. C
3. C
4. O
5. O
6. O

Exercise 14-2

1. B
2. N
3. L
4. LL

Exercise 14-3

a. NAV = (total market value of securities - liabilities)/number of shares
   NAV = ($10,500,000 - $2,000,000)/(1,500,000) = $5.67/share
b. $5.67 - $4.92 = .75

Exercise 14-4

1. H
2. F
3. C
4. B
5. D
6. E
7. A
8. G

Exercise 14-5

Approximate yield = Dividends + capital gains distributions + [(ending price - beginning price)/1 year period]/[(ending price + beginning price)/2]

Approximate yield Fund 1: $\dfrac{\$1.25 + \$0.75 + [(\$14.50 - \$13.25)/1]}{(\$14.50 + \$13.25)/2}$

$$= \frac{\$ 3.25}{\$13.88} = 23.4\%$$

Approximate yield Fund 2: $\dfrac{\$0.50 + \$0.10 + [(\$5.00 - \$4.00)/1]}{(\$5.00 + \$4.00)/2}$

$$= \frac{\$1.60}{\$4.50} = 35.6\%$$

Approximate yield Fund 3: $\dfrac{\$2.00 + \$0.05 + [(\$13.50 - \$12.00)/1]}{(\$13.50 + \$12.00)/2}$

$$= \frac{\$3.55}{\$12.75} = 27.8\%$$

Exercise 14-6

a. 25,000 lbs x .6275 = $15,687.50 total price of contract
$15,687.50 x .20 margin = $3,137.50
b. 25,000 lbs x (.64 - .6275) = $312.50
c. $312.50/$3,137.50 = 10% approximately

Exercise 14-7

A put is an option contract to sell a security over a set period of time at a specified price.

A call is an option contract to buy a security over a set period of time at a specified price.

(1) $55 - $45 = $10 gain per share
$10 x 100 shares = $1,000
$1,000 - $200 = $800 gain
Return = $800/$200 = 400%

(2) $55 - $35 = $20 gain per share
$20 x 200 shares = $4,000
$4,000 - $900 = $3,100 gain
Return = $3,100/$900 = 344%

(3) $75 - $65 = $10 gain per share
$10 x 300 shares = $3,000
$3,000 - $1,200 = $1,800 gain
Return = $1,800/$1,200 = 150%

(4) Since the striking price of the call option is higher than the current market price, the call option would not be exercised.

(5) Since the striking price of the put option is lower than the current market price, the put option would not be exercised.

Exercise 14-8

a) Return on investment = After tax profits/Total investment

$$ROI = \frac{\$20,000 \times (1 - .28)}{\$175,000} = 8.2\%$$

b) $$ROI = \frac{(\$20,000 - \$8,400^*)(1 - .28)}{\$105,000} = 8.0\%$$

* $70,000 x .12 = $8,400 interest

Since the ROI is higher if she purchases the duplex with cash, this method of financing is recommended.

SOLUTIONS TO CASE PROBLEMS

Case 14.1

1. The limited real estate partnership would require an investment of nearly all of his savings. Although annual returns on these types of investments in the past often ranged between 10-25 percent of the amount invested, there is no guarantee of the return or the safety of the principal. The liquidity of this investment is also very limited. Phil should diversify his portfolio into a variety of investments. If he could find a limited real estate partnership with a smaller minimum investment, it could become a part of a planned diversified portfolio.

2. The commodities future contract will require a $32,500 investment, a significant portion of Phil's savings. Trading in commodities is risky and there is great potential of losing his investment. From the given information, it is not likely that Phil has any experience in commodities trading. If Phil is not prepared to absorb losses, he should not invest in commodities.

3. Phil must risk either losing the market opportunity for his invention by not having enough savings to finance the project or risk losing some of his savings through speculative investing. Phil's friends have chosen two inappropriate investments for his situation; the real estate limited partnership absorbs too much of his total savings and the commodities future contract is too risky for a novice trader. Phil would be well-advised to find some middle ground between certificates of deposits and commodities - perhaps a portion of Phil's portfolio should be invested in a well diversified mutual fund with a focus on growth stocks.

CHAPTER 15

FILL IN THE BLANK ANSWERS

1. as soon as you begin working
2. setting retirement goals, developing an investment program
3. social security, income-producing assets, pension plans
4. Social Security
5. payroll taxes (FICA)
6. current funding, pension fund
7. 67
8. investment
9. 40
10. 62
11. survivor's benefits
12. Personal Earnings and Benefit Estimate Statement
13. $9,720, $1
14. sometimes
15. annuity
16. accumulation
17. single-premium
18. period certain
19. refund annuity
20. with no refund
21. annuity certain
22. temporary life annuity
23. fixed-dollar
24. variable annuity
25. Life insurance
26. attract and retain quality employees, meet demands of collective bargaining, provide benefits to owners and key managers
27. noncontributory
28. vested
29. vested
30. cliff, graded schedule
31. contribution
32. benefit
33. unfunded
34. funded
35. supplementary
36. reduction
37. Keogh
38. self-directed

SOLUTIONS TO EXERCISES

Exercise 15-1

1. N
2. C
3. N
4. C
5. N
6. C

Exercise 15-2

a. $40,000(.15) = $6,000
      $6,000(.28) = $1,680
b. $6,000 - $1,680 = $4,320

Exercise 15-3

Future Value of an Annuity for 30 years at 10 percent is 164 from Appendix C.

Money accumulated = $30,000 x 164 = $4,920,000.

SOLUTIONS TO CASE PROBLEMS

Case 15.1

1.   See following worksheet.

2.   This analysis only considers normal household expenditures and does not take into account the special goals of the Mescons. The approximate costs of these goals would have to be estimated and factored into the analysis.

3.   The Mescons have savings currently of $40,000. If they earn 8 percent on their investments over the next 35 years, they will have $588,000 ($40,000 x 14.7). This should be more than enough to cover their shortfall.

Case 15.2

Laura will become fully vested in two more years and will become eligible for pension benefits. If she accepts the higher level position and terminates her current employment, she will forfeit these pension benefits. Before finalizing her career decision, Laura should assess her financial situation. However, her situation is not as bad as it would have been several years ago. If we assume that the seven year vesting requirement means that her current employer offers a graded vesting plan, Laura could be about 60 percent vested right now so she should not lose all her pension benefits. This new law also means that Laura should receive pension benefits from her new employer if she works for five or seven years.

PROJECTING RETIREMENT INCOME AND INVESTMENT NEEDS

Name(s) **Robert & Debbie Mescon**　　Date **January 1993**

I.　Estimated Household Expenditures in Retirement:

A.　Approximate number of years to retirement **35**

B.　*Current* level of annual household
expenditures, excluding savings .... $ **62,000**

C.　Estimated household expenses in retirement *as a*
percent of current expenses .... **.75**

D.　Estimated annual household expenditures
in retirement (B x C) .... $ **46,500**

II.　Estimated Income in Retirement:

E.　Social security, annual income ..... **$1,676 × 12** .... $ **20,112**

F.　Company/employer pension plans,
annual amounts .... $ **20,000**

G.　Other sources, annual amounts .... $ **0**

H.　Total annual income (E + F + G) .... $ **40,112**

I.　Additional required income, or *annual* shortfall (D – H) .... $ **6,388**

III.　Inflation Factor:

J.　Expected average annual rate of inflation
over the period to retirement **5%**

K.　Inflation factor (in Appendix A):
Based on _____ years to retirement (A) and an expected
average annual rate of inflation (J) of _____ **5.51**

L.　Size of inflation-adjusted
annual shortfall (I x K) .... $ **35,198**

IV.　Funding the Shortfall:

M.　Anticipated return on assets held
after retirement **8%**

N.　Amount of retirement funds required—size of nest egg (L + M) .... $ **439,975**

O.　Expected rate of return on
investments *prior* to retirement **8%**

P.　Compound interest factor (in Appendix B):
Based on **35** years to retirement (A) and an expected
rate of return on investments of **8%** (O) **172**

Q.　Annual savings required to fund
retirement nest egg (N + P) .... $ **2,558**

Note: Parts I and II are prepared in terms of current (today's) dollars.

CHAPTER 16

FILL IN THE BLANK ANSWERS

1. state
2. People planning
3. $600,000
4. first-level
5. Second-level
6. liquidity
7. living death
8. estate
9. probate
10. gross
11. life insurance
12. Social security
13. will
14. Intestacy
15. testator
16. attorney
17. introductory
18. direction of payments
19. dispositive
20. pecuniary legacy
21. appointment
22. tax
23. common disaster
24. execution, attestation
25. two or three
26. mental competency, freedom of choice, proper execution
27. undue influence
28. codicil
29. right of election
30. lodging
31. letter of last instructions
32. probate process
33. joint tenancy, tenants by the entirety
34. trust, grantor, trustee, beneficiaries
35. trust principal, res
36. corporate trustee
37. testamentary
38. grantor
39. step-up
40. funded
41. gift, estate
42. $10,000
43. unified tax credit

44. inheritance, estate
45. credit, gap
46. divide, deduct, defer, discount

SOLUTIONS TO CASE PROBLEMS

Case 16.1

1. If Jonathon dies intestate, his separately-owned assets would be distributed one-third to his spouse and two-thirds to his children after deduction of debts, taxes and state family exemptions.

2. The key components of Jonathon's will should include: 1) the introductory clause, 2) directions of payments, 3) dispositive provisions, 4) appointment clause, 5) tax clause, 6) common disaster clause, 7) execution and attestation clause, and 8) witness clause.

3. In order to change an existing will, a codicil may be drawn up stating the new beneficiary. Or a will may be revoked by: 1) making a later will that expressly revokes prior wills, 2) making a codicil that revokes prior wills, 3) making a later will that is inconsistent with a prior will, and 4) physically mutilating, burning, tearing or defacing the will with the intention of revoking it.

4. No. For a will to be properly executed, it must be in writing and signed by the testator and witnesses at the logical end. Jonathon may create a video letter of last instructions if he feels compelled to leave a visual record with parting comments. He should have his will prepared as a written document.

5. The executor must collect the assets of the decedent, pay debts or provide the debt payments that are not currently due, and distribute any remaining assets to the persons entitled to them by will. Sid is probably a good choice since he is Jonathon's business partner, most likely is familiar with Jonathon's affairs, and should have good administrative skills.

Case 16.2

The worksheet solution follows this page.

COMPUTING NET FEDERAL ESTATE TAXES PAYABLE

Name _Connie Reisman_   Date _January 1993_

Line	Computation	Item	Amount	Total Amount
1		*Gross estate*		$3,575,657
	Subtract sum of:	(a) Funeral expenses	$ 7,900	
		(b) Administrative expenses	13,510	
		(c) Debts	215,000	
		(d) Taxes	0	
		(e) Losses	0	
2	Result:	*Adjusted gross estate*		$3,339,247
	Subtract sum of:	(a) Marital deduction	0	
		(b) Charitable deduction	25,000	
3	Result:	*Taxable estate*		$3,314,247
4	Add:	*Adjusted taxable gifts*		$ 0
5	Result:	*Tentative tax base*		$3,314,247
6	Compute:	*Tentative estate tax*	$ 1,463,636	
7	Subtract:	Gift taxes payable on post-1976 gifts	0	
8	Result:	*Estate tax payable before credits*		$1,463,636
9	Subtract sum of:	(a) Unified tax credit	$ 192,800	
		(b) State death tax credit	211,368	
		(c) Credit for tax on prior transfers	49,200	
		(d) Credit for foreign death taxes	0	$ 453,368
10	Result:	*Net federal estate tax payable*		$1,010,268

266

Cases

THE GARNETT CASE STUDY

Meet Scott and Paula Garnett! Scott and Paula are a young couple in their early 30's who after six years of marriage became the proud parents of twins--Jason and Amy. As you might expect, the twins (now two years old) have changed many aspects of Scott and Paula's lives--simple things like eating a full meal all at once, sleeping late in the morning, etc. But on a more serious note, Paula did quit her job as the Head Dietician at a local hospital and is now teaching Chemistry at Bowie High School so her schedule would be better suited to raising children. This career change resulted in a $10,000 reduction in after-tax income. Paula is able to make up some of that difference by working part time for the hospital during the summer. Scott, an engineer with the telephone company, has been able to reduce the amount of travel involved with his job in the past couple years.

Another change since the birth of Jason and Amy is that the Garnett's house which they purchased four years ago keeps getting smaller. Even though it is a 3-bedroom home, it is only 1300 square feet and there is almost no yard for the children. In fact, the need for a larger home and the desire to start saving for the twins' college education are the main reasons Scott and Paula are now interested in getting financial planning help.

Scott and Paula have decided to work with Sarah Harrison, C.F.P., a professional financial planner recommended by Paula's parents. After their initial meeting with Ms. Harrison, Scott and Paula felt very comfortable about her abilities to assist them with their goals. They also liked the fact that she is a fee-only planner and does not sell any financial products. Scott and Paula feel that since they are paying a flat fee of $1,500 for their original plan plus $350 a year for annual updates (if they want updates), they will get unbiased advise.

One of the purposes of the first meeting with the financial planner was for Ms. Harrision to find out "who" the Garnetts are. She asked both Scott and Paula to talk informally about their past as well as what they wanted for the future. From this discussion she learned the following:

--Both Scott and Paula grew up in middle class families where their fathers are professionals and their mothers are homemakers.

--Before the twins came, Scott and Paula had higher incomes and lower expenses than they do now. They are still trying to cope with the resulting new spending patterns. They used to pay off their revolving credit at the end of each month. Now they have nearly $6,000 in outstanding credit card debt.

--Neither Scott nor Paula are too knowledgeable about personal finances. In the past, they just paid their bills and tried to learn from their mistakes. Now that they are on a tighter budget, they want to take better control of their finances.

--Scott and Paula are struggling over how to manage their joint checking account. Since both of them write checks on the same account, they sometimes have difficulty remembering to record their checks. When they had more discretionary income, they just kept a larger balance in their checking account and didn't worry about the problem. Now they feel they must try to resolve this management problem.

--Because of their lack of investment knowledge, they are willing to take only low-to-moderate risks with their investments. They are willing to commit some of their investment funds to the stock market; however, they like the idea of doing this through mutual funds.

--Both Scott and Paula love to spoil Jason and Amy with presents and designer clothes, but lately when Scott has brought huge teddy bears and other expensive toys home from trips there have been "discussions" about overspending. Similar "discussions" have centered on the cost of eating out for lunch every day. Paula has to take her lunch to school (or eat at the school cafeteria) so she has noticed how much can be saved by brown-bagging rather than eating out. On the advice of a personal finance book they have just read, Scott and Paul have already decided to allocate $75 a month "fun money" to each of them in their 1993 budget. This will be money they can spend any way they want--no explanations required! This was a strategy recommended by the book to help couples who were having disagreements about how money was being spent.

--While the family is generally healthy, Paula suffers from allergies and has been taking allergy shots regularly. Scott is about 50 pounds overweight. His doctor is encouraging him to drop the extra weight especially since heart problems are present in his family. Although both of his parents are still living, Scott's father had a heart attack at age 45.

At the end of their first meeting with Ms. Harrison, she gave Scott and Paula a packet of forms to fill out and return to her before their next meeting. These forms are presented on the following pages. Read over the information Scott and Paula provided so that you can get to know them and their financial situation better.

PERSONAL FINANCIAL INFORMATION

CLIENT INFORMATION

NAME   Scott Allen Garnett

BIRTH DATE   3/7/61

SOCIAL SECURITY NO.   385-01-1658

BUSINESS PHONE   512/555-5800

SPOUSE INFORMATION

NAME   Paula Lynne Garnett

BIRTH DATE   1/12/62

SOCIAL SECURITY NO.   412-58-1711

BUSINESS PHONE   512/555-1144

RESIDENCE ADDRESS   5276 Sunset Blvd.

CITY, STATE & ZIP   Kingsland, USA 78732

RESIDENCE PHONE   512/555-5187

WEDDING DATE   4/28/85

CHILDREN

Name	Birth Date	Social Security No.	Grade
Jason Scott Garnett	1/15/91	456-86-3291	ABC Child Care
Amy Lynne Garnett	1/15/91	456-89-1661	ABC Child Care

EDUCATION

	School	Degree	Year Received
Scott	State University	B.S. Engineering	8/83
Paula	North State University	B.S. Nutrition	5/83

OCCUPATION

	Employer	Position	Years From To
Scott	General Telephone Corp.	Field Engineer	6/87 - present
Paula	Kingsland Ind. School Dist.	Chemistry Teacher	8/91 - present

CONSULTANTS FOR FINANCIAL PLANNING

	Name	Address	Phone
Bank Officer	Deana Hunter	Bank of the Hills Kingsland, USA 78704	555-4882
Insurance Agent	Warren Heaton	2169 6th Street Kingsland, USA 78701	555-2217
Securities Broker	Robert McDonald	First City Center, Suite 606 Kingsland, USA 78711	555-5808

LOCATION OF DOCUMENTS		
Wills/Trusts		None
Insurance:	Life	Group policies through General Telephone Corp. and Kingsland Ind. School Dist. Information booklets on file at home
	Health	Group policies through General Telephone Corp. and Kingsland Ind. School Dist. Information booklets on file at home
	Disability	Group policy through General Telephone Corporation Information booklet on file at home
	Auto & Home-owners	Files including policies at home
Deeds: Title to cars & Deed to house		File at home
Birth/Marriage/Other Certificates		Uncertain

ASSETS - January 1, 1993

All assets are joint/community property unless otherwise noted.

	LOCATION	BALANCE	RATE OF INTEREST	MATURITY
CHECKING:	Bank of the Hills	$1,750	3.0%	N/A
MONEY MARKET ACCOUNT:	General Telephone Credit Union	$6,663	4.5%	N/A
CD's:	Bank of the Hills	$2,200	5.0%	12/15/93
	General Telephone Credit Union	$ 750	5.2	12/12/93
CASH ON HAND:		$ 350		

	Year Purchased	Purchase Price	Current Market Value	Replacement Value
PERSONAL RESIDENCE:	1989	$75,000	$87,750	$90,000

SECURITY INVESTMENTS:

# Shares	Security	Cost or Basis			Current Value	
		Date Acquired	Per Share	Total	Per Share	Total
100	IBM Stock (High School graduation gift to Paula)	5/10/80	90-1/8	$9,013	64-1/2	$6,450
100	Walgreen's Stock	9/15/86	38-1/2	$3,850	43	$4,300
220.02	Kemper International	3/28/86	9.09	$2,000	8.24	$1,813
180.18	--reinvested dividends and capital gains distributions	quarterly thru reinvestment	varied	don't know	8.24	$1,485
183.48	Evergreen Fund (IRA-Scott)	3/25/85	10.90	$2,000	14.24	$2,613
109.65	--reinvested dividends and capital gains distributions	quarterly thru reinvestment	varied	don't know	14.24	$1,561

	Year	Make	Model	Cost	Current Value
AUTOMOBILES:	1987	Honda	Accord	$14,050	$ 4,500
	1991	Dodge	Caravan	$17,000	$13,000

PERSONAL PROPERTY:

	Market Value
Clothing	$ 8,525
Furniture & Appliances	$21,500
Stereo, TV, and Camera Equipment	$10,750
Fishing boat	$ 2,000
Jewelry --includes diamond ring ($5,600), gold watch ($1,000), diamond & ruby pin ($7,800), and antique diamond earrings ($5,300) in addition to costume jewelry (listed jewelry is Paula's separate property)	$24,500
Computer Equipment	$ 2,500

EMPLOYER-SPONSORED RETIREMENT ACCOUNTS:

Scott	$ 6,215
Paula	$ 1,575
Scott--401(k)	$ 6,516

LIABILITIES - January 1, 1993

LOANS:

To Whom Owed	Original Amount of Account	Property or Service Purchased	Interest Rate	Current Balance	Payment Amount	How often Paid	Total Number of Payments	Date for First Payment
Gen Tel Credit Union	$13,000	Dodge Caravan	11%	$6,939	$335.99	monthly	48	12/20/90
Gen Tel Credit Union	$ 3,500	Computer Equipment	9.5%	$2,442	$112.12	monthly	36	1/21/92
First Federal Savings	$ 7,485	Stafford Loan-Scott	5.5%	$1,023	$ 81.23	monthly	120	2/11/84
Kingsland National Bank	$67,500	Home	10.5%	$65,989	$617.45	monthly	360	3/16/89

CREDIT CARDS:

	Number	Annual Fee	Interest Rate	Maximum Line of Credit	Outstanding Balance	Minimum Monthly Payment	Grace Period	Calculation Method
Shamrock Gas	17 654 21176 51880	$ 0	18.5%	---	$ 0	Total balance on gasoline	yes	Av. Daily Bal.
Visa	2152 4619 2129 1781	$30	18.0%	$4,000	$1,363	10% of balance or $20, whichever is greater	yes	Adjusted Bal.
Mastercard Gold	2418 1781 4615 9063	$ 0	13.9%	$8,000	$2,360	5% of balance or $20, whichever is greater	no	Av. Daily Bal.
American Express	3280 34545 32189	$55	---	---	$ 0	Total balance	---	---
Dillards	1284 6675 8	$ 0	18.0%	$2,500	$ 843	10% of balance or $20, whichever is greater	yes	Av. Daily Bal.
Foleys	323 05 1762	$ 0	18.0%	$3,000	$ 529	5% of balance or $50 whichever is greater	yes	Av. Daily Bal.
Sears	465 323 621	$ 0	18.0%	$10,000	$ 825	3% of balance or $15, whichever is greater	yes	past due bal.

1992 INCOME

	Gross Income
Scott's salary	$41,000
Bonuses	0
Paula's salary	22,000
Summer job (June & July)	2,400
Interest[1]	543
Dividends[2]	622
Capital gains distributions[3]	208
Sale of Securities:	
Fidelity Puritan Mutual Fund[4]	3,532

Income after tax deductions but before insurance and retirement deductions (take-home pay):

Scott $2,574 per month
Paula $1,382 per month (Paula is paid over 12 months)
Paula $ 904 per month in June and July only

---

[1]Checking ($63 a year, paid monthly), money market account ($331 a year, paid monthly), CDs ($149 a year, paid in December).

[2]IBM ($484 a year), Walgreens ($52 a year), Kemper International Fund ($24 a year), and Evergreen Fund ($62 a year). All dividends are paid quarterly in March, June, September, and December.

[3]Kemper International Fund ($56 a year) and Evergreen Fund ($152 a year). Distributions are paid quarterly in March, June, September, and December.

[4]235 shares purchased on May 14, 1988 at $12.76 per share and sold January 5, 1992, at $15.03 per share.

1992 EXPENSES

	Cash Flow Monthly[5]	Cash Flow Annually
Medical/Dental Expenses (not covered by insurance)	$	$ 493
House payment ($449 principal & $6,955 interest annually)	617	7,404
Charitable contributions	25	300
Food/Groceries, etc.	330	3,960
Food away from home	110	1,320
Clothing	225	2,700
Utilities (electricity & water)	120	1,440
Telephone	30	360
Property taxes (paid as part of monthly house payment)	98	1,176
Furniture purchases (used proceeds of Fidelity Puritan sales)		2,500
Auto maintenance - gas, tires, etc.	140	1,680
Auto loan payments	336	4,032
Entertainment	75	900
August vacation (used proceeds of Fidelity Puritan sales)		1,000
Child care ($3,895 qualifies for child care credit)	350	4,200
Health & disability insurance	105	1,260
Life insurance	15	180
Auto insurance (paid semiannually in March & August)		1,195
Personal care	45	540
Federal income taxes withheld ($204/mo. extra in June & July)	893	11,124
Social Security taxes withheld ($92/mo. extra in June & July)	402	5,008
Stafford education loan payments	81	972
Computer loan payments	112	1,344
Interest paid on credit card debt (purchases are included in appropriate expenditure categories)	55	660
Homeowner's insurance (paid as part of monthly house payment)	38	456
Home maintenance & repair	65	780
Contributions to employer-sponsored retirement accounts	130	1560
Reinvested interest, dividends, & capital gains distributions		1373
Miscellaneous	150	1,800

[5]regular monthly expenditures

INSURANCE INFORMATION

LIFE INSURANCE:

*INSURED	Scott	Paula
Type of Life Insurance	Group Term	Group Term
Face amount	$82,000 (2 times salary)	$50,000
Beneficiary	Paula	Scott
Owner	Scott	Paula
Annual Premium	Employer paid	$15/month (payroll deduction)

DISABILITY INSURANCE:

*INSURED		Scott
Policy number		Employer group policy
Definition of Disability		Own job for 2 years, any job educationally suited for after 2 years
Mo. Benefit		65% of gross monthly salary
Waiting Period	Sick	90 days
	Accident	90 days
Benefit Period	Sick	to age 65
	Accident	to age 65
Premiums		$25/month (payroll deduction)
Comments		Policy includes a Social Security rider

MEDICAL INSURANCE:

*INSURED	Scott	Paula, Jason, & Amy
Company	Blue Cross Blue Shield	Prucare (HMO)
Policy Number	Group #251-365-2	Group # 248361
*HOSPITAL Room Rate	75% of semi-private rate	100% of semi-private rate
Number of Days	Unlimited	Unlimited
*Major Medical Maximum	$500,000/year	Unlimited
Deductible	$500/person/year	$15 copayment per doctor's visit $10 copayment per prescription
% participation	75/25	--
Cap on participation	$1,800/year	--
Maternity	Covered	Covered
Dental	No	No
Monthly Premiums	Employer paid for employee.	$80/month for Jason & Amy. Employer paid for employee.
*COMMENTS		
Scott's Policy:	Family members can be covered for $30/month/person. Coordination of benefits provision is included in policy.	
Paula's Policy:	Must use HMO facilities and selected hospitals. Family members can be covered for $40/month/person. Coordination of benefits provision is included in policy.	

AUTO INSURANCE:

*DESCRIPTION	(1) Honda Acord	(2) Dodge Caravan
Company	U.S. Casualty	U.S. Casualty
Policy Number	156-88876-AOB6	156-88876-AOB6
Liability	$40,000 or (20/40/15)	$40,000 or (20/40/15)
Medical Payments	$2,500/person	$2,500/person
Uninsured Motorist	$40,000 or (20/40/15)	$40,000 or (20/40/15)
Collision	(Actual Cash Value)	(Actual Cash Value)
Deductible	$250	$250
Comprehensive	(Actual Cash Value)	(Actual Cash Value)
Deductible	$50	$50
Annual Premium	$430	$765
Comments	Paid semi-annually in March and August	Same

HOMEOWNER'S INSURANCE:

*DESCRIPTION	Residence at 5276 Sunset Blvd.
Company	U.S. Property Insurance
Policy Number	368-11332-HO2
Type of Policy	HO-2
Coverages: --Dwelling --Other structures --Personal property --Loss of use --Personal liability --Medical payments	$70,000 $ 7,000 (10%) $35,000 (50%) $14,000 (20%) $25,000 $ 500/person
Deductible	$250
Annual Premium	$456

ESTATE PLANNING INFORMATION

Paula inherited the jewelry listed in the Personal Property section of this case from her maternal grandmother. Upon her death, Paula would like Amy to have the diamond ring and the antique diamond earrings. She would like Jason to have the gold watch and the diamond and ruby pin. With the above exceptions, Scott and Paula would like to leave all of their assets to each other. They would both like Jason and Amy to be their secondary beneficiaries. In case they both died, they would like Paula's parents to be Jason and Amy's legal guardians.

RETIREMENT INFORMATION

Person Covered	Scott	Paula
Type of pension plan	Qualified, non-contributory, defined benefits	Qualified, contributory, defined contribution, 8% average annual return over the past 5 years
Vesting	5 year cliff vesting, $6,215 currently vested	5 year cliff vesting, employer contribution not currently vested, $1,575 employee contributions currently accumulated
Mandatory employee contribution	Not applicable	3% of gross salary ($55/mo.) Contributions paid with before-tax income
Employer contribution	Unknown	5% of gross salary
Retirement age	Age 65	age 65 or 30 years of service (whichever comes first)
Annual benefits	3% of average annual salary over the last 5 years times the number of years of service	whatever annual annuity the funds in the account at retirement will buy
Death benefits	$100,000 received instead of retirement benefits	Same as retirement benefits
Beneficiary	Paula	Scott
Other plans available	401(k) - employer contributes $.50 for each $1.00 of employee contribution, 8% average return over the past 4 years	403(b)-no employer contribution, 8.6% average return over the past 2 years
Vesting	Immediate, $6,516 vested	Immediate
Employee contribution	Currently $75/month; maximum is 5% of salary	Currently $0; maximum is 10% of salary
Beneficiary	Paula	Not applicable

FINANCIAL GOALS

Short range (1 year):

> To start a regular savings plan, to have an adequate emergency fund, to buy a larger house, and to start saving for Jason and Amy's college educations.

Intermediate range (1-5 years):

> To pay off all revolving credit debt, and to buy a new car.

Long term (over 5 years):

> To take annual vacations and to be able to retire when Scott is 65 and live at least as well as they are now.

What is your single most important financial objective at this time:

> To buy a larger house.

- -

FINANCIAL PRIORITIES

	Scott	Paula
a. LIVING: paying monthly bills	1	1
b. PLEASURE: spending money	2	5
c. RETIREMENT: invest in future	8	8
d. DISABILITY: protect against	7	3
e. DEATH: take care of family	3	4
f. REDUCE TAXES: spend to save	6	7
g. INVESTING: accumulate assets	5	6
h. CHILDREN: future needs	4	2

Prioritized with 1 being most important and 8 being least important

OTHER INFORMATION

1.   Are you able to save regularly? <u>No, not voluntarily</u>

2.   How much are able to save annually? <u>approximately $2,900</u>
      Where? <u>In retirement accounts and through reinvestment of unearned income</u>

3.   Do you invest regularly? <u>No, not since the children's birth</u>

4.   Do feel that you are financially organized? <u>Yes--somewhat</u>

5.   Do you budget your money? <u>No written budget</u>

6.   If you were to die, could your spouse handle the finances?
                          Scott - <u>yes</u>

                          Paula - <u>yes</u>

7.   How do you feel about saving for retirement? <u>It's important, but other goals are more important right now.</u>

8.   If you had an extra $5,000 what would you do with it?
                          Scott - <u>buy a larger house</u>

                          Paula - <u>pay off the revolving debt</u>

9.   How do feel about taking investment risks?
                          Scott - <u>low- to-moderate</u>
                          Paula - <u>moderate</u>

10.   How is your health?   Scott - <u>Good except for weight problem</u>

                          Paula - <u>Very good except for allergies</u>

                          Jason - <u>Excellent</u>
                          Amy - <u>Excellent</u>

Scott and Paula Garnett would like your help in starting their financial plan. Review the Garnett's financial and personal information before answering the following questions.

1.   Using the January 1, 1993 asset and liability information, develop a balance sheet for Scott and Paula Garnett. Assume they have no unpaid bills.

2.   Using the income and expenditure information for 1992, complete an income and expenditures statement for Scott and Paula. Use the "cash flow" concept for this financial statement including all money inflows as income and all outflows as expenditures. Did Scott and Paula have a cash surplus or a cash deficit in 1992?

        What is the result of including the money received from selling assets (Fidelity Puritan Mutual Fund) as income? What is the result of including current saving (reinvested interest, dividends, capital gains distributions as well as contributions to employer-sponsored retirement accounts) as expenditures? What does an income and expenditures statement using the cash flow concept where all inflows and outflows are included show compared to a statement where investment inflows and savings are excluded?

3.   Based on the financial statements completed in Questions 1 and 2, calculate the savings, liquidity, solvency, and debt service ratios.

4.   Based on the information in the original case and in their financial statements, state at least 3 positive and 3 negative aspects of Scott and Paula's current financial position.

Scott and Paula would like to develop a budget to help them achieve one of their short term goals--to get better control of their spending. To start this process, they have restated their financial goal as follows:
        --to buy a larger home as soon as possible. They are willing to sell their stock to help pay for the downpayment and closing costs. They also plan to sell their current house.
        --to accumulate 3 month's after-tax income in money market accounts/funds within 2 years to be used as their emergency fund.
        --to pay off all of their revolving credit debt within the next 2 years.
        --to have the equivalent of $50,000 in today's dollar in 16 years for the twin's college education.
        --to continue contributing $900 a year to Scott's 401(k) plan.
        --to save $5,000 in 3 years for the downpayment on a new car.
        --to establish a regular savings program in the amount to accomplish their stated goals.

---

5.   Assuming that college expenses will increase at an annual rate of 6%, how much will Scott and Paula need in 16 years if they want the equivalent of $50,000 in today's dollar?

        How much will they need to have if college expenses increase 8% a year?

6.   Using future value calculations, how much would Scott and Paula have to save this year to be on track in meeting their goals for:
                --their emergency fund (remember they already have $6,663 in their money market account). They want to ignore Paula's extra summer income for the

purposes of calculating 3 month's after-tax income.
--the twin's college education fund (assuming college expenses increase 6% a year)
--the downpayment for a new car

Assume Scott and Paula can earn 5% on their emergency fund and car goals and 10% on their college savings goal.

7. Prepare a cash budget for the year of 1993 using the income and expenditure data from the original case as well as the figures needed to meet their goals (from Question 6). In addition, if they pay their current minimum monthly payments on their credit cards ($413), they will have these debts paid off in less than 2 years (assuming they pay off all future credit card purchases upon billing). The $413 monthly payments already include interest so do not budget additional money for interest on this credit card debt.

Assume that income and expenditures for 1993 will be the same as 1992 except:
--Scott's gross salary will be $42,500, Social Security withholding on his income will be $3,251, and income tax withholding will be $7,225.
--Paula's gross teaching salary will be $22,880, Social Security withholding on this income will be $1,750, and income tax withholding will be $3,890.
--Paula's contribution to her retirement plan will go up to $686 for the year.
--There will be no sale of securities.
--Furniture purchases and repairs are estimated to be only $500.
--They will take a short August vacation with an estimated cost of $450.
--They will allocate $150 a month for "fun money."
--They will pay the financial planning fee in four equal installments, $375 a month in January, February, March, and April.
--They will reduce miscellaneous expenditures to $50 a month.

8. Can Scott and Paula achieve all of their stated goals considering their income and expenditure patterns? If not, what recommendations would you make to help them achieve their goals?

9. Prepare a 1992 tax return for Scott and Paula using the financial data in the original case. (HINT: Subtract the $1,560 they contributed to their retirement plans from their gross salary before entering this income on the tax form. Also, remember that income earned on IRAs is tax-deferred.) Do they owe more taxes, or will Scott and Paula receive a refund? How much?

10. Assuming that 1993 will be similar to 1992 (except for the changes mentioned in Question 7), should Scott and Paula make any adjustments to their withholding allowances? If yes, should they increase or decrease the number of withholding allowances claimed?

11. What is Scott and Paula's average tax rate in 1992? What is their marginal tax rate?

12. Approximately how much did they save in taxes by investing $900 in Scott's 401(k) retirement account? (This move reduced their taxable income by $900.)

13. Given Scott and Paula's goals and risk tolerances, what tax strategies would you recommend to help them reduce their tax liability? Do they have enough money to implement the recommended tax strategies?

PART TWO: The Garnett Case Study

After reviewing their 1993 budget constructed in Part 1, Question 7, Scott and Paula have decided to:

1. pay off all their new credit card purchases upon billing.
2. reduce their dining out to $90 per month and clothing to $200 per month.
3. reduce their contribution to the children's college fund in 1993 to $2,400 ($200 per month). They plan to increase this in 1994 when Scott's Stafford Loan is paid off.
4. reduce their 1993 federal income tax withholding to $8,000. Reducing their income tax withholding increases their after-tax income to the following:

	Before-Tax Income	Social Security Tax Withheld	Federal Income Tax Withheld	After-Tax Income
Scott	$42,500	$3,251	$5,243	$34,006
Paula	22,880	1,750	2,517	18,613
Paula's summer job	2,400	184	240	1,976
TOTALS for 1993	$67,780	$5,185	$8,000	$54,595

----

1. Evaluate the amount of Scott and Paula's liquid assets. According to the general consensus of financial experts, do they currently have enough assets (3 - 6 months of after-tax income) in a highly liquid form? If no, how much should be added to liquid assets in order to meet the minimum requirements?

Scott and Paula have just received their January, 1993 bank statement for their NOW account. It contains the following information:

--ending balance	$1,562.15
--service charge	0.00
--interest earned	3.76

Their checkbook ledger shows a final balance of $1,389.34. However, the following checks and deposits are not listed on the bank statement and are, therefore, still outstanding:

check #1206 for $138.98
check #1210 for $65.99
deposit made on January 28 for $70.92
ATM withdrawal made January 29 for $35.00

----

2. Reconcile Scott and Paula's January bank statement. How much difference, if any, is there between the bank statement balance and the ending balance in their checkbook, after reconciliation?

Scott and Paula currently maintain their checking account at Bank of the Hills. However, they have other accounts and loans through Scott's credit union. They would like to compare the NOW accounts at these two financial institutions. Both are convenient and covered by federal deposit insurance.

Bank of the Hills
        --no service charge for accounts maintaining a minimum daily balance of $1,000
      --monthly service charge of $10 plus $.10 a check if the minimum daily balance falls
        below $1,000
        --3.0% (annual percentage rate) interest is paid monthly on the average daily balance
        --ATM fee of $.25 per transaction
        --stop payment fee of $15.00
        --insufficient funds fee of $15.00

General Telephone Credit Union
        --no service charge for accounts maintaining an average daily balance of $500
        --monthly service charge of $15 plus $.05 a check if average daily balance falls below $50
        --3.5% (annual percentage rate) interest is paid monthly on the average daily balance
        --ATM fee of $2.00 per month
        --stop payment fee of $20.00
        --insufficient funds fee of $20.00

Scott and Paula report that in an average month they write 40 checks and make 6 ATM transactions. They maintain an average daily balance in their checking account of $1,400, but the minimum daily balance falls to less than $1,000 about 2 months a year. They have used the stop payment service only once in the past 5 years, and they have never bounced a check.

----

3.   Using the above information, compare the positive and the negative aspects of these two accounts. How much interest would they earn in a year with each account? What would the service charges and ATM charges be in a year with each account? Which one would you recommend for Scott and Paula?

4.   Given Scott and Paula's problem with keeping track of their checking account (cited in the original case), would you recommend they continue to use a single joint account or should they open two individual checking accounts?

5.   Scott and Paula are wanting to start a regular savings program to help them achieve their goals. Assuming they want to make monthly contributions, what type of account would you recommend for their emergency fund?

6.   If Scott and Paula continue to contribute $900 each year to Scott's 401(k) retirement account earning 8% compounded annually, how much will they have accumulated in 28 years? Remember that they already have $6,516 in this account. Also note that Scott's employer contributes $.50 for every $1.00 Scott and Paula contribute.

          If Scott and Paula felt they needed to accumulate a total of $250,000 in this 401(k) in 28 years, how much would they have to contribute annually assuming an 8% annual return and the $6,516 that is already in the account?

One of Scott and Paula's short term goals is to buy a larger home as soon as possible. They have been house hunting for several months and have found a home they like that costs $128,000. While the lender requires only a 10% down payment, Scott and Paula plan on making a 15% down payment. They have also shopped for home mortgages and narrowed their choices to the following:

30-year fixed-rate mortgage
--8.5% interest with 1.5 points
--other closing costs of $3,100 (includes a 1% loan origination fee)
--monthly payments

30-year adjustable-rate mortgage (ARM)
--6.0% interest with 2 points
--other closing costs of $3,250 (includes a 1% loan origination fee)
--2.0% annual interest rate cap
--6.0% overall interest rate cap
--indexed to 1-year Treasury Bill rates
--monthly payments

Scott and Paula expect to have the following changes in expenditures associated with the purchase and maintenance of this house:
--property taxes of 1.6% of the house value ($2,048/year)
--homeowners insurance of $650/year
--private mortgage insurance of $180/year
--maintenance of 1.0% of the house value ($1,280/year)
--utility expenditures of $160/month
Scott and Paula expect to live in this house at least 10 years.

----

7. Compare and evaluate the two mortgages for Scott and Paula. What would be the front-end costs and the monthly payments for principal and interest on each of these mortgages? How much could the monthly payments for principal and interest go up on the ARM after the first year? Over the life of the loan? What are the characteristics of the T-Bill index used on the (ARM)? Keeping in mind their financial situation and risk tolerances, which mortgage would you recommend for Scott and Paula? Why?

8. Will Scott and Paula be able to qualify for the fixed-rate mortgage if the lender applies the following two affordability ratios:
    a. monthly mortgage payments cannot exceed 30% of the borrower's monthly before-tax income, and
    b. total monthly debt payments cannot exceed 36% of this same monthly before-tax income?
    c. If not, can they qualify for the adjustable-rate mortgage using these criteria?

    In figuring if Scott and Paula will qualify, use all of their income except the sale of securities and dividend income from the IBM and Walgreens stock that they may have to sell to buy the new house. Remember that they both received raises in 1993 (See beginning of Part 2). Also use the minimum required payments for the revolving credit ($413) as part of the monthly debt payments. The amount of their monthly house payment will be the sum of the following:

--monthly payment for principal and interest
--1/12 of their annual property taxes
--1/12 of their homeowners insurance premium
--1/12 of the annual private mortgage insurance premium

They expect to net at least $13,000 (after their current mortgage and selling expenses are paid) from the sale of their present house, and they are willing to sell all of their IBM and Walgreens stock to help pay for the front-end costs.

9. Assume the Garnetts sell their current house for $86,000 on February 26, 1993. The sales expenses, including real estate broker's commissions, are $6,160. After paying these expenses and paying off their mortgage balance (which would be down to $65,908), how much money will Scott and Paula have left to help with the purchase of their new home?

10. Assume Scott and Paula buy their new house February 28, 1993 using the adjustable-rate mortgage. They pay for the downpayment, points, and other closing costs with the net proceeds from the sale of their first house and with money from their IBM and Walgreens stock. They sell their IBM stock for $65.25 per share and the Walgreens Stock for $45.25 per share. The brokerage commissions on the sales are $163 for the IBM and $136 for the Walgreens. Any extra funds not needed to buy the house are deposited in their money market account.

Revise the Garnett's balance sheet as of February 28, 1993 to reflect the changes in their assets and liabilities. The new loan balances for their previous debts are: Dodge Caravan ($6,392), computer ($2,256), Stafford Loan ($869), bank credit cards ($3,523), and store credit cards ($2,067). Assume they made deposits of $516 per month to their money market account in January and February for their goals (emergency fund, car down payment, and college education). They also made regular contributions to their retirement plans both months. The market value of their Kemper International fund increased to $8.75 a share and their Evergreen Fund went up to $15.63 a share by February 28. While there would also be a slight increase in some of their assets due to reinvested interest income, disregard that on this balance sheet revision. Assume no other changes than the ones specifically mentioned in the evolving case. What is their new net worth? What is the primary reason Scott and Paula's net worth went down with the purchase of their new home?

11. Again assuming no other changes than the ones specifically mentioned (review Part 1 and Part 2), revise Scott and Paula's 1993 budget. Since they lived in their first home 2 months and their second home 10 months of the year, prorate all housing expenses accordingly. Note that since they sold their IBM and Walgreens stock they will receive no dividends from this stock. However, they will be receiving a tax refund (calculated in Part 1, Question 9) in 1993. How much is their new budget surplus (deficit)?

12. Estimate Scott and Paula's 1993 federal income taxes after the purchase of the new home. The mortgage interest paid on their first home before they sold it was $1,154 while the interest on their new home is expected to be $5,415 for 1993. Assume both the discount points and the loan origination fee paid on the purchase of their new home meet all the IRS rules to be deductible in the year paid. How does their 1993 tax estimate compare to their 1992 tax liability?

PART THREE: The Garnett Case Study

1. Calculate the minimum monthly payment for March, 1993 on each of Scott and Paula's credit cards using the following outstanding balances:

Visa	$1,188	Dillards	$743
MasterCard Gold	$2,335	Foleys	$499
		Sears	$825

2. What is Scott and Paula's debt safety ratio as of March, 1993? Evaluate their ability to handle their debt.

3. Calculate the finance charges on Scott and Paula's Visa and MasterCard Gold with the following monthly transactions:

	VISA			MASTERCARD GOLD	
Date	Transaction	Amount	Date	Transaction	Amount
4/1	Beginning balance	$1,089	4/1	Beginning balance	$1,698
4/15	Purchase	35	4/6	Purchase	23
4/20	Payment	154	4/23	Purchase	116
4/30	Purchase	60	4/25	Payment	256

4. If four of Scott and Paula's credit cards were stolen but only the following unauthorized charges were made before they reported the cards missing, how much would Scott and Paula's maximum liability be according to federal legislation?

Shamrock Gas	$ 46	MasterCard Gold	$193
Visa	$692	American Express	$ 71

5. After paying off all of their revolving credit debt, Scott and Paula plan on keeping only one bank credit card. Compare and evaluate their Visa and MasterCard Gold terms on the assumption that all charges made on the card they keep will be paid at the end of the billing cycle. They will not allow any charges to revolve. They expect their charges would produce an average daily balance of about $300 a month in a typical month. Recommend the card that would be less expensive for Scott and Paula under these conditions.

6. After moving into their larger home, Scott and Paula feel they need new furniture. They think the furnishings would cost about $4,000, but they are not sure if they can afford the furniture or if they should use cash or credit. The following loans are available:

    General Telephone
    Credit Union   Ace Furniture Company
    12% stated interest rate   10% stated interest rate
    simple interest loan   add-on interest loan
    36 monthly payments   36 monthly payments

    a. Compare the monthly payments, the total finance charges, and the APRs on the three above loans. Which would you recommend as the best loan for Scott and Paula? Why?

b.   (For students using the computer disk) Run the amortization table for the recommended loan. How much interest would be paid in the first year of this loan? During the second year? The third year?

c.   Before Scott and Paula decide on using credit, they want to compare the cost of using the loan you recommended with the cost of paying cash for the furniture. If they used cash, they would withdraw funds from their General Telephone Credit Union Money Market Fund (currently earning 4.5%) to pay for the furniture. Compare the relative cost of cash vs. credit (using the General Telephone Credit Union loan) for Scott and Paula. Would you advise Scott and Paula to buy the furniture at this time? If yes, would you recommend cash or credit?

7.   As of March 1993, Scott and Paula had approximately $5,600 outstanding on their credit cards. Would you recommend that they consolidate that debt onto one credit card or perhaps use the home equity loan outlined below to consolidate that debt? What are the advantages and disadvantages?

Home Equity Line
of Credit
prime + 2.5% interest rate formula (currently 8.5%, maximum rate 18%)
simple interest loan
$8,000 line of credit
$80 set up fee
amortized over 10 years

PART FOUR: The Garnett Case Study

After Scott and Paula purchase their new home, they are interested in reevaluating their insurance needs.

1. Use the multiple earnings approach and Exhibit 9.1 to estimate the total life insurance needs on Scott's life. How much additional life insurance (over the term life insurance policy and death benefit on his retirement plan) would this method suggest Scott buy?

2. Repeat the above procedure to estimate the amount of additional life insurance that should be purchased on Paula's life (assuming the current value of her retirement account is $1,689).

3. Use the needs approach to calculate the amount of additional insurance, if any, needed on Scott's life. Scott would like Paula to receive enough money from his life insurance to pay off all of their consumer debt (but not the home mortgage). Scott would also like his insurance to provide an extra $5,000 to add to their emergency fund, $4,000 to cover final expenses, and $30,000 to supplement Jason and Amy's college fund.

   With the consumer credit paid off, they estimate that Paula and the twins would need approximately $50,000 a year for living expenses during Period 1 (until the children are age 18). In Period 2 (after the children graduate from high school until Paula retires at age 65), they estimate her living expenses would be $36,000 a year. During retirement, they feel she could live comfortably on $30,000 a year (since the house would be paid off by then).

   Paula's gross monthly income while working is estimated to be $2,500 during Period 1 and $3,500 during Period 2, and her pension income after retirement should be about $1,100 a month. Investment income should average $100 a month for the rest of her life. They should receive approximately $1,500 a month from Social Security while the children are still home and $950 a month from Social Security once again when Paula retires. Social Security will pay nothing during Period 2. Assuming Paula retires at age 65, she has 34 years of work and 22 years of retirement to look forward to (given the average life expectancy of a woman her age).

   They expect that Paula would sell the Honda Accord for about $4,500 if Scott were to die. Out of all their other assets, they would like to use only the Evergreen Fund (Scott's IRA currently valued at $14.58 per share) and his 401(k)(current value of $6,742) to help support Paula and the children. All of these funds would be available without penalty if Scott died. In addition, Scott does have some life insurance and a retirement account death benefit through his employer.

4. Use the needs approach to calculate the amount of additional insurance, if any, needed on Paula's life. Use the same assumptions as above except that annual living needs would be $60,000 in Period 1 due to the need for additional child care and help around the house. Scott's gross monthly income while working would be $3,550. His income during retirement would be $5,700 a month (assuming he continues contributing to his 401(k) plan and he stays with his current employer). Because of Paula's lower income, they will receive only $1,300 a month from Social Security while the children are at home. However, due to Scott's higher income during his working years, he should receive

approximately $1,000 a month from Social Security when he retires. Assuming Scott retires at age 65, he has 33 years of work and 15 years of retirement ahead of him.

He also expects to sell the Honda for about $4,500 if Paula were to die. Out of all their other assets, they would like to use only Paula's retirement account (currently valued at $1,689) and her term life insurance to help support Scott and the children. In the case of Paula's death, Scott's 401(k) and IRA would not become available without penalty.

5. Compare and evaluate the multiple earnings approach and the needs approach of estimating life insurance needs.

6. Evaluate the group term life policies Scott and Paula currently have. Should they keep these policies and/or buy additional life insurance coverage? If you recommend they buy other policies, how much and what type of policies should they purchase? Using the examples in this text, approximately how much would the recommended policies cost?

7. Recommend appropriate beneficiary and settlement options for Scott and Paula's policies.

8. Evaluate Scott's disability income policy. Assume that he does not want to rely on Social Security or other government programs in case of a disability. Scott does have 45 days of paid sick leave accumulated. Does Scott need (and could he get) additional coverage? If yes, how much more is needed and how much would this coverage cost?

9. Calculate Paula's disability income needs. Use the same assumptions about government benefits as above. Paula has 30 days of paid sick leave accumulated, but there is no disability income policy available through her employer. Does Paula need disability coverage? If yes, how much coverage is needed? What waiting period and duration of benefits would you recommend? Approximately how much would it cost?

10. Evaluate Scott's group major medical policy in terms of maximum limit, deductible, participation, etc. What is the maximum dollar amount of covered expenses Scott would have to pay per year (assuming the insurance benefits remain below the maximum limit)? Is this an acceptable policy for Scott considering his health and financial conditions?

11. Evaluate Paula's group HMO coverage. What are the potential out-of-pocket costs under this coverage? Is this an acceptable policy for Paula and the children considering their health and financial conditions?

12. Would you recommend that Paula be covered under Scott's policy or vice versa? Why? If so, how much would it cost? Which policy should the children be covered under? Why?

13. Evaluate Scott and Paula's homeowner's insurance needs for their new house. Remember the policy in the original case was for their first home. Their new home is 2,400 square feet, and they have been told that replacement would cost $65/square foot. What form of HO insurance is appropriate for them? How much coverage do you recommend for their house, personal property, personal liability, etc.? Approximately how much will the recommended coverage cost?

14. Evaluate Scott and Paula's auto insurance policy. Is this coverage adequate for their insurance needs? Recommend any needed changes. Approximately how much would the recommended changes cost?

15. Do Scott and Paula need any other types of insurance coverage? If yes, what and why? About how much would it cost?

16. Revise Scott and Paula's budget to reflect the change in expenditures caused by your insurance recommendations. Assume all changes are effective in April, 1993 and that Scott and Paula pay premiums annually for all private insurance (not through their employers) except their auto insurance which is paid semi-annually and their homeowners policy that is paid with their monthly mortgage payment.

PART FIVE: The Garnett Case Study

1. Using the asset values on Scott and Paula's latest balance sheet (Part 2, Question 10) and the interest rates given in the original case, how much annual interest income should they receive in 1993 from (assuming the same balance was maintained all year):
   - --their checking account
   - --their money market account
   - --their certificate of deposit at Bank of the Hills
   - --their certificate of deposit at General Telephone Credit Union

2. Using the dividend income and current values from the original case, what was the current dividend yield in 1992 on the Kemper International mutual fund investment? On the Evergreen Fund (Scott's IRA)?

3. Scott and Paula purchased their Kemper International shares in March 1986. What was the approximate annual yield on this investment from March 1986 to March 1993 (See Part 2, Question 10 for a February 28, 1993 price quote)? Assume that the dividends and capital gains distributions paid in 1992 were typical of those paid over the years this investment was owned. Compare the annual yield on this stock mutual fund to the yield on Scott and Paula's less risky investments. Did the fund provide an adequate yield for the risk taken?

4. Repeat Question 3 for the Evergreen Mutual Fund?

5. Track the net asset value (NAV) of Kemper International and the Evergreen Fund over a two-week period. The needed information can be found in The Wall Street Journal and in many daily newspapers.

6. From looking at the mutual fund listings, does Kemper International Fund and Evergreen Fund charge front-end loads, 12(b)-1 fees, and/or redemption fees? If there is a front-end load on either fund, what percent load is charged?

7. In February 1993, Scott and Paula sold their IBM and Walgreens stock (See Part 2, Question 10 for details of the sale.) Calculate the before-tax capital gain (loss) on these shares.

8. Given their marginal tax bracket, approximately how much of their capital gain (loss) would be paid (saved) on federal income taxes in 1993?   (See your answer to Part 1, Question 11 for Scott and Paula's marginal tax bracket.)

9. Scott and Paul's certificates of deposit will mature in December 1993, and they are trying to decide how to reinvest the $2,950 plus interest. They are considering the following 2 different stock investments. What is the current dividend yield on each of these investments? What would the approximate annual yield be on each given the following assumptions? They plan to keep the investment about 7 years.

	Blue-chip stock	Aggressive growth stock
Current market value	$33.25	$25.87
Annual dividend income	$ 1.75	$ .75
Market value in 7 years	$43.00	$58.00

10. Scott and Paula are also considering investing this $2,950 plus interest in a corporate bond that is currently selling at discount for $3,000. It has a face value of $4,000, matures in 7 years, and has an AA rating from Moody's. It pays annual interest of $150. What is the current yield on this bond investment? What is the yield-to-maturity on this bond?

11. Given Scott and Paula's marginal tax rate, would a tax-free AA municipal bond with a current yield of 4% provided a higher after-tax current yield than the corporate bond in Question 10?

12. An acquaintance of Scott and Paula thought that they should invest in the aggressive growth stock on margin. Would you recommend that Scott and Paula buy stock on margin? Why or why not?

13. What type of savings/investment vehicle would you recommend for Scott and Paula--the blue-chip stock, the aggressive growth stock, the corporate bond, the municipal bond or something else? Remember their goals and their tolerance for risk when making the recommendation. Justify your recommendation.

PART SIX--CHAPTER 15: The Garnett Case Study

1.   Calculate Scott's annual retirement benefit from his employer pension plan. Assume his average salary over the last 5 years of work is $4,000 per month and he continues working for General Telephone Corporation until he is 65 years of age.

2   One of Scott and Paula's long term goals is to retire in 33 years when Scott is 65. Their current living expenses are approximately $60,000 (excluding savings), but they feel they would be able to live during retirement on about 90% of their current living expenses. Assuming Scott and Paula continue to work for their current employers, they expect to receive approximately $1,100 a month from Paula's retirement plan in addition to the retirement benefit from Scott's employer plan (See Question 1). If they continue contributing $75 a month to Scott's 401(k) plan, that should provide another $1,500 a month. They have decided they do not want to count on any Social Security benefits when calculating their retirement needs. They want to use Scott's IRA and any other investments for special goals so do not include them in the needs assessment either. Calculate Scott and Paula's retirement income and investment needs assuming an average rate of inflation of 5%, 5% return on investments after retirement, and 8% return on investments prior to retirement.

3.   Recalculate Scott and Paula's retirement needs using the information from the previous question except that they do not stay with their current employers the next 33 years. Assume that their annual income from employer pensions will be only $40,000 and their annual income from their 401(k) will be $12,000.

4.   As part of Scott and Paula's goals (Part One), they indicated that they wanted to continue contributing $900 a year to Scott's 401(k) retirement account. After looking at their retirement needs and reviewing the 401(k) arrangements for each of their employers, would you recommend this strategy? If not, what would you recommend? Why?

5.   Refer to Scott and Paula's most recent budget. Can they afford your recommendation? If yes, revise their budget to reflect any changes in expenditures resulting from your recommended investment strategy.

PART SIX--CHAPTER 16: The Garnett Case Study

Scott and Paula own their new house jointly with right of survivorship (community property in community property states).

1.   Referring to Scott and Paula's most recent balance sheet (Part 2, Question 10), would Scott's estate be subject to federal estate taxes if he were to die? If yes, what steps should be taken to reduce estate taxes?

2.   Which of Scott's assets would be probate and which would be non-probate assets?

3.   From their most recent balance sheet, would Paula's estate be subject to federal estate taxes if she were to die? If yes, what steps should be taken to reduce estate taxes?

4.   Which of Paula's assets would be probate and which would be non-probate assets?

5.   Since neither Scott nor Paula currently have wills, how would Scott's estate be distributed if he were to die? How would Paula's estate be distributed? Use Exhibit 16.3 to answer this question.

6.   Given the Garnett's estate planning needs, should Scott and Paula have wills written? If yes, what should be included in these wills?

7.   Scott and Paula have considered saving for Jason and Amy's college educations in the children's names rather than in Scott and Paula's names. Since the contributions to these accounts (currently $100 a month per child) would be considered gifts to the children, would Scott and Paula have to pay gift taxes on these gifts?

<u>REPRESENTATIVE ANSWERS</u>: The Garnett Case Study

The following answers are representative--but not the only right answers to the questions in the case. Also, the latter answers build upon previous solutions to the case.

<u>Part One</u>

1.   See computer printout.

2.   See computer printout. Scott and Paula had a cash surplus for 1992 of $8,588. Since this surplus included $3,532 from the sale of assets one might argue the surplus is overstated by $3,532. However, the cash surplus is less the $2,933 new retirement contributions and reinvested interest, dividends, and capital gains distributions. As we constructed this statement using the cash flow concept, it simply shows all the money coming in, all the money flowing out, and any funds that are left over. A statement that excluded income from the sale of assets as well as new savings expenditures would have shown a somewhat smaller cash surplus ($8,588 - $3,543 + $2,933 = $7,978). The $7,978 would be the increase in net worth on the balance sheet that results from the surplus.

3.   See computer printout.

4.   Positive Aspects:

      --They have a net worth of nearly $137,000.
      --They both appear to have stable incomes, and their income level is fairly high.
      --Their assets are well diversified.
      --They are reinvesting their investment income.
      --They have started saving for retirement.
      --Their solvency ratio is over 60%. Therefore, their assets could lose 60% of their value before Scott and Paula would become insolvent.
      --Their debt service ratio is only 20%. They should not have problems meeting their debt obligations.
      --Their financial records seem well organized except that they don't know where many of their official documents are located.
      --Scott and Paula are in fairly good agreement about their financial priorities and their risk levels.
      --Their savings ratio is over 15%.
      --Their liquidity ratio is nearly 60%. They could pay their current debt with their liquid assets for over 7 months.

      Negative Aspects:

      --They do not have a regular savings program to help them meet their goals.
      --They have nearly $6,000 in credit card debt at high rates of interest.
      --The liability coverage on both their homeowner's and their automobile insurance is too low.
      --Paula does not have disability income insurance.
      --Neither of them have wills.
      --They are having a large amount of federal income taxes withheld.

298

5. $127,018 and $171,297. See computer printout.

6.   See computer printout. $2,206 emergency fund
                                        3,533 college fund
                                        <u>1,586</u> car down payment
                                        $7,325 yearly savings required in 1993

7.   See computer printout. The savings and investment budget category includes contributions to Scott's 401(k), Paula's retirement plan, their money market account for their goals as well as reinvested interest, dividends, and capital gains distributions

8.   No, Scott and Paula will not be able to save for all of their goals and continue their current expenditure patterns on their after-tax income. Since Paula has already taken a job that pays less since the children were born, we can assume that being with the kids is very important to them. This probably rules out her making more money right now, but perhaps they are having too much federal income taxes withheld. This question will be answered after we do Question 9.

      Their most immediate goals are getting better control of their spending, starting a regular savings program to achieve their goals, accumulating an adequate emergency fund, and buying a larger house. Therefore, we should not cut the savings for the emergency fund. Also, we need to keep in mind that buying a larger house will probably increase housing expenditures soon. Some ideas about what they might want to do to reduce expenditures are:

      --See if they are having too much federal income tax withheld.
      --Make slight cuts in variable expenditures (such as food, clothing, recreation, etc.).
      --Give up their vacation for a year.
      --Shop around for a better buy on their auto and/or homeowners insurance.
      --Transfer all their credit card debt to the MasterCard and cancel their Visa and American Express cards. This would save them $85 a year in annual fees as well as lowering their interest expenses.
      --Quit using their credit cards as revolving debt. Use them for convenience only, paying the total balance upon billing to save interest costs.
      --Reduce (or eliminate for a year) the amount being saved for their long-term goals (retirement through Scott's 401(k) and the children's college fund).
      --Do their own financial planning rather than hiring a financial planner.

9.   Scott and Paula will receive a refund of approximately $3,145 (using the 1992 Tax Rate Schedule). See computer printout.

      Dividend income and capital gains distributions on the Evergreen Fund were not included because this is an IRA investment.

10.   Since they are getting such a large refund for 1992, Scott and Paula should reduce the amount of their federal income tax withholding to approximately $8,000. They would do this by increasing the number of withholding allowances being claimed.

11.   Average tax rate = tax liability/taxable income $7,979/$47,901 = 16.66%

        Marginal tax rate = rate paid on last dollar =   28%

12. $900   401(k) contribution
        x .28   marginal tax rate
        $252   tax savings

13.   Keeping in mind Scott and Paula's goals, their primary tax strategies would include buying a more expensive house (to get more interest and property tax deductions) and to continue saving for retirement using the 401(k) plan. Because of the level of their adjusted gross income and the fact that they are covered through employer retirement plans, IRA's would not provide a tax deduction. When they start saving for Jason and Amy's college educations, they should evaluate investment alternatives (such as Series EE US Savings Bonds and municipal bonds) that have tax advantages. They should also consider saving funds in Jason and Amy's names.

        Once Scott and Paula reduce the amount of federal income tax withholding and make other minor budget changes, they should be able to buy the larger house. They may also be able to do some savings for retirement and college.

Part 1, Question 1

```
+FP/PC------------------------------------------------------------ FP/PC+
|                                                                        |
|                        B A L A N C E   S H E E T                       |
|                                                                        |
+------------------------------------------------------------------------+
```

Scott and Paula Garnett   01/01/93

| ASSETS | LIABILITIES AND NET WORTH |

Liquid Assets: Current Liabilities
  Cash on hand.............   350   Utilities...............   0
  In checking..............   1750   Rent....................   0
  Savings accounts.........   0   Insurance premiums......   0
  Money market funds   Taxes...................   0
    and deposits...........   6663   Medical/dental bills....   0
  CDs < 1 yr. maturity.....   2950   Repair bills............   0
  Other....................   0   Bank crd. card balances..   3723
                             ------   Dept. store charge cards.   2197
    Total Liquid Assets.....   11713   Travel/entrtmt. card.....   0
                                           Gas/other credit cards...   0
Investments: Bank line of credit......   0
  Stocks I.................   6450   Other cur. liabilities...   0
         II.................   4300   ------
  Bonds I.................   0   Total Cur. Liabilities.   5920
         II.................   0
  CDs > 1 yr. maturity.....   0   Long-term Liabilities
  Mut. funds I.............   3298   Primary res. mortgage....   65989
            II.............   4174   Second home mortgage.....   0
  Real estate..............   0   Real estate investments..   0
  Retirement funds.........   14306   Auto loans...............   6939
  Other....................   0   Appliance/furn. loans....   0
                             ------   Home improvement loans...   0
    Total Investments......   32528   Educational loans........   1023
                                           Other I..................   2442
Real Property   II..................   0
  Primary residence........   87750   ------
  Second home..............   0   Total Long-term Liab...   76393
  Car I....................   4500
      II...................   13000
  Recreation equipment.....   2000
  Other....................   0

    Total Real Property..... 107250

Personal Property
  Furniture and appl.......   21500
  Stereos, TVs, etc........   10750
  Clothing.................   8525
  Jewelry..................   24500   (II) Tot. Liabilities.   82313
  Other....................   2500

    Total Personal Property. 67775   Net Worth [(II)-(III)]. 136953

    (I) Total Assets...... 219266   Total Liab. and Net Worth.. 219266
                            ======   ======

Part 1, Question 2

```
+FP/PC-------------------------------------------------------FP/PC+
|         I N C O M E   A N D   E X P E N D I T U R E S   S T A T E M E N T |
+-----------------------------------------------------------------+
```

Scott and Paula Garnett   for the year   ending 12/31/92

INCOME

Wages and salaries:	I...	41000
	II..	24400
Self-employment income...................................		0
Bonuses and commissions..................................		0
Pensions and annuities...................................		0
Investment income:	Interest received.............................	543
	Dividends received............................	622
	Rents received................................	0
	Sale of securities............................	3532
	Other...	208
Other income		0
(I) TOTAL INCOME.......................................		70305

EXPENDITURES

Housing:	Rent payment..................................	0
	Mortgage payment..............................	7404
	Repairs, maintenance, improvements............	780
Utilities:	Gas, electric, water..........................	1440
	Phone...	360
	Cable TV and other............................	0
Food:	Groceries and dining out......................	5280
Autos:	Loan payments.................................	4032
	License plates, fees, etc.....................	0
	Gas/oil/repairs/tires/maintenance.............	1680
Medical:	Health/major medical/disability insurance.....	1260
	Doctor/dent/hosp/medicine.....................	493
Clothing:	Clothes, shoes, and accessories...............	2700
Insurance:	Homeowner's...................................	456
	Life..	180
	Auto..	1195
Taxes:	Income and Social Security....................	16132
	Property......................................	1176
Appl/furn/other:	Loan payments.................................	0
	Purchases and repairs.........................	2500
Personal care:	Laundry, cosmetics, hair care.................	540
Recreation/entertmt:	Vacations.....................................	1000
	Other recreation and entertainment............	900
Other loans:	I. Stafford loan..............................	972
	II. Computer loan.............................	1344
Other expenditures:	I. Charitable contributions, child care, interest paid, miscellaneous	6960
	II. Retirement contributions; reinvested unearned income.	2933
(II) TOTAL EXPENDITURES................................		61717

```
      CASH SURPLUS (OR DEFICIT) [(I) - (II)]............................    8588
                                                                         ======
```

Part 1, Question 3

```
+FP/PC-------------------------------------------------------FP/PC+
|                                                                  |
|          F I N A N C I A L    S T A T E M E N T    R A T I O S   |
|                                                            `     |
+------------------------------------------------------------------+
```

Scott and Paula Garnett   12/31/92

                        Total net worth   136953
Solvency ratio   =   ---------------   = -------- = 62.46 %
                        Total assets   219266

                        Liquid assets   11713
Liquidity ratio   = ------------------ = ------- = 59.54 %
                       Total current debts   19672

                        Cash surplus   8588
Savings ratio   = ------------------ = ------- = 15.85 %
                       Income after taxes   54173

                        loan payments   1146
Debt service ratio = ------------------ = ------- = 19.56 %
                       Monthly gross   65400
                       (before-tax) income


```
------------------------------------------------------------------
```

Part 1, Question 5

```
+FP/PC----------------------------------------------------------FP/PC+
|         F U T U R E   V A L U E   O F   A   S I N G L E   C A S H   F L O W    |
+-----------------------------------------------------------------+

                 Single cash flow.............     50000.00
                 Rate of return...............        6.00%
                 Number of years..............       16.00

                 Future value.................    127017.59

---------------------------------------------------------------------

+FP/PC----------------------------------------------------------FP/PC+
|         F U T U R E   V A L U E   O F   A   S I N G L E   C A S H   F L O W    |
+-----------------------------------------------------------------+

                 Single cash flow.............     50000.00
                 Rate of return...............        8.00%
                 Number of years..............       16.00

                 Future value.................    171297.13

---------------------------------------------------------------------
```

Part 1, Question 6

```
+FP/PC---------------------------------------------------------------FP/PC+
|      F U T U R E   V A L U E   O F   A   S I N G L E   C A S H   F L O W      |
+-------------------------------------------------------------------------+
```

Emergency Fund

```
                Single cash flow.............    6663.00
                Rate of return...............       5.00%
                Number of years..............       2.00

                Future value.................    7345.96
```

```
+FP/PC---------------------------------------------------------------FP/PC+
|      YEARLY SAVINGS REQUIRED TO ACCUMULATE A GIVEN FUTURE VALUE          |
+-------------------------------------------------------------------------+
```

```
                Future value.................    4522.00
                Rate of return...............       5.00%
                Number of years..............       2.00

                Yearly savings required......    2205.86
```

```
+FP/PC---------------------------------------------------------------FP/PC+
|  SETTING INVESTMENT GOALS:  MAKING A SERIES OF INVESTMENTS OVER TIME     |
+-------------------------------------------------------------------------+
```

Emergency Fund

```
   Targeted financial goal..............................     11868
   Projected average return on investments..............      5.00
   Number of years to target date.......................      2.00
   Amount of initial investment (if any)................      6663

   Terminal value of initial investment.................      7346
   Balance to come from savings plan....................      4522
   Amount of each annual investment in the series.......      2206
```

Part 1, Question 6

```
+FP/PC------------------------------------------------------------------FP/PC+
|           YEARLY SAVINGS REQUIRED TO ACCUMULATE A GIVEN FUTURE VALUE        |
+----------------------------------------------------------------------------+
```
College education
```
                 Future value................    127018.00
                 Rate of return..............        10.00%
                 Number of years.............        16.00

                 Yearly savings required......      3533.21
```

```
------------------------------------------------------------------------------
```

```
+FP/PC------------------------------------------------------------------FP/PC+
|           YEARLY SAVINGS REQUIRED TO ACCUMULATE A GIVEN FUTURE VALUE        |
+----------------------------------------------------------------------------+
```
Car down payment
```
                 Future value................      5000.00
                 Rate of return..............         5.00%
                 Number of years.............         3.00

                 Yearly savings required......      1586.04
```

```
------------------------------------------------------------------------------
```

Yearly savings required

$2,206 emergency fund
3,533 College fund
1,586 Car down payment
─────
$ 7,325

Part 1, Question 7

```
+-FP/PC------------------------------------------------------------FP/PC-+
|            M O N T H L Y   C A S H   B U D G E T   S U M M A R Y       |
+-----------------------------------------------------------------------+
```

NAME(S): Scott and Paula Garnett   Page 1

FOR THE YEAR ENDING 12/31/93	JAN	FEB	MAR
Take-Home Pay: Source 1	2669	2669	2669
Take-Home Pay: Source 2	1437	1437	1437
Take-Home Pay: Source 3	0	0	0
Bonuses and Commissions	0	0	0
Pensions and Annuities	0	0	0
Interest	33	33	33
Dividends	0	0	155
Rents	0	0	0
Sale of Securities	0	0	0
Other *Capital gains distributions*	0	0	52
Other Income: Source 1	0	0	0
Other Income: Source 2	0	0	0
TOTAL INCOME	4139	4139	4346
Rent/Mortgage Payment	617	617	617
Repairs, Maintenance, Improvements	65	65	65
Gas, Utilities, Water	120	120	120
Phone	30	30	30
Cable TV and Other	0	0	0
Groceries	330	330	330
Dining Out	110	110	110
Loan/Lease Payments	336	336	336
License Plates, Fees, Etc.	0	0	0
Gas, Oil, Tires, Maintenance	140	140	140
Health Insurance, Etc.	105	105	105
Doctor, Dentist, Hospital, Medicine	41	41	41
Clothing, Shoes, Accessories	225	225	225
Homeowner's Insurance	38	38	38
Life Insurance	15	15	15
Automobile Insurance	0	0	598
Income and Social Security Taxes	0	0	0
Property Taxes	98	98	98
Loan Payments	0	0	0
Purchases and Repairs	42	42	42
Laundry, Cosmetics, Hair Care	45	45	45
Vacations	0	0	0
Other Recreation and Entertainment	75	75	75
Savings and Investments	775	775	982
Charitable Contributions	25	25	25
~~Gifts~~ *Miscellaneous*	50	50	50
~~Education Expenses~~ *Financial Planning Fee*	375	375	375
Subscriptions, Magazines, Books	0	0	0
Other Expenditures: Item 1 *Stafford, computer, Credit card debt*	606	606	606
Other Expenditures: Item 2 *Child care*	350	350	350
Fun Money	150	150	150
TOTAL EXPENDITURES	4763	4763	5568
CASH SUPLUS (OR DEFICIT)	-624	-624	-1222
CUMULATIVE CASH SUPLUS (OR DEFICIT)	-624	-1248	-2470

307

```
+-FP/PC--------------------------------------------------------------FP/PC-+
|            M O N T H L Y   C A S H   B U D G E T   S U M M A R Y         |
+-------------------------------------------------------------------------+
```
NAME(S): Scott and Paula Carnett   Page 2

FOR THE YEAR ENDING 12/31/93	APR	MAY	JUN
Take-Home Pay: Source 1	2669	2669	2669
Take-Home Pay: Source 2	1437	1437	1437
Take-Home Pay: Source 3	0	0	904
Bonuses and Commissions	0	0	0
Pensions and Annuities	0	0	0
Interest	33	33	33
Dividends	0	0	156
Rents	0	0	0
Sale of Securities	0	0	0
Other *Capital gains distributions*	0	0	52
Other Income: Source 1	0	0	0
Other Income: Source 2	0	0	0
TOTAL INCOME	4139	4139	5251
Rent/Mortgage Payment	617	617	617
Repairs, Maintenance, Improvements	65	65	65
Gas, Utilities, Water	120	120	120
Phone	30	30	30
Cable TV and Other	0	0	0
Groceries	330	330	330
Dining Out	110	110	110
Loan/Lease Payments	336	336	336
License Plates, Fees, Etc.	0	0	0
Gas, Oil, Tires, Maintenance	140	140	140
Health Insurance, Etc.	105	105	105
Doctor, Dentist, Hospital, Medicine	41	41	41
Clothing, Shoes, Accessories	225	225	225
Homeowner's Insurance	38	38	38
Life Insurance	15	15	15
Automobile Insurance	0	0	0
Income and Social Security Taxes	0	0	0
Property Taxes	98	98	98
Loan Payments	0	0	0
Purchases and Repairs	42	42	42
Laundry, Cosmetics, Hair Care	45	45	45
Vacations	0	0	0
Other Recreation and Entertainment	75	75	75
Savings and Investments	775	775	983
Charitable Contributions	25	25	25
~~Gifts~~ *Miscellaneous*	50	50	50
~~Education Expenses~~ *Financial Planning Fee*	375	0	0
Subscriptions, Magazines, Books	0	0	0
Other Expenditures: Item 1 *Stafford, computer, Credit*	606	606	606
Other Expenditures: Item 2 *Child care card debt*	350	350	350
Fun Money	150	150	150
TOTAL EXPENDITURES	4763	4388	4596
CASH SUPLUS (OR DEFICIT)	-624	-249	655
CUMULATIVE CASH SUPLUS (OR DEFICIT)	-3094	-3343	-2688

NAME(S): Scott and Paula Garnett   Page 3

FOR THE YEAR ENDING 12/31/93	JUL	AUG	SEP
Take-Home Pay: Source 1	2669	2669	2669
Take-Home Pay: Source 2	1437	1437	1437
Take-Home Pay: Source 3	904	0	0
Bonuses and Commissions	0	0	0
Pensions and Annuities	0	0	0
Interest	33	33	33
Dividends	0	0	155
Rents	0	0	0
Sale of Securities	0	0	52
Other *Capital gains distributions*	0	0	0
Other Income: Source 1	0	0	0
Other Income: Source 2	0	0	0
TOTAL INCOME	5043	4139	4346
Rent/Mortgage Payment	617	617	617
Repairs, Maintenance, Improvements	65	65	65
Gas, Utilities, Water	120	120	120
Phone	30	30	30
Cable TV and Other	0	0	0
Groceries	330	330	330
Dining Out	110	110	110
Loan/Lease Payments	336	336	336
License Plates, Fees, Etc.	0	0	0
Gas, Oil, Tires, Maintenance	140	140	140
Health Insurance, Etc.	105	105	105
Doctor, Dentist, Hospital, Medicine	41	41	41
Clothing, Shoes, Accessories	225	225	225
Homeowner's Insurance	38	38	38
Life Insurance	15	15	15
Automobile Insurance	0	597	0
Income and Social Security Taxes	0	0	0
Property Taxes	98	98	98
Loan Payments	0	0	0
Purchases and Repairs	42	42	42
Laundry, Cosmetics, Hair Care	45	45	45
Vacations	0	450	0
Other Recreation and Entertainment	75	75	75
Savings and Investments	775	775	982
Charitable Contributions	25	25	25
~~Gifts~~ *Miscellaneous*	50	50	50
~~Education Expenses~~ *Financial Planning Fee*	0	0	0
Subscriptions, Magazines, Books	0	0	0
Other Expenditures: Item 1 *Stafford, Computer credit* 'ard debt	606	606	606
Other Expenditures: Item 2 *Child care*	350	350	350
Fun Money	150	150	150
TOTAL EXPENDITURES	4388	5435	4595
CASH SUPLUS (OR DEFICIT)	655	-1296	-249
CUMULATIVE CASH SUPLUS (OR DEFICIT)	-2033	-3329	-3578

```
+-FP/PC--------------------------------------------------------------FP/PC-+
|        M O N T H L Y   C A S H   B U D G E T   S U M M A R Y           |
+------------------------------------------------------------------------+
NAME(S): Scott and Paula Garnett                              Page 4
```

FOR THE YEAR ENDING 12/31/93	OCT	NOV	DEC	TOTAL
Take-Home Pay: Source 1	2669	2669	2669	32028
Take-Home Pay: Source 2	1437	1437	1437	17244
Take-Home Pay: Source 3	0	0	0	1808
Bonuses and Commissions	0	0	0	0
Pensions and Annuities	0	0	0	0
Interest	33	33	182	545
Dividends	0	0	156	622
Rents	0	0	0	0
Sale of Securities	0	0	0	0
Other *Capital gains distributions*	0	0	52	208
Other Income: Source 1	0	0	0	0
Other Income: Source 2	0	0	0	0
TOTAL INCOME	4139	4139	4496	52455
Rent/Mortgage Payment	617	617	617	7404
Repairs, Maintenance, Improvements	65	65	65	780
Gas, Utilities, Water	120	120	120	1440
Phone	30	30	30	360
Cable TV and Other	0	0	0	0
Groceries	330	330	330	3960
Dining Out	110	110	110	1320
Loan/Lease Payments	336	336	336	4032
License Plates, Fees, Etc.	0	0	0	0
Gas, Oil, Tires, Maintenance	140	140	140	1680
Health Insurance, Etc.	105	105	105	1260
Doctor, Dentist, Hospital, Medicine	41	41	41	492
Clothing, Shoes, Accessories	225	225	225	2700
Homeowner's Insurance	38	38	38	456
Life Insurance	15	15	15	180
Automobile Insurance	0	0	0	1195
Income and Social Security Taxes	0	0	0	0
Property Taxes	98	98	98	1176
Loan Payments	0	0	0	0
Purchases and Repairs	42	42	42	504
Laundry, Cosmetics, Hair Care	45	45	45	540
Vacations	0	0	0	450
Other Recreation and Entertainment	75	75	75	900
Savings and Investments	775	775	1132	10279
Charitable Contributions	25	25	25	300
~~Gifts~~ *Miscellaneous*	50	50	50	600
~~Education Expenses~~ *Financial Planning Fee*	0	0	0	1500
Subscriptions, Magazines, Books	0	0	0	0
Other Expenditures: Item 1 *Stafford, computer, credit*	606	606	606	7272
Other Expenditures: Item 2 *Child care Card debt*	350	350	350	4200
Fun Money	150	150	150	1800
TOTAL EXPENDITURES	4388	4388	4745	56780
CASH SUPLUS (OR DEFICIT)	-249	-249	-249	-4325
CUMULATIVE CASH SUPLUS (OR DEFICIT)	-3827	-4076	-4325	-4325

Part 1, Question 1

| C A S H   B U D G E T   S U M M A R Y |
+--+

NAME(S): Scott and Paula Garnett
FOR YEAR ENDING 12/31/93

	Total Income	Total Expenses	Cash Surplus (Deficit)	Cumulative Cash Surplus (Deficit)
Jan	$ 4139	$ 4763	$ -624	$ -624
Feb	4139	4763	-624	-1248
Mar	4346	5568	-1222	-2470
Apr	4139	4763	-624	-3094
May	4139	4388	-249	-3343
Jun	5251	4596	655	-2688
Jul	5043	4388	655	-2033
Aug	4139	5435	-1296	-3329
Sep	4346	4595	-249	-3578
Oct	4139	4388	-249	-3827
Nov	4139	4388	-249	-4076
Dec	4496	4745	-249	-4325
TOTALS ..	$ 52455	$ 56780		$ -4325

+--+

Part 1, Question 9

```
        FEDERAL INCOME TAX WORKSHEET
        Scott and Paula Garnett
                                              1992          1993
```

	1992	1993
INCOME		
1. Wages, salaries, tips, etc.	$63,840	$0
2. Interest income	543	
3. Dividends	560	
4. Capital gains (losses)	589	
5. Net business income (loss)	0	
6. Income (deductible losses) from rental property	0	
7. Other income	0	
8. TOTAL INCOME (add lines 1 - 7)	$65,532	$0
ADJUSTMENTS		
9. Keogh contributions	$0	$0
10. AGI before IRA contributions (subtract line 9 from line 8)	65,532	0
11. Deductible IRA contributions	0	
12. ADJUSTED GROSS INCOME (subtract line 11 from line 10)	$65,532	$0
ITEMIZED DEDUCTIONS		
13. Deductible medical expenses	$0	$0
14. State and local income and property taxes	1,176	
15. Mortgage interest	6,955	
16. Other deductible interest	0	
17. Charitable contributions	300	
18. Deductible misc. expenses	0	
19. Casualty and theft losses	0	
20. TOTAL ITEMIZED DEDUCTIONS (add lines 13 - 21)	$8,431	$0
TAXABLE INCOME		
21. Write in the amount on line 20 or or your standard deduction, whichever is greater	$8,431	$0
22. Personal exemptions	9,200	
23. TAXABLE INCOME (substract lines 21 and 22 from line 12)	$47,901	$0
TAX LIABILITY		
24. Tax before credits (see tax tables)	$8,758	$0
25. Child care credit	779	
26. YOUR TAX (subtract line 25 from line 24)	$7,979	$0
TAX WITHHELD	$11,124	$0
TAX DUE or (REFUND)	($3,145)	$0

REPRESENTATIVE ANSWERS: The Garnett Case Study

Part Two

1. Excluding Paula's summer income (as Scott and Paula requested in Part I), 3 months of after-tax income would be $13,155 [($34,006 + $18,613)/4]. If her summer income is included, 3 months of after-tax income would be $13,649 ($54,595/4).

    Looking at Scott and Paula's balance sheet prepared in Part 1, Question 1, we see that they currently have $11,713 in liquid assets. Using either of the above figures, they do not currently have enough liquid assets to meet the minimum requirements. They need to add at least $1,442 ($13,155 - $11,713) to their liquid assets to satisfy the "financial experts." However, they are working on this in their latest budget by allocating savings to build up their emergency fund.

2. Scott and Paula's checking account is reconciled for January. See computer printout.

3. <u>Positive aspects of Bank of the Hills NOW account:</u>

    --Lower flat monthly service charge, but higher per check charge (if balance falls below the required minimum balance
    --Lower stop payment and insufficient funds fees

    <u>Positive aspects of General Telephone Credit Union NOW account:</u>

    --Defines balance for assessment of service charge as "average daily balance" rather than "minimum daily balance"
    --Lower minimum balance requirement to escape service charge
    --Slightly higher APR paid on average daily balance

	Bank of the Hills	General Telephone Credit Union
Annual interest income	$1,400 x .03 = $42.00	$1,400 x .035 = $49.00
Annual check service charge	[$10 + ($.10 x 40)] x 2 = $28.00	$ 0.00
Annual ATM charges	6 x 12 x $.25 = $18.00	12 x 2 = $24.00
Net income from account	($4.00)	$25.00

    I would recommend they switch their checking account to the General Telephone Credit Union as long as they are satisfied with the way that institution has handled their other accounts. Based on these estimates, they would make $25.00 (before taxes) rather than spending $4.00 on their checking account each year.

4. It is generally more expensive to maintain two accounts rather than one account. However, if Scott and Paula would move their checking to the General Telephone Credit Union, they could split their account balance in half and still have over the $500 in each

account to avoid monthly service charges. The only additional cost would be the $2 per month ATM fee if they both wanted to access their checking accounts through ATMs.

In addition to the extra cost, if anything happened to one of them, the other would not be able to withdraw funds from the other's account as quickly as with one joint account. And they would have to make decisions about what money would be deposited in each separate account and what payments would be made from each of the separate accounts.

On the other hand, having two separate accounts could make it easier to record their deposits and withdrawals and it would ensure that neither of them maliciously withdrew funds from a joint account (in case of divorce, etc.) In addition, it never hurts to have well managed accounts in one's own name, especially for women. I would recommend they try using two separate accounts and see how it works. They can always go back to the joint account if the separate accounts are not satisfactory.

5. If Scott and Paula are willing to open a new account, they should investigate the return on money market mutual funds compared to their money market deposit account. If they want to use one of their existing accounts, I would recommend they make the monthly contribution for the emergency fund (which is about $184/month) to their General Telephone Credit Union money market account. If they don't want the hassle of mailing a check each month, they could probably arrange for an automatic withdrawal from a checking account.

6. See computer printout.

7.

	30-year fixed-rate	30-year ARM
Downpayment	$19,200	$19,200
Points	1,632	2,176
Closing costs	3,100	3,250
Total front-end costs	$23,932	$24,626

See computer printout.

Monthly payment for principal & interest	$ 837	$ 652
maximum after first year	$ 837	$ 798
maximum over life of loan	$ 837	$ 1,119

The front-end costs for the fixed-rate mortgage is $694 less than the front-end costs for the ARM. In addition, the fixed-rate mortgage offers the security Scott and Paula would get from knowing that the payment for principal and interest would not go up. On the other hand, the current monthly payment on the ARM would be much more affordable on their tight budget, and it could possibly go down over the years (although it is historically quite low right now). In the worst possible case, the monthly payment on the ARM would be $282 higher than that of the fixed-rate mortgage. However, it would take at least 3 years for the payment to reach that level because of the 2% annual cap. The Treasury Bill Index used on this ARM is more volatile than some of the other indices used. It is probably not the best index when interest rates are already low and if one prefers more stability.

One could recommend either of these mortgages. The fixed-rate offers the lower front-end costs and the security of stable payments while the ARM offers significantly lower payments at this time and has decent interest rate caps. Overall, I would recommend the ARM. If they have a budget surplus, Scott and Paula could save the difference between the fixed-rate and ARM payments (currently $185/month) so funds would be available in case their monthly payments went up significantly later on.

8a.   See computer printout. Scott and Paula pass the first test. Their monthly house payment of $1,077 will be less than the $1,715 maximum monthly mortgage payment for their income.

Scott and Paula's monthly before-tax income for 1993 is estimated to be:

$67,780	salaries
543	interest income
86	dividend income
208	capital gains distributions
$68,617	annual income

$$\$68,617/12 = \$5,718 \text{ monthly income}$$
$$\times .30$$
$$\$1,715 \text{ maximum monthly mortgage payment}$$

Monthly house payment with fixed-rate mortgage:

$ 837	principal & interest
171	property taxes
54	homeowners insurance
15	private mortgage insurance
$1,077	total monthly payment

8b.   Scott and Paula just do pass the second test. Their total debt payments of $2,019 are below the maximum of $2,058 based on their income.

Maximum debt:

$$\$5,718 \text{ monthly income}$$
$$\times .36$$
$$\$2,058 \text{ maximum monthly debt payment}$$

Total monthly debt payments with fixed rate mortgage:

$1,077	house payment
413	credit card minimum payments
336	Dodge Caravan payment
81	Stafford Loan payment
112	computer payment
$2,019	total monthly payments

8c.   Since they qualify for the higher monthly payment on the fixed-rate loan, they would also qualify for the ARM.

9. $86,000 gross sales price
     - 6,160   sales expenses
      -65,908 loan balance
     $13,932 net proceeds

10.   See computer printout.

      $24,626 front-end costs with ARM
      -13,932 net proceeds from sale of house
      $10,694 needed from sale of stock

	IBM	Walgreens		
Market value	$65.25	$45.25		
Number of shares	x 100	x 100		
Gross proceeds	$6,525	$4,525		
Commissions	- 163	- 136		
Net proceeds	$6,362 +	$4,389	=	$10,751
Needed from sale of stock				-10,694
Added to money market account				$ 57

The additional value in the employer retirement accounts are from:
          $ 57 Paula's contribution went up slightly due to her raise
           113 Scott's $75 contribution is matched with $38 by his employer
          $170
          x 2 months
          $340 increase in value

Their net worth went down $10,053, primarily because of the transaction costs they had to pay to sell their first house and to buy their new home.

11.   See computer printout for their revised 1993 budget. Changes from the original 1993 budget completed in Part 1, Question 7 include:

      --higher after-tax salaries due to lower withholding for federal income taxes ($54,595)
      --lower dividends due to selling IBM and Walgreens stock
      --higher sales of securities due to selling IBM and Walgreens stock (net proceeds of $10,751)
      --other income from sale of the first house (net proceeds of $13,932))
      --other income from the 1992 income tax refund ($3,145)
      --mortgage payments, property taxes, homeowners and private mortgage insurance, house maintenance, and utilities were prorated with 2 months in their first house and ten months in their new house
      --reduced dining out expenses ($90 per month)
      --reduced clothing expenses ($200 per month)
      --reduced contribution to college fund ($200 per month)
      --funds from stock sale added to money market account ($57)
      --front-end costs for the new house ($24,626)

The savings and investment budget category includes contributions to Scott's 401(k), Paula's retirement plan, their money market account for their goals as well as reinvested interest, dividends, and capital gains distributions. The excess $57 from the sale of stock is also included in February. The net proceeds from the sale of the house, the stock proceeds, and the front-end costs on the new house were divided between 2 or 3 months because the computer program would not accept 5-digit numbers.

Scott and Paula's revised budget shows a cash surplus of $1,794 for 1993. This is due primarily to the reduction in federal income tax withholding, a tax refund, and some reductions in expenditures. Those sources of increased income were more than enough to offset the increased costs associated with their new home.

12. See computer printout for Scott and Paula's 1993 federal income tax estimate. The estimate was done using IRS estimates for the standard deduction ($6,200), personal exemption ($2,350), and marginal tax brackets (15% for $0 - $36,900 taxable income, 28% for $36,901 - $89,150 taxable income, and 31% for taxable income over $89,150). All of these numbers pertain to marrieds filing jointly.

The $1,586 contributed to retirement plans with before-tax income was deducted from wages ($67,780 - $1,586 = $66,194).

Mortgage interest was calculated by adding the interest paid on their 2 homes ($1,154 and $5,415), the $1,088 loan origination fee paid on the new home, and the $2,176 paid in discount points.

There was a $2,651 capital loss on the IBM stock ($6,525 - $163 - $9,013), a $539 capital gain on the Walgreens stock ($4,525 - $136 - $3,850), and capital gains distributions on the Kemper International Fund of $56. This produced a net capital loss of $2,056.

The dividends and capital gains distributions on the Evergreen Fund were not included since that is an IRA investment.

According to the 1993 tax estimate, Scott and Paula will pay about $1,441 less in taxes in 1993 than in 1992. Part of that savings can be attributed to the larger itemized deductions on the new house, but a large portion of the tax savings is a result of the net capital loss on their investments.

Part 2, Question 2

```
+FP/PC-----------------------------------------------------------FP/PC+
|          C H E C K I N G   A C C O U N T   R E C O N C I L I A T I O N          |
+---------------------------------------------------------------------+
```

For the Month of   January   , 1993

Accountholder Name(s):Scott and Paula Garnett

Type of Account:NOW

----

1. Ending balance shown on bank statement..................... $ 1562.15
   Add up checks and withdrawals still outstanding:

Check # or date	Amount	Check # or date	Amount	Check # or date	Amount
1206	138.98	1210	65.99	01/29/93	35.00
	0.00		0.00		0.00
	0.00		0.00		0.00
	0.00		0.00		0.00
	0.00		0.00		0.00
	0.00		0.00		0.00

                                              TOTAL $ 239.97

2. Deduct total checks/withdrawals still
   outstanding from bank balance............................. - $ 239.97

Date	Amount	Date	Amount	Date	Amount
01/28/93	70.92		0.00		0.00
	0.00		0.00		0.00
	0.00		0.00		0.00
	0.00		0.00		0.00
	0.00		0.00		0.00

                                              TOTAL $ 70.92

3. Add total deposits still outstanding
   to bank balance... + $ 70.92

|A| ADJUSTED BANK BALANCE (1-2+3)........................... $ 1393.10

4. Ending balance shown in checkbook.......................... $ 1389.34

5. Deduct any bank service charges for the period............ - $ 0.00

6. Add interest earned for the period......................... + $ 3.76

 B| NEW CHECKBOOK BALANCE (4-5+6)........................... $ 1393.10

Adjusted bank balance = new checkbook balance...the account IS reconciled.

Part 2, Question 6a

```
FP/PC----------------------------------------------------------------FP/PC+
      F U T U R E   V A L U E   O F   A   S I N G L E   C A S H   F L O W  |
----------------------------------------------------------------------------+

                Single cash flow.............      6516.00
                Rate of return...............         8.00%
                Number of years..............        28.00

                Future value.................     56214.23

-----------------------------------------------------------------------------


FP/PC----------------------------------------------------------------FP/PC+
        F U T U R E   V A L U E   O F   A N   A N N U I T Y            |
----------------------------------------------------------------------------+

                Annuity payment..............      1350.00
                Rate of return...............         8.00%
                Number of years..............        28.00

                Future value.................    128707.42

-----------------------------------------------------------------------------
```

$ 56,214.23
128,707.42
$ 184,921.65

Part 2, Question 6b

```
FP/PC----------------------------------------------------------------FP/PC+
    SETTING INVESTMENT GOALS:  MAKING A SERIES OF INVESTMENTS OVER TIME     |
----------------------------------------------------------------------------+

    Targeted financial goal................................    250000
    Projected average return on investments................      8.00
    Number of years to target date.........................     28.00
    Amount of initial investment (if any)..................      6516

    Terminal value of initial investment...................     56214
    Balance to come from savings plan......................    193786
    Amount of each annual investment in the series.........      2033

-----------------------------------------------------------------------------
```

$1,355 Scott's contribution
  678 Employer matching
$2,033

Part 2, Question 1

```
+FP/PC--------------------------------------------------------FP/PC+
|        MORTGAGE PAYMENT CALCULATION GIVEN PRINCIPAL, INTEREST RATE AND TIME    |
+-------------------------------------------------------------------------------+

                    Principal...................    108800.00
                    Interest rate...............        8.50%
                    Number of years.............       30.00

                    Monthly mortgage payment.....      836.58

------------------------------------------------------------------------------------

+FP/PC--------------------------------------------------------FP/PC+
|        MORTGAGE PAYMENT CALCULATION GIVEN PRINCIPAL, INTEREST RATE AND TIME    |
+-------------------------------------------------------------------------------+

                    Principal...................    108800.00
                    Interest rate...............        6.00%
                    Number of years.............       30.00

                    Monthly mortgage payment.....      652.31

------------------------------------------------------------------------------------

+FP/PC--------------------------------------------------------FP/PC+
|        MORTGAGE PAYMENT CALCULATION GIVEN PRINCIPAL, INTEREST RATE AND TIME    |
+-------------------------------------------------------------------------------+

                    Principal...................    108800.00
                    Interest rate...............        8.00%
                    Number of years.............       30.00

                    Monthly mortgage payment.....      798.34*

------------------------------------------------------------------------------------

+FP/PC--------------------------------------------------------FP/PC+
|        MORTGAGE PAYMENT CALCULATION GIVEN PRINCIPAL, INTEREST RATE AND TIME    |
+-------------------------------------------------------------------------------+

                    Principal...................    108800.00
                    Interest rate...............       12.00%
                    Number of years.............       30.00

                    Monthly mortgage payment.....     1119.13**

------------------------------------------------------------------------------------
```

* only $2/month more than using the balance at the end of the 1st year ($107,578) and amortizing it over the remaining 29 years.

** $15/month more than using the balance at the end of the 3rd year ($106,013) and amortizing over the remaining 27 years. With the 2% annual cap, this would be the soonest this ARM could reach its maximum cap.

Part 2, Question 8

```
+FP/PC-------------------------------------------------------FP/PC+
|            H O M E   A F F O R D A B I L I T Y   A N A L Y S I S      |
+---------------------------------------------------------------------+
 1  Amount of annual income.........................................  68617
 2  Monthly income (Item 1 - 12)....................................   5718
 3  Lender's affordability ratio (as a percent).....................    30%
 4  Maximum monthly mortgage payment (PITI) (Item 2 x Item 3)........   1715
 5  Estimated monthly tax and homeowner's insurance payment.........    240
 6  Maximum monthly loan payment (Item 4 - Item 5)..................   1475
 7  Approximate average interest rate on loan (as a percent)........ 8.500%
 8  Planned loan maturity (in years)................................     30
 9  Mortgage payment per $10,000 (using Items 7 and 8 and rounded)....    77
10  Maximum loan based on monthly income
    ($10000 x Item 6 - Item 9)...................................... 191884
11  Funds available for making a down pmt.&  paying closing costs..... 23750
12  Funds available for making a down payment (Item 11 x 2 - 3)....... 15833
13  Maximum purchase price based on available monthly income
    (Item 10 + Item 12)............................................. 207718
14  Minimum acceptable down payment (as a percent)..................    10%
15  Maximum purchase price based on down payment
    (Item 12 - Item 14)............................................. 158333
16  Maximum home purchase price (lower of Item 13 and Item 15)....... 158333
```

Part 2, Question 10

```
+FP/PC--------------------------------------------------------- FP/PC+
|                                                                     |
|                      B A L A N C E   S H E E T                      |
+---------------------------------------------------------------------+
```

Scott and Paula Garnett   02/28/93

```
---------------------------------------------------------------------
            ASSETS              |       LIABILITIES AND NET WORTH
---------------------------------------------------------------------
```

Liquid Assets:		Current Liabilities	
Cash on hand.............	350	Utilities.................	0
In checking..............	1750	Rent......................	0
Savings accounts.........	0	Insurance premiums........	0
Money market funds		Taxes.....................	0
and deposits...........	7752	Medical/dental bills.....	0
CDs < 1 yr. maturity.....	2950	Repair bills.............	0
Other....................	0	Bank crd. card balances..	3523
		Dept. store charge cards.	2067
Total Liquid Assets.....	12802	Travel/entrtmt. card.....	0
		Gas/other credit cards...	0
Investments:		Bank line of credit......	0
Stocks I.................	0	Other cur. liabilities...	0
II..................	0		
Bonds I.................	0	Total Cur. Liabilities.	5590
II..................	0		
CDs > 1 yr. maturity.....	0	Long-term Liabilities	
Mut. funds I.............	3502	Primary res. mortgage....	108800
II.............	4582	Second home mortgage.....	0
Real estate..............	0	Real estate investments..	0
Retirement funds.........	14646	Auto loans...............	6392
Other....................	0	Appliance/furn. loans....	0
		Home improvement loans...	0
Total Investments......	22730	Educational loans........	869
		Other I..................	2256
Real Property		II..................	0
Primary residence........	128000		
Second home..............	0	Total Long-term Liab...	118317
Car I....................	4500		
II....................	13000		
Recreation equipment.....	2000		
Other....................	0		
Total Real Property.....	147500		
Personal Property			
Furniture and appl.......	21500		
Stereos, TVs, etc........	10750		
Clothing.................	8525		
Jewelry..................	24500	(II) Tot. Liabilities.	123907
Other....................	2500		
		Net Worth [(II)-(III)].	126900
Total Personal Property.	67775		
		Total Liab. and Net Worth..	250807
(I) Total Assets......	250807		======
	======		

Part 2, Question 11

```
+-FP/PC------------------------------------------------------------FP/PC-+
|          M O N T H L Y   C A S H   B U D G E T   S U M M A R Y          |
+------------------------------------------------------------------------+
```

NAME(S): Scott and Paula Garnett   Page 1

FOR THE YEAR ENDING 12/31/93	JAN	FEB	MAR
Take-Home Pay: Source 1	2834	2834	2834
Take-Home Pay: Source 2	1551	1551	1551
Take-Home Pay: Source 3	0	0	0
Bonuses and Commissions	0	0	0
Pensions and Annuities	0	0	0
Interest	33	33	33
Dividends	0	0	21
Rents	0	0	0
Sale of Securities	5375	5376	0
Other *Capital gains distributions*	0	0	52
Other Income: Source 1 *Sale of house*	6966	6966	0
Other Income: Source 2 *Tax refund*	0	0	0
TOTAL INCOME	16759	16760	4491
Rent/Mortgage Payment	617	617	652
Repairs, Maintenance, Improvements	65	65	107
Gas, Utilities, Water	120	120	160
Phone	30	30	30
Cable TV and Other	0	0	0
Groceries	330	330	330
Dining Out	90	90	90
Loan/Lease Payments	336	336	336
License Plates, Fees, Etc.	0	0	0
Gas, Oil, Tires, Maintenance	140	140	140
Health Insurance, Etc.	105	105	105
Doctor, Dentist, Hospital, Medicine	41	41	41
Clothing, Shoes, Accessories	200	200	200
Homeowner's Insurance ¢ *Private mortgage insurance*	38	38	69
Life Insurance	15	15	15
Automobile Insurance	0	0	598
Income and Social Security Taxes	0	0	0
Property Taxes	98	98	171
Loan Payments	0	0	0
Purchases and Repairs	42	42	42
Laundry, Cosmetics, Hair Care	45	45	45
Vacations	0	0	0
Other Recreation and Entertainment	75	75	75
Savings and Investments	681	738	754
Charitable Contributions	25	25	25
~~Gifts~~ *Miscellaneous*	50	50	50
~~Education Expenses~~ *Financial planning fee*	375	375	375
~~Subscriptions, Magazines, Books~~ *Front-end cost*	8209	8209	8208
Other Expenditures: Item 1 *Stafford, computer, credit*	606	606	606
Other Expenditures: Item 2 *Child care Card debt*	350	350	350
Fun Money	150	150	150
TOTAL EXPENDITURES	12833	12890	13724
CASH SUPLUS (OR DEFICIT)	3926	3870	-9233
CUMULATIVE CASH SUPLUS (OR DEFICIT)	3926	7796	-1437

FOR THE YEAR ENDING 12/31/93	APR	MAY	JUN
Take-Home Pay:　Source 1	2834	2834	2834
Take-Home Pay:　Source 2	1551	1551	1551
Take-Home Pay:　Source 3	0	0	988
Bonuses and Commissions	0	0	0
Pensions and Annuities	0	0	0
Interest	33	33	33
Dividends	0	0	22
Rents	0	0	0
Sale of Securities	0	0	0
Other *Capital gains distributions*	0	0	52
Other Income:　Source 1 *Sale of house*	0	0	0
Other Income:　Source 2 *Tax refund*	3145	0	0
TOTAL INCOME	7563	4418	5480
Rent/Mortgage Payment	652	652	652
Repairs, Maintenance, Improvements	107	107	107
Gas, Utilities, Water	160	160	160
Phone	30	30	30
Cable TV and Other	0	0	0
Groceries	330	330	330
Dining Out	90	90	90
Loan/Lease Payments	336	336	336
License Plates, Fees, Etc.	0	0	0
Gas, Oil, Tires, Maintenance	140	140	140
Health Insurance, Etc.	105	105	105
Doctor, Dentist, Hospital, Medicine	41	41	41
Clothing, Shoes, Accessories	200	200	200
Homeowner's Insurance *& Private mortgage insurance*	69	69	69
Life Insurance	15	15	15
Automobile Insurance	0	0	0
Income and Social Security Taxes	0	0	0
Property Taxes	171	171	171
Loan Payments	0	0	0
Purchases and Repairs	42	42	42
Laundry, Cosmetics, Hair Care	45	45	45
Vacations	0	0	0
Other Recreation and Entertainment	75	75	75
Savings and Investments	681	681	755
Charitable Contributions	25	25	25
Gifts *Miscellaneous*	50	50	50
Education Expenses *Financial planning fee*	375	0	0
Subscriptions, Magazines, Books *Front-end costs*	0	0	0
Other Expenditures:　Item 1 *Stafford, computer, credit*	606	606	606
Other Expenditures:　Item 2 *Child care Card debt*	350	350	350
Fun Money	150	150	150
TOTAL EXPENDITURES	4845	4470	4544
CASH SUPLUS (OR DEFICIT)	2718	-52	936
CUMULATIVE CASH SUPLUS (OR DEFICIT)	1281	1229	2165

NAME(S): Scott and Paula Garnett   Page 3

FOR THE YEAR ENDING 12/31/93	JUL	AUG	SEP
Take-Home Pay: Source 1	2834	2834	2834
Take-Home Pay: Source 2	1551	1551	1551
Take-Home Pay: Source 3	988	0	0
Bonuses and Commissions	0	0	0
Pensions and Annuities	0	0	0
Interest	33	33	33
Dividends	0	0	21
Rents	0	0	0
Sale of Securities	0	0	0
Other *Capital gains distributions*	0	0	52
Other Income: Source 1 *Sale of house*	0	0	0
Other Income: Source 2 *Tax refunds*	0	0	0
TOTAL INCOME	5406	4418	4491
Rent/Mortgage Payment	652	652	652
Repairs, Maintenance, Improvements	107	107	107
Gas, Utilities, Water	160	160	160
Phone	30	30	30
Cable TV and Other	0	0	0
Groceries	330	330	330
Dining Out	90	90	90
Loan/Lease Payments	336	336	336
License Plates, Fees, Etc.	0	0	0
Gas, Oil, Tires, Maintenance	140	140	140
Health Insurance, Etc.	105	105	105
Doctor, Dentist, Hospital, Medicine	41	41	41
Clothing, Shoes, Accessories	200	200	200
Homeowner's Insurance *: private mortgage insurance*	69	69	69
Life Insurance	15	15	15
Automobile Insurance	0	597	0
Income and Social Security Taxes	0	0	0
Property Taxes	171	171	171
Loan Payments	0	0	0
Purchases and Repairs	42	42	42
Laundry, Cosmetics, Hair Care	45	45	45
Vacations	0	450	0
Other Recreation and Entertainment	75	75	75
Savings and Investments	681	681	754
Charitable Contributions	25	25	25
~~Gifts~~ *Miscellaneous*	50	50	50
~~Education Expenses~~ *Financial planning fee*	0	0	0
~~Subscriptions, Magazines, Books~~ *Front-end costs*	0	0	0
Other Expenditures: Item 1 *Stafford, computer credit*	606	606	606
Other Expenditures: Item 2 *Child care Cash debt*	350	350	350
Fun Money	150	150	150
TOTAL EXPENDITURES	4470	5517	4543
CASH SUPLUS (OR DEFICIT)	936	-1099	-52
CUMULATIVE CASH SUPLUS (OR DEFICIT)	3101	2002	1950

NAME(S): Scott and Paula Garnett   Page 4

FOR THE YEAR ENDING 12/31/93	OCT	NOV	DEC	TOTAL
Take-Home Pay: Source 1	2834	2834	2834	34008
Take-Home Pay: Source 2	1551	1551	1551	18612
Take-Home Pay: Source 3	0	0	0	1976
Bonuses and Commissions	0	0	0	0
Pensions and Annuities	0	0	0	0
Interest	33	33	182	545
Dividends	0	0	22	86
Rents	0	0	0	0
Sale of Securities	0	0	0	10751
Other *Capital gains distribution*	0	0	52	208
Other Income: Source 1 *Sale of house*	0	0	0	13932
Other Income: Source 2 *Tax refund*	0	0	0	3145
TOTAL INCOME	4418	4418	4641	83263
Rent/Mortgage Payment	652	652	652	7754
Repairs, Maintenance, Improvements	107	107	107	1200
Gas, Utilities, Water	160	160	160	1840
Phone	30	30	30	360
Cable TV and Other	0	0	0	0
Groceries	330	330	330	3960
Dining Out	90	90	90	1080
Loan/Lease Payments	336	336	336	4032
License Plates, Fees, Etc.	0	0	0	0
Gas, Oil, Tires, Maintenance	140	140	140	1680
Health Insurance, Etc.	105	105	105	1260
Doctor, Dentist, Hospital, Medicine	41	41	41	492
Clothing, Shoes, Accessories	200	200	200	2400
Homeowner's Insurance *& Private mortgage insurance*	69	69	69	766
Life Insurance	15	15	15	180
Automobile Insurance	0	0	0	1195
Income and Social Security Taxes	0	0	0	0
Property Taxes	171	171	171	1906
Loan Payments	0	0	0	0
Purchases and Repairs	42	42	42	504
Laundry, Cosmetics, Hair Care	45	45	45	540
Vacations	0	0	0	450
Other Recreation and Entertainment	75	75	75	900
Savings and Investments	681	681	904	8672
Charitable Contributions	25	25	25	300
~~Gifts~~ *Miscellaneous*	50	50	50	600
~~Education Expenses~~ *Financial planning fee*	0	0	0	1500
~~Subscriptions, Magazines, Books~~ *Points and costs*	0	0	0	24626
Other Expenditures: Item 1 *Stafford, computer credit*	606	606	606	7272
Other Expenditures: Item 2 *Child care (Car's 200)*	350	350	350	4200
Fun Money	150	150	150	1800
TOTAL EXPENDITURES	4470	4470	4693	81469
CASH SUPLUS (OR DEFICIT)	-52	-52	-52	1794
CUMULATIVE CASH SUPLUS (OR DEFICIT)	1898	1846	1794	1794

Part 2, Question 11

```
-FP/PC-----------------------------------------------------------------FP/PC-+
                    C A S H   B U D G E T   S U M M A R Y                    |
-----------------------------------------------------------------------------+
NAME(S): Scott and Paula Garnett
FOR YEAR ENDING 12/31/93
```

	Total Income	Total Expenses	Cash Surplus (Deficit)	Cumulative Cash Surplus (Deficit)
Jan	$ 16759	$ 12833	$ 3926	$ 3926
Feb	16760	12890	3870	7796
Mar	4491	13724	-9233	-1437
Apr	7563	4845	2718	1281
May	4418	4470	-52	1229
Jun	5480	4544	936	2165
Jul	5406	4470	936	3101
Aug	4418	5517	-1099	2002
Sep	4491	4543	-52	1950
Oct	4418	4470	-52	1898
Nov	4418	4470	-52	1846
Dec	4641	4693	-52	1794
TOTALS ..	$ 83263	$ 81469		$ 1794

```
   ----------------------------------------------------------------------+
```

Part 2, Question 12

FEDERAL INCOME TAX WORKSHEET
Scott and Paula Garnett

	1992	1993
INCOME		
1. Wages, salaries, tips, etc.	$63,840	$66,194
2. Interest income	543	543
3. Dividends	560	24
4. Capital gains (losses)	589	(2,056)
5. Net business income (loss)	0	
6. Income (deductible losses) from rental property	0	
7. Other income	0	
8. TOTAL INCOME (add lines 1 - 7)	$65,532	$64,705
ADJUSTMENTS		
9. Keogh contributions	$0	$0
10. AGI before IRA contributions (subtract line 9 from line 8)	65,532	64,705
11. Deductible IRA contributions	0	
12. ADJUSTED GROSS INCOME (subtract line 11 from line 10)	$65,532	$64,705
ITEMIZED DEDUCTIONS		
13. Deductible medical expenses	$0	$0
14. State and local income and property taxes	1,176	1,906
15. Mortgage interest	6,955	9,833
16. Other deductible interest	0	
17. Charitable contributions	300	300
18. Deductible misc. expenses	0	
19. Casualty and theft losses	0	
20. TOTAL ITEMIZED DEDUCTIONS (add lines 13 - 21)	$8,431	$12,039
TAXABLE INCOME		
21. Write in the amount on line 20 or or your standard deduction, whichever is greater	$8,431	$12,039
22. Personal exemptions	9,200	9,400
23. TAXABLE INCOME (substract lines 21 and 22 from line 12)	$47,901	$43,266
TAX LIABILITY		
24. Tax before credits (see tax tables)	$8,758	$7,317
25. Child care credit	779	779
26. YOUR TAX (subtract line 25 from line 24)	$7,979	$6,538
TAX WITHHELD	$11,124	$8,000
TAX DUE or (REFUND)	($3,145)	($1,462)

REPRESENTATIVE ANSWERS: The Garnett Case

<u>Part Three</u>

1. The following are the March minimum monthly payments for Scott and Paula's revolving credit:

Visa	$118.80	--the greater of ($1,188 x .10) or $20
MasterCard Gold	116.75	--the greater of ($2,335 x .05) or $20
Dillards	74.30	--the greater of ($ 743 x .10) or $20
Foleys	50.00	--the greater of ($ 499 x .05) or $50
Sears	24.75	--the greater of ($ 825 x .03) or $15
	$384.60	

2. Scott and Paula's debt safety ratio is 20%, a point that is considered an indicator of potential credit problems. Scott and Paula should concentrate on their goal of paying off their revolving credit and avoid taking on any new debt at this time.

Monthly consumer debt payment	Annual after-tax income
$385 credit cards	$34,006 Scott
336 Dodge Caravan	18,613 Paula
81 Stafford loan	1,976 Paula's summer job
112 computer	$54,595
$914	

$54,595/12 = $4,550

$914/$4,550 = 20%

3. Scott and Paula's Visa card has an 18.0% APR (.015/month), a grace period, and the finance charge is calculated using the adjusted balance method.

Date	Transaction	Amount	Balance	Finance Charge Calculation
4/1	Beginning Balance	$1,089	$1,089	
4/20	Payment	154	935	
	Total Finance Charge			$935 x .015 = $14.03

Their MasterCard Gold has a 13.9% APR (.0116/month), no grace period, and the finance charge is calculated using the average daily balance method.

Date	Transaction	Amount	Balance	Finance Charge Calculation
4/1	Beginning Balance	$1,698	$1,698	$1,698 x .0116 x 5 = $ 3.28 / 30
4/6	Purchase	23	1,721	$1,721 x .0116 x 17 = $11.31 / 30
4/23	Purchase	116	1,837	$1,837 x .0116 x 2 = $ 1.42 / 30
4/25	Payment	256	1,581	$1,581 x .0116 x 6 = $ 3.67 / 30
	Total Finance Charge			$19.68

4.   Since a card holder's legal liability is the lesser of $50 or the amount charged, Scott and Paula's maximum liability in this case would be $196.

5.   Visa   Annual cost for Scott and Paula
        Annual fee of $30   Total cost would be the $30 annual fee since they
        Interest rate of 18.0%   would pay off the total bill at the end of each
        A grace period   billing cycle.
        Adjusted balance method

        MasterCard Gold
        Annual fee of $0 $300.00 average daily balance
        Interest rate of 13.9%   x.139 APR
        No grace period $ 41.70
        Average daily balance method

        Under these use and payment conditions, the Visa card would be the less expensive bank card for Scott and Paula.

6a.   See computer printout.

        General Telephone Credit Union
        Monthly payment using Exhibit 8.8   Finance charge
                $ 33.22 payment per $1,000 $132.88 monthly payment
                x   4   x   36 months
                $132.88 monthly payment   4,784 total cost
                                                           - 4,000 principal
                                                            $ 784 finance charge

        On a simple interest loan, the APR is always equal to the stated rate (12%).

        Ace Furniture
        Finance charge = $4,000 x .10 x 3 = $1,200

        Monthly payment = ($4,000 + $1,200)/36 = $144.44

        $$APR = \frac{(12)\ [(95)(36) + 9]\ (\$1,200)}{(12)(36)(36+1)\ [(4)(\$4,000) + \$1,200]} = 17.96\%$$

        I would recommend the General Telephone Credit Union loan if Scott and Paula decide to borrow for furniture. It has the lower APR, monthly payment, and finance charges.

b.   See computer printout. $417 is paid in interest on the General Telephone loan the first year, $267 is paid the second year, and $99 is paid the third year.

c.   See computer printout. If Scott and Paul decide to buy furniture now, it would be less expensive to pay cash rather than to use credit. However, I recommend that they do not buy the furniture now. Their debt safety ratio is already very high, indicating they should not take on more debt. In addition, their liquidity level is low so they should not deplete their liquid assets.

7. See computer printouts. The MasterCard Gold is the only current credit card that could be used for consolidation of $5,600 because the credit line on the Visa is only $4,000. With the 18% rate of interest, Scott and Paula would not want to use the Visa for consolidation anyway.

	Without Consolidation	MasterCard Gold	Home Equity Line of Credit
Current APR	13.9% to 18% (av. 15.95%)	13.9%	8.5%
Minimum monthly payment	$385 (Ques. 1)	$5,600 x .05 $ 280	$69 (Computer printout)
Assuming 16-month payoff period:			
monthly payment	$392	$386	$372
total finance charge	$652	$566	$342
tax savings	$ 0	$ 0	$ 96 (28% MTR)
additional costs	$ 60	$ 0	$ 80
Total cost	$652	$566	$342
	- 0	- 0	- 96
	+ 60	+ 0	+80
	$712	$566	$326

I did the analysis using a 16-month payoff period since that is how long payoff would take if Scott and Paula did not consolidate their revolving debt but did continue to make close to the minimum monthly payment for March over the next 16 months.

Consolidation using the home equity line of credit is the least expensive option being considered. However, if they can't make the payments on this line, they could lose their home. I would recommend that Scott and Paula open the home equity line of credit and transfer all their revolving debt to this line of credit. In addition, I feel they should close (or at least not use) their MasterCard Gold. The Visa and retail credit cards should be used only to charge items that will be paid off upon billing each month. Scott and Paula need to be very careful about charging up their revolving accounts again.

Part 3, Question 6a

```
+FP/PC----------------------------------------------------------FP/PC+
|     A N A L Y S I S   O F   I N S T A L L M E N T   L O A N S :   A P R  |
+---------------------------------------------------------------------+
```
General Telephone Credit Union

```
              Loan principal............................  4000

              Annual interest rate (%)..................  12.00

              Length of the loan in years...............  3.00

              Is this an add-on loan (Y or N)?..........  N


              Total finance charge......................   783

              Monthly loan payment......................   133

              Approximate APR...........................  12.00%
```

```
---------------------------------------------------------------------
```

```
+FP/PC----------------------------------------------------------FP/PC+
|     A N A L Y S I S   O F   I N S T A L L M E N T   L O A N S :   A P R  |
+---------------------------------------------------------------------+
```
Ace Furniture Company

```
              Loan principal............................  4000

              Annual interest rate (%)..................  10.00

              Length of the loan in years...............  3.00

              Is this an add-on loan (Y or N)?..........  Y


              Total finance charge......................  1200

              Monthly loan payment......................   144

              Approximate APR...........................  17.96%
```

```
---------------------------------------------------------------------
```

Part 3, Question 66

MONTHLY PAYMENT ANALYSIS FOR A SIMPLE INTEREST LOAN

PAGE 1

General Telephone Credit Union

Month	Outstanding Loan Bal.	Monthly Payment	Interest Charges	Principal Reduction
1	4,000.00	132.86	40.00	92.86
2	3,907.14	132.86	39.07	93.79
3	3,813.35	132.86	38.13	94.73
4	3,718.62	132.86	37.19	95.67
5	3,622.95	132.86	36.23	96.63
6	3,526.32	132.86	35.26	97.60
7	3,428.72	132.86	34.29	98.57
8	3,330.15	132.86	33.30	99.56
9	3,230.59	132.86	32.31	100.55
10	3,130.04	132.86	31.30	101.56
11	3,028.48	132.86	30.28	102.58
12	2,925.90	132.86	29.26	103.60
13	2,822.30	132.86	28.22	104.64
14	2,717.67	132.86	27.18	105.68
15	2,611.98	132.86	26.12	106.74
16	2,505.24	132.86	25.05	107.81
17	2,397.43	132.86	23.97	108.89
18	2,288.55	132.86	22.89	109.97
19	2,178.57	132.86	21.79	111.07
20	2,067.50	132.86	20.68	112.18
21	1,955.32	132.86	19.55	113.31
22	1,842.01	132.86	18.42	114.44
23	1,727.57	132.86	17.28	115.58
24	1,611.98	132.86	16.12	116.74
25	1,495.24	132.86	14.95	117.91
26	1,377.34	132.86	13.77	119.09
27	1,258.25	132.86	12.58	120.28
28	1,137.97	132.86	11.38	121.48
29	1,016.49	132.86	10.16	122.70
30	893.80	132.86	8.94	123.92
31	769.87	132.86	7.70	125.16
32	644.71	132.86	6.45	126.41
33	518.30	132.86	5.18	127.68
34	390.62	132.86	3.91	128.95
35	261.67	132.86	2.62	130.24
36	131.43	132.74	1.31	131.43
TOTAL		4,782.84	782.84	4,000.00

Part 3, Question 6c

```
+FP/PC-------------------------------------------------------------FP/PC+
|                B U Y   O N   T I M E   O R   P A Y   C A S H           |
+-----------------------------------------------------------------------+
```

Cost of Borrowing:

1. Loan payments.

    Loan principal: 4000   Annual rate: 12.000% Length: 3.00 ....   132.86

2. Total loan payments (monthly PMT x loan length in months).......   4782.86

3. Less: Principal amount of loan.................................   4000.00

4. Total interest paid of life of loan (line 2 - line 3)..........   782.86
                                                                       ----

5. Tax considerations:

    ? Is this a home equity loan? (Y/N)...............................   N
    ? Do you itemize deductions on your federal tax returns? (Y/N).   Y

6. Your federal tax bracket (15, 28, or 31%).....................   28%

7. Taxes saved due to interest deductions (if applicable)..........   0.00

8. Total after-tax cost of borrowing (line 4 - line 7)............   782.86

Cost of Paying Cash:

9. Annual int. earned on savings. Annual interest rate: 4.500% ...   180.00

10. Annual after-tax int. earnings [line 9 x (1 - line 6)].........   129.60

11. Total after-tax int. earnings (line 10 x loan length in years)..   388.80

Net Cost of Borrowing:

12. Difference in cost of borrowing vs. cost of paying cash (line 4
    OR line 8 less line 11). If > 0, pay cash; if < 0, borrow......   394.06
                                                                       ========
```
```

Part 3, Question 1

```
FP/PC-------------------------------------------------------------FP/PC+
        A N A L Y S I S   O F   I N S T A L L M E N T   L O A N S :   A P R   |
--------------------------------------------------------------------------+
```

Without consolidation

```
          Loan principal.............................  5600

          Annual interest rate (%)...................  15.95

          Length of the loan in years................  1.33

          Is this an add-on loan (Y or N)?...........  N


          Total finance charge.......................   652

          Monthly loan payment.......................   392

          Approximate APR............................  15.95%
```

```
FP/PC-------------------------------------------------------------FP/PC+
        A N A L Y S I S   O F   I N S T A L L M E N T   L O A N S :   A P R   |
--------------------------------------------------------------------------+
```

Consolidation on MasterCard Gold

```
          Loan principal.............................  5600

          Annual interest rate (%)...................  13.90

          Length of the loan in years................  1.33

          Is this an add-on loan (Y or N)?...........  N


          Total finance charge.......................   566

          Monthly loan payment.......................   386

          Approximate APR............................  13.90%
```

```
FP/PC-------------------------------------------------------------FP/PC+
        A N A L Y S I S   O F   I N S T A L L M E N T   L O A N S :   A P R   |
--------------------------------------------------------------------------+
```

Consolidation on Home Equity Loan

```
          Loan principal.............................  5600

          Annual interest rate (%)...................  8.50

          Length of the loan in years................  1.33

          Is this an add-on loan (Y or N)?...........  N


          Total finance charge.......................   342

          Monthly loan payment.......................   372

          Approximate APR............................  8.50%
```

Part 3, Question 1

```
+FP/PC------------------------------------------------------FP/PC+
|        A N A L Y S I S   O F   I N S T A L L M E N T   L O A N S :   A P R  |
+------------------------------------------------------------------+
```

Minimum monthly payment on the Home Equity loan

Loan principal............................. 5600

Annual interest rate (%).................. 8.50

Length of the loan in years............... 10.00

Is this an add-on loan (Y or N)?.......... N

Total finance charge...................... 2732

Monthly loan payment...................... 69

Approximate APR........................... 8.50%

```
------------------------------------------------------------------
```

<u>REPRESENTATIVE ANSWERS:</u> <u>The Garnett Case</u>

<u>Part Four</u>

1.   Scott is 32 years old and has a gross annual income of $42,500. I used the closest factor in Exhibit 9.1, 8.4, for a 30-year-old earning $40,000.

$ 42,500 gross income
x   8.4 factor
$357,000 total life insurance needs
- 82,000 group term life insurance
-100,000 death benefit from retirement plan
$175,000 additional coverage needed

2.   Paula is 31 years old and has a gross annual income of $25,280. I used the closest factor, 7.4, for a 30-year-old earning $30,000.

$ 25,280 gross income
x   7.4 factor
$187,072 total life insurance needs
- 50,000 group term life insurance
-    1,689 retirement plan
$135,383 additional coverage needed

3.   No additional coverage is needed. See computer printout. This was calculated based on Scott and Paula's balance sheet after they bought their new house.

4.   No additional coverage is needed. See computer printout. This was also calculated based on their balance sheet after they bought their new house.

5.   While the multiple earnings approach is much easier to calculate than the needs approach, it is based on arbitrary assumptions and largely ignores the survivors' needs and the resources available to the survivors.

Using the multiple earnings approach and Exhibit 9.1 (based on replacing 75% of lost earnings for a married breadwinner with 2 children), we found that the Garnetts should buy $175,000 additional coverage on Scott and over $135,000 additional coverage on Paula. However, using the needs approach which considers the specific needs and resources of the family, we found that neither Scott nor Paula needed additional life insurance coverage.

6.   The following price comparisons are based on the premiums quoted in Exhibit 9.5 and 9.7 of the text.   Scott is currently receiving $82,000 life insurance coverage as well as a $100,000 death benefit through his retirement plan at no out-of-pocket cost to him. Therefore, I would recommend he keep this coverage. These employee benefits more than cover the Garnetts needs so I do not recommend additional life insurance on Scott's life. However, if Scott were to change jobs or otherwise lose these benefits, the situation should be quickly reevaluated.

Paula is currently paying $180 per year for $50,000 of term life insurance through her employer. This is expensive compared to the $131 per year she would pay for similar five-year renewable term coverage ($2.62 x 50). I recommend that she drop her group policy and replace it with individual five-year term coverage. Even though the life insurance needs analysis on Paula completed in Question 4 shows that there is no need for life insurance, upon closer analysis one notes that there are significant needs immediately to pay off debts, for final expenses, for the college education fund, and to build up the emergency fund as well as living expenses in Period 1. The negative life insurance need comes only after the children leave home. However, this excess which doesn't start for another 16 years will not help the family if Paula dies now. Within the next 16 years there is an income need of $63,707 and only $6,189 in resources assuming she drops her group life policy. I recommend that Paula buy $60,000 of five-year renewable term life insurance. This would cost approximately $157 per year ($2.62 x 60). I would not recommend the more expensive straight life policy ($12.47 x 60 = $748 per year) because the need for life insurance on Paula seems temporary. Paula's life insurance needs should also be regularly reevaluated as she and the family get older.

7. Scott should be the primary beneficiary on Paula's policy with Jason and Amy as the secondary beneficiaries. Paula should be the primary beneficiary on Scott's policy with the children named as secondary beneficiaries.

   I would recommend a lump-sum settlement option on both of their policies since they are each capable of handling the finances it the other dies. This option gives the greatest flexibility and perhaps enhanced investment return.

8. Based on the premiums quoted in Exhibit 10.6 of the text, Scott's current disability income policy is a very good buy. He is now paying $300 annually while the premium quoted in the text would be $541 per year for similar coverage--65% of gross monthly income ($3,542 x .65 = $2,302 per month), a 90-day waiting period, and coverage to age 65 ($23.50 x 23.02 = $541 per year). I recommend Scott keep the policy he has because of the good price and because he needs coverage for a long-term disability (to age 65) since he is the primary source of the family's income. While the 90-day waiting period would be tight given Scott and Paula's limited liquid assets, Scott does have 45 days of paid sick leave accumulated and they could come up with additional funds, if needed, from their investment assets.

9. Paula does not currently have a disability income policy, and the family does depend on her income (as shown in budget). I recommend that she purchase a private policy that covers 65% of her gross monthly income (as much as is generally available) and pays until age 65. Ignoring her summer job, Paula's gross monthly income is $1,907 so her coverage would be $1,240 per month. Paula has only 30 days of paid sick leave accumulated, but the lost of her salary would be less significant than the lost of Scott's salary so I recommend a 90-day waiting period on her policy as well. This would cost $291 per year ($23.50 x 12.40).

10. The maximum limit on Scott's major medical policy through his employer is $500,000 per year. A higher limit would be better, but this limit is adequate. With a $500 deductible and an $1,800 cap on the participation per year, Scott's maximum out-of-pocket cost on covered expenses would be $2,300 per year. This appears to be an acceptable health policy given their financial resources and Scott's health.

11. Paula's HMO seems to be very comprehensive with unlimited maximum coverage. While the exact out-of-pocket costs cannot be calculated, they should be quite low--$15 per doctor's visit and $10 per prescription. As long as there are good doctors and a good hospital associated with the HMO, this should provide very good health benefits.

12. I would not recommend that Scott be covered under Paula's HMO coverage even though it is more comprehensive. The extra cost ($480 per year) does not seem warranted since Scott is in good health. Nor would I recommend Paula be covered under Scott's policy. She would be paying more money ($360 per year) for what appears to be less coverage. There is no point in either of them being covered under both policies--especially since both policies have coordination of benefits provisions.

    While it does cost $120 per year more to cover Jason and Amy under Paula's HMO rather than Scott's major medical insurance, I recommend they continue doing this. Generally small children have enough colds, sickness, and accidents that it will probably be cost effective. This should be reevaluated as the children get older.

13. The HO-2 (Broad Form) should provide adequate coverage for their new home. I recommend the following coverages:

    House (replacement cost is 2,400 x $65 = $156,000)
          (80% of replacement cost is $124,800)
    Recommended coverage on house $150,000
    (somewhere between $124,800 & $156,000)

    Personal property   75,000
    (50% of $150,000 is standard for an HO-2 policy
      and should be adequate based on their balance sheet)

    Other structures (10% of dwelling)   15,000

    Loss of use (20% of dwelling)   30,000

    Personal liability (at least $100,000)   300,000

    Medical payments   1,000/person

    Deductible   500/occurrence

    Scott and Paula should check the policy to see if there are any special limitations on jewelry, boats, and computers that require additional consideration. They will probably find they want to purchase a scheduled personal property floater to cover their expensive pieces of jewelry. A $20,000 floater would cost approximately $350 annually. They also may want to consider replacement cost coverage on their personal property.

    Since there is nothing in the text to help estimate the cost of this insurance and the variations among states and regions are considerable, let's assume that the premium given in Part 2 ($650 per year) will purchase the basic policy. The personal property floater will cost an additional $350 a year.

14. I would recommend Scott and Paula increase their liability coverage to $300,000 (100/300/50 in split liability states). To keep the annual premium about the same as it currently is, they should increase their deductibles on both collision and comprehensive coverage to $500 per occurrence. They could easily handle the first $500 in damages with their liquid assets.

15. Scott and Paula really do not need umbrella liability coverage given their current financial condition. Given their professions, professional liability insurance in probably not needed either. The previously discussed insurance should adequately meet their needs for protection.

16. See computer printout. I used the budget from Part 2 and modified it for changes in insurance premiums. Increased insurance expenditures from my recommendations:

	Current Coverage	Recommended Coverage
Life insurance--Scott	$ 0	$ 0
Life insurance--Paula	180	157
Disability insurance--Scott	300	300
Disability insurance--Paula	0	291
Health insurance	960	960
Homeowners insurance	650	650
Personal property floater	0	350
Auto insurance	1,195	1,195
TOTAL	$3,285	$3,903

Increased expenditures from my recommendations are $618 per year.

Part 4, Question 3

Scott's Life Insurance

A. FAMILY INCOME NEEDS

1. DEBT LIQUIDATION   **Totals**
   a. Home mortgage.......................... 0
   b. Other loans............................ 15107
   c. Total debt (a + b).. 15107

2. FINAL E%4000PENSES... *4,000*

3. ANNUAL INCOME NEEDS   period1 Period2 Period3
   a. Monthly living expenses............... 4167   3000   2500
   b. Less: SS survivor's benefits......... 1500   0   950
   c. Less: Surviving spouse's income...... 2500   3500   1100
   d. Less: Other income................... 100   100   100
   e. Net monthly inc. needs (a-b-c-d)..... 67   -600   350
   f. Net yearly inc. needs (12 x e)....... 804   -7200   4200
   g. Number of years in period............ 16   18   22
   h. Total funding needed (d x e)......... 12864 -129600 92400
   i. Total living needs (h1 + h2 + h3)................................ -24336

4. Spouse reeducation fund... 0

5. Children's opportunity fund...................................... 30000

6. Other needs.. 5000

   TOTAL INCOME NEEDS (1c + 2 + 3i + 4 + 5 + 6)...................... 29771

_____

B. FINANCIAL RESOURCES AVAILABLE

1. Savings and investments *IRA and 401(k)*.... 11016

2. Group life insurance.................... 82000

3. Other life insurance *Retirement death benefit.* 100000

4. Other resources *Sale of Honda*...........   4500

   TOTAL RESOURCES AVAILABLE (1 + 2 + 3 + 4)...................... 197516

_____

C. ADDITIONAL LIFE INSURANCE NEEDS (A - B) (none if negative)......... -167745

_____

Part 4, Question 4

Paula's Life Insurance

A.   FAMILY INCOME NEEDS

  1. DEBT LIQUIDATION   Totals
     a. Home mortgage....................... 0
     b. Other loans.......................... 15107
     c. Total debt (a + b)....................................... 15107

  2. FINAL E%4000PENSES...*4,000*

  3. ANNUAL INCOME NEEDS   period1 Period2 Period3

	period1	Period2	Period3
a. Monthly living expenses..............	5000	3000	2500
b. Less: SS survivor's benefits.........	1300	0	1000
c. Less: Surviving spouse's income......	3550	3550	5700
d. Less: Other income...................	100	100	100
e. Net monthly inc. needs (a-b-c-d).....	50	-650	-4300
f. Net yearly inc. needs (12 x e).......	600	-7800	-51600
g. Number of years in period...........	16	17	15
h. Total funding needed (d x e).........	9600	-132600	-774000

     i. Total living needs (h1 + h2 + h3)............................. -897000

  4. Spouse reeducation fund... 0

  5. Children's opportunity fund.................................... 30000

  6. Other needs... 5000

     TOTAL INCOME NEEDS (1c + 2 + 3i + 4 + 5 + 6)...................... -842893

B.   FINANCIAL RESOURCES AVAILABLE

  1. Savings and investments *Retirement account.*   1689

  2. Group life insurance.................... 50000

  3. Other life insurance.................... 0

  4. Other resources *Sale of Honda*............ 4500

     TOTAL RESOURCES AVAILABLE (1 + 2 + 3 + 4)......................... 56189

C.   ADDITIONAL LIFE INSURANCE NEEDS (A - B) (none if negative)........ -899082

Part 4, Question 16

NAME(S): Scott and Paula Garnett   Page 1

FOR THE YEAR ENDING 12/31/93	JAN	FEB	MAR
Take-Home Pay: Source 1	2834	2834	2834
Take-Home Pay: Source 2	1551	1551	1551
Take-Home Pay: Source 3	0	0	0
Bonuses and Commissions	0	0	0
Pensions and Annuities	0	0	0
Interest	33	33	33
Dividends	0	0	21
Rents	0	0	0
Sale of Securities	5375	5376	0
Other *Capital gains distributions*	0	0	52
Other Income: Source 1 *Sale of house*	6966	6966	0
Other Income: Source 2 *Tax Refund*	0	0	0
TOTAL INCOME	16759	16760	4491
Rent/Mortgage Payment	617	617	652
Repairs, Maintenance, Improvements	65	65	107
Gas, Utilities, Water	120	120	160
Phone	30	30	30
Cable TV and Other	0	0	0
Groceries	330	330	330
Dining Out	90	90	90
Loan/Lease Payments	336	336	336
License Plates, Fees, Etc.	0	0	0
Gas, Oil, Tires, Maintenance	140	140	140
Health Insurance, Etc.	105	105	105
Doctor, Dentist, Hospital, Medicine	41	41	41
Clothing, Shoes, Accessories	200	200	200
Homeowner's Insurance *& Private mortgage insurance*	38	38	69
Life Insurance	15	15	15
Automobile Insurance	0	0	598
Income and Social Security Taxes	0	0	0
Property Taxes	98	98	171
Loan Payments	0	0	0
Purchases and Repairs	42	42	42
Laundry, Cosmetics, Hair Care	45	45	45
Vacations	0	0	0
Other Recreation and Entertainment	75	75	75
Savings and Investments	681	738	754
Charitable Contributions	25	25	25
~~Gifts~~ *Miscellaneous*	50	50	50
~~Education Expenses~~ *Financial planning fee*	375	375	375
~~Subscriptions, Magazines, Books~~ *Front-end costs*	8209	8209	8208
Other Expenditures: Item 1 *Stafford loan, computer*	606	606	606
Other Expenditures: Item 2 *Child care* *Credit card*	350	350	350
Fun Money	150	150	150
TOTAL EXPENDITURES	12833	12890	13724
CASH SUPLUS (OR DEFICIT)	3926	3870	-9233
CUMULATIVE CASH SUPLUS (OR DEFICIT)	3926	7796	-1437

FOR THE YEAR ENDING 12/31/93   APR   MAY   JUN

	APR	MAY	JUN
Take-Home Pay: Source 1	2834	2834	2834
Take-Home Pay: Source 2	1551	1551	1551
Take-Home Pay: Source 3	0	0	988
Bonuses and Commissions	0	0	0
Pensions and Annuities	0	0	0
Interest	33	33	33
Dividends	0	0	22
Rents	0	0	0
Sale of Securities	0	0	0
Other *Capital gains distributions*	0	0	52
Other Income: Source 1 *Sale of house*	0	0	0
Other Income: Source 2 *Tax refund*	3145	0	0
TOTAL INCOME	7563	4418	5480
Rent/Mortgage Payment	652	652	652
Repairs, Maintenance, Improvements	107	107	107
Gas, Utilities, Water	160	160	160
Phone	30	30	30
Cable TV and Other	0	0	0
Groceries	330	330	330
Dining Out	90	90	90
Loan/Lease Payments	336	336	336
License Plates, Fees, Etc.	0	0	0
Gas, Oil, Tires, Maintenance	140	140	140
Health Insurance, Etc.	396	105	105
Doctor, Dentist, Hospital, Medicine	41	41	41
Clothing, Shoes, Accessories	200	200	200
Homeowner's Insurance *+ Private mortgage insurance*	419	69	69
Life Insurance	157	0	0
Automobile Insurance	0	0	0
Income and Social Security Taxes	0	0	0
Property Taxes	171	171	171
Loan Payments	0	0	0
Purchases and Repairs	42	42	42
Laundry, Cosmetics, Hair Care	45	45	45
Vacations	0	0	0
Other Recreation and Entertainment	75	75	75
Savings and Investments	681	681	755
Charitable Contributions	25	25	25
~~Gifts~~ *Miscellaneous*	50	50	50
~~Education Expenses~~ *Financial planning fee*	375	0	0
~~Subscriptions, Magazines, Books~~ *Closing costs*	0	0	0
Other Expenditures: Item 1 *Student loan, computer,*	606	606	606
Other Expenditures: Item 2 *child care* *Credit cards*	350	350	350
Fun Money	150	150	150
TOTAL EXPENDITURES	5628	4455	4529
CASH SUPLUS (OR DEFICIT)	1935	-37	951
CUMULATIVE CASH SUPLUS (OR DEFICIT)	498	461	1412

M O N T H L Y   C A S H   B U D G E T   S U M M A R Y

NAME(S): Scott and Paula Garnett   Page 3

FOR THE YEAR ENDING 12/31/93	JUL	AUG	SEP
Take-Home Pay: Source 1	2834	2834	2834
Take-Home Pay: Source 2	1551	1551	1551
Take-Home Pay: Source 3	988	0	0
Bonuses and Commissions	0	0	0
Pensions and Annuities	0	0	0
Interest	33	33	33
Dividends	0	0	21
Rents	0	0	0
Sale of Securities	0	0	0
Other *Capital gains distributions*	0	0	52
Other Income: Source 1 *Sale of house*	0	0	0
Other Income: Source 2 *Tax refund*	0	0	0
TOTAL INCOME	5406	4418	4491
Rent/Mortgage Payment	652	652	652
Repairs, Maintenance, Improvements	107	107	107
Gas, Utilities, Water	160	160	160
Phone	30	30	30
Cable TV and Other	0	0	0
Groceries	330	330	330
Dining Out	90	90	90
Loan/Lease Payments	336	336	336
License Plates, Fees, Etc.	0	0	0
Gas, Oil, Tires, Maintenance	140	140	140
Health Insurance, Etc.	105	105	105
Doctor, Dentist, Hospital, Medicine	41	41	41
Clothing, Shoes, Accessories	200	200	200
Homeowner's Insurance *& Private mortgage insurance*	69	69	69
Life Insurance	0	0	0
Automobile Insurance	0	597	0
Income and Social Security Taxes	0	0	0
Property Taxes	171	171	171
Loan Payments	0	0	0
Purchases and Repairs	42	42	42
Laundry, Cosmetics, Hair Care	45	45	45
Vacations	0	450	0
Other Recreation and Entertainment	75	75	75
Savings and Investments	681	681	754
Charitable Contributions	25	25	25
~~Gifts~~ *Miscellaneous*	50	50	50
~~Education Expenses~~ *Financial planning fees*	0	0	0
~~Subscriptions,~~ Magazines, ~~Books~~ *front-end costs*	0	0	0
Other Expenditures: Item 1 *Stafford, Computer, credit*	606	606	606
Other Expenditures: Item 2 *Child care* *Cards*	350	350	350
Fun Money	150	150	150
TOTAL EXPENDITURES	4455	5502	4528
CASH SUPLUS (OR DEFICIT)	951	-1084	-37
CUMULATIVE CASH SUPLUS (OR DEFICIT)	2363	1279	1242

```
+-FP/PC--------------------------------------------------------------FP/PC-+
|              M O N T H L Y   C A S H   B U D G E T   S U M M A R Y       |
+-------------------------------------------------------------------------+
```

NAME(S): Scott and Paula Garnett   Page 4

FOR THE YEAR ENDING 12/31/93	OCT	NOV	DEC	TOTAL
Take-Home Pay: Source 1	2834	2834	2834	34008
Take-Home Pay: Source 2	1551	1551	1551	18612
Take-Home Pay: Source 3	0	0	0	1976
Bonuses and Commissions	0	0	0	0
Pensions and Annuities	0	0	0	0
Interest	33	33	182	545
Dividends	0	0	22	86
Rents	0	0	0	0
Sale of Securities	0	0	0	10751
Other *Capital gains distribution*	0	0	52	208
Other Income: Source 1 *Sale of house*	0	0	0	13932
Other Income: Source 2 *Tax refund*	0	0	0	3145
TOTAL INCOME	4418	4418	4641	83263
Rent/Mortgage Payment	652	652	652	7754
Repairs, Maintenance, Improvements	107	107	107	1200
Gas, Utilities, Water	160	160	160	1840
Phone	30	30	30	360
Cable TV and Other	0	0	0	0
Groceries	330	330	330	3960
Dining Out	90	90	90	1080
Loan/Lease Payments	336	336	336	4032
License Plates, Fees, Etc.	0	0	0	0
Gas, Oil, Tires, Maintenance	140	140	140	1680
Health Insurance, Etc.	105	105	105	1551
Doctor, Dentist, Hospital, Medicine	41	41	41	492
Clothing, Shoes, Accessories	200	200	200	2400
Homeowner's Insurance *& Private mortgage insurance*	69	69	69	1116
Life Insurance	0	0	0	202
Automobile Insurance	0	0	0	1195
Income and Social Security Taxes	0	0	0	0
Property Taxes	171	171	171	1906
Loan Payments	0	0	0	0
Purchases and Repairs	42	42	42	504
Laundry, Cosmetics, Hair Care	45	45	45	540
Vacations	0	0	0	450
Other Recreation and Entertainment	75	75	75	900
Savings and Investments	681	681	904	8672
Charitable Contributions	25	25	25	300
~~Gifts~~ *Miscellaneous*	50	50	50	600
~~Education Expenses~~ *Financial planning fee*	0	0	0	1500
~~Subscriptions, Magazines, Books~~ *Front-end costs*	0	0	0	24626
Other Expenditures: Item 1 *Stafford, computer, credit card*	606	606	606	7272
Other Expenditures: Item 2 *Child care*	350	350	350	4200
Fun Money	150	150	150	1800
TOTAL EXPENDITURES	4455	4455	4678	82132
CASH SUPLUS (OR DEFICIT)	-37	-37	-37	1131
CUMULATIVE CASH SUPLUS (OR DEFICIT)	1205	1168	1131	1131

Part 4, Question 16

```
+-FP/PC--------------------------------------------------------------FP/PC-+
|                  C A S H   B U D G E T   S U M M A R Y                    |
+--------------------------------------------------------------------------+
```

NAME(S): Scott and Paula Garnett
FOR YEAR ENDING 12/31/93

	Total Income	Total Expenses	Cash Surplus (Deficit)	Cumulative Cash Surplus (Deficit)
Jan	$ 16759	$ 12833	$ 3926	$ 3926
Feb	16760	12890	3870	7796
Mar	4491	13724	-9233	-1437
Apr	7563	5628	1935	498
May	4418	4455	-37	461
Jun	5480	4529	951	1412
Jul	5406	4455	951	2363
Aug	4418	5502	-1084	1279
Sep	4491	4528	-37	1242
Oct	4418	4455	-37	1205
Nov	4418	4455	-37	1168
Dec	4641	4678	-37	1131
TOTALS ..	$ 83263	$ 82132		$ 1131

```
+------------------------------------------------------------------------+
```

REPRESENTATIVE ANSWERS: The Garnett Case Study

Part Five

1.
Checking account ($1,750 x .03)	$ 52.50
General Tel. money market account ($7,752 x .045)	348.84
Bank of the Hills certificate of deposit ($2,200 x .05)	110.00
General Tel. certificate of deposit ($750 x .052)	39.00
TOTAL	$ 550.34

2.
Kemper International ($24/$3,298)   0.7%
Evergreen Fund ($62/$4,174)   1.5%

3. See computer printout. Over this particular 7 year period, Kemper International yielded only 1.7% per year. Since Kemper International is an international mutual fund with average risk, this return was definitely not adequate compensation for the risk.

$$\frac{.20 + \left[\dfrac{8.75 - 9.09}{7}\right]}{\left[\dfrac{8.75 + 9.09}{2}\right]} = 1.7\%$$

4. See computer printout. Evergreen Fund yielded an average of 9.96% annually over the 8 years Scott and Paula have owned this mutual fund. Evergreen is a growth mutual fund of average risk. This return is not phenomenal, but it is certainly better than the return on the Kemper International Fund.

$$\frac{.73 + \left[\dfrac{15.63 - 10.90}{8}\right]}{\left[\dfrac{15.63 + 10.90}{2}\right]} = 9.96\%$$

5. This could be done for any current 2-week period.

6. The following are quotes for December 14, 1992:

	NAV	Offer Price	Load	Load Percent
Kemper International	8.32	8.83	0.51	6%
Evergreen Fund	14.39	NL	0	0%

Neither of these funds have 12(b)-1 or redemption fees.

7.

	IBM	Walgreens
sales price per share	$ 65.25	$45.25
purchase price per share	- 90.125	- 38.50
gain (loss) per share	($24.875)	$ 6.75
number of shares	x 100	x 100
gross gain (loss)	($2,488)	$ 675
sales commissions	- 163	- 136
gain (loss)	($2,651)	$ 539

NET LOSS   ($2,112)

8. $2,112 capital loss
    x .28 marginal tax bracket
    $ 591 tax savings

9. Current dividend yield on blue-chip stock ($1.75/$33.25)   5.3%
    Current dividend yield on aggressive growth stock ($.75/$25.87)   2.9%

    See computer printouts for approximate annual yields.

    Blue Chip Stock

    $$\frac{1.75 + \left[\dfrac{43.00 - 33.25}{7}\right]}{\left[\dfrac{43.00 + 33.25}{2}\right]} = 8.2\%$$

    Aggressive Growth Stock

    $$\frac{.75 + \left[\dfrac{58.00 - 25.87}{7}\right]}{\left[\dfrac{58.00 + 25.87}{2}\right]} = 12.7\%$$

10. Current yield on corporate bond ($150/$3,000)   5.0%

    See computer printout for the yield-to-maturity.

    $$\frac{150 + \left[\dfrac{4,000 - 3,000}{7}\right]}{\left[\dfrac{4,000 + 3,000}{2}\right]} = 8.37\%$$

11. $$\frac{4.0\%}{1 - .28} = 5.56\% \text{ fully taxable equivalent yield}$$

    Yes, the tax-free bond has a higher after-tax current yield than the corporate bond, but without further information we can't compare the yield-to-maturity.

12. No, I would not recommend that Scott and Paula buy any stock on margin. The risk level is higher than their stated risk tolerance, their investment knowledge is not adequate, and they do not have enough liquid assets to comfortably meet a potential margin call.

13. Referring to Scott and Paula's goals (Part 1), they have fulfilled their primary goal of purchasing a larger home. Their current budget (Part 4) also includes savings for their emergency fund, retirement, and a new car as well as expenditures for paying off their credit card debt. It includes only partial funding for their college education goal. Therefore, I would recommend they designate the proceeds from the CDs to the college education fund.

   Since this is a long-term goal, I would recommend a growth-oriented investment. I feel that Scott and Paula's risk tolerance could handle this, but because of their limited funds, limited investment knowledge, and the lack of diversification inherent in a single stock purchase I would recommend they put the funds in a growth mutual fund. They could open the fund in December with the proceeds of the CD and the current savings that are now being put in their money market account. They could then start making their monthly contributions for this goal directly into the growth mutual fund.

Part 5, Question 3

```
+FP/PC-------------------------------------------------------------------FP/PC+
|  I N V E S T M E N T   R E T U R N S   F O R   A   M U T U A L   F U N D  |
+-----------------------------------------------------------------------------+

        Annual dividend and capital gains distribution...........   0.200
        Ending price per share...................................   8.750
        Beginning price per share................................   9.090
        Investment period in years...............................       7

        Return (approximate annual yield)........................   1.70%

-------------------------------------------------------------------------------
```

Part 5, Question 4

```
+FP/PC-------------------------------------------------------------------FP/PC+
|  I N V E S T M E N T   R E T U R N S   F O R   A   M U T U A L   F U N D  |
+-----------------------------------------------------------------------------+

        Annual dividend and capital gains distribution...........   0.730
        Ending price per share...................................  15.630
        Beginning price per share................................  10.900
        Investment period in years...............................       8

        Return (approximate annual yield)........................   9.96%

-------------------------------------------------------------------------------
```

Part 5, Question 9

```
+FP/PC-------------------------------------------------------FP/PC+
|            I N V E S T M E N T   R E T U R N S   F O R   A   S T O C K            |
+-----------------------------------------------------------------+

        Annual dividend.........................................    1.750
        (Future) selling price of the stock.....................   43.000
        (Current) market price of the stock....................   33.250
        Investment period in years..............................        7

        Return (approximate annual yield).......................    8.24%

-------------------------------------------------------------------
```

```
+FP/PC-------------------------------------------------------FP/PC+
|            I N V E S T M E N T   R E T U R N S   F O R   A   S T O C K            |
+-----------------------------------------------------------------+

        Annual dividend.........................................    0.750
        (Future) selling price of the stock.....................   58.000
        (Current) market price of the stock....................   25.870
        Investment period in years..............................        7

        Return (approximate annual yield).......................   12.73%

-------------------------------------------------------------------
```

Part 5, Question 10

```
+FP/PC-------------------------------------------------------FP/PC+
|            I N V E S T M E N T   R E T U R N S   F O R   A   B O N D            |
+-----------------------------------------------------------------+

        Annual interest income..................................    150.00
        Maturity value of the bond..............................   4000.00
        (Current) market price of the bond.....................   3000.00
        Years until maturity....................................         7

        Return (approximate yield to maturity)..................    8.37%

-------------------------------------------------------------------
```

Part Six--Chapter 15

1. $ 4,000 average monthly salary
        x   12
        $48,000 annual income
        x   .03
        $ 1,440
        x   39 number of years with employer
        $56,160 annual retirement benefit

2.   See computer printout.

3.   See computer printout.

4.   Scott and Paula's first retirement needs analysis (assuming they continue with their current employers until their retirement) indicates that they really do not need to continue contributing $75 per month to Scott's 401(k). However, this analysis is based on many assumptions over a very long period of time. The large retirement benefit Scott would receive if he stays with his present employer until he retires is the result of his working for the same company for 39 years. If he changes employers in the future, his retirement benefit could change dramatically as we saw in the second retirement needs analysis. Other assumptions, such as those for inflation and return on investments, could also be optimistic.

I recommend that Scott and Paula continue contributing $75 per month to Scott's 401(k) because of the tax deferral received on this type of investment and the fact that Scott's employer matches every $1.00 contribution with another $.50. If the children's college education fund is under-funded when they reach college age, Scott could consider borrowing from his 401(k) plan (assuming current tax laws are still effective).

5.   Scott and Paula's budget will not change since my recommendation is to continue with their current strategy.

Part 6, Chap. 15, Question 2

Estimated	A. Approximate number of yrs. to retirement.................	33
Household	B. Current level of an. household exp. excluding savings..	60000
Exp. in	C. Est. household exp. in retirement as % of current exp..	90
Retirement	D. Est. annual household exp. in retirement (B x C).......	54000
		=======
Estimated	E. Social security, annual income..........................	0
Income in	F. Company/employer pension plans-annual amounts..........	69360
Retirement	G. Other sources-annual amounts...........................	18000
	H. Total annual income (E + F + G).........................	87360
	I. Add'l. req'd. income or annual shortfall (D - H).......	-33360
		=======
Inflation	J. Expected avg. ann. rate of infl. until retirement (%)..	5
Factor	K. Infl. fac. based on 33 yrs. and 5% rate of inflation..	5.003
	L. Size of inflation-adjusted annual shortfall (I x K)....	-166906
		=======
Funding	M. Expected return on assets held after retirement (%)....	5
the	N. Amt. of retirement funds required (L - M)..............	%-333812
Shortfall	O. Expected return on assets prior to retirement (%)......	8
	P. Comp. int. factor based on 33 yrs. and 0% return......	145.951
	Q. Ann. savings req'd. for retirement nest egg (N - P)....	-22872
		=======

Part 6, Chap. 15, Question 3

Estimated	A. Approximate number of yrs. to retirement................	33
Household	B. Current level of an. household exp. excluding savings..	60000
Exp. in	C. Est. household exp. in retirement as % of current exp..	90
Retirement	D. Est. annual household exp. in retirement (B x C).......	54000
		=======
Estimated	E. Social security, annual income..........................	0
Income in	F. Company/employer pension plans-annual amounts..........	40000
Retirement	G. Other sources-annual amounts...........................	12000
	H. Total annual income (E + F + G).........................	52000
	I. Add'l. req'd. income or annual shortfall (D - H).......	2000
		=======
Inflation	J. Expected avg. ann. rate of infl. until retirement (%)..	5
Factor	K. Infl. fac. based on 33 yrs. and 5% rate of inflation..	5.003
	L. Size of inflation-adjusted annual shortfall (I x K)....	10006
		=======
Funding	M. Expected return on assets held after retirement (%)....	5
the	N. Amt. of retirement funds required (L - M)..............	200128
Shortfall	O. Expected return on assets prior to retirement (%)......	8
	P. Comp. int. factor based on 33 yrs. and 0% return......	145.951
	Q. Ann. savings req'd. for retirement nest egg (N - P)....	1371
		=======

REPRESENTATIVE ANSWERS: The Garnett Case

Part Six--Chapter 16

1. Scott's gross estate is well under the $600,000 needed before being subject to Federal Estate taxes. Roughly, it would consist of half of their $126,900 net worth (Paula's jewelry and retirement account would not be included but all of his IRA and 401(k) would be included). In addition, Scott's life insurance and retirement death benefit proceeds of $182,000 would be part of his estate.

2. (Given the limited information in this case) In a joint property state, all of his property would be probate property except the house, his life insurance, his retirement death benefit, his 401(k), and his IRA (the Evergreen Fund). These listed exceptions would be non-probate property.

   In a community property state, all of his property would be probate property except his life insurance, his employer retirement account, his 401(k), and his IRA. The house, as well as his other assets, would be probate.

3. Paula's estate would not be subject to Federal Estate taxes either. Her gross estate would be approximately half of their joint net worth (including all of her listed jewelry and retirement account contributions but not including Scott's IRA and 401(k) accounts) plus $50,000 in life insurance proceeds.

4. The same as the answer to Question 2 except that Paula does not have a 401(k) or an IRA.

5. Scott's assets with named beneficiaries (life insurance, retirement death benefit, 401(k) plan, and probably the IRA) would pass directly to Paula, the named beneficiary. In a joint property state, Paula would get sole ownership of the house. In a community property state, the house would probably be included with the other assets that pass according to the intestate laws. According to typical intestate laws (Exhibit 16.3), Scott's other assets would divided into thirds with Paula, Amy, and Jason each receiving one-third.

   The distribution of Paula's assets would follow the same system.

6. Each of them should definitely have a written will. If they die without valid wills, the intestacy laws for their state will control how their property is divided. In each of their wills, he/she should provide for the distribution of his/her property according to his/her wishes. They have previously stated they would each like the other to be the primary beneficiary with Jason and Amy being the secondary beneficiaries. However, Paula has specific wishes about who should inherit her jewelry. It is also very important that both Scott and Paula designate a legal guardian for the children in case both of them were to die. They have said they would like Paula's parents to be legal guardians. They should also appoint executors to administer their estates.

7. No, these gifts would not be subject to gift taxes because at their current level ($1,200 annually per child) they are well below the $10,000 per year ($20,000 if Scott and Paula join in the gift) that is allowed free of gift taxes.

EPILOGUE: The Garnett Case

Scott and Paula Garnett sought out financial planning assistance because, despite a net worth of nearly $137,000 and annual salaries totaling over $65,000, they were feeling financially squeezed. This was due primarily to the birth of twins and a subsequent reduction in Paula's income. Scott and Paula's goals were to:
- --buy a larger house
- --increase the amount of cash reserves in their emergency fund
- --pay off their revolving debt
- --save for their children's college educations
- --continue saving for retirement
- --save for a new car

Accomplishments

By selling their present house and liquidating their stock investments, Scott and Paula were able to purchase a larger house. This satisfied one of their most immediate goals.

After calculating their 1992 tax liability, it was found that they would be receiving a large tax refund. As a result they were able to adjust their withholding allowances for 1993 and increase their take-home incomes. This had a positive impact on their cash flow and helped make it possible to start saving for their other goals.

As the result of a comprehensive review of their insurance, Scott and Paula purchased additional disability insurance, a personal property floater for Paula's jewelry, and increased the liability coverage on their homeowners and auto policies. This will help protect their assets against insurable risks.

Scott and Paula each had a will written to provide for the orderly transfer of their assets and to name a guardian for the children.

Scott and Paula had enough cash surplus to fund their goals for the emergency fund, for paying off the revolving debt, for a new car, and for retirement savings. With financial planning, they were able to partially fund the college education goal.

Challenges

The only major goal that is still not being completely funded is the children's college education fund. They decided to use $2,950 plus interest from CDs that reached maturity to establish the education fund, and they will make monthly contributions to that account. Within the next two years, Scott and Paula will have their emergency fund at the desired level and their revolving debt as well as the Stafford loan paid off. Some of the funds now being used for those goals could then be directed to the college education fund.

Scott and Paula will need to monitor their budget monthly to make sure they stay on track with their spending and saving. If they do have the projected $1,131 cash surplus (Part 4, Question 16) at the end of 1993, they will be able to use that money to help meet their goals (or as a reward for the great financial planning job they did in 1993). They will also need to update their financial plans, including their budget regularly, as their family needs and the economy change. This reevaluation should be completed annually.

THE SIMMONS CASE STUDY

Lisa Simmons, age 34, is the mother of two children--Andy (13) and Karen (7). Last year the Simmons family was a typical two-income family faced with juggling the demands of two careers and a growing family. All that changed suddenly last June, however, when Lisa's husband, Tom, died in an automobile accident. Now Lisa is in the process of putting her and her children's lives back on an even keel--both psychologically and financially.

Despite the adversity, Lisa does have a great deal of support. Both her and Tom's parents live in the local area and have helped her handle her affairs. More importantly, they have provided the children with much time and attention. In addition, Tom's group medical insurance (under which the children are currently covered) has provided some needed counseling to help Andy deal with his father's sudden death. Financially, Lisa's salary plus Social Security survivor's benefits have been enough for the family to maintain their standard of living in the months following the death. However, Lisa feels that is in now time for her to look at her longer term financial plans.

Prior to his death, Tom and Lisa had done some financial planning for their family. Among their goals were to sell their current home and purchase a larger home, to buy a home computer, to buy a boat, to continue providing gymnastics lessons for Karen, to send the children to college, and to retire at age 65. As a result of their planning, they had started a regular savings plan and updated their insurance coverages and wills. Lisa feels very fortunate for the benefits of that planning (particularly the life insurance and wills), but she knows that she must now revise her financial goals and plans.

Last December Lisa's parents fulfilled one of the family's goals. They gave her and the children a new home computer and printer. Lisa has since purchased an assortment of software including a comprehensive financial management program. She has just finished entering her family's income, expenses, assets, liabilities, and other selected data into the program. The following pages are a summary of that information.

PERSONAL FINANCIAL INFORMATION

CLIENT INFORMATION

NAME   Lisa Andrews Simmons

BIRTH DATE   1/11/59

SOCIAL SECURITY NO.   365-55-1120

BUSINESS PHONE   512/555-4521

SPOUSE INFORMATION

NAME   Tom L. Simmons (deceased)

BIRTH DATE   6/8/55

SOCIAL SECURITY NO.   454-32-8763

BUSINESS PHONE   ---

RESIDENCE ADDRESS   288 Meadowbrook Court

CITY, STATE & ZIP   Newton, USA 78731

RESIDENCE PHONE   512/555-6821

WEDDING DATE   1/15/79

CHILDREN

Name	Birth Date	Social Security Number	Grade
Andrew (Andy) Simmons	2/14/80	454-01-7921	Eight grade
Karen Simmons	12/2/85	454-42-6637	Second grade

EDUCATION

	School	Degree	Year Received
Lisa	North State University	B.S. Advertising	5/85

OCCUPATION

	Employer	Position	Years From To
Lisa	J.& L. Advertising	Graphic Artist	4/87 - present

CONSULTANTS FOR FINANCIAL PLANNING

	Name	Address	Phone
Attorney	William Carlson	600 Congress Avenue Newton, USA 78701	555-7738
Securities Broker	Janice Sanders	1626 Shoal Creek Boulevard Newton, USA 78731	555-1611
Bank Officer	Sandra Ko	First National Bank of Newton Newton, USA 78704	555-8878
Insurance Agent	Tony Hernandez	3562 S. Lamar Newton, USA 78701	555-2341

LOCATION OF DOCUMENTS		
Wills/Trusts:	Will	Attorney's office (William Carlson)
Insurance:	Life	Group policy through J.& L. Advertising Information booklet in home file
	Health	Group policies through J.& L. Advertising and The Brookside Institute (Tom's former employer) Information booklets in home file
	Auto	Policy in home file
	House	Policy in home file
Deeds:	Auto House	In home file In home file
Birth/Marriage/Other Certificates		In home file

ASSETS - January 1, 1993

	LOCATION	BALANCE	RATE OF INTEREST	MATURITY
CHECKING	First National Bank[1] (opened 10/15/85)	$ 2,945	3.0%	N/A
MONEY MARKET ACCOUNTS/FUNDS	First National Bank[1] (opened 7/25/92)	$ 5,115	3.7%	N/A
	Fidelity Cash Reserves (opened 7/8/92)	$14,755	4.5%	N/A
CD	First National Bank[1]	$13,500	6.5%	12/13/93
SAVINGS ACCT.	First National Bank[1] (opened 3/15/83)	$ 5,687	3.5%	N/A
CASH ON HAND		$ 230		
LIFE INSURANCE (face value on Tom's policy which has not been distributed)	American Life,Inc.	$75,000	6.9%	N/A
VESTED PENSION	J.& L. Advertising	$ 8,908		

[1]Insured by FDIC.

SECURITY INVESTMENTS

Security	# Shares	Cost			Current Value	
		Date Acquired	Per Share	Total	Per Share	Total
Kroger	300	9/30/90	12-7/8	$ 3,863	13-1/2	$ 4,050
Fidelity Puritan Mutual Fund	200 115.86	10/28/83 reinvestment program	12.24 (13.02 average)	$ 2,448 $1,508	15.03 15.03	$ 3,006 $ 1,741
Merrill Lynch Phoenix A Mutual Fund	100 100 46.67	10/13/85 6/16/86 reinvestment program	12.15 12.86 (12.05 average)	$ 1,215 $ 1,286 $ 562	11.13 11.13 11.13	$ 1,113 $ 1,113 $ 519

REAL PROPERTY

	Year	Make	Model	Cost	Current Value
Automobile:	1991	Chevrolet	Lumina	$15,500	$ 9,600
House:	1988			$95,000	$115,500

PERSONAL PROPERTY

	Market Value
Clothing	$ 7,500
Furniture & appliances	$30,000
Stereo, TVs, cameras, etc.	$ 6,500
Computer, printer, & software	$ 3,500
Baseball card collection	$ 4,500
Exercise equipment	$ 2,700
Toys, books, and children's games	$ 3,200
Miscellaneous household items	$ 5,000

LIABILITIES - January 1, 1993

LOANS:

To Whom Owed	Original Amount of Account	Property or Service Purchased	Interest Rate	Current Balance	Payment Amount	How often Paid	Total Number of Payments	Date for First Payment
Guaranty Federal Savings	$85,500	House	10.75%	$83,066	$798.13 (PI)	monthly	360	3/12/88
GMAC	$13,000	Automobile	10.5%	$ 8,493	$332.84	monthly	48	6/10/91
First National Bank	$ 9,500	Debt Consolidation	13.5%	$ 6,252	$322.39	monthly	36	11/30/91

CREDIT CARDS:

	Number	Annual Fee	Interest Rate	Maximum Line of Credit	Outstanding Balance	Minimum Monthly Payment	Grace Period	Calculation Method
AT&T Universal MasterCard	4897 2301 5602 1927	$ 0	15.4%	$5,000	$ 493	2% of balance or $20, whichever is greater	yes	Av. Daily Bal.
Visa	4310 4516 3100 3259	$ 0	18.0%	$3,000	$ 0	5% of balance or $25, whichever is greater	no	Adjusted Bal.
MasterCard	3529 0317 2432 0917	$35	14.0%	$3,000	$ 0	5% of balance or $20, whichever is greater	yes	Av. Daily Bal.
American Express	2782 163539 62005	$45	---	---	$ 0	Total balance	---	---
Foley's	1626 5512 7	$ 0	18.0%	$1,500	$ 129	10% of balance or $10, whichever is greater	yes	Av. Daily Bal.
Montgomery Wards	0 50186 96182 0	$ 0	18.0%	$1,500	$ 0	3% of balance or $15 whichever is greater	yes	Av. Daily Bal.
Yaring's	361 05891	$ 0	18.0%	---	$ 275	10% of balance or $50, whichever is greater	yes	Past due bal.

1992 INCOME

		Gross Income
Lisa's salary		$29,500
Self employment		6,280
Tom's salary	(January through May)	16,470
Social Security benefits	($1,380/month June through December)	9,660
Life insurance proceeds	(June)	25,000
Interest[1]		3,703
Dividends[2]		356
Capital gains distributions[3]		178
Sale of Assets		
	Gabelli Growth Mutual Fund[4]	2,027
	1989 Jeep Cherokee[5]	8,575

Income after tax deductions but before insurance deductions (take-home pay):

Lisa's salary	$1,902 per month
Tom's salary	$2,548 per month (January through May)
Lisa's self employment	$ 386 per month

---

[1]Checking ($60/year), money market accounts/funds ($420/year), CD ($435/year paid in December),savings account ($200/year), life insurance ($2,588/year). All are paid monthly except the CD.

[2]Kroger ($0), Fidelity Puritan ($252), Merrill Lynch Phoenix ($104). All dividends paid quarterly in March, June, September, and December.

[3]Fidelity Puritan ($0) and Merrill Lynch Phoenix ($178). Distributions are paid quarterly in March, June, September, and December.

[4]100 shares purchased February 3, 1990 at $16.27/share and sold on February 15, 1992, at $20.27 share.

[5]Purchased June 16, 1989 for $16,500 and sold August 1, 1992 for $8,575.

1992 EXPENSES

	Cash Flow Monthly	Cash Flow Annually
House Payment (PI=$798, Property taxes=$205, Homeowners insurance=$50)	$1,053	$12,636
Utilities (electricity and water)	175	2,100
Telephone ($45) and Cable TV ($30)	75	900
House repairs ($45/mo. Jan.-May, $75/mo. June-Dec.)		750
Groceries ($600/mo. Jan.-May, $450/mo. June-Dec.)		6,150
Food away from home	150	1,800
Auto loan payments	333	3,996
Auto maintenance ($215/mo. Jan.-May, $125/mo. June-Dec.)		1,950
Medical/Dental Expenses (not covered by insurance)		310
Clothing ($250/mo. Jan.-May, $175/mo. June-Dec.)		2,475
Health insurance	250	3,000
Life insurance (January-May)	20	100
Auto insurance ($690 in February, $390 in August)		1,080
Income taxes ($931/mo. Jan.-May, $437/mo. June-Dec.)		7,714
Soc. Security taxes ($509/mo. Jan.-May, $257/mo. June-Dec.)		4,344
Appliance and furniture purchases		1,236
Personal care	50	600
Entertainment	100	1,200
Vacation (taken in March)		1,500
Children's activities (including $100/mo. for gymnastics)	200	2,400
Debt consolidation loan payments	322	3,864
Deductible child care ($100/mo. Sept.-May, $225/mo. June-Aug.)		1,575
Charitable contributions	75	900
Children's allowances ($50/mo. for Andy & $30/mo. for Karen)	80	960
Miscellaneous	275	3,300
Deductible business expenses (self-employment)	72	864
Funeral expenses (June)		3,850

INSURANCE INFORMATION

LIFE INSURANCE

*INSURED	Lisa	Tom (until his death)
Type of Life Insurance	Group Term	Group Term
Face amount	$59,000 (2 times salary)	$100,000
Beneficiary	Andy and Karen	Lisa
Owner	Lisa	Tom
Annual Premium	Employer paid	$20/month (payroll deduction)

DISABILITY INSURANCE:

*INSURED		Lisa
Policy number		Employer group policy
Definition of Disability		Own job
Mo. Benefit		70% of gross monthly salary
Waiting Period	Sick	30 days
	Accident	30 days
Benefit Period	Sick	3 years
	Accident	3 years
Premiums		Employer paid

MEDICAL INSURANCE

*INSURED	Lisa J.& L. Advertising	Andy and Karen The Brookside Institute
Company	Metropolitan Life	Health Care Plan (HMO)
Policy Number	Group #063-111	Group # 168521 AGC
*Hospitalization Room Rate	80% of semi-private rate	100% of semi-private rate
Number of Days	unlimited	unlimited
*Major Medical Maximum	$100,000/person/year	unlimited
Deductible	$500/person/year	$10 copayment per doctor's visit $ 5 copayment per prescription
% participation	80/20	--
Cap on participation	$1,000/person/year	--
Mental Health	80% for up to 30 visits	$10 copayment per visit
Dental	no	no
Annual Premiums	Employer paid for employee.	$250 per month paid for children. Employer paid for employee.

*COMMENTS	
Lisa's Policy:	Family member could be covered for $80/month. Coordination of benefits provision is included in policy.
Tom's Policy:	Must use HMO facilities and selected hospitals. Dependents can be covered for $125/person/month. Tom's dependents can be covered until 6/95 under COBRA regulations. Coordination of benefits provision is included in policy.

AUTO INSURANCE

*DESCRIPTION	(1) 1989 Jeep Cherokee	(2) 1991 Chevy Lumina
Company	AETNA Casualty	AETNA Casualty
Policy Number	156-88876-AOB6	same
Liability	$40,000 or (20/40/15)	$40,000 or (20/40/15)
Medical Payments	$2,500/person	$2,500/person
Uninsured Motorist	$40,000 or (20/40/15)	$40,000 or (20/40/15)
Collision	(Actual Cash Value)	(Actual Cash Value)
Deductible	$200	$200
Comprehensive	(Actual Cash Value)	(Actual Cash Value)
Deductible	$ 50	$ 50
Annual Premium	$600	$780
Comments	Paid semi-annual payment in February. Sold vehicle in August.	Paid semi-annually in February and August

HOMEOWNERS INSURANCE

Company	American Property Insurers
Policy Number/Type	33490-73798-88/HO-2
Dwelling	$100,000
Other Structures	$ 10,000 (10%)
Personal Property on Premises (actual cash value)	$ 50,000 (50%)
Personal Property off Premises	$ 5,000
Additional Living Expenses (annual limit)	$ 20,000 (20%)
Comprehensive Liability (per occurrence)	$100,000
Medical Payments (per person)	$ 500
Property Damage to Others (per occurrence)	$ 250
Deductible	$ 500 (1/2% of dwelling coverage)
Annual Premium	$ 600
Comments	Paid as part of monthly mortgage payment

RETIREMENT INFORMATION

Person Covered	Lisa
Type of pension plan	Qualified, non-contributory, defined benefits
Vesting	5-year vesting $8,908 currently vested
Benefit formula	2.5% of average annual salary over last 3 years times number of years of service.
Death benefit	Same as vested retirement benefit
Beneficiary	Andy and Karen
Other plans available	401(k) - no employer contribution, maximum employee contribution of 10% of gross salary. 8% average return over the past 4 years. Invested in a balanced mutual fund.
Vesting	Immediate
Current Value	$0

ESTATE PLANNING INFORMATION

Tom left his total estate to Lisa. Lisa would like Andy to get his father's baseball card collection and Karen to receive the exercise equipment. Lisa would like them to share equally in the remainder of her estate. Her father and mother are named as the children's guardians as well as co-executors of her estate. However, Lisa has not had her will updated since Tom's death. Her current will leaves all her assets to Tom.

FINANCIAL GOALS

Short range (1 year):
> To continue funding Karen's gymnastics lessons, to have an adequate emergency fund.

Intermediate range (1-5 years):
> To save for Andy's college education, to buy a new car.

Long term (over 5 years):
> To save for Karen's college education, to start her own business, to retire when she in 65.

What is your single most important financial objective at this time:
> To have an adequate emergency fund.

FINANCIAL PRIORITIES

	Lisa
a. LIVING: paying monthly bills	1
b. PLEASURE: spending money	5
c. RETIREMENT: invest in future	8
d. DISABILITY: protect against	2
e. DEATH: take care of family	3
f. REDUCE TAXES: spend to save	7
g. INVESTING: accumulate assets	6
h. CHILDREN: future needs	4

Prioritized with 1 being most important and 8 being least important.

OTHER INFORMATION

1. Are you able to save regularly? <u>Yes</u>

2. How much are able to save annually? <u>$3,000</u> Where? <u>Money market mutual fund</u>

3. Do you invest regularly? <u>Yes</u>

4. Do feel that you are financially organized? <u>Yes - somewhat</u>

5. Do you budget your money? <u>No written budget</u>

6. If you were to die, could your dependents handle their finances? <u>No</u>

7. How do you feel about saving for retirement? <u>It's important, but have other goals that are more important right now</u>

8. If you had an extra $5,000 what would you do with it? <u>Pay off the debt consolidation loan</u>

9. How do feel about taking investment risks? <u>Moderate risk taker</u>

PART ONE: The Simmons Case Study

Lisa Simmons would like your help in revising her financial plan. Review Lisa's financial and personal information before answering the following questions.

1. Using the January 1, 1993 asset and liability information, develop a balance sheet for Lisa Simmons. Assume that she has no unpaid bills.

2. Using the income and expenditure information for 1992, complete an income and expenditure statement for Lisa Simmons. Date this statement January through December of 1992. Use the "cash flow" concept for this financial statement including all money inflows as income and all outflows as expenditures. Did Lisa have a cash surplus or a cash deficit in 1992? What impact did Lisa's 1992 cash surplus (deficit) have on her balance sheet for January 1, 1993?

3. Based on Lisa's financial statements, calculate the following ratios:
   -- savings ratio
   -- liquidity ratio
   -- solvency ratio
   -- debt service ratio

4. Based on the information in the original case and in the financial statements just completed, list at least 3 positive and 3 negative aspects of Lisa's current financial position.

5a. If Lisa wants to provide the equivalent of $10,000 per year in today's dollars for Andy's college education and she feels that the rate of inflation will be 6% annually over the next 5 years, how much will she need to provide annually?

 b. If Lisa wants to provide the equivalent of $10,000 per year in today's dollars for Karen's college education and she feels that the rate of inflation will be 6% annually over the next 11 years, how much will she need to provide annually?

6a. How much money would Lisa need to have in Andy's college education fund in 5 years if Lisa wanted to be able to withdraw $13,500 a year for 5 years to help cover Andy's education expenses? Assume that she could earn 6% annually on the money left in the account.

 b. What is the present value of the above amount (from Question 6a) assuming an 8% discount rate?

 c. How much money would Lisa need to have in Karen's college education fund in 11 years if Lisa wanted to be able to withdraw $19,000 a year for 5 years to help cover Karen's education expenses? Assume that she could earn 6% annually on the money left in the account.

 d. What is the present value of the above amount (from Question 6c) assuming an 8% discount rate?

7. After reading Chapter 3, you now probably realize that Lisa's financial goals are not defined well enough in the original case to serve as the basis for her financial plan and cash budget. Upon further thought (and the calculations from Questions 5 and 6), she has restated her financial goals as follows:

--to save $20,000 for a new car within 3 years. Lisa plans to give Andy the Lumina when he turns 16. Lisa will get the new car.
--to accumulate $57,000 within 5 years for Andy's college education.
--to accumulate $50,000 in 8 years to start her own business.
--to accumulate $80,000 for Karen's college education within the next 11 years.
--to contribute $2,000 each year to her 401(k) retirement account.
--to contribute $2,000 annually to an IRA.
--to establish a regular savings program in an amount that will accomplish these stated goals.

Lisa would like to cash in the American Life Insurance policy ($75,000) and commit $25,000 to Andy's college fund, $15,000 to Karen's college fund, $10,000 for the car fund, and $25,000 for her business fund. Assuming she can earn 8% on the college funds, 5% on the car fund, and 9% on the business fund, will the life insurance proceeds provide enough to fulfill each of these goals? If not, how much extra will Lisa have to save annually for each of her stated goals?

8. Prepare a 1993 cash budget for Lisa using the income and expenditure data from the original case as well as the figures from Question 7 needed to meet her goals. Regarding income, assume that monthly Social Security benefits will increase 3 percent and they will receive the benefits for 12 months. Of course, in 1993 she will not receive Tom's salary, the sale of assets from 1992, or the life insurance proceeds received in 1992. Lisa expects her CD to earn $880 (rather than $435) in 1993, and the $75,000 from the American Life Insurance policy (which she will receive in 12 equal monthly payments during 1993) will earn approximately $6,000 interest (rather than $2,588). Assume all other income items, including her salary, will remain constant. All investment income (interest, dividends, and capital gains distributions) will be reinvested.

There will also be quite a change in expenditures as a result of Tom's death. For all expenditure categories that had one monthly figure for January through May 1992 and another figure for June through December (such as groceries and clothing), use the later amount for all months of the 1993 budget. There will be no funeral or life insurance expenditures, and auto insurance will be due on only one car. Assume all other expenditures are the same as 1992.

9. Can Lisa achieve all of her stated goals considering her family's current income and expenditure patterns? If not, list specific recommendations you would make to help her achieve these goals.

10. Lisa currently has a small consulting business which she has developed over the past 3 years to make a little extra income and to learn more about running a business. However since she is now a single parent, Lisa has less time for the business than she did before Tom's death. Use the work sheet presented in Exhibit 3.4 to analyze the financial benefit of her second income. Lisa estimates a gross income of $6,280, deductible business expenses of $864, Social Security taxes of $829, and federal income taxes of $812 from the business. In addition, approximately $500 of the child care expenses can be attributed to Lisa's second income. What is the net income from Lisa's consulting business? What other aspects should Lisa consider (other than the financial implications) in making the decision to continue consulting?

11. Prepare a 1992 tax return for Lisa (and Tom as her deceased husband) using the financial data in the original case. Will Lisa owe more taxes or receive a refund? How much?

   NOTES:
   -- The Gabelli Growth Mutual Fund is a no-load fund. This means there were no commissions paid when the fund was purchased or sold.
   -- Mortgage interest paid on Lisa's home in 1992 was $8,966.
   -- The Social Security tax liability on Lisa's self-employment income is $829 of the $4,344 paid in Social Security taxes.
   -- Lisa has not started contributing to her 401(k) plan or IRA yet so do not use this in calculating the 1992 tax liability.
   -- The Social Security benefits received are the children's income ($4,830 each) and are not included as income to Lisa.
   -- Lisa will file a joint return with her deceased husband in 1992. In 1993, she will be a qualifying widow (assuming she does not remarry).

12. What is Lisa's average tax rate in 1992? What is her marginal tax rate in 1992? In calculating the average tax rate, use the tax liability after credits rather than the tax liability before credits.

13. Approximately how much would Lisa have saved in taxes if she had invested $2,000 in her 401(k) retirement account and $2,000 in an IRA in 1992?

14. What tax strategies would you recommend to help Lisa reduce her tax liability? Remember her financial status, goals, and risk tolerance.

PART TWO: The Simmons Case Study

After reviewing her budget for 1993 and completing her 1992 taxes, Lisa has decided to make a few modifications in both income and expenditures.

- She will be receiving a tax refund of $2,918 in April.
- She will try to continue her consulting business at the same level as in 1992.
- Based on an estimate of her income tax liability for 1993, Lisa will reduce tax withholding and estimating to $3,100 (approximately $2,300 withholding on her salary and $800 estimated tax payments on her self-employment income). This will increase Lisa's monthly take-home income (after Social Security and income taxes) to $2,079 from salary and $388 from self-employment.
- Lisa will keep better track of her expenditures, and reduce miscellaneous expenses to $100 per month.
- She will let Andy assume more of the child care responsibility for Karen as both children are getting old enough to take on additional responsibilities. This will reduce deductible child care expenses for Karen to $125 per month.
- The family will make small reductions in selected monthly variable expenditures. The new budgeted amounts will be phone ($30), groceries ($425), dining out ($125), clothing ($125), entertainment ($75), and children's activities ($175). In addition, they will spend only $1,000 on a June vacation in 1993.

Assuming all of these revisions start in January, they should reduce Lisa's 1993 budget deficit to approximately $12,500. She will consider other changes (such as paying off loans, refinancing the mortgage, and changing contribution amounts for goals) as you continue to help Lisa with her financial plan.

1. Evaluate the amount of Lisa's liquid assets. If Lisa wants to keep 5 months of after-tax earned income (salary and self-employment income) in a highly liquid form, how much would this be? How much of her current liquid assets could then be used for other purposes or repositioned into other types of assets?

2. Lisa has just received her January, 1993 statement for her NOW account. It contains the following information:
    - --ending balance $1,568.36
    - --service charge (ATM fee)   2.70
    - --interest earned $ 5.06

    Her checkbook ledger shows a final balance of $1,145.63. However, the following checks and deposits are not listed on the bank statement:
    - --check #4521 for $333.00
    - --check #4523 for $24.57
    - --deposit made January 26 for $62.00
    - --ATM withdrawal made January 28 for $50.00
    - --ATM withdrawal made January 30 for $75.00

    Reconcile Lisa's January bank statement. How much difference, if any, is there between the bank statement balance and the ending balance in their checkbook after reconciliation?

3. Lisa is currently maintaining five separate liquid asset accounts. What are the positive and the negative characteristics of each of these accounts?

4. Lisa currently maintains a regular NOW account at First National Bank, and she also has several of her liquid investment accounts at this bank. First National just began offering a Super NOW account that pays a higher rate of interest on checking balances than the regular NOW account and does not charge for limited ATM usage. Lisa writes an average of 35 checks per month, makes approximately 10 ATM withdrawals per month, and maintains an average daily balance in her checking account of $2,000. The minimum balance in her NOW account has been as low as $1,100 since Tom's death. She would be willing to move funds from her First National savings account and/or money market account into the Super NOW account if this would be financially advantageous.

Regular NOW Account
   --no service charge for accounts maintaining a minimum daily balance of $1,000.
   --monthly service charge of $5 plus $.15 per check if the minimum daily balance falls below $1,000.
   --3.0% (annual percentage rate) interest is paid monthly on the average daily balance.
   --ATM fee of $.30 per transaction.

Super NOW Account
   --no service charge for accounts maintaining a minimum daily balance of $7,500.
   --monthly service charge of $15 plus $.15 per check if the minimum daily balance falls below $7,500.
   --4.0% (annual percentage rate) interest is paid monthly on the average daily balance.
   --no ATM fee on first 15 transactions.

Help Lisa evaluate these two checking accounts considering her liquid assets and use of checking services. What are the advantages and disadvantages of each NOW account? Which one would you recommend for Lisa?

5. In a recent magazine article, Lisa read about using U.S. EE Savings Bonds as a way to save for college. What are the advantages and disadvantages of using this investment for Andy's and Karen's college education funds? Would you recommend that Lisa invest in U.S. EE Savings Bonds?

6a. If Lisa contributes $2,000 per year to her 401(k) account for the next 30 years and the account continues to average an 8% annual return, how much will the account be worth in 30 years?

 b. If Lisa wanted to have $300,000 in her 401(k) account in 30 years, how much would she need to contribute each year assuming an 8% annual return?

Lisa has noticed that mortgage interest rates have fallen significantly since she and Tom purchased their home in 1988. She made a few phone calls and found that Guaranty Federal Savings offered very competitive refinancing terms. Since the outstanding balance on her current mortgage is well below 80 percent of her home's market value, Lisa was offered the following mortgage options:

25-year fixed-rate mortgage
--7.75% interest with 1-1/2 discount points
--other closing costs of $2,500 (this includes a 1% loan origination fee)
--monthly payments

<u>25-year adjustable-rate mortgage</u>
--5.5% interest with 3 discount points
--other closing costs of $2,500 (this includes a 1% loan origination fee)
--1% annual interest rate cap
--6% overall interest rate cap
--monthly payments

Lisa's current mortgage has a monthly payment for principal and interest of $798 with no prepayment penalties. Lisa expects to live in her home at least until Karen graduates from high school (10 years). She would refinance the current loan balance ($83,066) and would pay the front-end costs with money from her Fidelity Cash Reserves Money Market mutual fund.

----

7. Compare and evaluate the two mortgage alternatives for Lisa. What would be the front-end costs and the monthly payments for principal and interest on each of these mortgages? How much could the monthly payments for principal and interest go up on the adjustable rate mortgage after the first year? Over the lifetime of the loan? Keeping in mind her financial situation and risk tolerances, which mortgage would your recommend for Lisa? Why?

8. In addition to a 7.75% fixed-rate mortgage with 1-1/2 discount points, the lender offers an 8.5% fixed-rate mortgage with no discount points. Compare the difference in monthly payments and front-end costs for these two mortgage options (assuming all else remains the same). How many months would Lisa need to expect to keep the mortgage before it would be wise for her to consider paying the discount points? Which of these fixed-rate mortgages would you recommend for Lisa? Why?

9. Complete the mortgage refinancing analysis assuming Lisa selects the 7.75% fixed-rate mortgage with 1-1/2 discount points. Be sure to include discount points along with other closing costs in this calculation. How many months would it take before the lower monthly payments of the 7.75% mortgage "break even" with the front-end costs of refinancing with this mortgage? Would you recommend that Lisa refinance her current mortgage? Why or why not?

10. Will Lisa be able to qualify for the 7.75% fixed-rate mortgage if the lender applies the following two affordability ratios:
    --monthly mortgage payments cannot exceed 28% of the borrower's monthly before-tax income, and
    --total monthly debt payments cannot exceed 35% of the monthly before-tax income?

    In figuring if Lisa will qualify, use her projected 1993 earned income, investment income, and Social Security benefits. Use net self-employment income ($6,280-$864=$5,416) rather than Lisa's gross earnings from self-employment. Do not include the $75,000 life insurance proceeds since this is not an on going source of funds. Since Lisa pays her credit card balances in full each month, do not include them in total debt payments. The amount of her monthly mortgage payment will be the sum of the following:
    --monthly payment for principal and interest
    --1/12 of her annual property taxes
    --1/12 of her homeowners insurance premium
    Do not include the maintenance costs.

11. Assume that Lisa does refinance her home February 25, 1993 with the 7.75% fixed-rate mortgage using funds from her Fidelity Cash Reserve mutual fund to pay the front-end costs. As of this date, Lisa has received a total of $12,500 from the $75,000 life insurance policy, leaving $62,500 of the face value with the insurance company. The $12,500 was used to buy U.S. EE savings bonds for Andy's college education fund. Lisa has not started making additional monthly contributions towards her stated goals (Part 1, Question 7) as she wanted to take care of the house refinancing first. In late February, Lisa closed her regular NOW account and opened the Super NOW account considered in Question 4. She closed the savings account putting that money in the Super NOW account and transferred an additional $1,000 from her First Federal money market account to the Super NOW account. The current balance in the Super NOW account is $9,126, and she has $135 in cash on hand. The current share values of her Kroger stock, Fidelity Puritan Fund, and Merrill Lynch Phoenix Fund are $13.75, $16.25, and $10.75, respectively. The up-dated outstanding balances on her debt are $7,973 (auto loan), $5,745 (debt consolidation loan), $363 (bank cards), and $675 (retail cards). Revise Lisa's balance sheet to reflect the changes in her assets and liabilities. Date the new balance sheet March 1, 1993. Assuming no other changes than ones specifically mentioned in this case, what is Lisa's new net worth? How can a good financial decision, such as refinancing a home mortgage, have a negative impact on net worth, at least temporarily?

12. Assuming no other changes than the ones specifically mentioned in this case, redo Lisa's budget for 1993. See the beginning of Part 2 for planned changes in income and expenditures for 1993. With the funds taken out of the Fidelity Cash Reserves mutual fund for front-end costs and the funds transferred to open the Super NOW account, Lisa expects her monthly interest income to be approximately $557 in January and February, $540 monthly March through November, and $1,420 in December. (The ATM fees saved by opening the Super NOW account are already included in the reductions in miscellaneous expenditures.) Lisa wants to begin making planned monthly contributions to her goals in March. Lisa made 2 mortgage payments on her original mortgage before refinancing. As is typical, when a house is financed late in the month, the first monthly payment skips a month. Therefore, she makes only 9 payments on the new mortgage in 1993. Again, we will think of this income and expenditure statement as a cash flow statement. All sources of funds (including withdrawals from savings) should be included as income, and all expenditures of funds (including front-end costs of the house refinancing) should be included as expenditures. Tax refunds for 1992 should be included as income as well. How much is Lisa's projected cash surplus (deficit) now for 1993?

13. Estimate Lisa's 1993 income taxes after refinancing the house. Assume that included in the $2,500 closing costs paid was a 1% loan origination fee. Remember that she will be making only nine monthly house payments in 1993 on the new mortgage. Since IRS regulations require a taxpayer to deduct as interest only a pro-rata portion of both loan origination fees and discount points actually paid on a refinanced mortgage, Lisa will be able to deduct only 9/300 of these expenditures in 1993. The 1993 interest paid on the original mortgage was $1,488 while $4,807 will be paid on the new mortgage. Refer to Lisa's latest budget projections for other changes which impact on her 1993 tax liability. The projected standard deduction for qualifying widows in 1993 is $6,200, the personal exemption is expected to be worth $2,350 per person, and the 15% marginal tax bracket will go up to a taxable income of approximately $36,900. How has Lisa's tax liability changed (compared to the previous year)? Is Lisa having enough taxes withheld to avoid a tax penalty for under withholding?

PART THREE: The Simmons Case Study

Based on the 1993 tax estimate completed in Part 2, Question 13, Lisa has decided to increase her income tax withholding by $45 per month starting in March. This will make her total withholding for the year $3,550 ($3,100 + $450) and her after-tax monthly salary $2,034 ($2,079 - $45).

1. Calculate the minimum monthly payment for March, 1993 on each of Lisa's credit cards using the following outstanding balances:

AT&T Universal Master Card	$255
Visa	$108
Foley's	$322
Yaring's	$353

2. What is Lisa's debt safety ratio as of March, 1993? Evaluate her ability to handle her debt. Include Social Security benefits as part of Lisa's take-home pay.

3. Calculate the finance charges on Lisa's two bank cards using the following transaction data:

	AT&T UNIVERSAL			VISA	
Date	Transaction	Amount	Date	Transaction	Amount
3/1	Beginning balance	$255	3/1	Beginning balance	$108
3/5	Purchase	21	3/7	Purchase	100
3/10	Payment	255	3/10	Payment	108
3/15	Purchase	57	3/20	Purchase	263

   Payments on both of these cards were made before the due date for the billing cycle.

4. If five of Lisa's credit cards were stolen and the following unauthorized charges were made before she reported the cards missing, how much would Lisa's maximum liability be according to federal legislation?

Montgomery Wards	$256	Foley's	$ 34
Yaring's	$345	Visa	$ 75
MasterCard	$102		

5. In February, 1993 Lisa found a billing error on her MasterCard statement. There was a charge for $289 that she did not make. What should Lisa do to correct this situation?

6. Lisa currently has three bank credit cards and one travel and entertainment card. This made some sense when Tom was alive, but now Lisa feels she does not need this many cards for her limited credit use. She would like to keep only two of these four cards. Help Lisa evaluate the four cards and recommend the two that would be best for her to keep. Lisa estimates that in an average month, she would charge $500, approximately $250 on each card. She would always pay off the total balance upon billing.

7. Andy is graduating from junior high school in May, and he has an opportunity to go on a 2-week class trip to the East Coast in June. The $2,500 cost of the trip must be paid by April 1. Lisa's parents have said they would pay $500 as part of their graduation present for Andy, but Lisa is concerned about how to pay for the other $2,000. It has not been budgeted for in children's activities. She called First National Bank about their signature loans. Lisa also received an offer through the mail from Federal Consumer Finance Company.

First National Bank	Federal Consumer Finance Company
11% stated interest rate	10% stated interest rate
simple interest loan	add-on interest loan
24 monthly payments	24 monthly payments

a. Compare the monthly payment, the total finance charges, and the APRs on the two above loans. Which would you recommend as the better loan for Lisa?

b. Before deciding on a loan, Lisa wants to compare the cost of using the loan you recommended with the cost of paying cash for the trip. If she used cash, Lisa would withdraw the $2,000 from her Fidelity Cash Reserves mutual fund (currently earning 4.5%). Compare the relative cost of cash vs. credit. Would you recommend Lisa pay for the trip with cash or with credit?

8. Lisa has expressed some interest in looking at her debt consolidation loan ($5,745)and auto loan ($7,973). She could pay one or both of these loans off using some of her liquid assets or refinance using the following home equity line of credit. What are the advantages and disadvantages?

Home Equity Line of Credit
prime + 2% interest rate formula (currently 8.25%, maximum 18%)
simple interest rate
$10,000 line of credit
$75 set up fee
amortized over 7 years

PART FOUR: The Simmons Case Study

Following the financial planning completed in Part 3, Questions 7 and 8, Lisa has:
    -- withdrawn $2,000 from her Fidelity Cash Reserves mutual fund to pay for Andy's class trip.
    --closed her First National Bank money market account transferring that $4,115 into her
Fidelity Cash Reserves mutual fund.
    --paid off the auto loan using $7,973 from the Fidelity Cash Reserves mutual fund.
    --opened the home equity line of credit and borrowed $5,745 from it to pay off the debt
consolidation loan.

Lisa's employer, J.&L. Advertising, will convert its employee benefit plan into a cafeteria-style plan starting April, 1993. Each employee has been given a maximum of $250 per month to "spend" on selected employee benefits. If more than $250 coverage is desired, the additional cost will be deducted from the employee's pay check. If less than $250 is "spent," the excess will be contributed to the employee's 401(k) account. The following insurance products are being offered to J.&L. Advertising employees.

Coverage	Monthly premium for employee	Monthly premium for dependents
Major medical policy[1]	$125	$45/dependent[2]
HMO[1,3]	$155	$65/dependent[2]
Dental coverage	$ 17	$12/dependent
Vision coverage	$ 6	$2/dependent
Long term disability[1]	$.70 per $100 of coverage	----
Term life insurance[1,4]	$.09 per $1,000 of coverage	----
Accidental death[4]	$.024 per $1,000 of coverage	----

[1]Policy is outlined in original case.
[2]Dependents must be covered under the same medical plan as the employee.
[3]HMO is the same plan offered through the Brookside Institute.
[4]Available in 1, 2, 3, or 4 times salary.

Since Lisa must make her employee benefits decisions by the end of March, she has decided this would be a good time to do a complete insurance evaluation.

1.   Use the needs approach to calculate the amount of insurance, if any, needed on Lisa's life. Lisa would like her beneficiaries to receive enough money from her life insurance to provide $4,500 for final expenses, an additional $35,000 for Andy's college education, and an additional $50,000 to for Karen's college (above what was committed in Part 1, Question 7). She feels the house could be sold for $115,500. After paying the sales expenses and paying off the home equity line of credit and the home mortgage, it should net approximately $20,000.

The children would live with Lisa's parents if she passed away, but Lisa would like to provide funds to pay for their expenses. She estimates that they would need $22,000 annually during the 5 years until Andy graduates from high school (Period 1) and $11,000 annually during the next 6 years until Karen graduates from high school (Period 2). Their living expenses once they go to college would be provided through their college fund and other available assets.

The children should receive approximately $1,400 a month from Social Security until Andy graduates from high school and $700 a month from Social Security until Karen graduates from high school. Investment income would be approximately $7,500 a year, but Lisa wants this to be reinvested rather than used for living expenses.

Lisa's expects that the children would want to sell some of her personal property, and she estimates they would receive about $15,000 from that sale. Andy would keep the car so he had a vehicle when he turned 16. Of her other assets, she would want the children to use only the retirement funds for support. Lisa would like the other assets to be available for unexpected needs and for when the children are financially independent. Based on this analysis, how much life insurance coverage does Lisa need?

2. Evaluate the group term life policy being offered through Lisa's employee benefit plan. Should Lisa get life insurance as part of her employee benefits? If yes, how much and what will it cost? Will she need more life insurance coverage than she can get through her employee plan? If you recommend she buy other policies, how much and what type of policies should she purchase? Using the examples in the text, approximately how much would the additional recommended policies cost?

3. Recommend appropriate beneficiary and settlement options for Lisa's policy(s).

4. Lisa's employer is also offering an accidental death policy as a choice in her fringe benefit package. Should Lisa buy this coverage? If yes, how much and what would it cost? If no, why not?

5. Evaluate the disability income policy offered as part of Lisa's employee benefit plan. Assume that she does not want to rely on Social Security disability or other government programs in case of a disability. Lisa does have 35 days of paid sick leave accumulated. Would this policy provide the coverage Lisa needs? Should Lisa get this policy as part of her employee benefit plan or should she purchase a private policy? How much would the recommended coverage cost?

6. Evaluate the two medical insurance options now offered through Lisa's employee benefit plan. Lisa and the children are all very healthy. Last year (which was a representative year) Lisa had a general physical ($150) and went to the doctor twice for minor ailments ($50 per visit). Karen went to the doctor three times for colds and the flu ($55 per visit) and once for a sprained ankle ($75). Andy's only medical care was monthly counseling following his father's death ($90 per visit). Lisa feels this medical history is a good indicator of the upcoming year.

If the family were covered under the major medical plan, what is the maximum amount Lisa could have to pay per year for covered expenses (assuming the insurance benefits remain below the maximum limit)? How much would Lisa have to pay out-of-pocket if the family incurred the same medical care as last year?

What are the potential out-of-pocket costs under the HMO coverage? How much would Lisa have to pay out-of-pocket if the family experienced the same medical care as last year? Assuming Lisa has been satisfied with both plans in the past, which coverage (the major medical policy or the HMO) would you recommend? How much would the premiums cost?

7. Two new options under Lisa's cafeteria-style employee benefit plan are dental care and vision care. The dental plan pays 100% of the cost for one check up per year per person. For additional dental care, there is a $100 annual deductible per person and the insured pays 20% of the costs incurred over the deductible. For orthodontic care (braces, etc.), there is a $500 annual deductible per person and the insured pays 50% of the costs incurred over the deductible. Over the past 5 years, the family has spent approximately $60 per person each year on annual check ups. In addition, Lisa has had about $200 of dental work done annually. Lisa does not expect either of the children will need braces in the upcoming year.

   The vision care plan pays 100% of the cost for one eye exam per year per person. For additional care and equipment (glasses and contacts), there is a $75 annual deductible per person and the insured pays 20% of the costs incurred over the deductible. Lisa has had no vision expenses for her or the children over the past 5 years, and she has no reason to expect a change in the near future.

   Should Lisa select dental and/or vision coverage as part of her employee benefit plan? Why? How much will the premiums cost?

8. Review your recommendations in Questions 1 through 7. How much of the $250 provided by Lisa's employer for employee benefits will she spend if she follows your recommendations? Will there be money left over to go into her 401(k) account or will money be withheld from her monthly check to pay for the excess coverage?

9. Evaluate Lisa's homeowner's insurance needs. Her home is 2,200 square feet, and she has been told that replacement would cost $55 per square foot. What form of HO insurance is appropriate? How much coverage do you recommend for her house, personal property, personal liability, etc.? Approximately how much will the recommended coverage cost?

10. Evaluate Lisa's auto insurance policy. Is this coverage adequate for her insurance needs? Recommend any required changes. Approximately how much would these changes cost?

11. Does Lisa need any other types of insurance coverage? If yes, what and why? About how much would the premiums cost?

12. Revise Lisa's balance sheet to reflect changes listed at the beginning of Part 4 as well as the following:
    --the $6,250 March distribution from Tom's life insurance was deposited in the Fidelity Cash Reserves mutual fund.
    --cash on hand and checking account balances are $175 and $8,211, respectively.
    --bank credit card and department store credit card balances are $351 and $209, respectively.
    Date the new statement April 1, 1993. What is Lisa's new net worth?

13. Revise Lisa's budget to reflect the changes in income and expenditures caused by the actions listed at the beginning of Parts 3 and 4 and by your insurance recommendations. Assume all changes are effective in April, 1993 except for the change in take-home pay which started in March. Lisa pays premiums annually for all private insurance (not through her employer) except her auto insurance which is paid semi-annually and her homeowners policy that is paid with her monthly mortgage payment. Lisa will be paying $308 monthly on the new home equity line of credit. She estimates that interest income will decrease by approximately $35 per month because of the withdrawals from savings for Andy's trip and to pay off the auto loan.

PART FIVE: The Simmons Case Study

1. Using the asset values on Lisa's latest balance sheet (Part 4, Question 12), how much annual interest income should she earn in 1993 from her: (assume the same balance was maintained all year)

    --Super NOW account (4% APR)

    --money market mutual fund (4.5% APR)

    --certificate of deposit (6.5%)

2. Using the dividend income and current values from the original case, what was the current dividend yield in 1992 on the:

    --Kroger stock

    --Fidelity Puritan mutual fund

    --Merrill Lynch Phoenix mutual fund

3. What was the approximate annual yield on the Gabelli Growth mutual fund investment that was sold early in 1992 (See original case for details of purchase and sale)? Assume that dividends and capital gains distributions averaged $.50 annually per share.. Compare the annual yield on this stock mutual fund to the yield on Lisa's less risky investments. Did the fund provide an adequate yield for the risk taken?

4. Track the market price of Kroger stock over a two-week period. The needed information can be found in *The Wall Street Journal* and in many daily newspapers. What exchange does Kroger trade on? What is Kroger's price/earnings ratio and what does it mean?

5. Track the net asset value (NAV) of the Fidelity Puritan and the Merrill Lynch Phoenix A mutual funds over a two-week period. The needed information can be found in *The Wall Street Journal* and in many daily newspapers.

6. From looking at the mutual fund listings, does the Fidelity Puritan fund and/or the Merrill Lynch Phoenix A fund charge front-end loads, 12(b)-1 fees, and/or redemption fees? If there is a front-end load on either fund, what percent load is charged?

7. Lisa would like to update her investment knowledge on the stock and mutual fund shares she currently owns. Use reports available in the library (*Standard & Poor's Stock Report* or *Value Line*) or other sources mentioned in you text to learn more about Kroger. Use Morningstar's *Mutual Fund Values*, Wiesenberger's *Investment Companies*, or other sources mentioned in the text to learn more about Lisa's two mutual funds.

8. Lisa wants to limit her potential loss on the Kroger stock investment. She would like to sell it if the market price drops to $10. How could she easily implement this strategy?

9. If Lisa sold all of her Fidelity Puritan mutual fund shares, what would be her before-tax capital gain on these shares? The current net asset value is $14.76. Given her marginal tax bracket (Part 2, Question 13), how much would she have to pay in federal income taxes on this transaction?

10. If Lisa sold all of her Merrill Lynch Phoenix mutual fund shares, what would be her before-tax capital loss on these shares? The current net asset value is $11.79. Given her marginal tax bracket, how much would she save in federal income taxes on this transaction?

11. Looking at Lisa's most recent balance sheet (Part 4, Question 12), which investment risks are her assets most vulnerable to?

12. Lisa's certificate of deposit will mature in December 1993, and she is trying to decide how to reinvest the $13,500 plus interest. She is considering the following 2 different stock investments. What is the current dividend yield on each of these investments? What would the approximate annual yield be on each given the following assumptions? She plans to keep the investment about 5 years.

	Blue-chip stock	Aggressive growth stock
Current market value	$40.12	$22.50
Annual dividend income	$ 1.63	$ .50
Market value in 5 years	$57.00	$50.00

13. Lisa is also considering investing this $13,500 plus interest in 15 corporate bonds that are currently selling at discount for $953 each. They mature in 5 years and have an AA rating from Moody's. They pay annual interest of $75 each. What is the current yield on this bond investment? What is the yield-to-maturity on these bonds?

14. Over the past year, Lisa has become very interested in New York State. She is wondering if there are municipal bond funds that invest only in New York municipalities. If yes, what are some of their names? Given Lisa's marginal tax rate, would a tax-free AA municipal bond with a current yield of 6% provided a higher after-tax current yield than the corporate bond in Question 13?

15. A friend of Lisa's has become very involved in residential rental real estate as an investment. What would be some of the advantages and disadvantages of investing in residential rental property for Lisa?

16. Look again at Lisa's latest balance sheet (Part 4, Question 12), her most recent budget (Part 4, Question 13), her investment objectives (below), and her risk tolerance and financial priorities (original case). Assuming Lisa has made all the cuts in expenditures that are possible and that she will not be making additional income in 1993, how should Lisa handle her projected budget deficit?

In order to help get Lisa started with her investment planning, recommend general types of investments that would be appropriate for her stated goals:

New car, $20,000, 3 years
   --$10,000 of the American Life Insurance policy was committed to this goal.
   --Assuming a 5% rate of return, additional annual savings of $2,672 are required.

Andy's college education, $57,000, 5 years
   --$25,000 of the American Life Insurance policy was committed to this goal.
   --$12,500 of that has already been invested in U.S. EE savings bonds.
   --Assuming an 8% rate of return, additional annual savings of $3,455 are required.

Business, $50,000, 8 years
> --$25,000 of the American Life Insurance policy was committed to this goal.
> --Assuming a 9% rate of return, no additional annual savings are required.

Karen's college education, $80,000, 11 years
> --$15,000 of the American Life Insurance policy was committed to this goal.
> --Assuming an 8% rate of return, additional annual savings of $2,705 are required.

401(k) account, $2,000 per year
> Employer invests this in a growth & income mutual fund.

IRA, $2,000 per year

Structure an investment portfolio for Lisa. What percentage of her liquid and investment assets would you recommend Lisa put in:
   --liquid asset investments
   --stocks and stock mutual funds
   --bond and bond mutual funds
   --other

How should Lisa position her current liquid and investment assets? How should she invest her annual contributions to savings and investments?

PART SIX--CHAPTER 15: The Simmons Case Study

1. Assuming Lisa were to continue working for J.& L. Advertising until she was age 65 and her average annual salary over her last three years was equivalent to $40,000 in today's dollars, what would her annual retirement benefit be from this pension?

2. Lisa plans on starting her own business in 8 years. At that time, she wants to resign from her current job. If she does resign, she will have three choices in regard to her vested pension:
    a. take the vested amount (estimated to be about $25,000) and use it as she wishes.
    b. roll this $25,000 over into an IRA.
    c. leave the funds in the company pension plan until she is age 65. In this case, Lisa estimates
       her average salary over her last three years would be equivalent to $35,000 in today's dollars.
    What are the advantages and the disadvantages of these options?

3. If Lisa decided to roll the $25,000 over into an IRA and earned an average annual return of 9% over the 23 years between starting her business and retiring at age 65, how much would the IRA be worth at retirement?

4. If, at age 65, Lisa put the IRA funds (from Question 3) in a safer investment with an average annual return of only 6%, how much could she withdraw annually over the next 25 years? How does this compare with the annual benefits that would be received from the pension fund had she left the funds in the company pension plan (Question 2)?

5. If Lisa contributes $2,000 annually to her 401(k) from now until she is age 65 and it earns 8% per year, what will it be worth at retirement? How much could Lisa withdraw from this fund annually over a 25-year period if she rolls it into a 6% IRA when she retires?

6   One of Lisa's long term goals is to retire in 31 years when she is 65. Her current living expenses are approximately $55,000 (excluding savings), but she feels she would be able to live during retirement on about 80% of her current living expenses. Assume Lisa continues to work for her current employer until age 65 (Question 1) and she contributes $2,000 per year to her 401(k) over those years (use assumptions from Question 5). She has decided not to count on any Social Security benefits when calculating her retirement needs. She wants to use all other investments for special goals so do not include them in the needs assessment either. Calculate Lisa's retirement income and investment needs assuming an average rate of inflation of 5%, 6% return on investments after retirement, and 8% return on investments prior to retirement.

7. Recalculate Lisa's retirement needs using the information from the previous question except that she does not stay with her current employer the next 31 years. Assume that she does quite to start her own business in 8 years and she does roll the $25,000 vested retirement amount into an IRA (use assumptions from Questions 3 and 4). While she would not be able to continue with the 401(k) after she left J.& L. Advertising, assume she continues investing in a similar alternative and receives the same annual income after retirement as in Question 5.

8. After looking at this second retirement needs analysis, Lisa wants to at least consider potential Social Security benefits. Using Exhibit 15.6, how much would you estimate Lisa's first-year annual Social Security benefits would be? Recalculate Lisa's retirement needs (one last time) using the data in Question 7 but adding in Social Security benefits.

9, Review needs from Questions 6, 7, and 8. Given Lisa's goals, what would your recommend?

PART SIX--CHAPTER SIXTEEN: The Simmons Case Study

1.   Referring to Lisa's most recent balance sheet (Part 4, Question 12), would Lisa's estate be subject to federal estate taxes if she were to die? If yes, what steps should be taken to reduce estate taxes?

2.   Which of Lisa's assets would be probate and which would be non-probate assets?

3.   Since Lisa's will currently names Tom as her sole beneficiary, how would her estate be distributed if she were to die? Use Exhibit 16.3 to answer this question.

4.   Given Lisa's estate planning needs, should she update her will? If yes, what should be included in this will?

5.   Lisa has decided that she would like to be cremated upon her death. She is also concerned that no one knows the details of her personal finances. She has discussed both of these things with Andy, but he is still young and there is much he doesn't understand. What is the best way to handle these issues?

6.   Lisa has considered saving for Andy's and Karen's college educations in the children's names rather than in her name. Since the contributions to these accounts would be considered gifts to the children, would Lisa be subject to gift taxes on the contributions? What are the advantages and the disadvantages of saving in the children's names?

386

<u>REPRESENTATIVE ANSWERS:</u> The Simmons Case Study

The following answers are representative--but not the only right answers to the questions in the case. Also, the latter answers build upon previous solutions to the case.

<u>Part One</u>

1.   See computer printout. Lisa Simmons has a net worth of $226,974.

2.   See computer printout. (Life insurance proceeds and sale of auto were entered as "bonuses and commissions" because the computer program would not accept them as "other income.") Lisa had a cash surplus in 1992 of $30,195. This large cash surplus contributed to the large net worth shown for January 1, 1993. We see evidence of this in the original case when life insurance proceeds are received in June and two money market accounts/funds are opened in July.

3.   See computer printout.

4.   Positive aspects:
        --Lisa has a net worth of $226,974.
        --She had a positive cash flow in 1992, but there will be many changes with Tom's death.
        --Lisa appears to have a stable income and the ability to earn extra income through self-employment.
        --Lisa received/will receive monies from Tom's life insurance, and the children will receive Social Security benefits until they are 18 years old.
        --Lisa has a solvency ratio of nearly 70%, meaning that her assets could lose 70% of their value before she would become insolvent.
        --Lisa's saving ratio is over 33%, but this is due primarily to proceeds from Tom's life insurance and the sale of an automobile.
        --Lisa's debt ratio is only 17%, but again this is somewhat distorted by the extra income from the life insurance and auto sale. However, her use of debt does seem to be under control. The low balances on credit cards suggest that Lisa makes limited use of revolving credit.
        --It appears that Lisa did not make major financial decisions (such as plunging into risky investments, selling her home, etc.) immediately following Tom's death.
        --Lisa's financial information and documents are very well organized.
        --Lisa owns a home and has 28% equity in the home.
        --Lisa has a long term disability income policy, and the family has health insurance coverage.

        Negative aspects:
        --Lisa's liquidity ratio is too high. She needs help positioning her assets into investments that will give a higher rate of return over the long run.
        --Lisa may have trouble maintaining the family's current standard of living without Tom's income.
        --Lisa needs a safe deposit box to keep official papers such as deeds, titles, birth certificates, marriage certificates, death certificates, etc.
        --Lisa has only a small vested pension. She needs to start planning for her retirement.
        --The interest rate on Lisa's home loan is rather high considering current mortgage interest rates.

--Lisa's life insurance coverage is only $59,000. This may be too low, especially for a single parent.

--The liability coverage on Lisa's automobile insurance policy is too low.

--Lisa's will needs to be updated following Tom's death.

5a. See computer printout.

$10,000
x 1.3382 future value of a lump sum
$13,382

b. See computer printout.

$10,000
x 1.8983 future value of a lump sum
$18,983

6a. See computer printout.

$13,500
x 4.2124 present value of an annuity
$56,867

b. See computer printout.

$56,867
x .6806 present value of a lump sum
$38,704

c. See computer printout.

$19,000
x 4.2124 present value of an annuity
$80,036

d. See computer printout.

$80,036
x .4289 present value of an annuity
$34,327

7. See computer printouts.
(New car)

$10,000
x 1.1576 future value of a lump sum
$11,576

$20,000
- 11,576
$ 8,424/3.1525 = $2,672 needed to save annually

(Andy's college fund)

$25,000
x 1.4693 future value of a lump sum
$36,733

$57,000
-36,733
$20,267/5.8666 = $3,455 needed to save annually

(Business fund)

$25,000
x 1.9926 future value of a lump sum
$49,815

$50,000

-49,815

$ 185   (close enough/no annual savings required)

(Karen's college fund) $15,000

x 2.3316   future value of a lump sum

$34,974

$80,000

-34,974

$45,026/16.6455 = $2,705 needed to save annually

Annual savings required: $ 2,672   car

                                       3,455   Andy's college

                                           0   business

                                       2,705   Karen's college

                                       2,000   401(k)

                                       2,000   IRA

                         $12,832

8.   See computer printout. The "savings and investments" expenditure category includes the current savings required to meet Lisa's goals (from previous question), the $75,000 from Tom's insurance policy that Lisa wants to commit to her goals, and reinvested interest, dividends, and capital gains distributions.

9.   The $23,268 budget deficit indicates that Lisa cannot achieve all of her goals (in the manner suggested) and continue current spending patterns on her income. There are numerous recommendations Lisa can consider.

Ideas for increasing after-tax income:

--Ask for a raise at work. The 1993 budget assumes no increase in salary.

--Expand the consulting business.

--Checking her withholding allowances at work. Lisa may be having too much money withheld for federal income taxes.

Ideas for decreasing expenses:

--Cut back slightly on variable expenses such as food, food away from home, clothing, furniture purchases, entertainment, vacations, and children's activities. Since Karen's gymnastics lessons were mentioned as a short-term goal, we would assume Lisa would want to continue funding them.

--Look into those miscellaneous expenses. $275 per month is a fairly high amount to not know how it is being spent. Perhaps this could be reduced.

--Consider refinancing the home mortgage at a lower rate of interest.

--Reduce medical insurance premiums by covering the children under Lisa's policy rather than through Tom's former employer if the new coverage would be adequate.

--Use liquid assets to pay off the debt consolidation loan and perhaps even the car loan. This would save the interest being spent which is at a much higher rate than the liquid assets are earning. Lisa did say that if she had an extra $5,000, she would use it to pay off the debt consolidation loan.

Ideas for modifying savings needed to meet goals:

--Lisa could try to earn a higher rate of return on her investments. However, this would probably require her taking a higher level of risk.

--She could extend the time frame for some of her goals. For example, she could plan on starting her own business in 10 years rather than in 8 years.

--She could scale down the amount needed to meet some of the goals. For example, rather than trying to fund the children's educations for 5 years she could plan on 4.5 years. Or she could cut back on the amount needed each year.

--Lisa could cut back somewhat on the amount of retirement savings in her 401(k) and/or IRA.

10. See computer printout. The net income from Lisa's consulting business is projected to be $3,275. Lisa needs to consider whether that amount adequately compensates her for the time she spends making this money. She should consider the demands the business makes on her well being, on the children, and it's impact on her future plans (going into business for herself on a full-time basis).

11. See computer printout. Lisa will receive a tax refund of $2,918 (using 1992 personal exemption amounts and tax tables).

Net business income	$6,280 gross income
	- 864 deductible expenses
	$5,416

Capital gains	$ 20.27 sales price per share
	- 16.27 purchase price per share
	4.00 gain per share
	x 100 number of shares
	$ 400 gain on Fidelity Puritan Mutual Fund
	+ 178 capital gains distributions
	$ 578

12. $4,796 / $34,082 = 14% average tax rate

15% marginal tax rate (from the 1992 tax rate schedules)

13. 401(k) $2,000
              x .15 marginal tax rate
              $ 300 tax savings

    IRA   There would have been no tax savings on a $2,000 IRA contribution because Lisa was covered by an employer retirement plan, and her adjusted gross income for 1992 was above $50,000. Therefore, the contribution would not have been deductible.

14. Remembering Lisa's goals, she could invest in a 401(k), but I would not recommend the IRA contribution. Her employer allows 401(k) contributions up to 10% of gross income annually ($2,950 based on her $29,500 income). She could also invest a small amount for retirement in a Keogh account based on her net self-employment income.

Regarding the children's college funds, Lisa should consider saving through U.S. EE Savings bonds that provide tax free interest income when used for a child's college education (and other requirements are met). Before doing this, she should check the after-tax yield that could be earned on comparable investments. Another possibility would be to put all or some of the education funds in the children's names so the investment earnings would be taxed as their income. Since Lisa is in the lowest marginal tax bracket (15%), this may not be that beneficial, however, especially if the children have other income.

If Lisa decides not to pay off her debt consolidation loan and/or auto loan, she could get a home equity line of credit and use those funds to pay off the old loan(s). The interest on the home equity debt would be tax deductible. (This strategy would not apply in Texas as state law prevents home equity lines of credit.)

Part I, Question I

```
+FP/PC-------------------------------------------------------------- FP/PC+
|
|                    B A L A N C E   S H E E T
|
+-----------------------------------------------------------------------+
```

Lisa Simmons   01/01/93

```
-----------------------------------------------------------------------
              ASSETS            |      LIABILITIES AND NET WORTH
-----------------------------------------------------------------------
```

Liquid Assets:		Current Liabilities	
Cash on hand.............	230	Utilities...............	0
In checking.............	2945	Rent....................	0
Savings accounts........	5687	Insurance premiums......	0
Money market funds		Taxes...................	0
and deposits...........	19870	Medical/dental bills.....	0
CDs < 1 yr. maturity.....	13500	Repair bills............	0
Other...................	0	Bank crd. card balances..	493
	------	Dept. store charge cards.	404
Total Liquid Assets.....	42232	Travel/entrtmt. card.....	0
		Gas/other credit cards...	0
Investments:		Bank line of credit......	0
Stocks I................	4050	Other cur. liabilities...	0
II................	0		------
Bonds I.................	0	Total Cur. Liabilities.	897
II.................	0		
CDs > 1 yr. maturity.....	0	Long-term Liabilities	
Mut. funds I.............	4747	Primary res. mortgage....	83066
II.............	2745	Second home mortgage.....	0
Real estate.............	0	Real estate investments..	0
Retirement funds........	8908	Auto loans..............	8493
Other. *Life insurance*.....	75000	Appliance/furn. loans....	0
	------	Home improvement loans...	0
Total Investments......	95450	Educational loans........	0
		Other I. *Debt consolidation*...	6252
Real Property		II.................	0
Primary residence........	115500		------
Second home.............	0	Total Long-term Liab...	97811
Car I...................	9600		
II...................	0		
Recreation equipment.....	2700		
Other. *Baseball card collection*	4500		

Total Real Property.....	132300		
Personal Property			
Furniture and appl.......	30000		
Stereos, TVs, etc, *computer*	10000		
Clothing................	7500		
Jewelry.................	0	(II) Tot. Liabilities.	98708
Other. *Toys & miscellaneous*..	8200		
	------	Net Worth [(II)-(III)].	226974
Total Personal Property.	55700		
		Total Liab. and Net Worth..	325682
(I) Total Assets......	325682		======
	======		

Part 1, Question 2

```
+FP/PC-----------------------------------------------------------------------FP/PC+
|       I N C O M E   A N D   E X P E N D I T U R E S   S T A T E M E N T       |
+------------------------------------------------------------------------------+
```
Lisa Simmons   for the year   ending 12/31/92

INCOME

Wages and salaries:	I..	29500
	II...	16470
Self-employment income....		6280
Bonuses and commissions.. *Life insurance proceeds & sales of auto*.........		33575
Pensions and annuities.. *Social security benefits*.......		9660
Investment income:	Interest received........................	3703
	Dividends received.......................	356
	Rents received...........................	0
	Sale of securities.......................	2027
	Other. *Capital gains distributions*...............	178
Other income		0
(I) TOTAL INCOME............................		101749

EXPENDITURES

Housing:	Rent payment.............................	0
	Mortgage payment.........................	9576
	Repairs, maintenance, improvements.......	750
Utilities:	Gas, electric, water.....................	2100
	Phone....................................	540
	Cable TV and other.......................	360
Food:	Groceries and dining out.................	7950
Autos:	Loan payments............................	3996
	License plates, fees, etc................	0
	Gas/oil/repairs/tires/maintenance........	1950
Medical:	Health/major medical/disability insurance....	3000
	Doctor/dent/hosp/medicine................	310
Clothing:	Clothes, shoes, and accessories..........	2475
Insurance:	Homeowner's..............................	600
	Life.....................................	100
	Auto.....................................	1080
Taxes:	Income and Social Security...............	12058
	Property.................................	2460
Appl/furn/other:	Loan payments............................	0
	Purchases and repairs....................	1236
Personal care:	Laundry, cosmetics, hair care............	600
Recreation/entertmt:	Vacations................................	1500
	Other recreation and entertainment.......	1200
Other loans:	I..	3864
	II.......................................	0
Other expenditures:	I *Children's activities, child care, & children's allowances*.	4935
	II *Charitable contributions, misc., business exp., & funeral*.	8914
(II) TOTAL EXPENDITURES.............................		71554

CASH SURPLUS (OR DEFICIT) [(I) - (II)]............................. 30195
======

Part 1, Question 3

FINANCIAL STATEMENT RATIOS

Lisa Simmons   12/31/92

$$\text{Solvency ratio} = \frac{\text{Total net worth}}{\text{Total assets}} = \frac{226974}{325682} = 69.69\ \%$$

$$\text{Liquidity ratio} = \frac{\text{Liquid assets}}{\text{Total current debts}} = \frac{42232}{18333} = 230.36\ \%$$

$$\text{Savings ratio} = \frac{\text{Cash surplus}}{\text{Income after taxes}} = \frac{30195}{89691} = 33.67\ \%$$

$$\text{Debt service ratio} = \frac{\text{loan payments}}{\substack{\text{Monthly gross} \\ \text{(before-tax) income}}} = \frac{1453}{45970} = 17.14\ \%$$

Part 1, Question 5

```
+FP/PC--------------------------------------------------------FP/PC+
|    F U T U R E    V A L U E    O F    A    S I N G L E    C A S H    F L O W    |
+------------------------------------------------------------------+
```

(a) *Andy*

                    Single cash flow............   10000.00
                    Rate of return..............   6.00%
                    Number of years.............   5.00

                    Future value................   13382.26

```
------------------------------------------------------------------

+FP/PC--------------------------------------------------------FP/PC+
|    F U T U R E    V A L U E    O F    A    S I N G L E    C A S H    F L O W    |
+------------------------------------------------------------------+
```

(b) *Karen*

                    Single cash flow............   10000.00
                    Rate of return..............   6.00%
                    Number of years.............   11.00

                    Future value................   18982.99

```
------------------------------------------------------------------
```

Part 1, Question 6

```
+FP/PC--------------------------------------------------------------FP/PC
|              P R E S E N T   V A L U E   O F   A N   A N N U I T Y
+-------------------------------------------------------------------------
```

(a) *Andy*

```
                Annuity payment..............    13500.00
                Rate of return (%)...........        6.00
                Number of years..............        5.00

                Present value................        0.00
```

```
+FP/PC--------------------------------------------------------------FP/PC
|            P R E S E N T   V A L U E   O F   A N   A N N U I T Y
+-------------------------------------------------------------------------
```

(c) *Karen*

```
                Annuity payment..............    19000.00
                Rate of return (%)...........        6.00
                Number of years..............        5.00

                Present value................        0.00
```

```
+FP/PC--------------------------------------------------------------FP/PC
| P R E S E N T   V A L U E   O F   A   S I N G L E   F U T U R E   V A L U E
+-------------------------------------------------------------------------
```

(b) *Andy*

```
                Single future value.........    56867.00
                Rate of return (%)...........       8.00%
                Number of years..............        5.00

                Present value................    38702.73
```

```
+FP/PC--------------------------------------------------------------FP/PC
| P R E S E N T   V A L U E   O F   A   S I N G L E   F U T U R E   V A L U E
+-------------------------------------------------------------------------
```

(d) *Karen*

```
                Single future value.........    80035.00
                Rate of return (%)...........       8.00%
                Number of years..............       11.00

                Present value................    34325.64
```

Part 1, Question 7   *Fund for new car*

```
+FP/PC------------------------------------------------------------FP/PC+
|    F U T U R E   V A L U E   O F   A   S I N G L E   C A S H   F L O W  |
+------------------------------------------------------------------------+


              Single cash flow.............      10000.00
              Rate of return...............         5.00%
              Number of years..............         3.00

              Future value.................      11576.25


------------------------------------------------------------------------


+FP/PC------------------------------------------------------------FP/PC+
|    YEARLY SAVINGS REQUIRED TO ACCUMULATE A GIVEN FUTURE VALUE         |
+------------------------------------------------------------------------+


              Future value.................       8424.00
              Rate of return...............          5.00%
              Number of years..............          3.00

              Yearly savings required......       2672.17


------------------------------------------------------------------------


+FP/PC------------------------------------------------------------FP/PC+
|    SETTING INVESTMENT GOALS:  MAKING A SERIES OF INVESTMENTS OVER TIME |
+------------------------------------------------------------------------+

     Targeted financial goal..............................    20000
     Projected average return on investments..............     5.00
     Number of years to target date.......................     3.00
     Amount of initial investment (if any)................    10000

     Terminal value of initial investment.................    11576
     Balance to come from savings plan....................     8424
     Amount of each annual investment in the series.......     2672


------------------------------------------------------------------------
```

Part 1, Question 7 *Andy's College fund*

```
+FP/PC---------------------------------------------------------------FP/PC+
|        F U T U R E   V A L U E   O F   A   S I N G L E   C A S H   F L O W        |
+-------------------------------------------------------------------------+


                Single cash flow.............     25000.00
                Rate of return...............        8.00%
                Number of years..............        5.00

                Future value.................    36733.20


--------------------------------------------------------------------------

+FP/PC---------------------------------------------------------------FP/PC+
|     YEARLY SAVINGS REQUIRED TO ACCUMULATE A GIVEN FUTURE VALUE     |
+-------------------------------------------------------------------------+


                Future value.................     20267.00
                Rate of return...............        8.00%
                Number of years..............        5.00

                Yearly savings required......     3454.64


--------------------------------------------------------------------------

+FP/PC---------------------------------------------------------------FP/PC+
|     SETTING INVESTMENT GOALS:  MAKING A SERIES OF INVESTMENTS OVER TIME     |
+-------------------------------------------------------------------------+

   Targeted financial goal...............................     57000
   Projected average return on investments...............      8.00
   Number of years to target date........................      5.00
   Amount of initial investment (if any).................     25000

   Terminal value of initial investment..................     36733
   Balance to come from savings plan.....................     20267
   Amount of each annual investment in the series........      3455


--------------------------------------------------------------------------
```

Business fund

```
+FP/PC---------------------------------------------------------------FP/PC+
|        F U T U R E   V A L U E   O F   A   S I N G L E   C A S H   F L O W        |
+-------------------------------------------------------------------------+

                Single cash flow.............     25000.00
                Rate of return...............        9.00%
                Number of years..............        8.00

                Future value.................    49814.07


--------------------------------------------------------------------------
```

Part I, Question 7   Karen's college fund

```
+FP/PC------------------------------------------------------------FP/PC+
|      F U T U R E   V A L U E   O F   A   S I N G L E   C A S H   F L O W   |
+----------------------------------------------------------------------+

               Single cash flow.............    15000.00
               Rate of return...............        8.00%
               Number of years..............       11.00

               Future value.................    34974.59


- - - - - - - - - - - - - - - - - - - - - - - - - - - - - - - - - - - - -


+FP/PC------------------------------------------------------------FP/PC+
|      YEARLY SAVINGS REQUIRED TO ACCUMULATE A GIVEN FUTURE VALUE       |
+----------------------------------------------------------------------+

               Future value.................    45025.00
               Rate of return...............        8.00%
               Number of years..............       11.00

               Yearly savings required......     2704.94


- - - - - - - - - - - - - - - - - - - - - - - - - - - - - - - - - - - - -


+FP/PC------------------------------------------------------------FP/PC+
|      SETTING INVESTMENT GOALS:  MAKING A SERIES OF INVESTMENTS OVER TIME   |
+----------------------------------------------------------------------+

     Targeted financial goal...............................    80000
     Projected average return on investments...............     8.00
     Number of years to target date........................    11.00
     Amount of initial investment (if any).................    15000

     Terminal value of initial investment..................    34975
     Balance to come from savings plan.....................    45025
     Amount of each annual investment in the series........     2705


- - - - - - - - - - - - - - - - - - - - - - - - - - - - - - - - - - - - -
```

Part 1, Question 8

```
+-FP/PC------------------------------------------------------------FP/PC-+
|            M O N T H L Y   C A S H   B U D G E T   S U M M A R Y        |
+------------------------------------------------------------------------+
```

NAME(S): Lisa Simmons   Page 1

FOR THE YEAR ENDING 12/31/93   JAN   FEB   MAR

	JAN	FEB	MAR
Take-Home Pay: Source 1	1902	1902	1902
Take-Home Pay: Source 2	386	386	386
Take-Home Pay: Source 3	0	0	0
Bonuses and Commissions	0	0	0
Pensions and Annuities *Social Security benefits*	1421	1421	1421
Interest	557	557	557
Dividends	0	0	89
Rents	0	0	0
Sale of Securities	0	0	0
Other	0	0	44
Other Income: Source 1 *Life insurance proceeds*	6250	6250	6250
Other Income: Source 2	0	0	0
TOTAL INCOME	10516	10516	10649
Rent/Mortgage Payment	798	798	798
Repairs, Maintenance, Improvements	75	75	75
Gas, Utilities, Water	175	175	175
Phone	45	45	45
Cable TV and Other	30	30	30
Groceries	450	450	450
Dining Out	150	150	150
Loan/Lease Payments	333	333	333
License Plates, Fees, Etc.	0	0	0
Gas, Oil, Tires, Maintenance	125	125	125
Health Insurance, Etc.	250	250	250
Doctor, Dentist, Hospital, Medicine	26	26	26
Clothing, Shoes, Accessories	175	175	175
Homeowner's Insurance	50	50	50
Life Insurance	0	0	0
Automobile Insurance	0	390	0
Income and Social Security Taxes	0	0	0
Property Taxes	205	205	205
Loan Payments	0	0	0
Purchases and Repairs	103	103	103
Laundry, Cosmetics, Hair Care	50	50	50
Vacations	0	0	1500
Other Recreation and Entertainment	100	100	100
Savings and Investments	7876	7876	8009
Charitable Contributions	75	75	75
~~Gifts~~ *Children's activities*	200	200	200
~~Education Expenses~~ *Debt consolidation loan*	322	322	322
~~Subscriptions, Magazines, Books~~ *Child care*	225	225	225
Other Expenditures: Item 1 *Children's allowances*	80	80	80
Other Expenditures: Item 2 *Miscellaneous*	275	275	275
~~Fun Money~~ *Business expenses*	72	72	72
TOTAL EXPENDITURES	12265	12655	13898
CASH SUPLUS (OR DEFICIT)	-1749	-2139	-3249
CUMULATIVE CASH SUPLUS (OR DEFICIT)	-1749	-3888	-7137

NAME(S): Lisa Simmons

FOR THE YEAR ENDING 12/31/93	APR	MAY	JUN
Take-Home Pay: Source 1	1902	1902	1902
Take-Home Pay: Source 2	386	386	386
Take-Home Pay: Source 3	0	0	0
Bonuses and Commissions	0	0	0
Pensions and Annuities *Social Security benefits*	1421	1421	1421
Interest	557	557	557
Dividends	0	0	89
Rents	0	0	0
Sale of Securities	0	0	0
Other	0	0	45
Other Income: Source 1 *Life insurance proceeds*	6250	6250	6250
Other Income: Source 2	0	0	0
TOTAL INCOME	10516	10516	10650
Rent/Mortgage Payment	798	798	798
Repairs, Maintenance, Improvements	75	75	75
Gas, Utilities, Water	175	175	175
Phone	45	45	45
Cable TV and Other	30	30	30
Groceries	450	450	450
Dining Out	150	150	150
Loan/Lease Payments	333	333	333
License Plates, Fees, Etc.	0	0	0
Gas, Oil, Tires, Maintenance	125	125	125
Health Insurance, Etc.	250	250	250
Doctor, Dentist, Hospital, Medicine	26	26	26
Clothing, Shoes, Accessories	175	175	175
Homeowner's Insurance	50	50	50
Life Insurance	0	0	0
Automobile Insurance	0	0	0
Income and Social Security Taxes	0	0	0
Property Taxes	205	205	205
Loan Payments	0	0	0
Purchases and Repairs	103	103	103
Laundry, Cosmetics, Hair Care	50	50	50
Vacations	0	0	0
Other Recreation and Entertainment	100	100	100
Savings and Investments	7876	7876	8010
Charitable Contributions	75	75	75
~~Gifts~~ *Childrens' activities*	200	200	200
~~Education Expenses~~ *Debt consolidation loan*	322	322	322
~~Subscriptions, Magazines, Books~~ *Child care*	225	225	225
Other Expenditures: Item 1 *Children's allowances*	80	80	80
Other Expenditures: Item 2 *Miscellaneous*	275	275	275
~~Fun Money~~ *Business expenses*	72	72	72
TOTAL EXPENDITURES	12265	12265	12399
CASH SUPLUS (OR DEFICIT)	-1749	-1749	-1749
CUMULATIVE CASH SUPLUS (OR DEFICIT)	-8886	-10635	-12384

```
+-FP/PC--------------------------------------------------------------------FP/PC-+
|        M O N T H L Y   C A S H   B U D G E T   S U M M A R Y                    |
+--------------------------------------------------------------------------------+
NAME(S): Lisa Simmons                                                      Page 3

FOR THE YEAR ENDING 12/31/93                    JUL        AUG        SEP
```

	JUL	AUG	SEP
Take-Home Pay: Source 1	1902	1902	1902
Take-Home Pay: Source 2	386	386	386
Take-Home Pay: Source 3	0	0	0
Bonuses and Commissions	0	0	0
Pensions and Annuities *Social Security benefits*	1421	1421	1421
Interest	557	557	557
Dividends	0	0	89
Rents	0	0	0
Sale of Securities	0	0	0
Other	0	0	44
Other Income: Source 1 *Life insurance proceeds*	6250	6250	6250
Other Income: Source 2	0	0	0
TOTAL INCOME	10516	10516	10649
Rent/Mortgage Payment	798	798	798
Repairs, Maintenance, Improvements	75	75	75
Gas, Utilities, Water	175	175	175
Phone	45	45	45
Cable TV and Other	30	30	30
Groceries	450	450	450
Dining Out	150	150	150
Loan/Lease Payments	333	333	333
License Plates, Fees, Etc.	0	0	0
Gas, Oil, Tires, Maintenance	125	125	125
Health Insurance, Etc.	250	250	250
Doctor, Dentist, Hospital, Medicine	26	26	26
Clothing, Shoes, Accessories	175	175	175
Homeowner's Insurance	50	50	50
Life Insurance	0	0	0
Automobile Insurance	0	390	0
Income and Social Security Taxes	0	0	0
Property Taxes	205	205	205
Loan Payments	0	0	0
Purchases and Repairs	103	103	103
Laundry, Cosmetics, Hair Care	50	50	50
Vacations	0	0	0
Other Recreation and Entertainment	100	100	100
Savings and Investments	7876	7876	8009
Charitable Contributions	75	75	75
~~Gifts~~ *Children's activities*	200	200	200
~~Education Expenses~~ *Debt Consolidation Loan*	322	322	322
~~Subscriptions, Magazines, Books~~ *Child care*	225	225	225
Other Expenditures: Item 1 *Children's allowances*	80	80	80
Other Expenditures: Item 2 *Miscellaneous*	275	275	275
~~Fun Money~~ *Business expenses*	72	72	72
TOTAL EXPENDITURES	12265	12655	12398
CASH SUPLUS (OR DEFICIT)	-1749	-2139	-1749
CUMULATIVE CASH SUPLUS (OR DEFICIT)	-14133	-16272	-18021

NAME(S): Lisa Simmons   Page 4

FOR THE YEAR ENDING 12/31/93	OCT	NOV	DEC	TOTAL
Take-Home Pay: Source 1	1902	1902	1902	22824
Take-Home Pay: Source 2	386	386	386	4632
Take-Home Pay: Source 3	0	0	0	0
Bonuses and Commissions	0	0	0	0
Pensions and Annuities *Social Security benefits*	1421	1421	1421	17052
Interest	557	557	1437	7564
Dividends	0	0	89	356
Rents	0	0	0	0
Sale of Securities	0	0	0	0
Other	0	0	45	178
Other Income: Source 1 *Life insurance proceeds*	6250	6250	6250	75000
Other Income: Source 2	0	0	0	0
TOTAL INCOME	10516	10516	11530	127606
Rent/Mortgage Payment	798	798	798	9576
Repairs, Maintenance, Improvements	75	75	75	900
Gas, Utilities, Water	175	175	175	2100
Phone	45	45	45	540
Cable TV and Other	30	30	30	360
Groceries	450	450	450	5400
Dining Out	150	150	150	1800
Loan/Lease Payments	333	333	333	3996
License Plates, Fees, Etc.	0	0	0	0
Gas, Oil, Tires, Maintenance	125	125	125	1500
Health Insurance, Etc.	250	250	250	3000
Doctor, Dentist, Hospital, Medicine	26	26	26	312
Clothing, Shoes, Accessories	175	175	175	2100
Homeowner's Insurance	50	50	50	600
Life Insurance	0	0	0	0
Automobile Insurance	0	0	0	780
Income and Social Security Taxes	0	0	0	0
Property Taxes	205	205	205	2460
Loan Payments	0	0	0	0
Purchases and Repairs	103	103	103	1236
Laundry, Cosmetics, Hair Care	50	50	50	600
Vacations	0	0	0	1500
Other Recreation and Entertainment	100	100	100	1200
Savings and Investments	7876	7876	8890	95926
Charitable Contributions	75	75	75	900
~~Gifts~~ *Children's activities*	200	200	200	2400
~~Education Expenses~~ *Debt consolidation loan*	322	322	322	3864
~~Subscriptions, Magazines, Books~~ *Child care*	225	225	225	2700
Other Expenditures: Item 1 *Children's allowances*	80	80	80	960
Other Expenditures: Item 2 *Miscellaneous*	275	275	275	3300
~~Fun Money~~ *Business expenses*	72	72	72	864
TOTAL EXPENDITURES	12265	12265	13279	150874
CASH SUPLUS (OR DEFICIT)	-1749	-1749	-1749	-23268
CUMULATIVE CASH SUPLUS (OR DEFICIT)	-19770	-21519	-23268	-23268

Part 1, Question 8

```
+-FP/PC---------------------------------------------------------FP/PC-+
|                     C A S H   B U D G E T   S U M M A R Y           |
+--------------------------------------------------------------------+
```

NAME(S): Lisa Simmons
FOR YEAR ENDING 12/31/93

	Total Income	Total Expenses	Cash Surplus (Deficit)	Cumulative Cash Surplus (Deficit)
Jan	$ 10516	$ 12265	$ -1749	$ -1749
Feb	10516	12655	-2139	-3888
Mar	10649	13898	-3249	-7137
Apr	10516	12265	-1749	-8886
May	10516	12265	-1749	-10635
Jun	10650	12399	-1749	-12384
Jul	10516	12265	-1749	-14133
Aug	10516	12655	-2139	-16272
Sep	10649	12398	-1749	-18021
Oct	10516	12265	-1749	-19770
Nov	10516	12265	-1749	-21519
Dec	11530	13279	1749	-23268
TOTALS ..	$ 127606	$ 150874		$ -23268

```
+--------------------------------------------------------------------+
```

Part 1, Question 10

```
+FP/PC-----------------------------------------------------------FP/PC+
|                                                                      |
|            S E C O N D   I N C O M E   A N A L Y S I S               |
|                                                                      |
+----------------------------------------------------------------------+
```

MONTHLY CASH INCOME

```
Gross Pay....................  6280
Pretax Contributions........     0
Add'l Job-Related Income....     0

(1) TOTAL CASH INCOME......  6280
                             -----
```

EMPLOYER-PAID BENEFITS

```
Health Insurance............     0
Life Insurance..............     0
Pension Contributions.......     0
Thrift-Plan Contributions...     0
Social Security.............     0
Profit Sharing..............     0
Other Deferred Comp.........     0

(2) TOTAL BENEFITS.........      0
                             -----
```

MONTHLY JOB-RELATED EXPENSES

```
Federal Income Tax..........   812
Social Security Tax.........   829
State Income Tax............     0
Child Care..................   500
Clothing and Personal Care..     0
Dry Cleaning................     0
Meals Away From Home........     0
Public Transportation.......     0
Gasoline....................     0
Auto-related Expenses.......     0
Other *deductible expenses*....  864
```

```
(3) TOTAL EXPENSES.........   3005
                              -----

(4) NET INCOME (DEFICIT)
    [(1) + (2) - (3)]....   3275
                           ======
```

Part 1, Question 11

FEDERAL INCOME TAX WORKSHEET
Lisa Simmons & Tom Simmons (deceased)

	1992	1993
INCOME		
1. Wages, salaries, tips, etc.	$45,970	$0
2. Interest income	3,703	
3. Dividends	356	
4. Capital gains (losses)	578	
5. Net business income (loss)	5,416	
6. Income (deductible losses) from rental property	0	
7. Other income	0	
8. TOTAL INCOME (add lines 1 - 7)	$56,023	$0
ADJUSTMENTS		
9. One-half of self-employment tax	415	
10. Keogh contributions	0	
11. AGI before IRA contributions (subtract lines 9 & 10 from line 8)	55,608	0
12. Deductible IRA contributions	0	
13. ADJUSTED GROSS INCOME (subtract line 12 from line 11)	$55,608	$0
ITEMIZED DEDUCTIONS		
14. Deductible medical expenses	$0	$0
15. State and local income and property taxes	2,460	
16. Mortgage interest	8,966	
17. Other deductible interest	0	
18. Charitable contributions	900	
19. Deductible misc. expenses	0	
20. Casualty and theft losses	0	
21. TOTAL ITEMIZED DEDUCTIONS (add lines 14 - 20)	$12,326	$0
TAXABLE INCOME		
22. Write in the amount on line 21 or or your standard deduction, whichever is greater	$12,326	$0
23. Personal exemptions	9,200	
24. TAXABLE INCOME (substract lines 22 and 23 from line 13)	$34,082	$0
TAX LIABILITY		
25. Tax before credits (see tax tables)	$5,111	$0
26. Child care credit	315	
27. YOUR TAX (subtract line 26 from line 25)	$4,796	$0
TAX WITHHELD	$7,714	$0
TAX DUE or (REFUND)	($2,918)	$0

<u>REPRESENTATIVE ANSWERS:</u> The Simmons Case Study

<u>Part Two</u>

1.   With the given changes in tax withholding, Lisa's monthly after-tax earned income is
      $2,467 ($2,079 + $388). Five months of earned income would then be $12,335 ($2,467 x
      5). Since Lisa currently has $42,232 in liquid assets (Part 1, Question 1), $29,897 is then
      available for other purposes or for repositioning into other types of assets.

2.   See computer printout. Lisa's checking account is not reconciled, but it is only $.20 off.
      Since it is such a small amount, I would recommend she not waste time looking for the
      error. She should just subtract $.20 from her check book balance and go play with the
      children or do something for herself.

3.

Type of Account	Positive Features	Negative Features
NOW account	Unlimited checking writing, extremely liquid, interest paid on checking balance, federally insured	Very low rate of interest, minimum balance required to avoid service charge
Money market account	Limited checking writing, very liquid, federally insured	Low rate of interest, minimum balance required to avoid service charge and/or reduced interest rate
Money market mutual fund	Limited check writing, very liquid, safe, generally pays slightly higher interest rate than other liquid investments with no maturity	Not federally insured, invest through an investment company rather than at local financial institution, minimum deposit required to open account
Certificate of deposit	Generally pays higher rate of interest than more liquid accounts, federally insured	No check writing privileges, penalty if funds are withdrawn before maturity
Savings account	Very liquid, federally insured, very low minimum balance required to open account	No check writing privileges, very low rate of return

4.   To maintain the needed minimum daily balance on the Super NOW account, Lisa could
      close her savings account and transfer that $5,687 as well as $1,000 from her First
      National Bank money market deposit account to the Super NOW account. That would
      provide the needed minimum daily balance to avoid monthly service charges ($1,100 +
      $5,687 + $1,000 = $7,787). The interest on the Super NOW account is slightly higher
      than the rate paid on both the savings and the money market deposit account as well as
      that paid on the regular NOW account so Lisa's interest income would increase by
      approximately $51 annually.

Checking:	$2,000 average daily balance
	x .01 difference in interest
	$20.00 increase in interest

Savings account:	$5,687 balance
	x .005 difference in interest
	$28.44 increase in interest

Money market :	$1,000 transfer
	x .003 difference in interest
	$ 3.00 increase in interest

Lisa would also save about $36 annually (10 x $.30 x 12) in ATM fees with the Super NOW account. This would be a total financial gain of $87 ($51 + $36). In addition to the financial gain, Lisa would have one less account to keep track of. However, she should never let her balance drop below the $7,500 minimum daily balance since the service charge for a single month would be approximately $20.25 [$15 + ($.15 x 35)]. This is $10 per month higher than the service charge on the regular NOW account.

I would recommend Lisa open the Super NOW account. If she has trouble maintaining the minimum daily balance, she can transfer a little more money from the money market deposit account.

5. U.S. EE savings bonds are an extremely save investment because they are backed by the full faith and credit of the U.S. government. They have a guaranteed minimum return of 6% if held at least 5 years, but they can earn a higher rate of return when market rates of interest increase. The bonds are sold at one-half of their face value, and the interest accumulates and is received when the investor redeems the bonds. The interest is exempt from state and local income taxes and can be deferred on federal income taxes. When bonds are used by a single taxpayer with an adjusted gross income of $56,950 or less to pay for college education, the interest earned is tax free for federal income taxes, too.

While U.S. EE savings bonds have excellent tax advantages when used for college savings, the minimum guaranteed rate of 6% is equal to only a 7.06% return for a taxpayer like Lisa in the 15% marginal tax bracket [6%/(1-.15)]. Lisa was expecting to get an 8% yield on the children's college funds (Part 1, Question 7). In addition, each bond must be held at least 5 years in order to avoid an interest rate reduction penalty. This means that not all of Andy's college education fund should be put into U.S. EE savings bonds.

I would recommend that some of Andy's and Karen's college funds be invested in U.S. EE savings bonds. However, some of their college funds should be put into higher yielding investments. Lisa also must remember not to put money that will be needed within the next 5 years into U.S. EE savings bonds.

6a. See computer printout.

$ 2,000
x 113.282 future value of an annuity
$ 226,564

b. See computer printout.

$300,000/113.282 = $2,648

7.

	7.75% Fixed-Rate	5.5% ARM
Points	$1,246	$2,492
Closing costs	2,500	2,500
Total front-end costs	$3,746	$4,992

See computer printout.

Monthly payment for principal & interest	$ 627	$ 510
maximum after first year	$ 627	$ 561
maximum over life of loan	$ 627	$ 844

The front-end costs on the fixed-rate mortgage are $1,246 less than those on the ARM, and the fixed-rate mortgage offers a stable payment for principal and interest over the life of the loan. However, the initial monthly payment on the ARM is $117 per month less than that of the fixed-rate mortgage. This could help Lisa's overextended budget. Under the worst scenario, it would take 3 years before the monthly payment on the ARM exceeded the monthly payment on the fixed-rate mortgage. At it's maximum, the ARM could have a monthly payment that was approximately $217 higher than the fixed-rate loan.

One could reasonably recommend either of these mortgages. Overall, however, I would recommend the fixed-rate mortgage because of the historically low rate of interest, the stable monthly payments, the lower front-end costs, and the fact that Lisa plans to keep the house for at least 10 more years.

8.   See computer printout.

	7.75% Fixed-Rate	8.5% Fixed-Rate	Difference
Front-end costs	$3,746	$2,500	$1,246
Monthly payment	$ 627	$ 669	$ 42

It would take about 30 months ($1,246/$42) for the lower monthly payments on the 7.75% loan to break even with the higher front-end costs paid on that mortgage. Since Lisa plans to live in the house another 10 years and she has liquid assets from which she can pay the discount points on the 7.75% mortgage, I recommend she get the 7.75% mortgage with 1 1/2 discount points.

9.   See computer printout. The computer analysis shows that it would take about 22 months to break even with the front-end costs of refinancing Lisa's current mortgage with the 7.75% fixed-rate mortgage. I would definitely recommend she refinance the mortgage. She will save a substantial amount of interest payments over the life of the loan.

10.   Lisa's monthly before-tax income for 1993 is estimated to be:
$29,500 salary
5,416 net income from self-employment
17,052 Social Security benefits
7,564 interest income
356 dividends
178 capital gains distributions
$60,066 annual income

$60,066/12 = $5,006$ monthly income
$$\begin{array}{r} \text{x} \quad .28 \\ \hline \$1,402 \end{array} \text{ maximum monthly mortgage payment}$$

Monthly house payment with 7.75% fixed-rate mortgage:
$627 principal and interest
205 property taxes
  50 homeowners insurance
$882 total monthly payment

Lisa passes the first test since the monthly payment on the loan is less than the maximum monthly payment for her level of income.

Maximum monthly debt payments: $5,006 monthly income
$$\begin{array}{r} \text{x} \quad .35 \\ \hline \$1,752 \end{array} \text{ maximum monthly debt payment}$$

Total monthly debt payment:
$ 882 house payment
333 auto loan payment
  322 debt consolidation loan payment
$1,537 total monthly payments

Lisa also passes the second test since her total monthly debt payments are less than the maximum for her level of income. Lisa qualifies for the 7.75% fixed-rate mortgage.

11. See computer printout. Lisa's net worth as of March 1, 1993 is $223,881. This is $3,093 less that her net worth on January 1, 1993. Although there were small changes in numerous assets and liabilities, the major cause for the lower net worth was the withdrawal of $3,746 from the money market deposit account to pay for the front-end costs of refinancing Lisa's home mortgage. As we saw in Question 9, it will take nearly 2 years before her lower monthly payments will offset the cost of refinancing. In the short run refinancing reduces Lisa's net worth, but in the long run this decision should enhance her financial position.

12. See computer printout. Lisa's projected budget deficit is now only $7,947 (compared to $23,268 from Part 1, Question 8). It is lower than projected after the changes detailed at the beginning of Part 2 for the following reasons:
--No monthly house payment for principal and interest was made in March ($798).
--Lower house payments for 9 months due to refinancing the mortgage (1,539).
--No monthly contributions for goals in January and February ($2,138).

13. See computer printout. Lisa's projected tax liability for 1993 is $3,549, $1,247 less than for 1992. This is due to her lower income as a result of Tom's death. However, Lisa decided to lower the amount of withholding before refinancing the house, and it appears that she is now not having enough taxes withheld to avoid a tax penalty for under withholding. In order to avoid this penalty, Lisa should have withheld at least 90% of her projected tax liability ($3,549 x .9 = $3,194).

Deduction for loan origination fee and discount points: $2,077 x 9/300 = $62

Part 2, Question 2

```
+FP/PC-------------------------------------------------------------------FP/PC+
|          C H E C K I N G   A C C O U N T   R E C O N C I L I A T I O N        |
+------------------------------------------------------------------------------+
```

For the Month of   January   , 1993

Accountholder Name(s):Lisa Simmons

Type of Account:NOW
----

1. Ending balance shown on bank statement.................... $ 1568.36
   Add up checks and withdrawals still outstanding:

Check # or date	Amount	Check # or date	Amount	Check # or date	Amount
4521	333.00	4523	24.57	1/28/93	50.00
1/30/93	75.00		0.00		0.00
	0.00		0.00		0.00
	0.00		0.00		0.00
	0.00		0.00		0.00
	0.00		0.00		0.00

                                              TOTAL $ 482.57

2. Deduct total checks/withdrawals still
   outstanding from bank balance............................. - $ 482.57

Date	Amount	Date	Amount	Date	Amount
01/26/93	62.00		0.00		0.00
	0.00		0.00		0.00
	0.00		0.00		0.00
	0.00		0.00		0.00
	0.00		0.00		0.00

                                              TOTAL $ 62.00

3. Add total deposits still outstanding
   to bank balance.. + $ 62.00

|A| ADJUSTED BANK BALANCE (1-2+3)........................... $ 1147.79

4. Ending balance shown in checkbook......................... $ 1145.63

5. Deduct any bank service charges for the period........... - $ 2.70

6. Add interest earned for the period........................ + $ 5.06

|B| NEW CHECKBOOK BALANCE (4-5+6)........................... $ 1147.99

Adjusted bank balance not = new checkbook balance...account NOT reconciled.

411

Part 2, Question 6

```
+FP/PC--------------------------------------------------------------------FP/PC+
|             F U T U R E   V A L U E   O F   A N   A N N U I T Y              |
+-----------------------------------------------------------------------------+

                    Annuity payment..............      2000.00
                    Rate of return...............         8.00%
                    Number of years..............        30.00

                    Future value.................    226566.42


------------------------------------------------------------------------------

+FP/PC--------------------------------------------------------------------FP/PC+
|      YEARLY SAVINGS REQUIRED TO ACCUMULATE A GIVEN FUTURE VALUE              |
+-----------------------------------------------------------------------------+

                    Future value.................    300000.00
                    Rate of return...............         8.00%
                    Number of years..............        30.00

                    Yearly savings required......      2648.23


------------------------------------------------------------------------------
```

Part 2, Question 7

```
+FP/PC--------------------------------------------------------------FP/PC+
|          MORTGAGE PAYMENT CALCULATION GIVEN PRINCIPAL, INTEREST RATE AND TIME          |
+------------------------------------------------------------------------+

                    Principal....................      83066.00
                    Interest rate................         7.75%
                    Number of years..............        25.00

                    Monthly mortgage payment.....        627.42


------------------------------------------------------------------------

+FP/PC--------------------------------------------------------------FP/PC+
|          MORTGAGE PAYMENT CALCULATION GIVEN PRINCIPAL, INTEREST RATE AND TIME          |
+------------------------------------------------------------------------+

                    Principal....................      83066.00
                    Interest rate................         5.50%
                    Number of years..............        25.00

                    Monthly mortgage payment.....        510.10


------------------------------------------------------------------------

+FP/PC--------------------------------------------------------------FP/PC+
|          MORTGAGE PAYMENT CALCULATION GIVEN PRINCIPAL, INTEREST RATE AND TIME          |
+------------------------------------------------------------------------+

                    Principal....................      83066.00
                    Interest rate................         6.50%
                    Number of years..............        25.00

                    Monthly mortgage payment.....        560.87 *


------------------------------------------------------------------------

+FP/PC--------------------------------------------------------------FP/PC+
|          MORTGAGE PAYMENT CALCULATION GIVEN PRINCIPAL, INTEREST RATE AND TIME          |
+------------------------------------------------------------------------+

                    Principal....................      83066.00
                    Interest rate................        11.50%
                    Number of years..............        25.00

                    Monthly mortgage payment.....        844.34 **


------------------------------------------------------------------------
```

* only $.58/month more than calculating the payment using the outstanding balance at the end of the 1st year ($81,610) and amortizing over the remaining 24 years.

** $26/month more than calculating the payment using the outstanding balance at the end of the 6th year ($75,649 assuming a 1%/year in interest each year) and amortizing over the remaining 19 years.

413

Part 2, Question 8

```
+FP/PC--------------------------------------------------------------FP/PC
|         MORTGAGE PAYMENT CALCULATION GIVEN PRINCIPAL, INTEREST RATE AND TIME
+--------------------------------------------------------------------------

                Principal.....................      83066.00
                Interest rate.................          8.50%
                Number of years...............         25.00

                Monthly mortgage payment......        668.87


--------------------------------------------------------------------------
```

Part 2, Question 9

```
+FP/PC--------------------------------------------------------------FP/PC+
|         M O R T G A G E   R E F I N A N C I N G   A N A L Y S I S        |
+--------------------------------------------------------------------------+

     1   Current monthly payment....................................    798
     2   Anticipated additional years in house......................     10
     3   Additional months in house (Item 2 x 12)...................    120
     4   Total payment (Item 1 x Item 3)............................  95760
     5   New mortgage payment.......................................    627
     6   New total payment (Item 3 x Item 5)........................  75240
     7   Potential savings (Item 4 - Item 6)........................  20520
     8   Prepayment penalty on current mortgage.....................      0
     9   Closing costs on new mortgage..............................   3746
    10   Refinancing cost (Item 8 + Item 9).........................   3746
    11   Total savings (Item 7 - Item 10)...........................  16774
    12   Monthly savings (Item 1 - Item 5)..........................    171
    13   Months to break even (Item 10/Item 12).....................     22


--------------------------------------------------------------------------
```

Part 2, Question 11

```
+FP/PC-------------------------------------------------------------- FP/PC+
|                                                                          |
|                        B A L A N C E   S H E E T                         |
|                                                                          |
+--------------------------------------------------------------------------+
```

Lisa Simmons   03/01/93

```
--------------------------------------------------------------------------
            ASSETS              |        LIABILITIES AND NET WORTH
--------------------------------------------------------------------------
```

ASSETS		LIABILITIES AND NET WORTH	
Liquid Assets:		**Current Liabilities**	
Cash on hand............	135	Utilities...............	0
In checking.............	9126	Rent....................	0
Savings accounts........	0	Insurance premiums......	0
Money market funds		Taxes...................	0
and deposits...........	15124	Medical/dental bills....	0
CDs < 1 yr. maturity.....	13500	Repair bills............	0
Other...................	0	Bank crd. card balances..	363
	------	Dept. store charge cards.	675
Total Liquid Assets.....	37885	Travel/entrtmt. card....	0
		Gas/other credit cards...	0
Investments:		Bank line of credit......	0
Stocks I................	4125	Other cur. liabilities...	0
II................	0		------
Bonds I................	0	Total Cur. Liabilities.	1038
II................	0		
CDs > 1 yr. maturity.....	0	**Long-term Liabilities**	
Mut. funds I............	5133	Primary res. mortgage....	83066
II...........	2652	Second home mortgage.....	0
Real estate.............	0	Real estate investments..	0
Retirement funds........	8908	Auto loans..............	7973
Other.*Life insurance & U.S. E E*	75000	Appliance/furn. loans....	0
Savings Bonds ------		Home improvement loans...	0
Total Investments......	95818	Educational loans........	0
		Other I. *Debt Consolidation*.	5745
Real Property		II.................	0
Primary residence.......	115500		------
Second home.............	0	Total Long-term Liab...	96784
Car I...................	9600		
II...................	0		
Recreation equipment.....	2700		
Other.*Baseball Card Collection*.	4500		

Total Real Property.....	132300		
Personal Property			
Furniture and appl.......	30000		
Stereos, TVs, etc,*Computer*	10000		
Clothing................	7500		
Jewelry.................	0	(II) Tot. Liabilities.	97822
Other. *Toys & Miscellaneous*.	8200		

Total Personal Property.	55700	Net Worth [(II)-(III)].	223881
(I) Total Assets......	321703	Total Liab. and Net Worth..	321703
	======		======

Part 2, Question 12

```
+-FP/PC----------------------------------------------------------------FP/PC-+
|           M O N T H L Y   C A S H   B U D G E T   S U M M A R Y            |
+----------------------------------------------------------------------------+
```

NAME(S): Lisa Simmons   Page 1

FOR THE YEAR ENDING 12/31/93   JAN   FEB   MAR

		JAN	FEB	MAR
Take-Home Pay:	Source 1	2079	2079	2079
Take-Home Pay:	Source 2	388	388	388
Take-Home Pay:	Source 3	0	0	0
Bonuses and Commissions		0	0	0
Pensions and Annuities *Social Security benefits*		1421	1421	1421
Interest		557	557	540
Dividends		0	0	89
Rents		0	0	0
Sale of Securities *Withdrawal from Fidelity Cash Reserves*		0	3746	0
Other		0	0	44
Other Income:	Source 1 *Life insurance*	6250	6250	6250
Other Income:	Source 2 *Tax refund*	0	0	0
TOTAL INCOME		10695	14441	10811
Rent/Mortgage Payment *& front-end cost of refinancing*		798	4544	0
Repairs, Maintenance, Improvements		75	75	75
Gas, Utilities, Water		175	175	175
Phone		30	30	30
Cable TV and Other		30	30	30
Groceries		425	425	425
Dining Out		125	125	125
Loan/Lease Payments		333	333	333
License Plates, Fees, Etc.		0	0	0
Gas, Oil, Tires, Maintenance		125	125	125
Health Insurance, Etc.		250	250	250
Doctor, Dentist, Hospital, Medicine		26	26	26
Clothing, Shoes, Accessories		125	125	125
Homeowner's Insurance		50	50	50
Life Insurance		0	0	0
Automobile Insurance		0	390	0
Income and Social Security Taxes		0	0	0
Property Taxes		205	205	205
Loan Payments		0	0	0
Purchases and Repairs		103	103	103
Laundry, Cosmetics, Hair Care		50	50	50
Vacations		0	0	0
Other Recreation and Entertainment		75	75	75
Savings and Investments		6807	6807	7992
Charitable Contributions		75	75	75
~~Gifts~~ *Children's activities*		175	175	175
~~Education Expenses~~ *Debt consolidation loan*		322	322	322
~~Subscriptions, Magazines, Books~~ *Child care*		125	125	125
Other Expenditures: Item 1 *Children's allowances*		80	80	80
Other Expenditures: Item 2 *Miscellaneous*		100	100	100
~~Fun Money~~ *Business expenses*		72	72	72
TOTAL EXPENDITURES		10756	14892	11143
CASH SUPLUS (OR DEFICIT)		-61	-451	-332
CUMULATIVE CASH SUPLUS (OR DEFICIT)		-61	-512	-844

NAME(S): Lisa Simmons   Page 2

FOR THE YEAR ENDING 12/31/93	APR	MAY	JUN
Take-Home Pay: Source 1	2079	2079	2079
Take-Home Pay: Source 2	388	388	388
Take-Home Pay: Source 3	0	0	0
Bonuses and Commissions	0	0	0
Pensions and Annuities *Social Security benefits*	1421	1421	1421
Interest	540	540	540
Dividends	0	0	89
Rents	0	0	0
Sale of Securities	0	0	0
Other	0	0	45
Other Income: Source 1 *Life insurance*	6250	6250	6250
Other Income: Source 2 *Tax refund*	2918	0	0
TOTAL INCOME	13596	10678	10812
Rent/Mortgage Payment	627	627	627
Repairs, Maintenance, Improvements	75	75	75
Gas, Utilities, Water	175	175	175
Phone	30	30	30
Cable TV and Other	30	30	30
Groceries	425	425	425
Dining Out	125	125	125
Loan/Lease Payments	333	333	333
License Plates, Fees, Etc.	0	0	0
Gas, Oil, Tires, Maintenance	125	125	125
Health Insurance, Etc.	250	250	250
Doctor, Dentist, Hospital, Medicine	26	26	26
Clothing, Shoes, Accessories	125	125	125
Homeowner's Insurance	50	50	50
Life Insurance	0	0	0
Automobile Insurance	0	0	0
Income and Social Security Taxes	0	0	0
Property Taxes	205	205	205
Loan Payments	0	0	0
Purchases and Repairs	103	103	103
Laundry, Cosmetics, Hair Care	50	50	50
Vacations	0	0	1000
Other Recreation and Entertainment	75	75	75
Savings and Investments	7859	7859	7993
Charitable Contributions	75	75	75
~~Gifts~~ *Children's activities*	175	175	175
~~Education Expenses~~ *Debt consolidation loan*	322	322	322
~~Subscriptions,~~ Magazines, ~~Books~~ *Child care*	125	125	125
Other Expenditures: Item 1 *Children's allowances*	80	80	80
Other Expenditures: Item 2 *Miscellaneous*	100	100	100
~~Fun Money~~ *Business expenses*	72	72	72
TOTAL EXPENDITURES	11637	11637	12771
CASH SUPLUS (OR DEFICIT)	1959	-959	-1959
CUMULATIVE CASH SUPLUS (OR DEFICIT)	1115	156	-1803

```
+-FP/PC--------------------------------------------------------------------FP/PC--
|              M O N T H L Y   C A S H   B U D G E T   S U M M A R Y
+------------------------------------------------------------------------------
 NAME(S): Lisa Simmons                                                    Page
```

FOR THE YEAR ENDING 12/31/93   JUL   AUG   SEP

Take-Home Pay: Source 1	2079	2079	2079
Take-Home Pay: Source 2	388	388	388
Take-Home Pay: Source 3	0	0	0
Bonuses and Commissions	0	0	0
Pensions and Annuities *Social Security benefits*	1421	1421	1421
Interest	540	540	540
Dividends	0	0	89
Rents	0	0	0
Sale of Securities	0	0	0
Other	0	0	44
Other Income: Source 1 *Life insurance*	6250	6250	6250
Other Income: Source 2	0	0	0
TOTAL INCOME	10678	10678	10811
Rent/Mortgage Payment	627	627	627
Repairs, Maintenance, Improvements	75	75	75
Gas, Utilities, Water	175	175	175
Phone	30	30	30
Cable TV and Other	30	30	30
Groceries	425	425	425
Dining Out	125	125	125
Loan/Lease Payments	333	333	333
License Plates, Fees, Etc.	0	0	0
Gas, Oil, Tires, Maintenance	125	125	125
Health Insurance, Etc.	250	250	250
Doctor, Dentist, Hospital, Medicine	26	26	26
Clothing, Shoes, Accessories	125	125	125
Homeowner's Insurance	50	50	50
Life Insurance	0	0	0
Automobile Insurance	0	390	0
Income and Social Security Taxes	0	0	0
Property Taxes	205	205	205
Loan Payments	0	0	0
Purchases and Repairs	103	103	103
Laundry, Cosmetics, Hair Care	50	50	50
Vacations	0	0	0
Other Recreation and Entertainment	75	75	75
Savings and Investments	7859	7859	7992
Charitable Contributions	75	75	75
~~Gifts~~ *Children's activities*	175	175	175
~~Education~~ Expenses *Debt consolidation Loan*	322	322	322
~~Subscriptions, Magazines, Books~~ *Child care*	125	125	125
Other Expenditures: Item 1 *Children's allowances*	80	80	80
Other Expenditures: Item 2 *Miscellaneous*	100	100	100
~~Fun Money~~ *Business expenses*	72	72	72
TOTAL EXPENDITURES	11637	12027	11770
CASH SUPLUS (OR DEFICIT)	-959	-1349	-959
CUMULATIVE CASH SUPLUS (OR DEFICIT)	-2762	-4111	-5070

```
+-FP/PC--------------------------------------------------------------FP/PC-+
|                                                                          |
|       M O N T H L Y   C A S H   B U D G E T   S U M M A R Y              |
+--------------------------------------------------------------------------+

NAME(S): Lisa Simmons                                               Page 4

FOR THE YEAR ENDING 12/31/93              OCT      NOV      DEC     TOTAL

Take-Home Pay:    Source 1               2079     2079     2079    24948
Take-Home Pay:    Source 2                388      388      388     4656
Take-Home Pay:    Source 3                  0        0        0        0
Bonuses and Commissions                     0        0        0        0
Pensions and Annuities  Social Security benefits  1421  1421  1421  17052
Interest                                  540      540     1420     7394
Dividends                                   0        0       89      356
Rents                                       0        0        0        0
Sale of Securities  Withdrawal from Fidelity Cash Reserves 0   0    0  3746
Other                                       0        0       45      178
Other Income:     Source 1 Life insurance  6250     6250     6250    75000
Other Income:     Source 2 Tax refund        0        0        0     2918

TOTAL INCOME                            10678    10678    11692   136248

Rent/Mortgage Payment: Front-end cost of refinancing  627   627   627  10985
Repairs, Maintenance, Improvements         75       75       75      900
Gas, Utilities, Water                     175      175      175     2100
Phone                                      30       30       30      360
Cable TV and Other                         30       30       30      360
Groceries                                 425      425      425     5100
Dining Out                                125      125      125     1500
Loan/Lease Payments                       333      333      333     3996
License Plates, Fees, Etc.                  0        0        0        0
Gas, Oil, Tires, Maintenance              125      125      125     1500
Health Insurance, Etc.                    250      250      250     3000
Doctor, Dentist, Hospital, Medicine        26       26       26      312
Clothing, Shoes, Accessories              125      125      125     1500
Homeowner's Insurance                      50       50       50      600
Life Insurance                              0        0        0        0
Automobile Insurance                        0        0        0      780
Income and Social Security Taxes            0        0        0        0
Property Taxes                            205      205      205     2460
Loan Payments                               0        0        0        0
Purchases and Repairs                     103      103      103     1236
Laundry, Cosmetics, Hair Care              50       50       50      600
Vacations                                   0        0        0     1000
Other Recreation and Entertainment         75       75       75      900
Savings and Investments                  7859     7859     8873    93618
Charitable Contributions                   75       75       75      900
Gifts  Children's activities              175      175      175     2100
Education Expenses Debt consolidation loan  322    322      322     3864
Subscriptions, Magazines, Books — Child care  125  125      125     1500
Other Expenditures:    Item 1 Children's allowances  80   80   80    960
Other Expenditures:    Item 2 Miscellaneous  100   100      100     1200
Fun Money  Business expenses               72       72       72      864

TOTAL EXPENDITURES                      11637    11637    12651   144195

CASH SUPLUS (OR DEFICIT)                 -959     -959     -959    -7947

CUMULATIVE CASH SUPLUS (OR DEFICIT)     -6029    -6988    -7947    -7947
```

Part 2, Question 12

```
+-FP/PC-------------------------------------------------------------------FP/PC-+
|                    C A S H   B U D G E T   S U M M A R Y                      |
+------------------------------------------------------------------------------+
```

NAME(S): Lisa Simmons
FOR YEAR ENDING 12/31/93

	Total Income	Total Expenses	Cash Surplus (Deficit)	Cumulative Cash Surplus (Deficit)
Jan	$ 10695	$ 10756	$ -61	$ -61
Feb	14441	14892	-451	-512
Mar	10811	11143	-332	-844
Apr	13596	11637	1959	1115
May	10678	11637	-959	156
Jun	10812	12771	-1959	-1803
Jul	10678	11637	-959	-2762
Aug	10678	12027	-1349	-4111
Sep	10811	11770	-959	-5070
Oct	10678	11637	-959	-6029
Nov	10678	11637	-959	-6988
Dec	11692	12651	-959	-7947
TOTALS ..	$ 136248	$ 144195		$ -7947

```
+------------------------------------------------------------------------------+
```

Part 2, Question 13

FEDERAL INCOME TAX WORKSHEET
Lisa Simmons & Tom Simmons (deceased)

	1992	1993
INCOME		
1. Wages, salaries, tips, etc.	$45,970	$29,500
2. Interest income	3,703	7,394
3. Dividends	356	356
4. Capital gains (losses)	578	178
5. Net business income (loss)	5,416	5,416
6. Income (deductible losses) from rental property	0	0
7. Other income	0	0
8. TOTAL INCOME (add lines 1 - 7)	$56,023	$42,844
ADJUSTMENTS		
9. One-half of self-employment tax	415	415
10. Keogh contributions	0	0
11. AGI before IRA contributions (subtract lines 9 & 10 from line 8)	55,608	42,429
12. Deductible IRA contributions	0	0
13. ADJUSTED GROSS INCOME (subtract line 12 from line 11)	$55,608	$42,429
ITEMIZED DEDUCTIONS		
14. Deductible medical expenses	$0	$0
15. State and local income and property taxes	2,460	2,460
16. Mortgage interest	8,966	6,295
17. Other deductible interest	0	62
18. Charitable contributions	900	900
19. Deductible misc. expenses	0	0
20. Casualty and theft losses	0	0
21. TOTAL ITEMIZED DEDUCTIONS (add lines 14 - 20)	$12,326	$9,717
TAXABLE INCOME		
22. Write in the amount on line 21 or or your standard deduction, whichever is greater	$12,326	$9,717
23. Personal exemptions	9,200	7,050
24. TAXABLE INCOME (substract lines 22 and 23 from line 13)	$34,082	$25,662
TAX LIABILITY		
25. Tax before credits (see tax tables)	$5,111	$3,849
26. Child care credit	315	300
27. YOUR TAX (subtract line 26 from line 25)	$4,796	$3,549
TAX WITHHELD	$7,714	$3,100
TAX DUE or (REFUND)	($2,918)	$449

421

Part Three

1. The following are the March minimum monthly payments for Lisa's revolving credit cards:

AT&T Universal MasterCard	$ 20.00	--the greater of ($255 x .02 = $5.10) or $20
Visa	25.00	--the greater of ($108 x .05 = $5.40) or $25
Foley's	32.20	--the greater of ($322 x .1 = $32.20) or $10
Yaring's	50.00	--the greater of ($353 x .1 = $35.30) or $50
	$127.20	

2. Lisa's debt safety ratio is 20%, a point that is considered an indicator of potential credit problems. Lisa should avoid taking on any additional debt at this time.

Monthly consumer debt payment		Monthly after-tax income	
$127	credit cards	$2,034	salary
333	auto loan	388	self-employment
322	debt consolidation loan	1,421	Social Security
$782		$3,843	

    $782/$3,843 = 20.3%

3. Lisa's AT&T Universal MasterCard has a 15.4% APR (.0128/month), a grace period, and the finance charge is calculated using the average daily balance method. There would be no finance charge for March because there is a grace period and the full balance was paid before the end of the billing cycle.

    Lisa's Visa card has an 18% APR (.015/month), no grace period, and the adjusted balance method is used to calculated the finance charge. Since there is no grace period and the balance at the end of the billing cycle is $363, the finance charge for March would be $5.45 ($363 x .015).

4. Since a card holder's legal liability on each credit card is $50 or the amount charged (whichever is less), Lisa's maximum legal liability would be $234 [$34 + (4 x $50)].

5. Lisa needs to write MasterCard notifying them within 60 days of the date she received the statement of the error on her statement. She should not pay the disputed portion of the balance ($289) while the issue is being investigated. MasterCard is required to respond within 30 days to Lisa's inquiry and resolve the issue within 90 days. MasterCard cannot collect the $289 or issue an unfavorable credit report as a result of the disputed charge.

6.

Card	APR	Annual Fee	Typical Finance Charge	Credit Line	Other Considerations
AT&T Universal MasterCard	15.4%	$ 0	$ 0	$5,000	Revolving credit line, no individual receipts returned, accepted by 7,800,000 outlets worldwide, cash advances available
Visa	18%	$ 0	$250 x .18 $ 45	$3,000	Revolving credit line, no individual receipts returned, accepted by 7,900,000 outlets worldwide, cash advances available
MasterCard	14%	$35	$ 0	$3,000	Revolving credit line, no individual receipts returned, accepted by 7,800,000 outlets worldwide, cash advances available
American Express	NA	$45	$ 0	None	Balance due upon billing, individual receipts returned, accepted by 3,100,000 outlets worldwide, no cash advances

I recommend the AT&T Universal MasterCard. It is the lowest cost card with a high credit line and is widely accepted. The second choice is a closer call. However, I would recommend the American Express card. It is $10 per year more expensive than the MasterCard, but all the second MasterCard offers is an additional $3,000 credit line. The American Express has an unlimited credit line and individual receipts are returned monthly. This could be useful to Lisa for her business expenses.

7a.   See computer printout.

   First National Bank

   Monthly payment using Exhibit 8.8
   $46.73 payment per $1,000
   x   2
   $93.46 monthly payment

   Finance charge
   $93.46 monthly payment
   x   24 months
   $2,243 total cost
   -2,000 principal
   $ 243 finance charge

On a simple interest loan, the APR is always the same as the stated rate (11%).

<u>Federal Consumer Finance Company</u>

Finance charge = $2,000 x .08 x 2 = $320

Monthly payment = ($2,000 + $320)/24 = $96.67

$$\text{APR} = \frac{(12) \ [(95)(24) + 9] \ (\$320)}{(12)(24)(24 +1) \ [(4)(\$2,000) + \$320]} = 14.67\%$$

The First National Bank loan is definitely the better of these two loans. The finance cost on it is $77 less than that of the Federal Consumer Finance Company loan.

b. See computer printout. Using cash withdrawn from the Fidelity Cash Reserves mutual fund would be $84 less than the cost of borrowing $2,000 from First National Bank. If Lisa feels that this is an important expenditure, I would recommend she use cash from her Fidelity fund. It is less expensive than financing the expenditure, and Lisa's debt safety ratio is already too high, indicating she should not take on additional debt.

8.

	Current Loan	Current Loan	Home Equity Loan	Home Equity Loan	Pay off with liquid assets	Pay off with liquid assets
	Auto	Debt	Auto	Debt	Auto	Debt
Interest rate	10.5% fixed rate	13.5% fixed rate	8.25% variable	8.25% variable	---	---
Monthly payment	$ 333	$ 322	$ 325	$ 308	---	---
Finance charge	$ 333 x 27 $8,991 -7,973 $1,018	$ 332 x 20 $6,640 -5,745 $ 895	$ 325 x 27 $8,775 -7,973 $ 802	$ 308 x 20 $6,160 -5,745 $ 415	---	---
Tax savings	$ 0	$ 0	$ 802 x .15 $ 120	$ 415 x .15 $ 62	---	---
Additional costs	$ 0	$ 0	$ 25	$ 0	$ 25	$0
After-tax cost of interest foregone	---	---	---	---	$7,973 x .038 $ 302	$5,745 x .038 $ 218
Total cost	$1,018	$895	$707	$353	$ 327	$ 218

The monthly payments are all based on the current pay off period for both loans, 27 months on the auto loan and 20 months on the debt consolidation loan. The after-tax cost of interest foregone is 3.8% [4.5% x (1 - .15)]. If Lisa decides to open the home equity line of credit, there will also be a $75 set up fee in addition to the costs detailed above; however, the line of credit could to used in the future as well.

The least expensive option is to pay off both of these loans. However, that would take $13,718. Lisa needs to keep at least $12,335 in liquid assets (Part 2, Question 1) for her emergency fund. Based on her most recent balance sheet (Part 2, Question 11), Lisa has the following liquid assets:

$	135	Cash on hand
	9,126	Super NOW account ($7,500 minimum balance requirement)
	4,115	First National Bank money market account
	11,009	Fidelity Cash Reserves mutual fund
	13,500	Certificate of deposit (matures in 12/93)
	$37,885	

If Lisa uses $2,000 from the Fidelity Cash Reserves mutual fund to pay for Andy's school trip, she will have only $9,009 in her Fidelity Cash Reserves mutual fund and total liquid assets of $35,885. But because of the minimum balance requirement on her Super NOW account and the maturity date on the certificate of deposit, Lisa does not comfortably have $13,718 available to pay off both of these two debts.

I recommend that Lisa withdraw $7,973 from the Fidelity Cash Reserves mutual fund to pay off the auto loan. This would save $691 ($1,018 - $327) over the next 27 months. It would leave a balance of $1,036 ($11,009 - $2,000 - $7,973) in the Fidelity Cash Reserves mutual fund. In addition, Lisa should open the home equity line of credit and borrow $5,745 from it to pay off the debt consolidation loan. This would save $467 ($895 - $353 - $75), and the home equity line would be available for future use. Total savings for these financial transactions would be $1,158 ($691 + $467).

If Lisa didn't want the balance on her Fidelity fund to be so low, she could withdraw $5,745 from the Fidelity Cash Reserves mutual fund to pay off the debt consolidation loan. This would save $677 ($895 -$218) over the next 20 months. It would leave a balance of $3,264 ($11,009 - $2,000 - $5,745) in the Fidelity Cash Reserves mutual fund. In addition, Lisa could open the home equity line of credit and borrow $7,973 from it to pay off the current auto loan. This would save $236 ($1,018 - $707 - $75). Total savings for these moves would be $913 ($677 + $236).

Lisa could also go with my original recommendation to pay off the auto loan and refinance the debt consolidation loan, and then transfer the money now in her First National Bank money market account into the Fidelity Cash Reserves mutual fund. This would consolidate her liquid assets into one less account and increase her interest income slightly. If she did this, the new balance on the Fidelity mutual fund would be $5,151 ($1,036 + $4,115).

Part 3, Question 7a

```
+FP/PC----------------------------------------------------------------------FP/PC+
|      A N A L Y S I S   O F   I N S T A L L M E N T   L O A N S :     A P R      |
+--------------------------------------------------------------------------------+


         Loan principal............................. 2000

         Annual interest rate (%)................... 11.00

         Length of the loan in years............... 2.00

         Is this an add-on loan (Y or N)?.......... N


         Total finance charge......................   237

         Monthly loan payment......................    93

         Approximate APR........................... 11.00%

----------------------------------------------------------------------------------
```


```
+FP/PC----------------------------------------------------------------------FP/PC+
|      A N A L Y S I S   O F   I N S T A L L M E N T   L O A N S :     A P R      |
+--------------------------------------------------------------------------------+


         Loan principal............................. 2000

         Annual interest rate (%)...................  8.00

         Length of the loan in years............... 2.00

         Is this an add-on loan (Y or N)?.......... Y


         Total finance charge......................   320

         Monthly loan payment......................    97

         Approximate APR........................... 14.67%

----------------------------------------------------------------------------------
```

Part 3, Question 76

```
          B U Y   O N   T I M E   O R   P A Y   C A S H
```

+--+

Cost of Borrowing:

1. Loan payments.

   Loan principal: 2000   Annual rate: 11.000% Length: 2.00 ....   93.22

2. Total loan payments (monthly PMT x loan length in months).......   2237.18

3. Less: Principal amount of loan.................................   2000.00

4. Total interest paid of life of loan (line 2 - line 3)..........   237.18
                                                                    ----

5. Tax considerations:

   ? Is this a home equity loan? (Y/N)............................   N
   ? Do you itemize deductions on your federal tax returns? (Y/N). Y

6. Your federal tax bracket (15, 28, or 31%).....................   15%

7. Taxes saved due to interest deductions (if applicable)........   0.00

8. Total after-tax cost of borrowing (line 4 - line 7)...........   237.18

Cost of Paying Cash:

9. Annual int. earned on savings. Annual interest rate: 4.500% ...   90.00

10. Annual after-tax int. earnings [line 9 x (1 - line 6)].........   76.50

11. Total after-tax int. earnings (line 10 x loan length in years)..   153.00

Net Cost of Borrowing:

12. Difference in cost of borrowing vs. cost of paying cash (line 4
    OR line 8 less line 11). If > 0, pay cash; if < 0, borrow......   84.18
                                                                    ========

Part 3, Question 8

```
+FP/PC--------------------------------------------------------------FP/PC+
|        A N A L Y S I S   O F   I N S T A L L M E N T   L O A N S :   A P R   |
+-------------------------------------------------------------------------+
```

Auto loan - minimum payment using home equity loan

```
        Loan principal............................  7973

        Annual interest rate (%)..................  8.25

        Length of the loan in years...............  7.00

        Is this an add-on loan (Y or N)?..........  N


        Total finance charge......................  2549

        Monthly loan payment......................   125

        Approximate APR...........................  8.25%
```

```
--------------------------------------------------------------------------
```

```
+FP/PC--------------------------------------------------------------FP/PC+
|        A N A L Y S I S   O F   I N S T A L L M E N T   L O A N S :   A P R   |
+-------------------------------------------------------------------------+
```

Auto loan - 27 month pay off using home equity loan

```
        Loan principal............................  7973

        Annual interest rate (%)..................  8.25

        Length of the loan in years...............  2.25

        Is this an add-on loan (Y or N)?..........  N


        Total finance charge......................   790

        Monthly loan payment......................   325

        Approximate APR...........................  8.25%
```

```
--------------------------------------------------------------------------
```

Part 3, Question 8

```
+FP/PC-------------------------------------------------------FP/PC+
|        A N A L Y S I S   O F   I N S T A L L M E N T   L O A N S :    A P R         |
+-----------------------------------------------------------------+
```

Debt consolidation loan — minimum payment using home equity loan

```
            Loan principal............................  5745

            Annual interest rate (%)..................  8.25

            Length of the loan in years...............  7.00

            Is this an add-on loan (Y or N)?..........  N


            Total finance charge......................  1837

            Monthly loan payment......................    90

            Approximate APR...........................  8.25%
```

```
+FP/PC-------------------------------------------------------FP/PC+
|        A N A L Y S I S   O F   I N S T A L L M E N T   L O A N S :    A P R         |
+-----------------------------------------------------------------+
```

Debt consolidation — 20 month pay off using home equity loan

```
            Loan principal............................  5745

            Annual interest rate (%)..................  8.25

            Length of the loan in years...............  1.67

            Is this an add-on loan (Y or N)?..........  N


            Total finance charge......................   425

            Monthly loan payment......................   308

            Approximate APR...........................  8.25%
```

<u>REPRESENTATIVE ANSWERS:</u> The Simmons Case Study

<u>Part Four</u>

1. According to this analysis, Lisa needs $87,196 of life insurance coverage. See computer printout.

2. If Lisa buys life insurance through her employee benefit plan, $88,500 (three times salary) is the closest amount to what Lisa actually needs. At a rate of $.09 per $1,000 coverage, it will cost $8 per month ($88,500/1,000 x $.09) or $96 per year. Using Exhibit 9.5 and 9.7 of the text, $88,500 of renewable term life insurance would cost $246 ($88,500/1,000 x $2.78) annually. The same amount of straight life insurance would cost $1,222 ($88,500/1,000 x $13.81) annually.

   Lisa can get all the life insurance she needs through her employee benefit plan and at a very low price. Although some experts feel life insurance needs should not be met through employee benefit plans because of the temporary nature of employment, Lisa's budget is very tight and she has been with this company several years. I recommend Lisa purchase $88,500 of group term life for $8 per month through her cafeteria-style benefit plan.

3. Andy and Karen should be the primary beneficiaries on Lisa's policy. Lisa's parents are named as the children's guardians in Lisa's will and would be the ones actually controlling the children's money if Lisa were to die.

   I would recommend a lump-sum settlement option assuming Lisa's parents are capable of handling finances. This option gives the greatest flexibility and perhaps enhanced investment return.

4. Despite its low cost, I would not recommend the purchase of accidental death insurance. Since it pays only when one dies in an accident, there is no rational reason to have it. Lisa's children will need a given level of benefits regardless of how Lisa dies.

5. Lisa's monthly take-home pay is currently $2,422 ($2,034 + $388). The disability policy offered in Lisa's fringe benefit plan would provide only $1,721 monthly ($29,500/12 x .7). This would be $701 per month less than Lisa is used to living on.

   The cost of the group disability income policy would be $12 per month ($1,721/100 x $.70) or $144 per year. Using Exhibit 10.6, $1,721 of coverage with a 30 day waiting period and a 3 year benefit period (like the group policy) would cost $303 annually ($1,721/100 x $17.60).

   Despite the fact that the group coverage is less expensive, I would not recommend it for two reasons. First, the 3 year benefit period is too short. For financial security, Lisa needs a policy that will pay until age 65 in case of long term disability. Second, Lisa needs a higher level of monthly benefits. A private policy would recognize Lisa's self-employment income as a basis for disability income coverage. Lisa's total earned income is $35,780 ($29,500 + $6,280); therefore, 70% of monthly income would be $2,087 ($35,780/12 x .7). This would be just $335 less than Lisa's current take-home pay.

In order to reduce the premium on a private disability income policy, Lisa should select at least a 90 day waiting period. She has 35 days of paid sick leave and enough liquid assets to cover the remaining 55 days. According to Exhibit 10.6, $2,087 per month coverage with a 90 day waiting period payable to age 65 would cost $490 per year ($2,087/100 x $23.50).

6. The maximum limit on the major medical policy offered through Lisa's employer is $100,000 per person per year. A higher limit would be better, but this limit is adequate. With a $500 annual deductible per person and a $1,000 annual cap on the participation per person, Lisa's maximum out-of-pocket cost on covered expenses for the family would be $4,500 per year.

Based on last year's medical history, Lisa's out-of-pocket medical costs with the major medical policy would be $1,106.

	Lisa	Karen	Andy
Cost of Care	$150	$ 55	$ 90
	50	55	x 12
	50	55	$1,080
	$250	75	
		$240	
Insurance Reimbursement	$250	$240	$1,080
	- 500	- 500	- 500
	$ 0	$ 0	$ 580
			x .8
			$ 464
Out-of-pocket Cost	$250	$240	$ 616

The combined cost of major medical premiums plus out-of-pocket costs would be $3,686 ($1,106 + $2,580).

The HMO offered through Lisa's employer seems to be very comprehensive with unlimited maximum coverage. While the exact annual out-of-pocket costs cannot be calculated, they should be quite low--$10 per doctor's visit and $5 per prescription. As long as there are good doctors and a good hospital associated with the HMO, this should provide very good health benefits.

Based on last year's history, Lisa's out-of-pocket medical costs with the HMO would be $190 ($10 x 19 visits). The combined cost of HMO premiums plus out-of-pocket expenses would be $3,610 ($190 + $3,420).

I would recommend the HMO coverage. The combined cost of premiums plus projected out-of-pocket costs based on the family's medical history is slightly lower with the HMO compared to the major medical plan. However, the potential out-of-pocket costs with the HMO are much lower than with the major medical plan. In addition, the maximum coverage is unlimited under the HMO, and there would be less paperwork because one does not have to file claims with an HMO. The premiums for the HMO would be $285 a month.

7. The annual cost of dental care premiums would be $204 for Lisa and $144 each for Andy and Karen, a total of $492. Based on their dental history the cost of dental care with no insurance would be $380. The cost of dental insurance premiums and out-of-pocket dental expenses would be $612. I recommend that Lisa budget for the family's dental care rather than buying dental insurance.

	Lisa	Karen	Andy
Cost of Care	$ 60 200 $260	$ 60	$ 60
Insurance Reimbursement	$200 -100 $100 x .8 $ 80 + 60 $140	$ 60	$ 60
Out-of-pocket Cost	$120	$ 0	$ 0

The annual premium for vision care would be $72 for Lisa and $24 for each of the children, a total of $120. While the price of this coverage is quite low, I recommend Lisa not purchase it since none of the family seems to need vision care at this time. The premiums saved would pay for an eye exam (or two) if needed.

8. Assuming Lisa follows my recommendations, she would purchase $88,500 of life insurance coverage on her life ($8 a month) and HMO coverage for her and the children ($285 a month) through her cafeteria-style plan. Since this is more than the $250 per month provided by her employer, $43 will be deducted from her monthly pay check to pay for the difference.

9. The HO-2 (Broad Form) should provide adequate coverage for Lisa's home. I recommend the following coverages:

House (replacement cost is 2,200 x $55 = $121,000)
    (80% of replacement cost is $96,800)
Recommended coverage on house $100,000
(somewhere between $96,800 & $121,000)

Personal property   60,000
(50% is standard for an HO-2 policy but it should
be raised to 60% based on Lisa's balance sheet)

Other structures (10% of dwelling)   10,000
Loss of use (20% of dwelling)   20,000
Personal liability (at least $100,000)   300,000
Medical payments   1,000/person

Deductible   500/occurrence

This is basically the coverage Lisa already has except the personal property coverage and the liability limits are higher. Lisa should check the policy to see if there are any special limitations on collections (such as baseball cards) and computers that require additional consideration. She also may want to consider replacement cost coverage on her personal property.

Since there is nothing in the text to help estimate the cost of this insurance and the variations among states and regions are considerable, let's assume that the increased coverage could be purchased for an additional $50 bringing the annual total of $650.

10. I would recommend Lisa increase her liability coverage to $300,000 (100/300/50 in split liability states) as $40,000 is definitely too low. To keep the annual premium about the same as it currently is, she should increase her deductibles on both collision and comprehensive coverage to $500 per occurrence. She could easily handle the first $500 in damages with her liquid assets.

11. Lisa really does not need umbrella liability coverage with her current financial condition. Given her profession, professional liability insurance in probably not needed either. The previously discussed insurance should adequately meet Lisa's needs for protection.

12. See computer printout. Lisa's new net worth is $221,484. It has decreased largely because of the withdrawal from savings for Andy's school trip.

13. See computer printout. Lisa's budget deficit is now only $3,937, $4,010 less than the previous budget. The following changes were made since the last revision of her 1993 budget (Part 2, Question 12):
--monthly after-tax salary decreased to $2,034 starting in March.
--$2,000 was withdrawn from savings and spent on Andy's school trip in April.
--$7,973 was withdrawn from savings and used to pay off the auto loan. Therefore, there were no auto loan payments after it was paid off in April.
--both interest income and reinvested interest income (savings & investments) went down $35 per month starting in April.
--the $308 home equity loan payment replaced the $322 debt consolidation loan payment starting in April.
--homeowners insurance increased to $54 per month starting in April.
--the annual disability income insurance premium of $490 was paid in April.
--the $43 per month payment for Lisa's cafeteria-style benefit plan replaced the $250 per month health insurance premium in April.

Overall insurance expenditures decreased by $1,944 per year largely because the children are now covered under the HMO as part of Lisa's employee benefit plan ($65 per month per dependent) rather than through Tom's fringe benefit plan ($125 per month per dependent). In addition, Lisa's employer pays for part of the children's coverage with its $250 monthly contribution to the cafeteria-style benefits.

Part 4, Question 1

```
+FP/PC----------------------------------------------------------------FP/PC+
|        P L A N N I N G   L I F E   I N S U R A N C E   N E E D S          |
+--------------------------------------------------------------------------+
```

A. FAMILY INCOME NEEDS

  1. DEBT LIQUIDATION   Totals
       a. Home mortgage........................   0
       b. Other loans..........................   0
       c. Total debt (a + b)...   0

  2. FINAL E%4500PENSES...$4,500

  3. ANNUAL INCOME NEEDS   period1 Period2 Period3
       a. Monthly living expenses..............   1833   917   0
       b. Less: SS survivor's benefits.........   1400   700   0
       c. Less: Surviving spouse's income......   0   0   0
       d. Less: Other income...................   0   0   0
       e. Net monthly inc. needs (a-b-c-d).....   433   217   0
       f. Net yearly inc. needs (12 x e).......   5196   2604   0
       g. Number of years in period............   5   6   0
       h. Total funding needed (d x e)......... 25980   15624   0
       i. Total living needs (h1 + h2 + h3)............................. 41604

  4. Spouse reeducation fund..   0

  5. Children's opportunity fund....................................   85000

  6. Other needs..   0

     TOTAL INCOME NEEDS (1c + 2 + 3i + 4 + 5 + 6)..................... 131104

B. FINANCIAL RESOURCES AVAILABLE

  1. Savings and investments. *Retirement funds*...   8908

  2. Group life insurance.....................   0

  3. Other life insurance.....................   0

  4. Other resources. *Sale of house & personal property* 35000

     TOTAL RESOURCES AVAILABLE (1 + 2 + 3 + 4)........................   43908

C. ADDITIONAL LIFE INSURANCE NEEDS (A - B) (none if negative)........   87196

Part 4, Question 12

```
+FP/PC--------------------------------------------------------------- FP/PC+
|                                                                          |
|                       B A L A N C E   S H E E T                          |
|                                                                          |
+--------------------------------------------------------------------------+
```

Lisa Simmons   04/01/93

         ASSETS | LIABILITIES AND NET WORTH

ASSETS		LIABILITIES AND NET WORTH	
Liquid Assets:		**Current Liabilities**	
Cash on hand.............	175	Utilities................	0
In checking..............	8211	Rent.....................	0
Savings accounts.........	0	Insurance premiums.......	0
Money market funds		Taxes....................	0
and deposits............	11401	Medical/dental bills.....	0
CDs < 1 yr. maturity.....	13500	Repair bills.............	0
Other....................	0	Bank crd. card balances..	351
	------	Dept. store charge cards.	209
Total Liquid Assets.....	33287	Travel/entrtmt. card.....	0
		Gas/other credit cards...	0
Investments:		Bank line of credit......	0
Stocks I.................	4125	Other cur. liabilities...	0
II.................	0		------
Bonds I..................	0	Total Cur. Liabilities.	560
II.................	0		
CDs > 1 yr. maturity.....	0	**Long-term Liabilities**	
Mut. funds I.............	5133	Primary res. mortgage....	83066
II.............	2652	Second home mortgage.....	0
Real estate.............	0	Real estate investments..	0
Retirement funds.........	8908	Auto loans...............	0
Other *Life insurance & U.S. EE*	68750	Appliance/furn. loans....	0
Savings Bonds ------		Home improvement loans...	0
Total Investments......	89568	Educational loans........	0
		Other I *Home equity line of credit*	5745
Real Property		II.................	0
Primary residence........	115500		------
Second home..............	0	Total Long-term Liab...	88811
Car I....................	9600		
II....................	0		
Recreation equipment.....	2700		
Other *Baseball card collection*.	4500		

Total Real Property.....	132300		
Personal Property			
Furniture and appl.......	30000		
Stereos, TVs, etc, *computer*.	10000		
Clothing.................	7500		
Jewelry..................	0	(II) Tot. Liabilities.	89371
Other. *Toys & miscellaneous*..	8200		

Total Personal Property.	55700	Net Worth [(II)-(III)].	221484
(I) Total Assets......	310855	Total Liab. and Net Worth..	310855
	======		======
```

435
```

Part 4, Question 13

```
+-FP/PC-----------------------------------------------------------------FP/PC-
|            M O N T H L Y   C A S H   B U D G E T   S U M M A R Y
+-----------------------------------------------------------------------------
```

NAME(S): Lisa Simmons   Page

FOR THE YEAR ENDING 12/31/93	JAN	FEB	MAR
Take-Home Pay: Source 1	2079	2079	2034
Take-Home Pay: Source 2	388	388	388
Take-Home Pay: Source 3	0	0	0
Bonuses and Commissions	0	0	0
Pensions and Annuities *Social Security Benefits*	1421	1421	1421
Interest	557	557	540
Dividends	0	0	89
Rents	0	0	0
Sale of Securities *Withdrawal from savings*	0	3746	0
Other	0	0	44
Other Income: Source 1 *Life insurance*	6250	6250	6250
Other Income: Source 2 *Tax refund*	0	0	0
TOTAL INCOME	10695	14441	10766
Rent/Mortgage Payment *+front-end costs of refinancing*	798	4544	0
Repairs, Maintenance, Improvements	75	75	75
Gas, Utilities, Water	175	175	175
Phone	30	30	30
Cable TV and Other	30	30	30
Groceries	425	425	425
Dining Out	125	125	125
Loan/Lease Payments	333	333	333
License Plates, Fees, Etc.	0	0	0
Gas, Oil, Tires, Maintenance	125	125	125
Health Insurance, Etc.	250	250	250
Doctor, Dentist, Hospital, Medicine	26	26	26
Clothing, Shoes, Accessories	125	125	125
Homeowner's Insurance	50	50	50
Life Insurance	0	0	0
Automobile Insurance	0	390	0
Income and Social Security Taxes	0	0	0
Property Taxes	205	205	205
Loan Payments	0	0	0
Purchases and Repairs	103	103	103
Laundry, Cosmetics, Hair Care	50	50	50
Vacations	0	0	0
Other Recreation and Entertainment	75	75	75
Savings and Investments	6807	6807	7992
Charitable Contributions	75	75	75
~~Gifts~~ *Children's activities*	175	175	175
~~Education Expenses~~ *Debt consolidation/home equity loan*	322	322	322
~~Subscriptions, Magazines, Books~~ *Child care*	125	125	125
Other Expenditures: Item 1 *Children's allowances*	80	80	80
Other Expenditures: Item 2 *Miscellaneous*	100	100	100
~~Fun Money~~ *Business expenses*	72	72	72
TOTAL EXPENDITURES	10756	14892	11143
CASH SUPLUS (OR DEFICIT)	-61	-451	-377
CUMULATIVE CASH SUPLUS (OR DEFICIT)	-61	-512	-889

FOR THE YEAR ENDING 12/31/93	APR	MAY	JUN
Take-Home Pay: Source 1	2034	2034	2034
Take-Home Pay: Source 2	388	388	388
Take-Home Pay: Source 3	0	0	0
Bonuses and Commissions	0	0	0
Pensions and Annuities *Social Security benefits*	1421	1421	1421
Interest	505	505	505
Dividends	0	0	89
Rents	0	0	0
Sale of Securities *Withdrawal from savings*	9973	0	0
Other	0	0	45
Other Income: Source 1 *Life insurance*	6250	6250	6250
Other Income: Source 2 *Tax refund*	2918	0	0
TOTAL INCOME	23489	10598	10732
Rent/Mortgage Payment	627	627	627
Repairs, Maintenance, Improvements	75	75	75
Gas, Utilities, Water	175	175	175
Phone	30	30	30
Cable TV and Other	30	30	30
Groceries	425	425	425
Dining Out	125	125	125
Loan/Lease Payments	7973	0	0
License Plates, Fees, Etc.	0	0	0
Gas, Oil, Tires, Maintenance	125	125	125
Health Insurance, Etc.	533	43	43
Doctor, Dentist, Hospital, Medicine	26	26	26
Clothing, Shoes, Accessories	125	125	125
Homeowner's Insurance	54	54	54
Life Insurance	0	0	0
Automobile Insurance	0	0	0
Income and Social Security Taxes	0	0	0
Property Taxes	205	205	205
Loan Payments	0	0	0
Purchases and Repairs	103	103	103
Laundry, Cosmetics, Hair Care	50	50	50
Vacations	0	0	1000
Other Recreation and Entertainment	75	75	75
Savings and Investments	7824	7824	7958
Charitable Contributions	75	75	75
~~Gifts~~ *Children's activities*	2175	175	175
~~Education Expenses~~ *Debt consolidation/home equity loan*	308	308	308
~~Subscriptions, Magazines, Books~~ *Child care*	125	125	125
Other Expenditures: Item 1 *Children's allowances*	80	80	80
Other Expenditures: Item 2 *Miscellaneous*	100	100	100
~~Fun Money~~ *Business expenses*	72	72	72
TOTAL EXPENDITURES	21515	11052	12186
CASH SUPLUS (OR DEFICIT)	1974	-454	-1454
CUMULATIVE CASH SUPLUS (OR DEFICIT)	1085	631	-823

```
|
+----------------------------------------------------------------------
         M O N T H L Y   C A S H   B U D G E T   S U M M A R Y
+----------------------------------------------------------------------
```

NAME(S): Lisa Simmons   Page

FOR THE YEAR ENDING 12/31/93	JUL	AUG	SEP
Take-Home Pay: Source 1	2034	2034	2034
Take-Home Pay: Source 2	388	388	388
Take-Home Pay: Source 3	0	0	0
Bonuses and Commissions	0	0	0
Pensions and Annuities *Social Security benefits*	1421	1421	1421
Interest	505	505	505
Dividends	0	0	89
Rents	0	0	0
Sale of Securities *Withdrawal from savings*	0	0	0
Other	0	0	44
Other Income: Source 1 *Life insurance*	6250	6250	6250
Other Income: Source 2 *Tax refund*	0	0	0
TOTAL INCOME	10598	10598	10731
Rent/Mortgage Payment	627	627	627
Repairs, Maintenance, Improvements	75	75	75
Gas, Utilities, Water	175	175	175
Phone	30	30	30
Cable TV and Other	30	30	30
Groceries	425	425	425
Dining Out	125	125	125
Loan/Lease Payments	0	0	0
License Plates, Fees, Etc.	0	0	0
Gas, Oil, Tires, Maintenance	125	125	125
Health Insurance, Etc.	43	43	43
Doctor, Dentist, Hospital, Medicine	26	26	26
Clothing, Shoes, Accessories	125	125	125
Homeowner's Insurance	54	54	54
Life Insurance	0	0	0
Automobile Insurance	0	390	0
Income and Social Security Taxes	0	0	0
Property Taxes	205	205	205
Loan Payments	0	0	0
Purchases and Repairs	103	103	103
Laundry, Cosmetics, Hair Care	50	50	50
Vacations	0	0	0
Other Recreation and Entertainment	75	75	75
Savings and Investments	7824	7824	7957
Charitable Contributions	75	75	75
~~Gifts~~ *Children's activities*	175	175	175
~~Education Expenses~~ *Debt consolidation/home equity loan*	308	308	308
~~Subscriptions, Magazines, Books~~ *Child care*	125	125	125
Other Expenditures: Item 1 *Children's allowance*	80	80	80
Other Expenditures: Item 2 *Miscellaneous*	100	100	100
~~Fun Money~~ *Business expenses*	72	72	72
TOTAL EXPENDITURES	11052	11442	11185
CASH SUPLUS (OR DEFICIT)	-454	-844	-454
CUMULATIVE CASH SUPLUS (OR DEFICIT)	-1277	-2121	-2575

NAME(S): Lisa Simmons   Page 4

FOR THE YEAR ENDING 12/31/93	OCT	NOV	DEC	TOTAL
Take-Home Pay: Source 1	2034	2034	2034	24498
Take-Home Pay: Source 2	388	388	388	4656
Take-Home Pay: Source 3	0	0	0	0
Bonuses and Commissions	0	0	0	0
Pensions and Annuities *Social Security benefits*	1421	1421	1421	17052
Interest	505	505	1385	7079
Dividends	0	0	89	356
Rents	0	0	0	0
Sale of Securities *Withdrawal from savings*	0	0	0	13719
Other	0	0	45	178
Other Income: Source 1 *Life insurance*	6250	6250	6250	75000
Other Income: Source 2 *Tax refund*	0	0	0	2918
TOTAL INCOME	10598	10598	11612	145456
Rent/Mortgage Payment *:front-end costs of refinancing*	627	627	627	10985
Repairs, Maintenance, Improvements	75	75	75	900
Gas, Utilities, Water	175	175	175	2100
Phone	30	30	30	360
Cable TV and Other	30	30	30	360
Groceries	425	425	425	5100
Dining Out	125	125	125	1500
Loan/Lease Payments	0	0	0	8972
License Plates, Fees, Etc.	0	0	0	0
Gas, Oil, Tires, Maintenance	125	125	125	1500
Health Insurance, Etc.	43	43	43	1627
Doctor, Dentist, Hospital, Medicine	26	26	26	312
Clothing, Shoes, Accessories	125	125	125	1500
Homeowner's Insurance	54	54	54	636
Life Insurance	0	0	0	0
Automobile Insurance	0	0	0	780
Income and Social Security Taxes	0	0	0	0
Property Taxes	205	205	205	2460
Loan Payments	0	0	0	0
Purchases and Repairs	103	103	103	1236
Laundry, Cosmetics, Hair Care	50	50	50	600
Vacations	0	0	0	1000
Other Recreation and Entertainment	75	75	75	900
Savings and Investments	7824	7824	8838	93303
Charitable Contributions	75	75	75	900
~~Gifts~~ *Children's activities*	175	175	175	4100
~~Education Expenses~~ *Debt consolidation/home equity loan*	308	308	308	3738
~~Subscriptions, Magazines, Books~~ *Child care*	125	125	125	1500
Other Expenditures: Item 1 *Children's allowances*	80	80	80	960
Other Expenditures: Item 2 *Miscellaneous*	100	100	100	1200
~~Fun Money~~ *Business expenses*	72	72	72	864
TOTAL EXPENDITURES	11052	11052	12066	149393
CASH SUPLUS (OR DEFICIT)	-454	-454	-454	-3937
CUMULATIVE CASH SUPLUS (OR DEFICIT)	-3029	-3483	-3937	-3937

Part 4, Question 13

```
+-FP/PC-----------------------------------------------------------FP/PC-
|                   C A S H   B U D G E T   S U M M A R Y
+------------------------------------------------------------------------
```

NAME(S): Lisa Simmons
FOR YEAR ENDING 12/31/93

	Total Income	Total Expenses	Cash Surplus (Deficit)	Cumulative Cash Surplus (Deficit)
Jan	$ 10695	$ 10756	$ -61	$ -61
Feb	14441	14892	-451	-512
Mar	10766	11143	-377	-889
Apr	13516	11542	1974	1085
May	10598	11052	-454	631
Jun	10732	12186	-1454	-823
Jul	10598	11052	-454	-1277
Aug	10598	11442	-844	-2121
Sep	10731	11185	-454	-2575
Oct	10598	11052	-454	-3029
Nov	10598	11052	-454	-3483
Dec	11612	12066	-454	-3937
TOTALS ..	$ 135483	$ 139420		$ -3937

```
+------------------------------------------------------------------------+
```

REPRESENTATIVE ANSWERS: The Simmons Case Study

Part Five

1. Super NOW account ($8,211 x .04) $ 328
    Fidelity Cash Reserves mutual fund ($11,401 x .045)   513
    Certificate of deposit ($13,500 x .065)   878
    TOTAL $1,719

2. Kroger ($0/$4,050)   0.0%
    Fidelity Puritan mutual fund ($252/ $4,747)   5.3%
    Merrill Lynch Phoenix ($104/$2,745)   3.8%

3. See computer printout. Over this particular 2 year period, Gabelli Growth mutual fund yielded 13.7% per year. Since Gabelli Growth is a growth mutual fund with below-average risk, this return was adequate compensation for the risk.

$$\frac{.50 + \left[\dfrac{20.27 - 16.27}{2}\right]}{\left[\dfrac{20.27 + 16.27}{2}\right]} = 13.7\%$$

4. This could be done for any 2-week period. Kroger trades on the New York Stock Exchange. It's price/earnings ratio was 18 in early January, 1993 meaning that its market value was 18 times its last year's earnings per share. Investors look at the P/E ratio as an indicator of value, whether or not the stock is a good buy at its current price. It should be compared to the P/E ratios of other companies in the same industry as well as the company's historical P/E ratio.

5. This could be done for any current 2-week period.

6. The following are quotes for January 7, 1993:

	NAV	Offer Price	Load	Load Percent
Fidelity Puritan	14.76	NL	0	0%
Merrill Lynch Phoenix A	11.79	12.61	0.82	7%

    Neither of these funds have 12(b)-1 or redemption fees.

7. The Kroger Company is one of the nation's largest retail grocery chains operating primarily in the Midwest, South and West. Kroger is currently not paying dividends and has traded in a fairly wide price range over the last 52 weeks, a high of $21.125 and a low of $11.25. According to a January 1, 1993 Value Line report, Krogers currently rates a C++ in financial strength. On a scale of 1 to 5 with 1 being the best, Krogers ranks 3 in safety and 4 on timeliness. It has a beta of 1.55. Projected 3 - 5 year average annual return is expected to be only 4%.

Fidelity Puritan is one of the approximately 142 funds in the Fidelity family of funds. Fidelity Puritan seeks as much income as possible, consistent with the preservation and conservation of capital. The fund (over $5.2 billion in assets) invests in common stocks, preferred stocks, and bonds, seeking diversity in terms of both companies and industries. It is given a 4-star rating (above average) by Morningstar and has an above-average return with only average risk. Both its 3- and 5-year return is over 9% annually, while its 10-year return is 17% annually. *Forbes* rates Fidelity Puritan's performance A in an up market and B in a down market. Annual expenses per $100 of assets are $0.65. Fidelity Puritan requires a $2,500 initial purchase, $250 minimum subsequent purchases, and allows telephone switch privileges.

Merrill Lynch Phoenix is one of the 92 funds in the Merrill Lynch family. This fund seeks long-term growth of capital rather than current income. The fund (241 million in assets) invests in equity and fixed-income securities of issuers in weak financial condition or those experiencing poor operating results which are, therefore, undervalued. Morningstar gives Merrill Lynch Phoenix a 3-star (neutral) rating. It has average risk with average return. *Forbes* rates its performance a B in up markets and a C is down markets. Annual expenses per $100 assets are $1.42 The fund shares are sold in two classes. Class A shares (which Lisa has) have a front-end load while Class B shares are subject to a contingent deferred sales charge and a 12b-1 fee. The fund requires a $1,000 minimum initial purchase and a $50 minimum subsequent purchase.

8   The best way for Lisa to limit a loss (or protect a gain) is to place a stop-loss order with her broker. If Lisa places a stop-loss order for Kroger at $10 per share, the order will automatically turn into a market order if Kroger drops to $10. The stock will then be sold at the prevailing market price (presumably somewhere around $10). There is no cost unless the stock is sold, and then Lisa would have to pay regular brokerage commissions.

9.   (200 x $14.76) - $2,448 = $504
     (115.86 x $14.76) - $1,508 =   202
                                    $706 before-tax capital gains
                                    x .15 marginal tax rate
                                    $106 tax liability

10. (100 x $11.79) - $1,215 =   ($ 36)
     (100 x $11.79) - $1,286 =   (107)
     (46.67 x $11.79) - $562 =   (12)
                                    ($155) before-tax capital loss
                                    x .15   marginal tax rate
                                    $ 23   tax savings

11. --Liquid assets--purchasing power risk
     --Stock--market, business, and financial risks
     --Stock mutual funds--market, business, and financial risks (but diversification tends to lessen the business and financial risks)
     --U.S. EE savings bonds--some liquidity risk because they cannot be liquidated for the first 6 months after purchase, and within the first 5 years they are subject to a reduction in interest earnings if liquidated.
     --Primary residence and baseball card collection--liquidity and market risks

12. Current dividend yield on blue-chip stock ($1.63/$40.12)   4.1%
    Current dividend yield on aggressive growth stock ($.50/$22.50)   2.2%

See computer printouts for approximate annual yields.

Blue Chip Stock

$$\frac{1.63 + \left[\dfrac{57.00 - 40.12}{5}\right]}{\left[\dfrac{57.00 + 40.12}{2}\right]} = 10.3\%$$

Aggressive Growth
Stock

$$\frac{.50 + \left[\dfrac{50.00 - 22.50}{5}\right]}{\left[\dfrac{50.00 + 22.50}{2}\right]} = 16.6\%$$

13. Current yield on corporate bond ($75/$953)   7.9%

See computer printout for the yield-to-maturity.

$$\frac{75 + \left[\dfrac{1,000 - 953}{5}\right]}{\left[\dfrac{1,000 + 953}{2}\right]} = 8.6\%$$

14. Morningstar reports on 15 municipal bond funds that investment primarily in New York state products. Among the top rated funds over the past 5 years are Rochester Fund Municipals, Shearson New York Municipals, Fidelity New York Tax-Free High Yield, Franklin New York Tax-Free Income, and Dreyfus New York Tax-Exempt Bond funds.

$$\frac{6.0\%}{1 - .15} = 7.1\% \text{ fully taxable equivalent yield}$$

No, the tax-free bond has a slightly lower fully taxable equivalent yield than the corporate bond, but without further information we can't compare the yield-to-maturity.

15. Residential real estate can provide a positive cash flow if it can be rented for more than its costs. It also has the potential for capital gain, it can be highly leveraged, and it can provide tax advantages for middle income investors like Lisa (if they are actively involved in managing the property). On the other hand, it carries moderate to high risk levels, low liquidity, and generally requires moderate to high levels of personal management.

Residential real estate would be a good investment for Lisa only if she thought she would enjoy managing property. Otherwise, I would recommend she select investments that don't take as much of her time.

16.   According to Lisa's latest budget, her 1993 cash deficit is approximately $4,000. Since her number one financial priority is "paying monthly bills" and since nothing more can be done with income or expenses, the $4,000 will have to come from the "savings and investments" category. I recommend Lisa cut this deficit in two ways:

--Lisa's 8th (and last) financial priority is investing for her retirement. Although retirement planning is important, I recommend she <u>not</u> start putting $2,000 a year in an IRA. She has other goals and priorities which she sees as more important at this time, and she doesn't have enough money for everything. The 401(k) gives a greater tax advantage than the IRA and has been earning a respectable return.

--Lisa expects to earn over $7,000 interest income in 1993 (about $1,700 of that on her liquid assets and the rest on the funds being distributed from the American Life Insurance policy). These are currently being reinvested and are, therefore, budgeted as "savings and investments." I recommend that she use $2,000 of this interest income for living expenses rather than reinvesting all of it.

Cutting the "savings and investments" expenditure category by $4,000 will give Lisa a small budget surplus for 1993.

General types of investments appropriate for a short term goals such as the new car would include money market mutual funds, money market deposit accounts, and 1, 2, or 3 year certificates of deposit. For Andy's college education with a 5 year time frame, certificates of deposit as well as a limited amount of U.S. EE savings bonds and some stock and bond mutual funds would be appropriate. The longer term goals (the business, Karen's college, and retirement) should be funded primarily with growth-oriented investments such as stock mutual funds and/or individual stock investments. U.S. EE savings bonds and corporate bonds with maturities corresponding with her college years could be used to diversify Karen's college fund. Real estate would also be appropriate to diversify the long-term investments.

Given Lisa's age, family status, risk tolerance, goals, and knowledge of investment products, I would recommend the following target portfolio mix:

liquid assets	25%
moderate term CDs	10%
stock mutual funds	
--balanced	20%
--growth	25%
high quality bonds (including U.S. EE savings bonds)	20%

Not including the vested retirement funds, house, or baseball card collection, Lisa currently has liquid and investment assets totaling $113,947. Lisa's assets are distributed as follows: (based on balance sheet in Part 4, Question 12)

liquid assets	29%
stock	4%
stock mutual funds	
--balanced	7%
U.S. EE savings bonds	11%
life insurance	49%

Generally speaking, as the funds are distributed from the life insurance, the monies should be invested in moderate term CDs, stock mutual funds, and high quality bonds. I would also recommend selling the Kroger stock ($4,125) and investing those funds in one of the above investment types. Individual stock does not fit into Lisa's investment portfolio (primarily because of lack of investment knowledge). This stock has not performed well and is not expected to improve much in the near future. She might also consider selling the Merrill Lynch Phoenix fund as it has not been a great performer either.

Following are my recommendations for Lisa's investment portfolio. While the percentages are not exactly at the targeted level, they are very close. I believe this portfolio is appropriate for Lisa's current needs. The final step in this process would be to implement Lisa's investment strategy by selecting and investing in good performing securities.

Goals/ Funds	Liquid Assets	Moderate Term CDs	Balanced Stock Funds	Growth Stock Funds	High Quality Bonds[1]
New car --$10,000 from life insurance --$ 2,672 annual investment	$ 2,672	$10,000			
Andy's college --$25,000 from life insurance --$ 3,455 annual investment		$ 6,250	$ 6,250 $ 3,455		$12,500
Business --$25,000 from life insurance			$ 6,250	$18,750	
Karen's college --$15,000 from life insurance --$ 2,705 annual investment			$ 3,750	$3,750	$ 7,500 $ 2,705
401(k) --$ 2,000 annual investment			$ 2,000		
Sell Kroger stock --$ 4,125				$ 4,125	
Sell Merrill Lynch Phoenix fund --$ 2,652				$ 2,652	
Current investments --$27,037 liquid assets[2] --$ 5,133 Fidelity Puritan fund	$27,037		$ 5,133		
TOTAL ($124,779)	$29,709	$16,250	$26,838	$29,277	$22,705
Percent of total	24%	13%	22%	23%	18%

[1]Includes U.S. EE savings bonds.
[2]$6,250 which was temporarily placed in Fidelity Cash Reserves mutual fund in March has been moved to Andy's college fund.

Port 5, Question 3

```
+FP/PC--------------------------------------------------------------FP/PC-
| I N V E S T M E N T   R E T U R N S   F O R   A   M U T U A L   F U N D
+------------------------------------------------------------------------
```
Gabelli mutual fund
```
       Annual dividend and capital gains distribution..........     0.500
       Ending price per share.................................    20.270
       Beginning price per share.............................     16.270
       Investment period in years............................          2

       Return (approximate annual yield).....................     13.68%
```

```
--------------------------------------------------------------------------
```

Question 12
```
+FP/PC--------------------------------------------------------------FP/PC-
|        I N V E S T M E N T   R E T U R N S   F O R   A   S T O C K
+------------------------------------------------------------------------
```
Blue-chip stock
```
       Annual dividend.......................................      1.630
       (Future) selling price of the stock...................     57.000
       (Current) market price of the stock...................     40.120
       Investment period in years............................          5

       Return (approximate annual yield).....................     10.31%
```

```
--------------------------------------------------------------------------
```

```
+FP/PC--------------------------------------------------------------FP/PC-
|        I N V E S T M E N T   R E T U R N S   F O R   A   S T O C K
+------------------------------------------------------------------------
```
Aggressive growth stock
```
       Annual dividend.......................................      0.500
       (Future) selling price of the stock...................     50.000
       (Current) market price of the stock...................     22.500
       Investment period in years............................          5

       Return (approximate annual yield).....................     16.55%
```

```
--------------------------------------------------------------------------
```

Question 13
```
+FP/PC--------------------------------------------------------------FP/PC-
|        I N V E S T M E N T   R E T U R N S   F O R   A   B O N D
+------------------------------------------------------------------------
```
Corporate bond
```
       Annual interest income................................      75.00
       Maturity value of the bond............................    1000.00
       (Current) market price of the bond....................     953.00
       Years until maturity..................................          5

       Return (approximate yield to maturity)................      8.64%
```

```
--------------------------------------------------------------------------
```

<u>REPRESENTATIVE ANSWERS:</u> The Simmons Case Study

<u>Part Six--Chapter 15</u>

1.　　$40,000　annual income
　　　　x　.025
　　　　$ 1,000
　　　　x　　37　number of years with employer
　　　　$37,000　annual retirement benefit

2.　　*Option a*: Lisa could use the money any way she wanted. She may need it to help start the new business.

Assuming the tax laws are similar to current ones in 8 years, there would be a 10% penalty for premature withdrawal of retirement funds plus income tax would be due on the amount withdrawn. About half of the $25,000 would be taxed at the 15% marginal tax rate and the other half at the 28 marginal tax rate if her other income stayed at the same level as 1993. After penalties and taxes, Lisa would get only $17,125 of the $25,000 ($25,000 - $2,500 - $1,875 - $3,500).

$25,000	$12,500	$12,500
x　.01　penalty rate	x　.15　marginal tax rate	x　　.28　marginal tax rate
$ 2,500　penalty	$ 1,875　tax	$ 3,500　tax

Option b: By rolling over into an IRA, the $25,000 would not be penalized or taxed (at this point). Lisa could select from a wide range of investment alternatives and manage the investment choices over the years. Assuming Lisa could average a 9% annual return, the $25,000 would be worth $281,448 by the time she was 65 years old. See computer printout.

　　　　$ 25,000
　　　　x 7.2579　future value of a lump sum
　　　　$181,448

Lisa would have to take responsibility for investing the $25,000 and managing it over the years. She might have to pay an annual fee, depending on where the money was invested. However, mutual fund companies typically charge only $10 to $30 annually.

Option c: If Lisa leaves the money in the company pension, she will not have to worry about managing it and there will not be taxes, penalties, or fees. She could expect an annual income at retirement of $12,250 for the rest of her life.

　　　　$35,000　annual income
　　　　x　.025
　　　　$　875
　　　　x　　14　number of years with employer
　　　　$12,250　annual retirement benefit

This annual retirement benefit may not be as high as she could achieve by investing the money herself through an IRA. In addition, if J.& L. Advertising were to experience financial difficulties, the worst possible outcome is that Lisa might lose some or all of the promised retirement benefit.

3. The IRA would be worth $181,447 at retirement. See computer printout and Question 2.

4. Lisa could withdraw $14,194 annually ($181,448/12.7834) from the IRA. See computer printout.

   Using these assumptions, the IRA produces a $1,944 ($14,194 - $12,250) larger annual payment than the company pension. But Lisa could outlive the IRA payments if she lived past age 90 while the company pension pays for the rest of her life. On the other hand, if Lisa were to die after age 65 but before age 90, the company pension benefits would stop and nothing would be paid out to beneficiaries. The remaining funds in the IRA would be passed on to Lisa's beneficiaries.

5. The 401(k) would be worth $246,692 at retirement. She could withdraw $19,298 annually. See computer printouts.

   $$\begin{array}{r} \$2,000 \\ \underline{\times 123.3459} \text{ future value of an annuity} \\ \$246,692 \end{array}$$

   $246,692/12.7834 = $19,298

6. No additional retirement savings are required. See computer printout.

7. $6,443 additional savings are required. See computer printout.

8. Lisa's first-year Social Security benefits would be about $10,260 ($855 x 12) according to Exhibit 15.6. Lisa should call for her *Personal Earnings and Benefit Estimate Statement* from the Social Security Administration to get a more accurate estimate.

   With Social Security benefits, only $152 additional annual savings are required.

9. There is little more Lisa can do about retirement planning in 1993. There is no more room in her budget. She does need to make the $2,000 annual contribution to her 401(k) as planned in Part 5. If Lisa still wants to start her own business in 8 years and if it makes sense financially at that time, I recommend she do it. But Lisa must realize that while she is self-employed she needs to set aside retirement funds for herself to replace the lost retirement benefits from her former employer. Her retirement funding should be fully analyzed at that time.

Part 6, Chapter 15

```
+FP/PC-------------------------------------------------------FP/PC+
|         F U T U R E   V A L U E   O F   A   S I N G L E   C A S H   F L O W         |
+-------------------------------------------------------------------+
```

Question 2 and 3
```
                  Single cash flow............   25000.00
                  Rate of return...............      9.00%
                  Number of years.............      23.00

                  Future value................  181446.86
```

```
-------------------------------------------------------------------
```

```
+FP/PC-------------------------------------------------------FP/PC+
|      YEARLY PAYMENTS PRODUCED FROM A GIVEN PRESENT VALUE       |
+-------------------------------------------------------------------+
```

Question 4
```
                  Present value...............  181448.00
                  Rate of return (%)..........       6.00
                  Number of years.............      25.00

                  Yearly savings required.......   14194.08
```

```
-------------------------------------------------------------------
```

```
+FP/PC-------------------------------------------------------FP/PC+
|         F U T U R E   V A L U E   O F   A N   A N N U I T Y         |
+-------------------------------------------------------------------+
```

Question 5
```
                  Annuity payment.............    2000.00
                  Rate of return..............       8.00%
                  Number of years.............      31.00

                  Future value................  246691.73
```

```
-------------------------------------------------------------------
```

```
+FP/PC-------------------------------------------------------FP/PC+
|      YEARLY PAYMENTS PRODUCED FROM A GIVEN PRESENT VALUE       |
+-------------------------------------------------------------------+
```

Question 5
```
                  Present value...............  246692.00
                  Rate of return (%)..........       6.00
                  Number of years.............      25.00

                  Yearly savings required.......   19297.91
```

```
-------------------------------------------------------------------
```

Part 6, Chapter 15, Question 6

Estimated	A.	Approximate number of yrs. to retirement................ 31
Household	B.	Current level of an. household exp. excluding savings.. 55000
Exp. in	C.	Est. household exp. in retirement as % of current exp.. 80
Retirement	D.	Est. annual household exp. in retirement (B x C)....... 44000
		=======
Estimated	E.	Social security, annual income........................ 0
Income in	F.	Company/employer pension plans-annual amounts......... 37000
Retirement	G.	Other sources-annual amounts.......................... 19298
	H.	Total annual income (E + F + G)....................... 56298
	I.	Add'l. req'd. income or annual shortfall (D - H)...... -12298
		=======
Inflation	J.	Expected avg. ann. rate of infl. until retirement (%).. 5
Factor	K.	Infl. fac. based on 31 yrs. and 5% rate of inflation.. 4.538
	L.	Size of inflation-adjusted annual shortfall (I x K).... -55809
		=======
Funding	M.	Expected return on assets held after retirement (%).... 6
the	N.	Amt. of retirement funds required (L - M).............. -930147
Shortfall	O.	Expected return on assets prior to retirement (%)...... 8
	P.	Comp. int. factor based on 31 yrs. and 0% return...... 123.346
	Q.	Ann. savings req'd. for retirement nest egg (N - P).... -7541
		=======

Question 7

Estimated	A.	Approximate number of yrs. to retirement................ 31
Household	B.	Current level of an. household exp. excluding savings.. 55000
Exp. in	C.	Est. household exp. in retirement as % of current exp.. 80
Retirement	D.	Est. annual household exp. in retirement (B x C)....... 44000
		=======
Estimated	E.	Social security, annual income........................ 0
Income in	F.	Company/employer pension plans-annual amounts......... 14194
Retirement	G.	Other sources-annual amounts.......................... 19298
	H.	Total annual income (E + F + G)....................... 33492
	I.	Add'l. req'd. income or annual shortfall (D - H)...... 10508
		=======
Inflation	J.	Expected avg. ann. rate of infl. until retirement (%).. 5
Factor	K.	Infl. fac. based on 31 yrs. and 5% rate of inflation.. 4.538
	L.	Size of inflation-adjusted annual shortfall (I x K).... 47686
		=======
Funding	M.	Expected return on assets held after retirement (%).... 6
the	N.	Amt. of retirement funds required (L - M).............. 794762
Shortfall	O.	Expected return on assets prior to retirement (%)...... 8
	P.	Comp. int. factor based on 31 yrs. and 0% return...... 123.346
	Q.	Ann. savings req'd. for retirement nest egg (N - P).... 6443
		=======

Part 6, Chapter 15, Question 8

```
+FP/PC-------------------------------------------------------------FP/PC+
|         S E T T I N G   F U T U R E   R E T I R E M E N T   N E E D S    |
+------------------------------------------------------------------------+


Estimated      A. Approximate number of yrs. to retirement...............      31
Household      B. Current level of an. household exp. excluding savings..   55000
Exp. in        C. Est. household exp. in retirement as % of current exp..      80
Retirement     D. Est. annual household exp. in retirement (B x C).......   44000
                                                                          =======
Estimated      E. Social security, annual income........................   10260
Income in      F. Company/employer pension plans-annual amounts.........   14194
Retirement     G. Other sources-annual amounts..........................   19298
               H. Total annual income (E + F + G)........................   43752
               I. Add'l. req'd. income or annual shortfall (D - H).......     248
                                                                          =======
Inflation      J. Expected avg. ann. rate of infl. until retirement (%)..       5
Factor         K. Infl. fac. based on 31 yrs. and  5% rate of inflation..   4.538
               L. Size of inflation-adjusted annual shortfall (I x K)....    1125
                                                                          =======
Funding        M. Expected return on assets held after retirement (%)....       6
the            N. Amt. of retirement funds required (L - M).............   18757
Shortfall      O. Expected return on assets prior to retirement (%)......       8
               P. Comp. int. factor based on 31 yrs. and  0% return...... 123.346
               Q. Ann. savings req'd. for retirement nest egg (N - P)....     152
                                                                          =======

------------------------------------------------------------------------
```

Part Six--Chapter 16

1.   Lisa's gross estate is well under the $600,000 needed before being subject to Federal Estate taxes. Roughly, it would consist of her $221,484 net worth plus her $88,500 life insurance.

2.   (Given the limited information in this case), all of her property would be probate property except the life insurance, the retirement death benefit, and the 401(k), assuming Lisa names beneficiaries when she opens the 401(k). These listed exceptions would be non-probate property.

3.   Lisa's assets with named beneficiaries (life insurance, retirement death benefit, and the 401(k) plan, assuming Lisa names beneficiaries) would pass directly to Andy and Karen, the named beneficiaries. According to typical intestate laws (Exhibit 16.3), Lisa's other assets would be divided equally between Andy and Karen with each receiving one-half.

4.   Lisa should definitely have her will updated. If she dies without a valid will, the intestacy laws for her state will control how her property is divided. In her will, she should provide for the distribution of her property according to her wishes. She has previously stated she would like Karen to receive the exercise equipment and Andy to receive the baseball card collection. She would like the children to share equally in the remainder of the estate. It is also very important that Lisa designate a legal guardian for the children since she is a single parent. She has said she would like her parents to be legal guardians as well as executors of her estate.

5.   Lisa needs to talk with her parents and Tom's parents about what she would prefer in the case of her death and the details of her finances. It is especially important that Lisa's parents understand her finances, how funds have been allocated for the children, and her wishes regarding the children since they have been named as guardians for the children in the event of Lisa's death. In addition, Lisa needs to draft a letter of last instructions that includes this financial information, the location of her will, instructions regarding cremation, and any other information she would like to convey upon her death.

6.   Any contributions that exceed $10,000 per year per child would be subject to gift taxes. Therefore, if Lisa does decide to save in Andy's and Karen's names, she should transfer no more than $10,000 annually to each of them.

Gifts to children are generally made to remove assets from one's estate before death in order to reduce estate taxes and/or to reduce income tax on income produced by the assets. Since Lisa does not have an estate tax liability, the first reason is not appropriate. There could be a limited amount of tax savings from gifting to the children, but not as much as for many parents because Lisa is in the 15% marginal tax bracket just like the children would be.

As long as the children have no other taxable income, there could be some tax savings by gifting each child enough assets to produce $600 of investment income, the current standard deduction for dependent taxpayers. Assuming an investment earned an 8% return, that would be a gift of $7,500 ($600/.08) for each child. The tax savings to Lisa would be $180 ($600 x 2 x .15). If the children have any other income (excluding Social Security which is not taxable at their levels of income), however, they will have to pay taxes on this income, probably at a 15% rate.

The primary disadvantage of gifting to the children is that Lisa would no longer own the investment asset gifted. She could not control how it was used. If, at age 18, Andy decided to buy a fancy sports car rather than go to college, he would have the money to buy the car.

EPILOGUE: The Simmons Case Study

Lisa Simmons began serious financial planning after being recently widowed. She was faced with numerous important decisions about income and expenditures, savings and investments, taxes, insurance, retirement, and estate planning. Through sound financial planning before Tom died, Lisa and the children were left with insurance proceeds to help with living expenses and to meet their goals. However, Lisa realized that it would take a lot of serious planning to make the best use of those resources. Lisa's major goals were to save for a new car, for the children's college educations, to start a business, and for her retirement.

Accomplishments

By developing a budget, Lisa learned valuable information about the family's cash flow and was able to make reductions in selected expenditure categories. Over the course of the financial planning process, Lisa's budget went from a $23,268 deficit to a $63 surplus for 1993.

Through tax planning, Lisa lowered her income tax withholding and increased her take-home pay. This had a positive impact on her cash flow and helped make it possible to start saving for her goals.

Lisa restructured her liquid assets with fewer accounts to keep track of. The remaining accounts provide a somewhat higher level of interest income and lower expenses as well.

Lisa refinanced her home mortgage at a lower rate of interest, thus reducing her monthly house payment significantly. She also paid off her auto loan and refinanced her debt consolidation loan using a home equity line of credit that offered a lower rate of interest as well as tax deductible interest.

She was able to provide money for Andy to take advantage of a class trip to the East Coast following his graduation from junior high school.

With the help of a cafeteria-style benefit plan offered through her employer, Lisa was able to buy excellent health coverage at a much lower cost than she had been paying. She also increased her life, disability income, homeowner's, and auto insurance coverages. With all these improvements, total insurance expenditures still decreased by nearly $2,000 annually.

Lisa became more knowledgeable about her current investments and made important decisions regarding how and where to invest her considerable assets. She now has a sound investment plan that should accomplish her stated goals.

She completed several retirement needs analyses that provided information about the adequacy of her retirement savings. Finally, Lisa updated her will, wrote a letter of last instructions, and began considering several other estate planning issues.

Challenges

Lisa's major challenge in the short run will be living within her budget. She will need to monitor the budget monthly to make sure she is staying on track with her spending and savings. In the longer run, Lisa's retirement planning will be a challenge, particularly if she does go into business for herself.